C++ FOR GAME PROGRAMMERS

SECOND EDITION

LIMITED WARRANTY AND DISCLAIMER OF LIABILITY

THE CD-ROM THAT ACCOMPANIES THIS BOOK MAY BE USED ON A SINGLE PC ONLY. THE LICENSE DOES NOT PERMIT THE USE ON A NETWORK (OF ANY KIND). YOU FURTHER AGREE THAT THIS LICENSE GRANTS PERMISSION TO USE THE PRODUCTS CONTAINED HEREIN, BUT DOES NOT GIVE YOU RIGHT OF OWN-ERSHIP TO ANY OF THE CONTENT OR PRODUCT CONTAINED ON THIS CD-ROM. USE OF THIRD-PARTY SOFTWARE CONTAINED ON THIS CD-ROM IS LIMITED TO AND SUBJECT TO LICENSING TERMS FOR THE RESPECTIVE PRODUCTS.

CHARLES RIVER MEDIA, INC. ("CRM") AND/OR ANYONE WHO HAS BEEN IN-VOLVED IN THE WRITING, CREATION, OR PRODUCTION OF THE ACCOMPANYING CODE ("THE SOFTWARE"), OR THE THIRD-PARTY PRODUCTS CONTAINED ON THIS CD-ROM, CANNOT AND DO NOT WARRANT THE PERFORMANCE OR RE-SULTS THAT MAY BE OBTAINED BY USING THE SOFTWARE. THE AUTHOR AND PUBLISHER HAVE USED THEIR BEST EFFORTS TO ENSURE THE ACCURACY AND FUNCTIONALITY OF THE TEXTUAL MATERIAL AND PROGRAMS CONTAINED HEREIN; WE, HOWEVER, MAKE NO WARRANTY OF THIS KIND, EXPRESS OR IM-PLIED, REGARDING THE PERFORMANCE OF THESE PROGRAMS. THE SOFTWARE IS SOLD "AS IS" WITHOUT WARRANTY (EXCEPT FOR DEFECTIVE MATERIALS USED IN MANUFACTURING THE DISC OR DUE TO FAULTY WORKMANSHIP); THE SOLE REMEDY IN THE EVENT OF A DEFECT IS EXPRESSLY LIMITED TO REPLACE-MENT OF THE DISC, AND ONLY AT THE DISCRETION OF CRM.

THE AUTHOR, THE PUBLISHER, DEVELOPERS OF THIRD-PARTY SOFTWARE, AND ANYONE INVOLVED IN THE PRODUCTION AND MANUFACTURING OF THIS WORK SHALL NOT BE LIABLE FOR DAMAGES OF ANY KIND ARISING OUT OF THE USE OF (OR THE INABILITY TO USE) THE PROGRAMS, SOURCE CODE, OR TEXTUAL MA-TERIAL CONTAINED IN THIS PUBLICATION. THIS INCLUDES, BUT IS NOT LIMITED TO, LOSS OF REVENUE OR PROFIT, OR OTHER INCIDENTAL OR CONSEQUENTIAL DAMAGES ARISING OUT OF THE USE OF THE PRODUCT.

THE SOLE REMEDY IN THE EVENT OF A CLAIM OF ANY KIND IS EXPRESSLY LIMITED TO REPLACEMENT OF THE BOOK AND/OR CD-ROM, AND ONLY AT THE DISCRETION OF CRM.

THE USE OF "IMPLIED WARRANTY" AND CERTAIN "EXCLUSIONS" VARY FROM STATE TO STATE, AND MAY NOT APPLY TO THE PURCHASER OF THIS PRODUCT.

C++ FOR GAME PROGRAMMERS

SECOND EDITION

MICHAEL J. DICKHEISER

CHARLES RIVER MEDIA

Boston, Massachusetts

Copyright 2007 Career & Professional Group, a division of Thomson Learning Inc.
Published by Charles River Media, an imprint of Thomson Learning Inc.
All rights reserved.

No part of this publication may be reproduced in any way, stored in a retrieval system of any type, or transmitted by any means or media, electronic or mechanical, including, but not limited to, photocopy, recording, or scanning, without prior permission in writing from the publisher.

Cover Design: Tyler Creative
Cover Image: © Applied Research Associates, Inc.

CHARLES RIVER MEDIA
25 Thomson Place
Boston, Massachusetts 02210
617-757-7900
617-757-7969 (FAX)
crm.info@thomson.com
www.charlesriver.com

This book is printed on acid-free paper.

Mike Dickheiser. *C++ for Game Programmers, Second Edition.*
ISBN: 1-58450-452-8

All brand names and product names mentioned in this book are trademarks or service marks of their respective companies. Any omission or misuse (of any kind) of service marks or trademarks should not be regarded as intent to infringe on the property of others. The publisher recognizes and respects all marks used by companies, manufacturers, and developers as a means to distinguish their products.

Library of Congress Cataloging-in-Publication Data
Dickheiser, Michael, 1970-
  C++ for game programmers / Michael Dickheiser. -- 2nd ed.
     p. cm.
  Rev. and expanded ed. of : C++ for game programmers / Noel Llopis.
  Includes index.
  ISBN 1-58450-452-8 (pbk. with cd-rom : alk. paper)
  1. C++ (Computer program language) 2. Computer games--Programming.
I. Llopis, Noel. C++ for game programmers. II. Title.

  QA76.73.C153L62 2007
  005.13'3--dc22

2006029183

Printed in the United States of America
06 7 6 5 4 3 2 First Edition

CHARLES RIVER MEDIA titles are available for site license or bulk purchase by institutions, user groups, corporations, etc. For additional information, please contact the Special Sales Department at 800-347-7707.

Requests for replacement of a defective CD-ROM must be accompanied by the original disc, your mailing address, telephone number, date of purchase and purchase price. Please state the nature of the problem, and send the information to CHARLES RIVER MEDIA, 25 Thomson Place, Boston, Massachusetts 02210. CRM's sole obligation to the purchaser is to replace the disc, based on defective materials or faulty workmanship, but not on the operation or functionality of the product.

To Sukie, for her support, wisdom, and love.

CONTENTS

CHAPTER 10 **STANDARD TEMPLATE LIBRARY: ALGORITHMS AND ADVANCED TOPICS**   **233**

ACKNOWLEDGMENTS

This book wouldn't exist without the efforts of Noel Llopis, who wrote the first edition and provided the fertile ground for my own thoughts on the subject. Naturally, I thank Noel for his contribution to the literature and for making it so easy to extend what has become a popular and well-received book on C++.

Next I must thank (profusely) Jenifer Niles, my publisher, for her ongoing support and endless patience, and for giving me the opportunity to take on this second edition. Also thanks to Lance Morganelli for his words of encouragement near the end when I was running on fumes and obscene amounts of caffeine.

I'd also like to thank some folks at Applied Research Associates, Inc., particularly Graham Rhodes and Rob Phillips, for their advice and support, including the daily reminders that I had a book to write, and "when was it going to be finished," and all that. Special thanks goes to Kevin Jones for providing the cover image, in spite of my many reworks and "tweaks" that a programmer has no business suggesting.

Finally, as always, I thank my wife, Sukie. I don't know how she puts up with these projects, but her steady patience and encouragement kept me sane even when everything else was a little crazy.

INTRODUCTION

WELCOME TO THE SECOND EDITION

Welcome to the second edition of *C++ for Game Programmers*! With the success of the first edition by Noel Llopis, it was inevitable that an updated version be written to address a number of questions and suggestions submitted by readers of all varieties of experience in game development. Through reader feedback in forums, blogs, reviews, and word-of-mouth, numerous ideas for improvement were considered in the writing of this new edition. The result is the book you now hold in your hands.

Aside from numerous emendations and improved examples and illustrations, the second edition offers three new chapters to satisfy the most popular demands of readers past. Chapter 8, "C++ Design Patterns," covers in detail some of the high-level problem-solving constructs that are most commonly found in games and other interactive applications. After the introductory chapters on the Standard Template Library, Chapter 11, "Beyond STL: Structures and Algorithms," provides a detailed hands-on discussion of using C++ to create efficient solutions to often difficult problems in a highly structured manner. Finally, Chapter 14, "C++ and Scripting," covers the ever-increasing use of embedded scripting languages and the many ways scripting can increase productivity without compromising the power and philosophy of C++.

It is hoped that this new edition will serve the needs of game programmers better than ever, particularly those who are new to C++, as well as those who are new to game development.

WHY THIS BOOK?

There are a lot of C++ books out there. Hundreds. Some of them are excellent, classic books in the field, and you'll see them mentioned quite often here. Others are not quite so good, and memories of them quickly fade into mediocrity. So why add yet another C++ book to the mix? The answer is that very few of these books deal with the unique problems we encounter as game programmers. In short, even the best books on the subject leave the reader ill-equipped to developed high-end games.

The better C++ books do offer excellent advice; they can improve your C++ programming and your ability to design solid C++ programs. But for the most part, they offer nothing more than *general* advice, and although a lot of it applies to game programming, much of it does not. Not only that, but some of the advice is even counterproductive for game development. By the time you realize this, you might be too far into your project to do anything about it.

That is where this book comes in. It does not intend to replace all the great C++ books out there. Instead, it supplements them by putting everything into perspective from a game-development point of view. This book points out the most effective C++ practices and steers you away from the potentially dangerous ones. It describes common C++ techniques to solve specific problems that most game developers have to face. It is an experienced hand to guide you along the way and help you quickly become an experienced C++ game developer.

When in doubt, this book takes a pragmatic approach to C++ development. Some recent books and articles expound the cleverness of certain techniques and language tricks while glossing over the fact that there are hardly any compilers that actually support these techniques, and that they actually make the code more confusing. This book focuses on the techniques that have been proven in real project environments that resulted in successfully shipped games, while steering clear of the more experimental and unproven approaches.

Is game development really any different than general application development? You can always find examples of applications that have some of the same requirements as games; but no other class of commercial software takes on *all* the difficult issues at the same time. These are some of the characteristics that games often have:

- Run at interactive speeds, even across the network
- Maintain a minimum acceptable frame rate (30–60 frames per second)
- Use most (or virtually all) of the system's hardware components
- Use a ton of audio, visual, and other data resources
- Employ cross-platform development

For example, it might be acceptable to spend 50 ms allocating some memory buffers in response to pressing a button to check your email, but it is clearly not acceptable to do that in the middle of a game running at 60 frames per second (where every frame is at most 16.7 ms).

Those characteristics shape how we approach the development of games. It is a mix of shrink-wrapped application development, real-time development, and operating system development. To make things even more interesting, throw in the mix the need to create gigabytes of resources and the fact that game development teams are made up of very diverse people, and you end up with a truly unique development process.

C++ FOR GAME DEVELOPMENT

Just a few years ago in the mid- to late 1990s, C was clearly the language of choice for game development. Nowadays, C++ has taken its place as the preferred language. It also happens to be really convenient: because C is just a subset of C++, it offers an easy upgrade path.

Notice that just because a program has been written in C++ it does not mean it is object oriented. A lot of code is being written in C++ as just a "better version of C." Also, there are still platforms where C++ development is not the norm; these are usually severely limited environments, such as handhelds and cell phones.

There were two main reasons for the transition from C to C++. The first one was complexity. As programs got more and more complex, people looked for solutions that would allow them to deal with the added complexity. In a way, this is the same reason that motivated the change from assembly to C as the primary development language over a decade ago.

The second reason is maturity. During the 1990s, C++ finally reached a more stable state. The standard was completed, the compiler support improved, and more C++ compilers appeared for different platforms, including new game consoles.

Those two reasons, along with faster computers and more easily available memory, made transitioning to C++ an easy choice. However, it does not mean that C++ is perfect. Far from it! C++ has its share of problems. Some of them are caused by the C baggage it carries around for backward compatibility, and a few are caused by poor design decisions. Even so, with all its problems, C++ is still the best tool we have at hand today. This book is not intended as a language advocacy book; it simply helps you use C++ as effectively as possible for game development.

For all the bad things that can be said about C++, its strength is that it is extremely powerful. Using it effectively is difficult, and so it comes with a steep learning curve. However, the benefits that can be reaped are well worth the effort. C++ is one of the few languages that allow high-level programming while still allowing really low-level access to the computer when necessary. It is a perfect mix for systems programming, and it is also perfect for game development. The trick is to know how to avoid getting tangled up in little unnecessary details and look at the big picture. C++ programming is all about tradeoffs: there are many ways of implementing the same functionality, so successful programming and design is all about finding the right balance between efficiency, reliability, and maintainability.

Another great advantage of C++ is that it is quite platform independent. Being able to develop for multiple platforms using the same source code is becoming more of an issue every year in light of the wide variety of game consoles as well as a significant PC market. Good C++ compilers are available for all the major game platforms as well as STL implementations and other major libraries. However, most of the low-level graphics, user interfaces, and sound APIs are still platform specific; so abstracting out the details becomes a useful practice for development on multiple platforms.

FOR WHOM IS THIS BOOK INTENDED?

This book is primarily intended for software engineers who are using C++ for game development or a similar field, such as real-time graphics or systems development. Both industry veterans with some C++ experience and people new to the industry who have a strong programming background can benefit from this book.

To get the most out of this book, you should have been using C++ for a few years, maybe even through a full project. You should have the C++ mechanics down and be ready to move on to the next step. If you have an extensive C background and are looking to move to C++, and you are ready to move at a fast pace, this book can also benefit you. Along with some basic C++ books, this book should shorten your learning curve by several years.

Specifically, at a minimum, you should have written several C++ programs, be comfortable with the syntax, and be familiar with some of the basic object-oriented concepts, such as inheritance. If you are not at that point, it would be best to put this book aside for a few weeks, start with some of the introductory C++ references listed in "Suggested Reading" at the end of Chapter 1, "Inheritance," and then come back here. Although not necessary, a comfortable familiarity with the concepts of pointers, memory layouts, CPU registers, and basic computer architecture is helpful for getting the maximum out of this book.

SOME GROUND RULES

Throughout this book, you'll see certain terms used over and over. These are terms with which most C++ programmers are familiar, but which escape exact definitions. However, most of the time, their exact meaning is very important in understanding the concepts presented here. Instead of explaining them every time they come up, here is an explanation of the most important terms:

- **Class:** The abstract specification of a user-defined type. It includes both the data and the operations that can be performed on that data.
- **Instance:** A region of memory with associated semantics used to store all the data members of a class. There can be multiples of these for each class.
- **Object:** Another name of an instance of a class. Objects are created by *instantiating* a class.

```
// This is an object of the class MyClass
MyClass object1;
// This is another one
MyClass object2;
// The pointer points to an object of the class MyClass
MyClass * pObj = new MyClass;
```

- **Declaration:** The part of the source code that introduces one or more names into a program. The following code is the declaration for a class:

```
class MyClass
{
public:
    MyClass();
    void MyFunction();
};
```

- **Definition:** The part of the code that specifies the implementation of a function or class. The following code defines the function `MyFunction()` from the previous declaration:

```
void MyClass::MyFunction()
{
    for (int i=0; i<10; ++i)
    {
    // Do something...
    }
}
```

ON THE CD

Small code snippets are in almost every chapter, in addition to the full source code on the CD-ROM. In writing the code, I have tried to maintain a plain, consistent style, with as few distractions as possible from the concepts that the code is trying to present. In the code, you will see all variables and function names using the MixedCaseApproach. In addition, I have used some basic prefixing in variable names that I think greatly increases readability (no, do not run away, it is not a full Hungarian notation!):

Scope Prefixes

m_	Class member variable. Hence, it is possible to, at a glance, distinguish a member variable from a local (stack) variable— for example: m_HitPoints.
s_	Class static variable—for example: s_HeapName.
g_	Global variable. Hopefully, you will not see many of those around—for example: g_UserInfo.

Type Prefixes

b	Boolean variable—for example: bAlive.
i	Integer—for example: iNumItems.
f	Floating point—for example: fRatio.
p	Pointer—for example: pItem.

The scope and type prefixes can be combined to create variables, such as m_bCanFly and s_pHeap.

SOURCE CODE

This is primarily a book about ideas and concepts. This is not a source of C++ code that you can just drop into your game project without knowing what it does. Instead, this book covers how things work in detail, what tradeoffs are involved, and what are some good rules to follow.

ON THE CD

The source code on the CD-ROM that accompanies this book is intended to illustrate the concepts explained in the chapters. It is one thing to talk about a construct and show a few code snippets and another to actually see a small program working in tandem to illustrate that specific construct.

To keep the source code as clear and to the point as possible, it is implemented in a somewhat austere manner. The code samples usually have no error-handling support or a clear abstraction between different layers. It is not the type of code you want to drop straight into a commercial product, but it *is* the type you want to read in a book that seeks to teach you the important concepts.

However, you can use the code on the CD-ROM as a starting point. Modify it, experiment with it, and eventually adapt it to fit your needs; or rewrite it from scratch to fit into your game engine with the knowledge you acquire from this book.

ABOUT THE COVER IMAGE

The cover image includes screen shots of a prototype serious game application, *Nemesis*, developed by Applied Research Associates, Inc. (ARA). The game is based on the Nemesis Advanced Demining System (Nemesis ADS), a U.S. Army Night Vision and Electronic Sensors Directorate (NVESD) research and development project being performed by ARA. The supporting program for the Nemesis ADS project is the U.S. Army Humanitarian Demining Program. The Nemesis ADS integrates mine-detection and neutralization technologies on a remotely controlled robotic platform. The objective of the game is to train operators in the decision-making and psycho-motor skills required for humanitarian demining. The prototype has partial support for the embedded hardware components used with the actual system and simulates the basic demining CONOPS defined by the Nemesis ADS program. The U.S. Army and the Night Vision and Electronic Sensors Directorate do not endorse the prototype game.

I

C++ ESSENTIALS

Ask your favorite basketball player what the secret of his success is. Chances are he will say it is all founded on the basics. He took the time to practice the basics over and over: dribbling with the right hand, dribbling with the left hand, making jump shots—over and over for many years. By learning those basic moves and concepts to the point that they became second nature to him, he was able to put together some of the most effective and spectacular plays on the court.

In that respect, C++ is fairly similar to basketball or any other skill-based activity. It is possible to create large, breathtaking programs in C++, but that requires a very solid foundation rooted in a solid grasp of the basic elements of the language. Before we can jump into creating full-blown games in C++ that awe players with their silky-smooth animation and efficient use of the hardware, we must first learn the ins and outs of the language.

In this first part, we cover the major features that differentiate C++ from C. We see how those features are used, how they are implemented internally and, most importantly, what their tradeoffs are and when they should be used. Knowing when *not* to use a specific feature is just as important as knowing the mechanics of how to use it.

INHERITANCE

In This Chapter

- Classes
- Inheritance
- Polymorphism and Virtual Functions
- To Inherit or Not to Inherit?
- When to Use and When to Avoid Inheritance
- Inheritance Implementation (Advanced)
- Cost Analysis (Advanced)
- Alternatives (Advanced)
- Program Architecture and Inheritance (Advanced)

*I*nheritance is a fundamental concept that is used often in advanced C++ topics, and it appears repeatedly throughout this book. Inheritance allows us to create new classes based on an existing class. Understanding exactly how inheritance works and how it is correctly (and incorrectly) used is an important step toward effective game development in C++.

1.1 CLASSES

To a beginner, the main difference between C and C++ is usually the concept of classes. C++ code written by an experienced C programmer with little exposure to C++ will often be referred to as "C with classes." But classes, in themselves, are little more than syntactical sugar.

In a nutshell, classes are ways of associating data with functions. *Objects* are specific instances of a class, each holding its own data, but sharing functionality with other objects of the same class.

The data part of a class is no different from a plain C structure. The only thing new is that C++ offers three levels of access: *public, protected,* and *private*. Additionally, by default, the items of a class are private, while the items of a structure are public. The following data structures are exactly the same. Notice how we had to explicitly add the `public` keyword to the class in order to make the member variables accessible from the outside.

```
struct Point3d
{
    float x;
    float y;
    float z;
};

class Point3d
{
public:
    float x;
    float y;
    float z;
};
```

As we will see later on, compilers vary a fair amount among themselves and from one platform to another in their code-generation rules. Compilers also vary in the types of optimizations they perform. In spite of this, both the `struct` and the `class` shown above generates an identical assembly sequence and will have the same performance characteristics on just about any platform.

What about being able to associate functions and data as part of the same data structure? That is where the syntactical sugar that makes classes unique comes in. It is certainly a very nice feature to have; it allows us to clearly express what operations we want to perform on a set of data. For example, to get the length of a vector, it's much more natural to write `objToCamera.Length()` than `Length(objToCamera)`.

But this is nothing more than an illusion. Internally, the C++ compiler quickly rewrites member function calls as plain C function calls, with the difference that the first parameter passed to the function is a pointer to the object to which the function is applied. The following code shows a member function call and how the compiler interprets it internally.

```
Vector3d objToCamera = object.GetPos() — camera.GetPos();

// This function call…
float fDist = objToCamera.Length();
```

```
// …would be transformed to something like this:
float fDist = Vector3d_Length(&objToCamera);
```

This is not to say that classes are only trivially different from structures. They are the basis for some other C++ features that allow us to do very powerful object-oriented programming in a natural way. They are also a pleasure to work with—our taste of syntactical sugar. To really see where the power of C++ comes from, we must look at the concept of inheritance.

1.2 INHERITANCE

Inheritance allows us to easily create new classes that are variations of an existing class. This is achieved with minimum work and without having to modify the original class in any way.

Inheritance comes in handy for representing concepts in an intuitive way. For example, we might have just finished creating a class that represents a normal enemy character in our game. The class takes care of animating the character on the screen, keeping track of its hit points, running the artificial intelligence (AI) for that character, and so forth.

```
class Enemy
{
public:
    void SelectAnimation();
    void RunAI();
    // Many more functions…
private:
    int m_iHitPoints;
    // Many more member variables here
};
```

When it comes time to add boss characters at the end of the level, we are faced with a tough decision: we would like to reuse a lot of the functionality of the Enemy class (e.g., tracking hit points, running animations, and so on), but the boss character is going to do a lot more than a regular enemy unit. We could move a lot of the functions out of the Enemy class and write a Boss class that also uses them. Unfortunately, that would mean breaking up the nice, encapsulated class we just created, which results in more maintenance headaches down the line.

This is where inheritance comes into play. We can create a new Boss class that *inherits* from the Enemy class. That means that the Boss class is going to adopt all the functionality of the Enemy class by default; in addition, we can override particular sections to give the boss the unique behavior we want. In this case, we can override the AI to do something completely different that gives the boss his unique character. This is how the Boss class would look using inheritance:

```
class Boss : public Enemy
{
public:
    void RunAI();
};
```

In a situation like this, Enemy would be called a *parent class*, and Boss would be a *child class*, because Boss inherits from Enemy. Now we can use both enemies and bosses like this:

```
Enemy enemy1;
Boss boss;

// Tell the enemy and boss to do their thing
enemy.RunAI();
boss.RunAI();
```

The variables and functions in a public section in a class are exposed to everybody using that class. The protected section can be used by the class itself and by all classes that derive from it. Finally, the private section is available only to that class, not even to the classes that derive from it. Refer to one of the C++ references at the end of this chapter for the specific syntax details of those keywords if you are not already familiar with them.

Sometimes we do not want to completely override a particular function in the parent class; instead, we just want to add some functionality to it. For example, we might want the Boss class to still behave like an enemy, but we want it to do some extra AI computations on top of that. The implementation of RunAI() would look like this:

```
void Boss::RunAI()
{
    // First run the generic AI of an enemy
    Enemy::RunAI();

    // Now do the real boss AI on top of that
    // ....
}
```

As you can see from the code, to call a function in the parent class that we are overriding, we prefix the call with the parent's class name followed by two colons (::). That is the C++ *scope operator*, and it specifies where a function, variable, or class resides. In this case, we are saying we want to call the RunAI() function in the parent Enemy class, not in the current Boss class.

There is nothing stopping us from inheriting from a child class to create a new child class. For example, we might want to create a really special boss for the end of the game, so we create the SuperDuperBoss. A derived class is not limited to overriding functions from its immediate parent class; it can override public and protected functions from *any* of its parent classes. In this case, we will override another function from the Enemy parent class.

```
class SuperDuperBoss : public Boss
{
public:
    void RunAI();
};
```

It quickly gets cumbersome to talk about classes inheriting from each other and from other classes in turn just by trying to describe how they are connected. Sentences quickly become a collection of the words *parent*, *child*, and *derived* mentioned over and over, making very little sense. This is not all that different from trying to explain a distant family relation: "It was my stepsister's twice-removed cousin's brother who. . . ." Just like a family tree, class diagrams can be used to give the same information in a much more concise way. The diagram in Figure 1.1 shows the relationship between the three classes we have constructed so far.

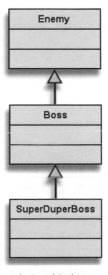

FIGURE 1.1   Inheritance relationship between three enemy classes.

We will be using the type of diagram shown in Figure 1.1 throughout this book. You will find similar diagrams used extensively in other C++ literature.

1.3 POLYMORPHISM AND VIRTUAL FUNCTIONS

So far, the inheritance examples we have covered are very simple but already very useful. However, if we were to begin using inheritance in a real project in the way described, our code will quickly become limiting and cumbersome. The main drawback is that pointers to objects have to be of the exact same type as the object to which they point. It sounds strange, doesn't it? After all, an int has always been of the type int, and nobody has complained about not being able to use a float pointer to refer to it. Read on. . . .

If, in the enemy/boss example, we have 20 different types of enemies and 5 different bosses, and we want to call the ExecuteFrame() function once for all the enemies currently in the level, we must keep track of the type of each enemy unit. That means keeping a list for each type of enemy and boss, and then iterating through each list. Every time we add a new unit type, we have to remember to add a new list and iterate through it. This could prove quite cumbersome. Wouldn't it be nice if there were a way to just keep a list of enemy units and call the ExecuteFrame() function on all of them, regardless of what type they really are?

That is exactly what *polymorphism* gives us: the ability to treat an object of one class as if it were an object of another class in the same inheritance hierarchy. Polymorphism is an extremely important fundamental concept to understand in order to follow along in this chapter and the rest of the book—as well as for any work you do in C++. Here is a short example of what polymorphism allows us to do:

```
// We can create an object of type Enemy:
Enemy * pEnemy1 = new Enemy

// And we can create an object of type Boss:
Boss * pBoss = new Boss;

// We can also create a pointer of type Enemy to refer to
// the boss!
Enemy * pEnemy2 = pBoss;
```

Even though it does not sound all that impressive, polymorphism is an extremely powerful feature. It allows us to forget about the true type of the object we are manipulating and to decouple the code that deals with that object from the specific implementations of each derived class. For instance, we could have a function that takes an enemy as a parameter and figures out whether or not we can shoot at it. This function could look something like this:

```
// Determine if the given enemy can be shot at
bool CanShootAtEnemy( Enemy& enemy );
```

As soon as we add a boss to the game, we must determine whether or not we can shoot at it. Without polymorphism, we are either forced to write a similar function that takes an object of type Boss as a parameter, or do something very dangerous, such as passing a void pointer and a flag indicating what type of variable it is:

```
// Bad: ignore polymorphism and write a new function to
// determine
// if a boss can be shot at
bool CanShootAtBoss (Boss& boss);

// Worse: try to write a generic function that uses the
// type of
// object and a void pointer
bool CanShootAtEnemyOrBoss(void* pEnemyOrBoss, bool
bIsEnemy);
```

Things can only get worse when we add new types of enemy classes. Polymorphism helps us by allowing us to have only one function that takes a reference to an enemy class, regardless of what type of enemy it is. This is also the mechanism we will use in later chapters to write plug-ins and to extend the functionality of the game without recompiling it (great for patching or even user-created "mods").

Going back to the enemy example, we can take advantage of polymorphism to make our program a lot simpler by keeping all the enemy units in a single array, regardless of whether they are plain enemies, bosses, or the final special boss. This allows us to treat all three types exactly the same way.

But there is potential for trouble here. Remember that we wrote a RunAI() function for both the Enemy class and the Boss class (which inherits from Enemy). Consider the following code snippet that uses polymorphism:

```
Enemy * pEnemy = new Enemy;
pEnemy->RunAI();      // Enemy::RunAI() gets called
```

```
Enemy * pBoss = new Boss;
pBoss->RunAI();     // Which function gets called??
                    // Boss::RunAI() or Enemy::RunAI()?
```

When both the pointer and the object are of the Enemy type, calling RunAI() clearly calls Enemy::RunAI(). But what happens when the pointer is of the Enemy type, and the object is of the Boss type? The answer is, it depends on whether RunAI() is a *virtual function* or not.

A function marked as virtual indicates that the type of the object should be used to determine which function should be called in case inherited classes override that function. Otherwise, the type of the pointer will always be used.

In our example, we want the bosses to run the Boss AI, and we want each enemy to run the correct type of AI based on its object type; so, we should make the RunAI() function virtual. Here is the revised Enemy class:

```
class Enemy
{
public:
    void SelectAnimation();
    virtual void RunAI();
    // Many more functions could go here…
private:
    int m_iHitPoints;
    // Many more member variables could go here…
};
```

Now we can finally act on all enemies with the same code, independent of whether or not they are a boss.

```
Enemy * pEnemies[256];          // Create an array of enemies
enemies[0] = new Enemy;
enemies[1] = new Enemy;
enemies[2] = new Boss;          // A Boss is an enemy,
                                    so this works
enemies[3] = new FlyingEnemy;   // Another type of enemy
                                    also works
enemies[4] = new FlyingEnemy;
// etc...

// Inside the game loop
   for ( int i=0; i < iNumEnemies; ++i )
   pEnemies[i]->RunAI();
```

1.4 To Inherit or Not to Inherit?

When you have a hammer, everything looks like a nail. Inheritance is a very powerful tool. A natural, initial reaction is to try to use it for everything. However, used incorrectly, inheritance can cause more problems than it solves, so you should consider using it only when appropriate, and when there is no other, simpler solution. There are two basic rules of thumb to consider when using inheritance, discussed next.

1.4.1 Rule 1: Containment versus Inheritance

Usually, the creation of a new class that inherits from another class models the "is a" relationship. If class B inherits from class A, it means that an object of type B is also of type A. In our previous example, the Boss "is an" Enemy, so it follows the rule correctly.

Imagine that someone suggests that the Enemy class should in turn inherit from the Weapon class; that way, the enemy can shoot and do all the things a weapon does. Tempting, but does it follow the rule? Is an enemy a weapon? Clearly not. It is more accurate to say that an enemy "has a" weapon. This kind of relationship is called *containment*, and it means that the Enemy class should probably have a member variable of type Weapon, but it should not inherit from it. The first rule is: *inheritance must model the "is a" relationship*.

Why bother making the distinction? The program will compile and run correctly even if Enemy inherits from Weapon. It might even save us some typing in the short term. The problems will arise later when we try to maintain it or make changes to the program. What if enemies can switch between different weapons? What if they can have multiple weapons? What if some of them have no weapons at all? A good, logical design makes all of these changes a breeze. Using inheritance incorrectly will make your life in effecting these changes much more difficult.

When in doubt about whether to use inheritance or not for a particular situation, avoid it—especially at the beginning when you are still learning its long-term effects on a large project. Many more projects were ruined by badly used inheritance than by using it too conservatively.

1.4.2 Rule 2: Behavior versus Data

Armed with the inheritance tool and our previous rule, an eager programmer creates a new class, EnemyTough, which inherits from Enemy, but which has twice as many hit points. It fits the previous rule perfectly: EnemyTough is an Enemy. So is there anything wrong with this arrangement?

Things will probably start looking strange when the EnemyTough class is fleshed out—the class is almost empty. The only new content will reside in the constructor, which assigns more hit points than the Enemy class. It looks useless, and in fact it *is* rather useless.

The reason that EnemyTough should not be a new class is that the only thing that changed is data, not the behavior of the object. If EnemyTough is not going to have any different behavior, then it is no different than an Enemy object that was initialized with more hit points.

This gives us our second rule: inherit from a class only when you want to modify the behavior of the class, not to change the data.

Apart from not doing anything that couldn't be accomplished in a much easier way, one of the main drawbacks of inheriting from classes in order to change data is the combinatorial explosion that can occur. Maybe we have an invulnerable enemy. Suppose that, instead of using a flag in the Enemy class, we create a new class, EnemyInvulnerable. What if we want a tough, invulnerable enemy? What about bosses and tough, invulnerable bosses? Also, data is something that can change easily during the course of the game. Maybe the enemy can use special powers and become invulnerable for a short period of time, or perhaps the enemy can get extra hit points and become "tough." If you have modeled those concepts through classes instead of through data, it will be very cumbersome to change the enemy object type while the game is running.

1.5 WHEN TO USE AND WHEN TO AVOID INHERITANCE

The previous section explained when it is correct to use inheritance as opposed to other types of construction. Normally, that is all you need to know, and that is as far as most other books take the subject.

You also need to be aware that there is a slight performance penalty associated with virtual functions. The following section, "Inheritance Implementation (Advanced)," deals with the gory details of how inheritance and virtual functions are implemented. For the time being, let's just say that our program will run a bit slower when using virtual functions.

The first consequence of this realization is that we should not use virtual functions unless we have to. This might sound really obvious, but sometimes people are tempted to make every function a virtual one just in case somebody, sometime, somewhere decides to inherit from that class and extend it. Planning for the future like that is commendable, but in most cases it is better not to open up that many possibilities. Maybe no object will inherit from those classes and will not override those functions. It would be great if compilers were smart enough to optimize virtual functions into plain functions when the virtual mechanism is not needed, but the C++ language was not designed that way. So for now, every time we make a virtual function call, we are paying a small penalty in performance.

Apart from the performance hit, there are still really good reasons not to make every function virtual. We cannot predict the future; so, unless we are aware of a pressing need to derive from a particular class, avoid doing so. By the time somebody does decide to derive a new class, things might have changed enough that the original class must be rewritten anyway. Also, it is much easier and faster to create a class without thinking of future extensibility, private functions, and member variables. As soon as we make them protected, public, or virtual, we need to start worrying about how they are going to be used, split them correctly, and maintain a consistent state. In other words, do not make a function virtual unless you are aware of a reason to do so *right now*. Most of the time, this is all we need to worry about. With current hardware, the overhead of virtual function calls is pretty small, so we can almost forget about it.

As it happens, sometimes we just cannot afford for a particular function to be virtual. Maybe it is a function deep inside an inner loop that gets called thousands and thousands of times per frame. This can be particularly true if it is a simple function that could otherwise be *inlined* (see Chapter 6, "Performance," for more information on inlining functions and dealing with performance). Before we get ready to replace this function with something else, we should really verify that it is the "virtualness" that is hurting performance. If that is the case, we should replace the virtual function with a nonvirtual function. Remember that just putting in an `if` statement and calling separate nonvirtual functions probably will not be any faster. We might need to make several copies of our inner loop, one for each function that is called. Even better, we might want to consider moving that inner loop into a class, and ensure that we call the correct loop based on a virtual function; that way there is only one virtual function call's worth of overhead for the whole loop.

Another potential performance drain is when the program crosses the virtual boundary many times. This is different from the case described before in that it is not just one virtual function that is called over and over again, but a whole set of functions. For example, imagine a virtual interface to a graphics renderer module. All the functions in the interface are virtual functions.

```
class GraphicsRenderer
{
public:
    virtual SetRenderState(...);
    virtual SetTextureState(...);
    virtual SetLight(...);
    virtual DrawTriangle(...);
    //...
};
```

Unfortunately, the abstraction for the renderer class was not chosen at the correct level, so every time we want to draw a triangle on the screen, we end up calling the sequence of virtual functions: `SetRenderState()`, `SetTextureState()`, `SetLights()`, and `DrawTriangle()`. Multiply that by the number of triangles rendered in each frame these days, and the virtual function overhead quickly adds up.

That is an extreme example, and the cost of drawing one triangle at a time on current PC graphics hardware would kill the game, but imagine for a moment that the main cost comes from the virtual function calls. How can we fix this problem? We can solve it by moving the abstraction to a higher level. Instead of the previous interface, we can come up with a new abstract interface that draws an initial mesh (set of triangles), like this:

```
class GraphicsRenderer
{
public:
    virtual SetMaterial(...);
    virtual DrawMesh(...);
    //...
};
```

Now, to draw a set of triangles, we call only two functions: `Set Material()`, and `DrawMesh()`. We have reduced the number of virtual functions called from four or five per triangle to only two per hundreds or thousands of triangles. Notice how the change we had to make was a major one. Completely changing such an interface has major consequences in all the code that calls it as well as in the program architecture in general, so this is something we should carefully consider when designing the interface for the first time.

1.6 Inheritance Implementation (Advanced)

In order to go any further in our understanding of the tradeoffs of inheritance, it is imperative to learn exactly how inheritance is implemented under the hood. Compiler writers have a fair amount of freedom in how they decide to implement inheritance; as long as they comply with the standard, they can pretty much do anything they want. Fortunately, just about every compiler we will come across on the PC and modern consoles will implement inheritance in roughly the same way, with only minor differences.

First, let's start with nonvirtual functions. These are easy because a particular function call always maps to a particular part of the code. The compiler can calculate the address of that function at compile and link time; at runtime, all it does is make a call to a fixed address.

Virtual functions are tricky because the code called depends not only on the specific function call made, but also on the type of the object that the function is called on. Usually, this is solved through the use of *virtual tables*, which are more often referred to as *vtables*. The vtable is nothing more than a table of pointers to functions. Every class with at least one virtual function has one of these vtables, and indexing into the correct slot of the table determines which function needs to be called at runtime.

An important thing to know about the vtable is that it only contains pointers to virtual functions; nonvirtual function addresses are still computed at compile time and are called directly in the code. That means that we pay only a few extra bytes and a small performance penalty per virtual function, but we are not affecting the performance of nonvirtual functions. This has been one of the guiding design principles of C++ from the start: you do not have to pay for features you are not using.

It is also important to note that there is only one vtable per class, not per object. This is extremely important because we typically have many instances of objects for a single class. For example, if we have a tile-based terrain, we might have a class that represents a terrain tile. If the map is 256×256, we will have 65,536 objects, but fortunately only one vtable (assuming all those terrain tiles are of the same class and have at least one virtual function).

The vtable for all the objects of a particular class will be the same, so instead of each object having a vtable of its own, each object has a pointer to the vtable for that class. Otherwise, how is the program going to know what class that object belongs to at runtime? Usually, this pointer is the first entry of the object. Consequently, the size of an object containing at least one virtual function increases at least by the size of a pointer. In current platforms, a pointer is usually four bytes. In the previous terrain example, that means we will be using an extra 64 KB just in vtable pointers, plus a few bytes for the vtable itself. That is a rather modest memory consumption considering the benefits we get out of it, but it is something we should be aware of nonetheless, especially on platforms with more limited memory.

To be correct, not every object has a pointer to a vtable—not even every object that belongs to a class with inheritance. Only objects that belong to a class with virtual functions have a vtable. It is a small but important distinction. It means that we are free to use inheritance for small, basic classes, such as a vector or a matrix, as long as we do not have any virtual functions in the class. Again, the same design principle is at work: if we are not using a feature, we are not paying any performance or memory penalties for it.

Figure 1.2 shows roughly how the memory layout looks for a class with virtual functions. For all of the gory details of virtual function implementation, refer to the resources in "Suggested Reading," at the end of this chapter.

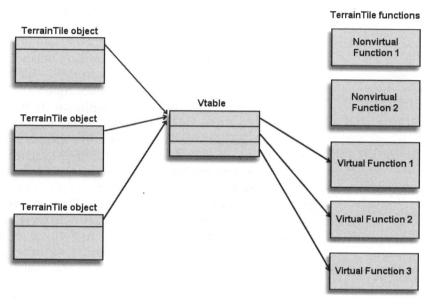

FIGURE 1.2   Memory layout of nonvirtual functions, virtual functions, a class vtable, and objects from that class.

1.7 Cost Analysis (Advanced)

Throughout this chapter, we have talked about a performance penalty for using virtual functions. We have been waving our hands, saying that the cost is not too great; but this penalty is not something we can totally ignore at all times, either. How much of a penalty is that exactly? Do you pay it every time you call a virtual function? How does it vary from platform to platform? Here is what happens at runtime when we call a virtual function through a pointer of a base class:

Step 1. Everything starts with an innocent-looking function call.

```
pEnemyUnit->RunAI();
```

Step 2. The vtable pointer of that object is fetched (see Figure 1.3).
Step 3. The entry at the offset corresponding to the function we are calling is fetched from the vtable (see Figure 1.4).

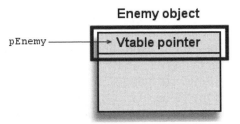

FIGURE 1.3   The vtable pointer of the object is fetched.

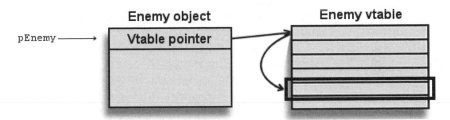

FIGURE 1.4   The correct entry in the vtable is fetched.

Step 4. A function call is made to the address specified by the vtable entry (see Figure 1.5).

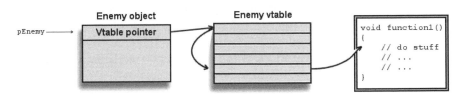

FIGURE 1.5   The function pointed to by the vtable entry is called.

Step 4 is the same as for a nonvirtual function, so the added cost in using a virtual function comes from steps 2 and 3. Those steps make the sequence look more expensive, but exactly how expensive is it? Unfortunately, it is very hard to answer that question accurately these days. Not only does the cost vary greatly from platform to platform, but different cache levels, speculative execution, and deep pipelining make it almost impossible to come up with a good answer.

We could just ignore any performance penalties, write the game, and then profile it to find out whether we have a bottleneck caused by virtual functions. Even though leaving optimizations for the end is a very good general rule, it falls short here. First of all, it is difficult to determine that things are being slowed down by virtual functions. Unlike an expensive inner loop, the use of virtual functions is not going to show up as hot spots in the profiler output. The consequences of virtual function overhead are going to be much more subtle and much more widespread. Most important, even if we narrow the bottleneck down to virtual function overhead, it might be too late to change it. If the whole game is architected to use inheritance and virtual functions to override specific behaviors, it is going to be extremely difficult to radically change this structure and remove all the virtual function calls that are slowing us down.

The best approach is to have some reasonable expectations of the impact virtual function calls have on our program and to keep those in mind when writing the game. Still, theoretical knowledge of virtual functions is no substitute for getting our hands dirty after the game is running; we'll have to do some real profiling and make sure our assumptions were in the ballpark.

Most of the time the added cost of using virtual functions is negligible. Sometimes the program does not run any slower (assuming the CPU was waiting for some other results to complete in the FPU unit, for example). Yet at other times—in very deep, frequently called loops, for example— we might feel the extra performance hit.

The greatest performance penalty often comes from what we do not get, rather than from the overhead of steps 2 and 3. Virtual functions are usually not inlined, so if the function could have been otherwise inlined, that might amount to a significant hit. We should avoid making functions virtual that we want to be inlined; it probably means we are trying to set an interface at too low a conceptual level anyway, so it is probably time to rethink that design.

Another big issue is the impact of the vtable lookup in the data cache. If we have many different types of classes, and all are being executed in a random order, we will find ourselves looking up entries in many different vtables during the course of a frame. This could cause the data cache to eject some other data we need, or even to consistently have cache misses for vtables we need to look up. In this situation, or on a platform with little or no data cache, the penalty added by virtual functions is much more noticeable and can lead to significant performance degradation of the game.

Do we always pay the cost of the extra indirection for virtual function calls? Surprisingly, the answer is not always. Compiler writers are very crafty and go out of their way to make sure our programs run as fast as possible. So if there is a shortcut they can take to make our program faster, they usually take it.

As it turns out, we need to go through the vtable jumps only for the most general (but also most common) cases. It is possible that we will be calling a function marked as virtual on an object directly (instead of through a pointer or a reference). In that case, the compiler notices it and invokes a nonvirtual function call. A similar thing happens if we are using a pointer or reference of the same type as the object itself; the compiler can optimize away the vtable jump and call the function directly.

```
Enemy * pEnemy1 = new Boss;
pEnemy1->RunAI(); // We pay the virtual function cost

Boss * pEnemy2 = new Boss;
pEnemy2->RunAI(); // Virtual function call optimized out
```

1.8 ALTERNATIVES (ADVANCED)

You have reached this point, and you are still not convinced you want to use inheritance. The extra memory overhead and performance hit really look like too much for what you are trying to do. Besides, you have managed to program perfectly fine in C without using inheritance, so why would you need it now?

That is a fair question. The best way to address it is to think about how we would go about doing a similar implementation in C without the help of inheritance. There are a variety of ways to do it.

- **One structure and many conditional statements:** We could create one C structure containing all possible data we might need for all inherited classes, add a type field, and everywhere we use it, have many conditional checks on the type field, doing different things depending on the type. Apart from how ugly the code will get and the maintenance nightmare if we use this approach, memory is wasted because all our structures are the same size (the size of the largest set of data we want to represent). Performance is also much worse than using virtual functions as soon as there are more than a few `if` statements because the performance cost of several conditional jumps quickly adds up.
- **One structure, but use `switch` statements instead of conditional statements:** In this approach, the source code looks a bit tidier, but chances are the compiler will produce the same code as for the

`if` statements, resulting in the same drawbacks. In some very rare instances, the compiler might be able to replace all the conditional jumps with a jump table. In that case, at best, performance will be the same as for virtual functions. Unfortunately, there is usually no easy way to reliably coerce the compiler into generating a jump table out of `switch` statements.

- **Tables of pointers:** We could create a table of function pointers for each type of object and then put a pointer to the appropriate table in each structure. We would have to take extreme care to fill it correctly for each structure, and it would not be particularly easy to read or pleasant to debug. Does this approach sound familiar? Of course it does; we are just re-implementing virtual functions except that we are not getting any of the other benefits of inheritance (different object sizes, private-protected members, and so on). Performance is the same with this approach as when using virtual functions and inheritance, except that it requires a lot of work. Let the compiler do the busy work for you instead.

The conclusion we should take away from this is that if we need the features of inheritance and virtual functions, we should just use them instead of trying to re-implement them all from scratch. Chances are the compiler will do a better job than we could at optimizing the code and doing all the bookkeeping.

1.9 PROGRAM ARCHITECTURE AND INHERITANCE (ADVANCED)

You might recall some warning comments in an earlier section in this chapter mentioning the potential dangers of inheritance. The problem goes way beyond "little" things such as unnecessary performance penalties or increased memory consumption. The real problem is what extensive use of inheritance can do to your source code.

The purpose of a class is to model self-contained concepts and to abstract out their implementation. This is done by providing the smallest public interface necessary and by hiding all the complexity inside private functions and member variables. Keeping that in mind, creating a class with a clean public interface is a challenge. We must make decisions about what should be exposed and what should be hidden; we must decide how to minimize the interface while providing all the flexibility we need. It is not an easy or straightforward job.

Adding inheritance to that mix is like fighting a war on two fronts. Not only do we have to worry about the current users of the class, we also have to worry about future extensibility and the protected interface we should expose. Things just got a lot more difficult all of a sudden.

The other major problem with inheritance has to do with its effect on the overall architecture of the program. Use of inheritance can quickly turn into deep inheritance chains—whole inheritance trees spanning dozens or hundreds of classes, some of them five, six, or more levels deep. Even though each class might have been modeled correctly, and even though it follows all the rules for correct inheritance, this situation is still undesirable. Large inheritance trees with many levels of inheritance make it hard for programmers to understand what the code is doing. Function calls need to be traced up and down the inheritance tree, and it might be difficult to know exactly what function is being called, depending on which functions specific classes override.

Worst of all, inheritance tends to "harden" the program design. Software in general (and games a bit more so) needs to be flexible. Things change—new requirements come from the publisher, new features need to be added to stay competitive, or something needs to be changed to make it more fun. Having a code base that can easily adapt to change is a worthy goal. The last thing we want to happen is to be two weeks away from shipping the game and not be able to make a crucial change that *should* have been trivial, but isn't.

What are our alternatives? We previously mentioned containment as being different from inheritance. Containment models the "has a" relationship, while inheritance models the "is a" relationship. Inheritance should never be used to model the "has a" relationship. However, sometimes we might want to use containment when inheritance would have been appropriate.

Containment, unlike inheritance, does not have the tendency to harden the program design. Things stay flexible and malleable. Because objects are contained within other objects, they do not need to know anything about who is holding them; they just need to worry about doing their job when they are told to do it. In a way, we are back to pure encapsulation. And the simpler the classes can be, the easier they are to use, develop, maintain, and change over time.

This does not mean that we should replace all inheritance with containment, only the problematic uses of inheritance. In a situation with a really deep inheritance chain, we might want to consider using containment judiciously in a few places just to break that chain into two or three smaller chains.

Look at the diagram in Figure 1.6 for an example of such a transformation. A deep inheritance chain five levels deep was transformed to use containment, and now the largest inheritance chain only has three levels. Notice how the arrows for inheritance are different than the arrows for containment.

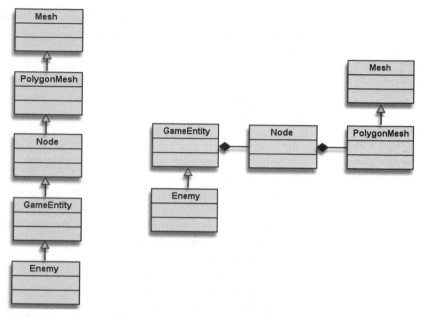

FIGURE 1.6   A deep inheritance chain can be modeled with containment.

1.10 CONCLUSION

After a quick review of C++ classes and objects, we saw how to create new classes based on existing classes through the use of inheritance. Then we saw a key concept behind object-oriented programming: polymorphism, the ability to refer to different types of objects through a pointer of the type of one of their parent classes. Virtual functions go hand in hand with polymorphism because they let us specify whether we want to call a function based on the pointer type or based on the object type.

We then examined how and when inheritance should be used, considered the correct uses of inheritance, presented alternatives, and looked at the potential drawbacks of inheritance. Specifically, we detailed how inheritance and virtual functions are implemented and what performance penalties they can cause.

SUGGESTED READING

Following are some excellent introductory C++ texts. You might want to browse through them as a refresher for some of the concepts in this chapter or as a starting point if you have no previous C++ experience.

Cline, Marshall, *C++ FAQ Lite*. Available online at *http://www. parashift.com/c++-faq-lite/*.

Eckel, Bruce, *Thinking in C++*. Prentice Hall, 2000. Also available online at *http://www.mindview.net/Books/TICPP/ThinkingInCPP2e.html*.

Lippman, Stanley B., *C++ Primer*. Addison-Wesley, 1998.

The following books give some good advice on how to use and not use inheritance:

Cargill, Tom, *C++ Programming Style*. Addison-Wesley, 1992.

Murray, Robert B., *C++ Strategies and Tactics*. Addison-Wesley, 1993.

For a really in-depth look at how inheritance and virtual functions are implemented, this is one of the best references out there:

Lippman, Stanley B., *Inside the C++ Object Mode*. Addison-Wesley, 1996.

MULTIPLE INHERITANCE

In This Chapter

- Using Multiple Inheritance
- Multiple Inheritance Problems
- Polymorphism
- When to Use Multiple Inheritance and When to Avoid It
- Multiple Inheritance Implementation (Advanced)
- Cost Analysis (Advanced)

Multiple inheritance is another new concept to C++. Single inheritance allowed us to create new classes from a parent class; multiple inheritance extends that capability by allowing us to create a class based on two or more parent classes. It is not as widely used as single inheritance, and it has its share of problems, but when used properly, multiple inheritance can be an effective tool in your design repertoire. In particular, specific idioms of multiple inheritance, such as abstract interfaces, can be very useful.

2.1 USING MULTIPLE INHERITANCE

Let us consider a simple design scenario, how we would implement it with the different tools we have at hand, and how it could be addressed with multiple inheritance. For this example, we are designing the basic

`GameEntity` class. This is the class from which all our game types will in-herit: enemy units, items, triggers, cameras, and so forth. In particular, we must implement two requirements: all game objects must be able to receive a message, and all game objects must be able to be linked as part of a tree. Forgetting about all other aspects of the `GameEntity` class, how can we go about implementing those two requirements?

2.1.1 The All-in-One Approach

The most obvious approach is to implement those requirements as part of the `GameEntity` class itself. There we can add the functions to receive mes-sages and to link the game object to any part of the tree.

As usual with C++, there are many different solutions to any given problem. Unfortunately, the first one that comes to mind—adding every-thing we need to the same class—is not usually the best way to go. This "all-in-one" approach is clearly very simple and straightforward, which is a big plus, but it also has some major drawbacks.

The simplicity of a class is a double-edged sword. On the one hand, it is very easy to add functionality without having to create new classes, change inheritance chains, or make any other structural changes. On the other hand, if we keep adding directly to the class definition, the `GameEntity` class will continue to grow in size and complexity every time we add a new concept. Soon, a fundamental base class such as `GameEntity` could balloon to an unmanageable size and a tangle of functions, difficult to both use and maintain. In our attempt to keep things simple in the short term, we have made things much more complicated over the long term.

Another problem with including all the functionality in a single class is code duplication. Is `GameEntity` the only class that will receive mes-sages? Maybe the `Player` class will also receive messages without being a game entity itself. Is `GameEntity` the only class that will be part of a tree? Probably other objects, such as scene nodes or animation bones, might be organized in a similar way. It would be a pity, as well as bad software en-gineering practice, not to reuse that code. Simply copying the relevant code everywhere it is needed is not a viable solution because doing so leads to major maintenance headaches as the architecture evolves.

2.1.2 Containment Considered

It is clear that each of the object types just mentioned should be repre-sented by its own class. In this case, we could have `MessageReceiver` and `TreeNode` classes. The question remains: how should these classes be re-lated to the `GameEntity` class?

The game object class could contain one of each of those objects and provide functions in its interface to use them. This approach is called *containment* (see Chapter 1, "Inheritance"), because a GameEntity object contains a MessageReceiver and a TreeNode object (Figure 2.1). As we will see in a later section in this chapter, containment is often an excellent solution. It leads to great reuse, without adding too much complexity to the classes that are extended in this way.

The only drawback with containment is that many interface functions, whose only purpose is to call a member function of another object, must be created and maintained. Those functions are tedious to maintain, particularly if the interfaces change often, and slightly degrade performance because of the extra function-call overhead. This is how the GameEntity class looks with containment:

```
class GameEntity
{
public:
    // MessageReceiver functions
    bool ReceiveMessage(const Message & msg);

    // TreeNode functions
    GameEntity * GetParent();
    GameEntity * GetFirstChild();
    // ...

private:
    MessageReceiver m_MsgReceiver;
    TreeNode        m_TreeNode;
};

inline bool GameEntity::ReceiveMessage(const Message & msg)
{
    return m_MsgReceiver.ReceiveMessage(msg);
}
inline GameEntity * GameEntity::GetParent()
{
    return m_TreeNode.GetParent();
}
inline GameEntity * GameEntity::GetFirstChild()
{
    return m_TreeNode.GetFirstChild();
}
```

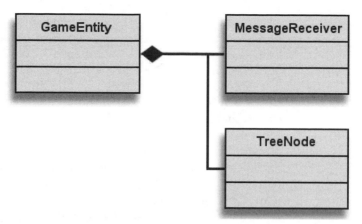

FIGURE 2.1   GameEntity class using containment.

We could use containment, as in the preceding code, but instead of providing member functions to interact with the objects inside GameEntity, we could just expose the objects themselves. That would certainly cut down on the maintenance of the dummy interface functions, but it exposes more information than necessary about how GameEntity is really implemented. If later we were to change its implementation to a more efficient way that did not use one of those classes, all the code that used GameEntity would have to be changed as well. Because this is not an attractive prospect, let's keep the private members of GameEntity private for the moment.

2.1.3 The Single-Inheritance Approach

Let's approach the problem using a technique we learned in Chapter 1: single inheritance. We saw that single inheritance very easily allows us to create a class that is a variation of a parent class. We could declare that a GameEntity object is a MessageReceiver and that it inherits from Message Receiver. But what about TreeNode? In a way, GameEntity also is a TreeNode. This concept cannot be modeled easily with single inheritance. We might be tempted to create an inheritance chain like the one shown in Figure 2.2.

On the surface, the inheritance chain solution seems to work. The program will run correctly, but it is a really ugly design that will only cause trouble later on. Is a TreeNode a MessageReceiver? It does not have to be, so why does it inherit from it? Reversing the relationship does not seem right, either. Besides, doing such an inheritance tree prevents us from reusing TreeNode elsewhere without it being a MessageReceiver as well. So, we'll have to come up with a better idea.

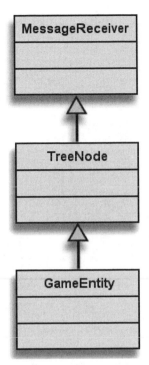

FIGURE 2.2   Single inheritance is not always enough; sometimes an inheritance chain is helpful.

2.1.4 Multiple Inheritance to the Rescue

Multiple inheritance is the solution to our problem. It works just like single inheritance, except that a class is allowed to inherit from multiple parent classes. In our case, we can have GameEntity inherit both from MessageReceiver and from TreeNode, and GameEntity will automatically have the interface, member variables, and behavior of all its parent classes. This is how we define the GameEntity class using multiple inheritance in code:

```
class GameEntity : public MessageReceiver, public TreeNode
{
public:
    // Game entity functions...
};
```

The corresponding inheritance diagram is shown in Figure 2.3.

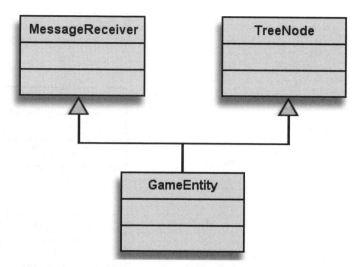

FIGURE 2.3   `GameEntity` modeled with multiple inheritance.

An object created with multiple inheritance can be used just as if it had been implemented using single inheritance:

```
GameEntity entity;
//...
GameEntity * pParent = entity.GetParent();
```

2.2 MULTIPLE INHERITANCE PROBLEMS

As you might expect, introducing new functionality and new features also introduces new complexities and problems. Multiple inheritance is no exception. As a matter of fact, some people might argue that multiple inheritance introduces more problems than it solves. Let's consider some of the main problems:

- Ambiguity
- Topography
- Program Architectures

2.2.1 Ambiguity

The first problem with multiple inheritance is ambiguity. What happens if two classes we inherited from contain a member function that has the exact same name and parameters? In our previous example, imagine that both `MessageReceiver` and `TreeNode` have a public member function called `IsValid()`, which is used for debugging and checks whether the object is in a correct state. What is the result of calling `IsValid()` on a `GameEntity` object? The result is a compile error because the call is ambiguous.

To solve the ambiguity, we must prefix the function call with the class name of the function we want to call. If we want to call those functions from within the `GameEntity` class, we use the *scope operator* (::) and write it like this:

```
void GameEntity::SomeFunction()
{
    if (MessageReceiver::IsValid() && TreeNode::IsValid())
    {
        //...
    }
}
```

Things get worse if we want to call those functions from *outside* the `GameEntity` class. We must also prefix those function calls with the class they belong to, so now the calling code needs to know about the parent classes of `GameEntity`:

```
bValid = entity.MessageReceiver::IsValid() &&
         entity.TreeNode.IsValid();
```

2.2.2 Topography

An even larger problem with multiple inheritance is the topography of some of the possible inheritance trees that can be created. Consider the following situation: we have an AI class that deals with moving entities on land (`LandAI`), and another class that deals with moving entities through the air (`FlyingAI`). Our game designers just came up with a new type of hybrid entity that needs to move both on land and through the air, and we need to create an AI class for it. A possible solution would be to inherit from both `LandAI` and `FlyingAI` (see Figure 2.4).

Everything goes well until we realize that both `LandAI` and `FlyingAI` inherit from the same base class. The inheritance tree we have just unknowingly created is shown in Figure 2.5.

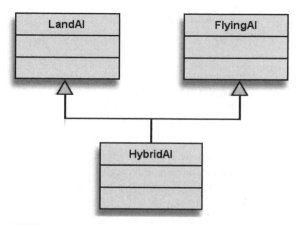

FIGURE 2.4   An innocent-looking multiple inheritance tree.

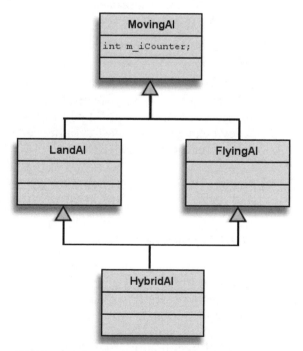

FIGURE 2.5   A diamond-shaped inheritance tree.

In code, the same class structure would be represented like this:

```
class MovingAI
{
```

```
    // ...
protected:
    int m_iCounter;
};

class FlyingAI : public MovingAI
{
    // ...
};

class LandAI : public MovingAI
{
    // ...
};

class HybridAI : public FlyingAI, public LandAI
{
    // ...
};
```

This is the dreaded diamond-shaped inheritance tree, also referred to as the DOD (Diamond Of Death). MovingAI is a parent class for HybridAI, but through two different paths. This arrangement has several unexpected consequences:

- The contents of MovingAI appear twice in HybridAI because HybridAI is created from two different classes, each of which already contains MovingAI. So, surprisingly, HybridAI will contain two m_iCounter variables.
- Trying to use a member variable of MovingAI from within HybridAI is ambiguous. We need to specify the inheritance path through which we want to access the member variable. It sounds redundant, since both paths seem to lead to the same variable, but as we saw in the previous point, this is not the case.

A representation of a HybridAI object, showing how it is composed of different sections from its parent classes, is shown in Figure 2.6.

To solve this problem with multiple inheritance, C++ introduces a new concept: *virtual inheritance,* which is a totally different concept than virtual functions. Virtual inheritance allows a parent class to appear only once in its children's object structures, even in the presence of the diamond inheritance hierarchy. But virtual inheritance comes with a runtime cost, as well as a small space cost. There is a lot of pointer fix-up and table dereferencing that must happen under the hood for everything to work as expected at runtime.

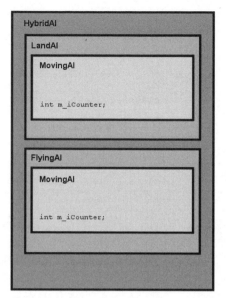

FIGURE 2.6   An object structure with multiple inheritance.

So, what is the best solution? It is best to avoid the diamond inheritance hierarchy at all costs. Usually, it is the sign of a bad class design, and it will cause more problems in the long run than it will solve. If you are absolutely convinced that a diamond-shaped hierarchy is the best design for your program, then make sure you and your team are aware of all the details and side effects of virtual inheritance. The "Suggested Reading" section at the end of this chapter is a great place to start. As for the rest of this book, we will avoid both virtual inheritance and the diamond-shaped hierarchy.

2.2.3 Program Architectures

As if that were not enough, multiple inheritance presents one last, fundamental problem: its correct but careless use can lead to a horrible program architecture. Over-reliance on multiple inheritance, and to a lesser extent on single inheritance, ends up causing deep inheritance hierarchies with large objects, bloated interfaces, and very tight coupling between classes. All this translates into your not being able to easily reuse individual classes in different contexts, a difficulty in maintaining and adding new features to existing code, and increased compile and link times.

Multiple inheritance is a complex, difficult tool to use. Whenever possible, it is best to look for alternative solutions such as composition, and to use multiple inheritance only when it is the best of all alternatives. Later in this chapter, we will examine some specific cases where multiple inheritance is the preferred solution.

2.3 POLYMORPHISM

Just as you can with single inheritance, in multiple inheritance you can refer to an object through a pointer of the parent class type. However, unlike single inheritance, with multiple inheritance we have to be much more careful in how we obtain and manipulate those pointers.

We can always cast a pointer to a class further up the hierarchy, as in the case of single inheritance. We can use the old-style C casting or the preferred C++-style casting.

```
GameEntity * pEntity = GetEntity();
MessageReceiver * pRec;
pRec = (MessageReceiver *)(pEntity); // C cast
pRec2 = static_cast<MessageReceiver *>(pEntity); // C++ cast
```

Things get more complicated when we cast down or across the hierarchy. With single inheritance, all we had to do was to make sure that the object we were pointing to was of the right type and then cast as usual. With multiple inheritance, this approach does not work. The reason has to do with the structure of the object with multiple inheritance—specifically, of the vtable. With single inheritance, the beginning of the vtable was the same for all the classes in the hierarchy, but derived classes would use entries further down in the vtable. With a multiple-inheritance hierarchy, different base classes will have different entry points in the vtable, so the cast will actually return a different pointer than the one it was cast from. This is covered in more detail in the section, "Multiple Inheritance Implementation," later in this chapter.

How is this casting accomplished? It is typically accomplished through the use of dynamic_cast, one of the new casting styles. Unlike the other forms of casting, dynamic_cast introduces some runtime code that actually does any necessary pointer arithmetic and adjusts for different vtable offsets. Additionally, dynamic_cast returns NULL if our casting is not legal given the object or the inheritance hierarchy.

```
GameEntity * pEntity = GetEntity();

// Normal dynamic cast. Works fine.
MessageReceiver * pRec;
pRec = dynamic_cast<MessageReceiver*>(pEntity);
```

```
// Also works fine, but pNode will have a different value
// than pEntity
TreeNode * pNode;
pNode = dynamic_cast<TreeNode*>(pEntity);

// This is not a valid cast because the entity we have is not
// actually a player object. It will fail and return NULL.
Player * pPlayer;
pPlayer = dynamic_cast<Player*>(pEntity);
```

Unfortunately, not only does `dynamic_cast` introduce a slight performance penalty, it also requires RTTI (runtime type information) to be enabled in the compiler settings. That means that the compiler will create and keep information at runtime about all the C++ classes, enough to be able to perform `dynamic_cast` correctly. It is not a huge amount of memory per class, but every single class will have that information, which can add up. That is particularly unfortunate because we probably do not need that information in every single class, especially not in simple, lightweight classes such as matrices or vectors. In Chapter 15, "Runtime Type Information," we will examine the default RTTI system in detail and present a custom-made alternative that might be better suited to games.

2.4 When to Use Multiple Inheritance and When to Avoid It

So far, the picture we have presented of multiple inheritance has not been particularly promising. You might even be wondering why there is a whole chapter dedicated to it. After all, the conclusion so far seems to be that it is better to avoid it as much as possible. However, if applied carefully, multiple inheritance can be a useful tool.

The most important thing to remember is not to use multiple inheritance indiscriminately. Just because it is the first solution that comes to mind does not mean it is the best one. We saw that multiple inheritance carries several potential problems with it: it can cause ambiguities that increase the complexity of the program, and it can also cause a small performance hit.

Whenever possible, consider using containment as an alternative to multiple inheritance. Most often, containment is a better solution for your intended design. If containment is not possible or is really cumbersome, do not apply single inheritance unless it fits right in. Trying to twist a single-inheritance chain to solve a problem that requires multiple inheritance is even worse because it creates useless temporary classes without real meaning, and it makes the program even harder to understand and maintain.

As we will see in more detail in Chapter 12, "Abstract Interfaces," abstract interfaces are a great application of multiple inheritance. By putting a few restrictions on the type of classes we can inherit from, abstract interfaces can use multiple inheritance without any of the problems described in this section. Abstract interfaces are the basis for switching implementations at runtime, extending the game after it has shipped, and for creating plug-ins, which are covered in Chapter 13, "Plug-Ins."

Avoid multiple inheritance in deep, complex hierarchies. Single inheritance makes things confusing enough when you are trying to find out where things are implemented and what the flow of the program is. Multiple inheritance makes such sleuthing that much harder. When you create deep, complicated hierarchies, it is very easy for the dreaded diamond-shaped hierarchy to rear its ugly head. That should be avoided at all costs until you are absolutely sure you need it to be that way.

Some good examples of multiple inheritance that have come up in the past in game development are simple, general extensions to a class. A reference-counted class is a good example of a function that can be used freely with multiple inheritance. Any function that inherits from this class will become reference-counted through the `AddRef` and `Release` functions. Such a class is usually perfectly fine to inherit from because it is very simple and because it does not inherit from any other classes in turn.

2.5 Multiple Inheritance Implementation (Advanced)

Multiple inheritance is implemented in a very similar way to single inheritance, but with some added complexity. Unfortunately, multiple inheritance does not result in nearly as neat and efficient an implementation as single inheritance does.

One of the most elegant aspects of single-inheritance implementation is that objects are always backward compatible with objects of parent classes. Because only one vtable pointer is needed, all extra elements added by derived classes are tacked on at the end, so a parent class simply ignores them. This allows us to easily cast up and down the inheritance hierarchy as long as we know the types of the objects (see Figure 2.7).

Under multiple inheritance, things are a bit more complicated. Because of polymorphism, a derived class should be able to be addressed like any of its parent classes after it has been correctly cast. Just appending the member variables and keeping one vtable (as you can with single inheritance) does not work because we cannot make the derived class look like all of its parent classes, no matter how hard we try.

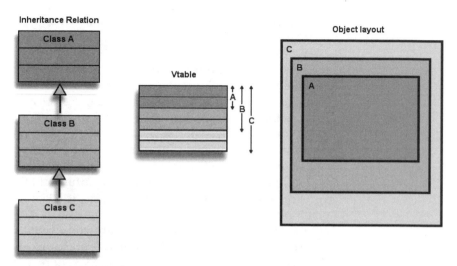

FIGURE 2.7   Parent class and derived classes using single inheritance.

Instead, along with the data, we must also append one vtable for each parent class. Now it becomes possible to cast a derived object to any of its parents by adding an offset to the pointer (see Figure 2.8).

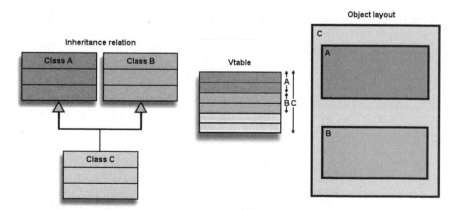

FIGURE 2.8   Two parent classes and a derived class with multiple inheritance.

From a memory standpoint, multiple inheritance adds an extra pointer to every object for every parent class. This memory hit is usually not a big deal considering the large amounts of RAM in today's computers, but it is something to keep in mind. In some applications, some objects are created many thousands of times, and we should be aware of this extra space requirement. As in the case of single inheritance, the vtable pointer is necessary only if there are some virtual functions in the parent class from which we are inheriting. Otherwise, only the member variables are appended.

One last thing to notice is that the order in which those classes are appended to create the derived class is completely implementation dependent. Most compilers append the classes in the order in which they are declared in the inheritance statement, but some compilers shuffle classes around a bit to gain a slight performance improvement.

2.6 COST ANALYSIS (ADVANCED)

Multiple inheritance has the same performance characteristics as single inheritance except for two cases: casting and virtual functions of the second parent class.

2.6.1 Casting

In the case of single inheritance, casting a pointer up and down the hierarchy is a free operation. Casting just identifies an object to the compiler as being of a particular class. The compiler makes sure that all operations on that pointer are legal, and that any virtual functions are using the correct vtable.

With multiple inheritance, things are more complex. Because the derived object is made out of multiple concatenated objects, each of them with its own vtable, some pointer adjustment is needed when casting between different types. Specifically, when casting a pointer from a derived class to the second (or later) parent class, or vice versa, a small offset is added to the pointer to point to the "correct" part of the object.

Casting to and from the first parent class has no effect on the pointer; it is a free operation, just as it is with single inheritance. Casting from the derived class to the first parent class is a similar operation without any effect on the pointer (see Figure 2.9a).

```
Parent1 * pParent1 = new Child;
Child * pChild = dynamic_cast<Child*>(pParent1);
assert (pParent1 == pChild);    // Unchanged
```

Casting from a parent class other than the first to the derived class changes the pointer. In this case, it adds a negative offset to point to the "real" beginning of the object (see Figure 2.9b).

```
Parent2 * pParent2 = new Child;
Child * pChild = dynamic_cast<Child*>(pParent2);
assert (pParent2 != pChild);    // Not the same!
```

Finally, casting from the derived class to the second parent class also changes the pointer. Now it adds a small offset that points to the subsection of the object that corresponds to that parent class (see Figure 2.9c).

```
Child * pChild = new Child;
Parent2 * pParent2 = dynamic_cast<Parent2*>(pChild);
assert (pChild != pParent2);    // Not the same!
```

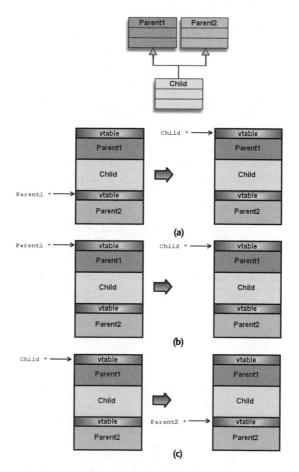

FIGURE 2.9 **(a)** Casting a pointer down the hierarchy from the first parent class. **(b)** Casting a pointer from the second parent class to the derived class. **(c)** Casting a pointer from the derived class to the second parent class.

How much of a performance hit can that extra pointer offset cause? Not much. The offset needed to add or subtract from the pointer is known at compile time, so it does not even require a data access somewhere else in memory (with potential data-cache-thrashing problems). The overhead of the vtable access and eventual function call more than overshadows the cost of adding an offset.

The more serious performance hit comes from the `dynamic_cast` itself. At runtime, the program must determine whether it is possible to cast between the original pointer type and the class to which we are trying to cast. For that, the program needs to take into account the type of the pointer we are casting, the type of object referenced by the pointer, and the final class type to which we want to cast. Depending on the implementation, the larger and more complicated the inheritance tree becomes, the slower the operation will be. In Chapter 15, we will examine dynamic casting and RTTI more closely and implement a custom version with better performance characteristics.

2.6.2 Virtual Functions of the Second Parent Class

The extra performance cost of multiple inheritance is not limited to `dynamic_cast`. A small performance cost is involved whenever a virtual function is invoked that belongs to a parent class other than the first one.

Look again at Figure 2.8 and notice how the derived object has multiple vtables. Whenever one of the functions in a vtable other than the first one is called, the pointer must be adjusted accordingly before the call. As it turns out, the pointer adjustment is exactly like what happens during the casting, as described in the previous section. Fortunately, this time there is no need to involve `dynamic_cast`, so the actual performance cost is negligible and can easily be ignored most of the time.

2.7 CONCLUSION

In this chapter, we examined the concept of multiple inheritance. It allows us to create a new class based on two or more parent classes and works very similarly to single inheritance.

Unfortunately, multiple inheritance has many problems: the ambiguity introduced by diamond-shaped inheritance trees, the need for virtual inheritance to solve that problem, a slight performance penalty, and, worst of all, a lot of complexity in what should be a simple building block.

Because of these problems, it is often better to look for other constructs when designing our programs. However, one good use of multiple inheritance is in abstract interfaces and their applications, such as plug-ins. We will cover these options in detail in later chapters.

SUGGESTED READING

For general advice about multiple inheritance, its uses and abuses, refer to the following resources:

Cargill, Tom, *C++ Programming Style*. Addison-Wesley, 1992.
Meyers, Scott, *Effective C++*. 2nd ed. Addison-Wesley, 1997.
Meyers, Scott, *More Effective C++*. Addison-Wesley, 1995.
Murray, Robert B., *C++ Strategies and Tactics*. Addison-Wesley, 1993.

For all the gory details about how multiple inheritance is implemented, including a discussion of virtual inheritance, refer to this resource:

Lippman, Stanley B., *Inside the C++ Object Mode*. Addison-Wesley, 1996.

3

CONSTNESS, REFERENCES, AND A FEW LOOSE ENDS

In This Chapter

- Constness
- References
- Casting

This chapter deals with some of the new concepts introduced in C++ that are not present in C. They are not fundamental concepts with major consequences, such as inheritance or templates, which will be covered in Chapter 4, "Templates." Rather, they are concepts with a more limited scope, and they are not going to radically affect the program architecture. This chapter should be a nice interlude after dealing with the complexities of multiple inheritance and before tackling the mind-bending subject of templates.

Specifically, the concepts covered in this chapter are: constness, which allows us to mark objects as read-only; references, which are a safer, nicer form of pointer; and the new casting operators, which even though they are a bit verbose, have some clear advantages over the brute-force approach of C-style casts.

All these concepts are useful in everyday programming. They are used throughout this book and in most C++ code written for today's games. Becoming familiar with these new concepts and knowing how to use them effectively is the focus of this chapter.

3.1 CONSTNESS

The const keyword is not new to C++, but you will see it a lot more often than in plain C programs. In addition to its old meaning, the keyword has been extended to work on references and member functions.

3.1.1 Concept

The concept of const is straightforward: it indicates that the "part" marked const cannot be changed (that is, will be constant) during program execution. The extremely vague word *part* was used on purpose to leave the definition sufficiently general to deal with all the different things we can flag as const, as we will see shortly.

By itself, const is only moderately useful. What makes it really an outstanding feature is that the compiler will enforce that rule in a very similar way to flagging parts of a class as private or protected. If anybody tries to modify the contents of an area marked as const, the compiler reports it right away as a compile-time error. Compile time is the best possible time to find out about these errors. And the sooner we find them, the sooner they can be corrected. Let's start by reviewing const variables.

```
const int MAX_PLAYERS = 4;
const char * pcAppName = "MyApp";
```

The variables are marked as const so that any attempt to modify them results in a compile-time error:

```
MAX_PLAYERS = 2;    // Error, MAX_PLAYERS is declared const
```

Experienced C programmers will no doubt wonder what the advantage of const is over using the #define preprocessor directive. Functionally, they are very similar, but using const allows the compiler to apply the usual C++-type safety, which might help catch errors and potential problems. Using #define just results in a straight text substitution with no type checking whatsoever. As a general rule, we should try to rely on the compiler as much as possible to check things for us. If the compiler can handle this busy work, our time is better spent elsewhere, rather than in tracking down strange typecasting problems.

Another added advantage of using const identifiers is that they are entered in the symbol table as they are compiled, which means they will be available in the debugger. It makes debugging a lot easier to see the symbolic name of the constant in the debugger as opposed to trying to guess what #define a certain number belongs to. Anyone who has had to debug and make sense of Win32 error codes and flags will immediately appreciate this advantage.

3.1.2 Pointers and `const`

Pointers are always a bit tricky when combined with `const`. Consider the four possibilities:

```
int * pData1;
const int * pData2;
int * const pData3;
const int * const pData4;
```

The easy ones are the first and last lines. Clearly, `pData1` is a non-const pointer to non-const data, meaning you are free to modify either one. The last one, `pData4`, is the opposite; you cannot modify either the pointer or the data pointed to by it. But what about the other two?

Remember: the `const` refers to what follows immediately to the right of it. So `pData2` is a non-const pointer to `const` integers. On the other hand, `pData3` has a `const` immediately to the left of the pointer variable, so the pointer is a `const`, but not the data it points to. Drawing mental parentheses to group the `const` keyword and what it affects helps make things clearer:

```
// Not C++ code, just a mental aid
(const int *) pData2;
int * (const pData3);
```

As if this were not complex enough, C++ adds yet another syntax variation to express the same concept. Otherwise, it would be hard to come up with tricky interview questions. What do you think this third form means?

```
int const * pData5;
```

It is a syntactically correct statement, but the `const` is between the data type and the asterisk. Drawing mental parentheses as before, we get `(int const *) pData5`, which should give us the right answer. This is a non-const pointer to `const` data. It is no different than `pData2`; it just has the `const` in a slightly different place. This style is not as common, but you might come across it sometime, so it is a good idea to at least be aware it exists as an alternative form.

3.1.3 Functions and `const`

One of the most useful applications of const is to flag function parameters and result values. Whenever we need to pass a function parameter that is large or expensive to copy, we usually pass a pointer to it instead (or a reference, as we will see in the next section). Using a pointer will avoid any copying costs and is very efficient. However, doing so has changed the behavior of the program. We initially intended to pass a copy of the original data; but now, to make things faster, we are passing the original data itself. We have changed from passing parameters by value to passing them by reference, purely for performance reasons.

Without using `const`, we have no way of distinguishing when a pointer to data is passed because of performance reasons and when it is passed so the function can modify the original data. This distinction is extremely important when maintaining a large code base. Even worse, a function might originally just read the data passed to it, but somewhere down the line, the function can be changed to actually modify that data. That could be disastrous if other parts of the program assume that the data will not change.

Using `const` solves all those problems. It removes any assumptions about when data changes and makes it totally explicit. Not only does `const` help us by flagging violations of the rule as a compile error, it lets a human reader of the source code quickly see the intent of a pointer (or a reference) parameter:

```
// Clearly pos is read-only
void GameEntity::SetPosition (const Point3d * pos);

// Vector entities will not be modified
int AI::SelectTarget (const vector<GameEntity*> * pEnts);
```

If a parameter is passed by value to a function, there is no need to use `const` at all. We are already passing a copy of the data, so there is no point in preventing the function from modifying that data if it wants to for its internal computations. That is an implementation detail, and the code that calls it should not have to care about it.

The same concept is applied to `return` values. Imagine a function that returns a rather expensive object to copy, such as a string or a matrix. The normal optimization is to return a pointer to the object instead of a new copy. Now the object can be modified directly through the pointer that was returned by the function. If that was our original intent, then all is well and good. However, maybe in our design we did not want people to be able to modify the object in such a direct fashion. In that case, we have created a potential loophole in our design. Consider the following `Player` class as an example:

```
// Player class with some constness problems
class Player
{
```

```
public:
    void SetName (char * name);
    char * GetName();
    //...
private:
    char m_name[128];
};

void Player::SetName (char * name)
{
    ::strcpy(m_ name, name);
}

char * Player::GetName()
{
    return m_ name;
}
```

At first glance everything looks good. We can set the name (probably in response to the player typing his or her name on the user interface), and we can retrieve the name to print it out or to send it along with chat messages over the network. The class will work as it stands.

However, as it is written, the class has the potential for many problems. Anybody can call GetName(), retrieve the pointer to the actual character array in the player object, and not only read from it, but modify it with impunity. Is that a problem? Most likely, yes. Chances are the class was designed to expect any player-name changes to happen by calling the SetName() member function. Maybe the new name is set to all the other players over the network, or maybe the new name is changed on the user interface. In either case, changing the name directly on the pointer we got from calling GetName() will not cause the desired effects. It can also be a hard bug to track down because it does not result in a crash or in any immediately apparent problem. Things that just get mysteriously out of synch are some of the hardest bugs to track down.

A way to get around that potential problem is to check every frame for whether the player name has changed, and if so, do whatever we need to in response to that change. But this is a lot of work and complexity for something that should be much simpler.

We could document the function profusely and explain that the pointer to the character array returned by GetName() is not supposed to be modified directly. But there is always the potential that someone will misuse the function, especially when people are in a hurry to meet their approaching deadlines.

A much better approach is to let the compiler enforce the fact that the object cannot be modified. We can do that by using `const` as part of the type of the `return` value of the function:

```cpp
// A better Player class without const problems
class Player
{
public:
    void SetName (const char * name);
    const char * GetName();
    //...
private:
    char m_name[128];
};

void Player::SetName (const char * name)
{
    ::strcpy(m_name, name);
}

const char * Player::GetName()
{
    return m_name;
}
```

Now, the only way to change the `Player` name is to go through `SetName()`, and the code should be greatly simplified. If somebody forgets and tries to write on the pointer returned by `GetName()`, they will get an immediate reminder from the compiler.

Incidentally, the `Player` class still leaves much to be desired, even in the previous two functions. A cleaner implementation would use references instead of pointers (which are covered in the next section), and it would use a string class instead of a character pointer (see the discussion on strings in Chapter 10, "Standard Template Library: Algorithms and Advanced Topics"). Even with these changes, the use of `const` remains the same.

3.1.4 Classes and `const`

So far, this chapter has been a recap of how the C keyword `const` should be used. But this is a book on C++, so why the recap? First, because `const` is not widely used in C code—or not as often as it is in C++ code, anyway. Second, because C++ extends its meaning to deal with class member functions, it is a good idea to become familiar with the const concept before covering new ground. C++ allows us to flag a class member function as a const. For example:

```
// An even better Player class
class Player
{
public:
    void SetName (const char * name);
    const char * GetName() const;
    //...
private:
    char m_name[128];
};

const char * Player::GetName() const
{
    return m_name;
}
```

Notice that both the declaration and the implementation of the member function GetName() were flagged as const. A member function marked as const indicates that executing it will not change the state of the object to which it was applied.

In our example, by flagging GetName() as const, we are telling the readers of the program (and the compiler) that nothing will be changed in the Player just by calling that function. And it is true; notice that all we do is return a pointer. On the other hand, the SetName() function is not marked as const. This is because SetName() changes the internal state of that Player object by changing its name.

This is important for the same reasons that it was important to flag variables or function arguments as const—actually, even more important. We are adding more information about the intentions of a function to the source code. It will make things more readable for other programmers, and it will let the compiler enforce the rules.

The compiler is actually pretty smart. If we had tried to implement the GetName() function returning a non-const character pointer, the compiler would have flagged that as a compile error because a member function that is marked as const is making an internal variable available to the caller without any guarantees of constness. So the const in the return value and the const in the member function go hand in hand.

The same thing applies to calling other functions. A member function flagged as const cannot call a member function of an object that is non-const. In other words, a const function cannot modify data in the object it is applied to or call any non-const functions in other objects.

The consequences of this rule are very important. It means that to use `const` effectively, you must use it everywhere possible. If only some classes mark `const` functions correctly, those functions cannot call other parts of the program that are not marked as `const`, even though they should have been marked that way. This fact makes interacting with older libraries that do not use `const` correctly somewhat annoying. Fortunately, the constness can be cast away (more on this later in this chapter). Needless to say, it should be cast away only when it is absolutely necessary; otherwise, we are defeating the whole point and foregoing all the advantages that the compiler provides us.

3.1.5 `mutable`: `const` but Not `const`

Notice that throughout this discussion, we have talked about the "status" of an object, but we were never more specific about what that meant. The compiler takes the literal meaning and interprets "status" as any member variable of that object changing. Usually, that interpretation matches exactly with what we mean, so everything works as it should.

However, sometimes some member variables do not reflect the status of an object at all, or at least not the logical state. This situation arises most often when an object keeps some internal information about its physical implementation. A simple example is an object that keeps track of how many times a certain query function has been called.

In our `Player` example, maybe each `Player` object wants to keep track of how many times the function `GetName()` has been called. The first thought would be to simply increment an internal counter every time the function is called. But the `GetName()` function is marked as `const`, so any attempt to change a member variable will result in a compile error. Another option might be to demote the function and not mark it as `const`, but this does not make any sense. For all intents and purposes, the `Player` object has the same state that it did before the function was called. Why should someone using the `Player` class care whether or not we are keeping some statistics inside?

Another, more complex example could be caused by the object caching some data. Maybe the object has a large amount of data and wants to load and unload it explicitly whenever necessary. To the outside world, the object should always appear to be present, with all its data; so a simple query function should clearly be marked as `const`, even though we will be loading a lot of data inside.

Fortunately, C++ has a clean solution to this problem: the keyword `mutable`. A member variable marked as `mutable` can be changed from any member function, whether it is marked as `const` or not. So we can mark any member variable that does not represent the object's logical status as `mutable`, and this would solve our problem of changing the variable from a const function.

Going back to the `Player` class example, let's add a `mutable` variable that keeps count of how many times the function `GetName()` has been called.

```
class Player
{
public:
    void SetName (const char * name);
    const char * GetName() const;
    //...
private:
    char m_name[128];
    mutable int m_iTimesGetNameCalled;
};

const char * Player::GetName() const
{
    ++m_iTimesGetNameCalled; // OK because it is mutable
    return m_name;
}
```

3.1.6 const Advice

The best advice with respect to the use of `const` is to use it as much as possible—everywhere: variables, arguments, return values, and member functions. The more extensively it is used, the more useful it becomes, and the easier it is to enforce.

There are no drawbacks at all for using `const`. It makes the intent of our code clearer for other programmers and lets the compiler enforce some added rules. The only time it can become a bit of a chore is when we start to use `const` with an existing code base. Until enough parts of the code have been correctly labeled as `const`, we will have to do a fair amount of casting away of constness. But it will all be worth it once most of the code has been converted to using `const` correctly.

3.2 REFERENCES

A *reference* is simply an alternative name for an object. Any operations done on a reference affect the original object it is referring to. Surprisingly, such a simple concept can become an extremely useful tool to manage complexity.

The syntax for references is simple. Aside from using the & symbol to specify a reference, references behave almost completely like regular objects. References work the same way with built-in data types and with objects.

```
int a = 100;
int & b = a;     // b is a reference to a
b = 200;         // both a and b are 200 now

Matrix4x4 rot = camera.GetRotation();
Matrix4x4 & rot2 = rot; // rot2 is a reference to rot
rot2.Inverse();         // inverses both rot and rot2
```

References are very much like pointers. They refer to an object such that all the operations affect the object that is pointed to by the reference. Also, creating a reference to an object is a very efficient operation, just like creating a pointer.

3.2.1 References versus Pointers

There are several major, very important differences between references and pointers:

- When working with a reference, we use the same syntax as when working with an object. Instead of using the operator -> to dereference the pointer and access member functions and variables, a reference uses a dot (.), just like a regular object.
- References can be initialized only once. A pointer can point to a certain object and then, at any time, be changed to point to a different object. References are different. After they have been initialized to refer to an object, they cannot be changed. In that sense, they behave like const pointers.
- References must be initialized as soon as they are declared. Unlike a pointer, we cannot create a reference and wait until a later time to initialize it. The initialization must happen right away.
- References cannot be NULL. This is a consequence of the first two points. Because references must be initialized right away with a real object, and because they cannot be changed, they can never be NULL like a pointer. Unfortunately, this does not mean that what they point to is valid. It is always possible to delete the object a reference is pointing to or to trick a reference through some casting to point to NULL.
- References cannot be deleted or created like a pointer. In that sense, they are just like an object.

3.2.2 References and Functions

Two of the main uses of references are to pass arguments and to return values from functions. In the previous section about `const` pointers as function arguments, we saw how, for efficiency's sake, it was advantageous to pass a pointer to large objects instead of passing a copy of the object. Although using a `const` pointer solved all the potential problems, having to change an object for the sake of a pointer just because of performance is awkward. References solve that problem. By passing a `const` reference as a parameter into a function, we accomplish the same goal as passing that object by value, without incurring any of the performance costs and with the same syntax. Notice that all the advice about using `const` pointers also applies to using references.

```
// SetRotation takes a const reference to a new rotation
// matrix
void GameEntity::SetRotation (const Matrix4x4 & rot)
{
    if (!rot.IsIdentity)
        // ...
}


// A matrix is a relatively expensive object to copy
Matrix4x4 rot;


// But we can call SetRotation without copying the matrix
// because the matrix is passed as a reference
entity.SetRotation(rot);
```

References can also be used to return objects from a function in an efficient manner. We must be careful what we do with the returned reference however, because if we assign it to an object, a copy will take place. If we just want to keep that reference around while we do some calculations, we must save it into a reference itself:

```
const Matrix4x4 & GameEntity::GetRotation() const
{
    return m_rotation; // Cheap. It's just a reference
}


// Watch out. This is making a new copy of the matrix
Matrix4x4 rot = entity.GetRotation();


// This just holds the reference. Very cheap.
const Matrix4x4 & rot = entity.GetRotation();
```

```
// We can pass the reference straight from a return
// value into a parameter too. Very efficient also.
camera.SetRotation (entity.GetRotation());
```

As with pointers, however, we must make sure that the object we are returning a reference to does not go out of scope when the function disappears. The most common situation is that of returning a reference to an object that was created on the stack. Doing so makes the reference point to an invalid memory location and causes the program to crash as soon as the reference is used. Fortunately, most compilers seem to detect this situation and issue a warning.

Even if you are not yet sold on the idea of references, it is almost impossible to avoid them altogether. You will see references popping up in copy constructors and in binary operators, so you should at least be familiar with their use. Hopefully, the rest of this section will convince you to use them in your own code, also.

```
// Copy constructor
Matrix4x4::Matrix4x4 (const Matrix4x4 & matrix);

// Binary operator
const & Matrix4x4 Matrix4x4::operator*(
                      const Matrix4x4 & matrix);
```

3.2.3 Advantages of References

If references are just like pointers with some different syntax, why use them? Why not stick to pointers? There are several reasons, even though as far as the compiler is concerned, they are pretty much just pointers. The reasons all have to do with making life easier for us, the programmers.

The first advantage of references is their syntax. Even the most experienced C programmer has to admit that it is a lot cleaner to use references than pointers, without asterisks and arrows all over the place. For example, which of these two lines of code do you find more readable?

```
 // Using pointers
position = *(pEntity->GetPosition());

// Using references
position = entity.GetPosition();
```

The next advantage of references is that they can never be NULL like a pointer. They always have to be pointing to an object, or at least to something the compiler was tricked into thinking was an object. In any case, it is usually a lot more difficult to pass an invalid reference than it is to pass a NULL or uninitialized pointer.

Just because a reference was pointing to a valid object at some point does not mean that the object will still be valid by the time it is accessed. The same problem occurs with pointers. This is called the "dangling pointer" problem, in which we keep a pointer to a place in memory that is freed, but the pointer is unchanged, and buggy code can attempt to dereference the pointer. However, recall that references must be initialized when they are first created and can never change values. Thus, it is usually harder to keep a reference around, pointing to some object in memory, after the object is destroyed. Most references go in the stack and disappear when they fall out of scope, so the problem is alleviated to some extent.

Another advantage of references is that there is never any doubt as to whether or not the object pointed to by the reference should be freed by the code that is using the reference. This can be done only through a pointer, not a reference. So if we are working with a reference, it is safe to assume that somebody else will free it.

All these advantages can be summarized by saying that using references is a slightly higher-level way of manipulating objects. It allows us to forget about the details of memory management and object ownership so that we can simply concentrate on the logic of the problem we are trying to solve. After all, we have to remember why we are writing a program in the first place. It is not to show our technical prowess in dealing with low-level details or to use all the latest features of C++; it is to create a great game. The more we can focus on the game and the less we have to worry about memory leaks and other implementation details, the faster we will finish, and the more robust the game will be.

Some people argue that one of the drawbacks of using references instead of pointers is that it is unclear whether objects are passed by reference or value just by looking at the calling code. It can be argued that it is not particularly useful for the calling code to know whether objects are passed by value or by reference. The important point is whether or not they can be modified by the function, and *that* depends on whether or not the reference (or the pointer) is a const. In either case, examining the function declaration reveals that information. With today's code-browsing tools, which are often integrated into the development environment, looking up that information takes nothing more than a mouse click.

Another slightly more sensible, often repeated bit of advice is to use const references for objects that will not be modified by the function, and to use pointers for those objects that will be modified by the function. The argument, again, is that there is no need to look at the function declaration to know more about what the function's intentions are with respect to its parameters. Although it might be true to a certain extent, there are still times when we want to pass a pointer to a function even though the object will not be modified. Besides, not everybody is going to follow this convention, which means that we must check the function declaration in any case.

3.2.4 When to Use References

Are pointers obsolete then? Should we use references all the time? Not at all. A good rule of thumb is to use references whenever possible. They are the cleaner, less error-prone interface. However, some situations still require pointers.

If an object must be created or deleted dynamically, we have to use a pointer to that object. Usually, the owner of a dynamically created object keeps a pointer to it. If anybody else has to use that object, they can use a reference to make it clear that they are not responsible for freeing that object. If at some point the ownership of the object must be transferred, it should be done through a pointer instead of a reference.

Sometimes we have to change the object we are pointing to. In that case, unless we change the structure of the program, a pointer is the only way to go because a reference can never point to a different object.

At other times we actually rely on the fact that a pointer can be NULL, either by returning a NULL pointer from a function as a sign that the function failed, or as an optional parameter to a function. References cannot point to nothing (NULL), so they do not serve that purpose. It is questionable whether or not a good program design relies on pointers sometimes being NULL. A better solution might be to refactor the program to indicate failed functions in a different way, and to use references instead.

The last reason for using a pointer over a reference is pointer arithmetic. With pointer arithmetic, we can iterate through a section of memory, interpreting its contents based on the type of pointer we are using. This is an extremely low-level way of working, has a high risk of introducing bugs, and could be a maintenance nightmare. When possible, avoid it at all costs. But if you must introduce pointer arithmetic at times, then you just have to do it. There might come an occasion, deep in your inner loops, when the extra overhead of iterating through a loop in a type-safe manner becomes unacceptable, and your profiler has clearly shown that a significant amount of time is wasted there. Then, and only then, would a technique such as pointer arithmetic be justified. Until then, avoid it at all costs.

Some studies have shown that a very large percentage of bugs in C++ are caused by memory leaks. The more we can work with objects in a higher level by using references instead of pointers, the more reliable and robust our programs will be.

3.3 CASTING

A conversion is the process of changing some data into a different type of data. In this case, the vague term *data* refers to anything from built-in types to user-created objects. The compiler has a set of rules to determine when a conversion is possible and should take place. For example, just assigning a float to an int triggers a conversion.

```
int a = 200;
float b = a;    // Conversion from int to float

char txt[] = "Hello";
float c = txt;    // No conversion possible
```

Casting is a directive we add to the source code to force the compiler to apply a particular conversion. It is done by adding the type we want to cast to in parentheses before the variable that is to be cast.

```
int n = 150;

// n is an integer, which divided by an integer results
// in another integer. f1 == 1.0
float f1 = n / 100;

// n is cast to a float, and when divided by an integer,
// the result is a float. f2 == 1.5
float f2 = (float)n / 100;    // cast to a float
```

3.3.1 The Need for Casting

Casting is an often-despised practice by most programmers. In truth, there are usually better, cleaner ways of accomplishing the same purpose. Every time we cast an object into a different type, we forego the C++ strong-typed language benefits. We are telling the compiler, "forget what you know about the type of this object and assume it is a different type instead." Because people make mistakes a lot more often than computers, it is a good idea to minimize the use of casting.

Sometimes, however, casting is the way to go. One reason for casting is to interface with a different section of the code. The interface expects a particular type, but we want to feed it data of a different type that is already in the correct format. A type cast does the job just fine in that case. This is most common in C libraries because they do not use inheritance or polymorphism.

Imagine a generic function that takes some data and a flag indicating how to interpret that data. Admittedly, this is a pretty terrible function, and the same could be accomplished in a much safer way using some C++ features, but it serves as an example of why casting is sometimes necessary:

```
void SerializeWrite (DataType type, void * pData);

char txt[] = "This is a string";
::SerializeWrite (SerializeString, (void *)txt);

float fPitch;
::SerializeWrite (SerializeFloat, (void *)&fPitch);

const Matrix4x4 & rot = camera.GetRotation();
::SerializeWrite (SerializeMatrix4x4, (void *)&rot);
```

Another reason for casting arises from the polymorphic use of objects. Imagine we have an extensive inheritance tree, and most of the code deals with objects through a pointer of the type of a common parent class. Sometimes it is necessary for the code to find out exactly what type of object it is dealing with and call a specific function in that object. This is often a sign of poor design, but it will happen. Assuming there is no runtime type information (RTTI) enabled, the program must find out the type of the object by calling some function and then casting it to the appropriate type:

```
void GameEntity::OnCollision (GameEntity & entity)
{
    if (entity.IsType(GameEntity::PROJECTILE))
    {
        GameProjectile & projectile = (GameProjectile &)
            entity;
        projectile.BlowUp();
    }
    // ...
}
```

3.3.2 C++-Style Casting

It seems that we can cast anything we want to our hearts' content with the C-style casts. Why do we need a new type of casts from C++? The new casts offer finer control over the casting process, allowing us to control different types of casting.

There are four types of cast operators in C++, depending on what we are casting: static_cast, const_cast, reinterpret_cast, and dynamic_cast.

The C++ cast operators also have a slightly different syntax than the traditional cast. They are a little more verbose than the old cast, and they tend to stand out from the source code. But do not be put off by the extra typing; it is also more readily apparent what the code is doing than with the C-style casts. The new casts follow this format:

```
static_cast<type>(expression)
```

The following code uses the C++-style cast:

```
// C++-style cast
float f2 = static_cast<float>(n) / 100;    // cast to a float
```

The other advantage of C++ casts is that they are more explicit in what they do. A programmer can glance at the code and immediately determine the purpose of a cast. Yes, this type of cast requires more typing, but it is worth it.

3.3.2.1 static_cast

The operator static_cast is a restricted version of its C counterpart. It tells the compiler to attempt to convert between two different data types. Like the C cast, it converts between built-in data types, even when there is some potential loss of precision. However, unlike the C cast, static_cast converts only between related pointer types. It is possible to cast pointers up and down the inheritance hierarchy, but not to a type outside of the hierarchy.

```
class A
{
};

class B : public A
{
};

// Unrelated to A and B
class C
{
};

A * a = new A;
```

```
// OK, B is a child of A
B * b = static_cast<B*>(a);

// Compile error. C is unrelated to A
C * c = static_cast<C*>(a);

// The old C cast would work just fine (but what would
// the program do?)
C * c = (C*)(a);
```

The only other difference is that static_cast cannot involve a change in constness. As with the C cast, if it is not possible to convert one type into another, the conversion fails.

3.3.2.2 const_cast

The operator const_cast cannot cast between different types. Instead, it just changes the constness of the expression to which it is applied. It can make something const that was not const before, or it can cast the const-ness away. Usually, there is no need to change something from non-const to const. That conversion happens automatically, because it is a less-restrictive change. Going the other way, from const to non-const, can be done only through a cast. Having to use const_cast is a sign that something does not fit correctly in the program design. It is like filing a square peg to make it fit in a round hole. Hopefully, most instances of const_cast are occasioned by calling older C-style functions with const expressions. If you find yourself using const_cast when calling your own program, immediately stop and rethink your design.

3.3.2.3 reinterpret_cast

The operator reinterpret_cast has the same power as the C-style cast. It can convert from any built-in data type to any other, and from any pointer type to another pointer type. It can even convert between built-in data types and pointers without any regard to type safety or constness. The results of reinterpret_cast are totally implementation dependent and rely on the particular memory layout of each of the objects being cast. Use reinterpret_cast extremely sparingly, and only when absolutely necessary and when the other types of casts are not enough.

3.3.2.4 dynamic_cast

In our discussion on multiple inheritance in Chapter 2, "Multiple Inheritance," the dynamic_cast operator was briefly covered. All the other cast operators are evaluated at compile time by the compiler, and the cast is either successful or it results in a compile error. In either case, there is no runtime cost involved. But `dynamic_cast` is quite different. It can be applied only to pointers or references—no built-in data types—but the key difference is that at runtime it checks whether the conversion is possible. And it does not just check whether two pointers are part of the same inheritance tree, as `static_cast` does; it checks the actual type of the objects referred to by those pointers, evaluates whether the conversion is possible, and if so, returns a new pointer, even accounting for any offsets necessary to deal with multiple inheritance. In the case that it is not possible to convert between the two types, the cast fails and it returns a `NULL` pointer. Clearly, to be able to do that, runtime type information must be enabled in the compiler. If you prefer not to have RTTI enabled, you must find alternatives to `dynamic_cast`. We explore these alternatives in Chapter 15, "Runtime Type Information."

3.4 CONCLUSION

In this chapter, we covered three new concepts introduced in C++:

- The keyword `const` allows us to mark a variable as read-only. Any attempts to modify it cause a compile-time error. This variable can be a simple data type, or it can be an object of a complex class type. Flagging a member function as `const` indicates that the function will not modify the state of the object, so we are allowed to call `const` member functions on `const` objects. And `const` is particularly useful as a tool for passing objects to and from functions in combination with pointers or references.
- References are alternate names for an object. They behave in very similar ways to pointers, but with some clear differences. In general, references allow us to deal with objects in a higher level, rather than passing memory locations around as pointers.
- The new casting operators introduced by C++ allow us to be much more specific with respect to what we are casting and how we are doing it. The casting operators also provide some compiler checking. In addition, `dynamic_cast` introduces some new functionality for casting with multiple inheritance.

SUGGESTED READING

Following are sources of several good opinions and guidelines on the use of `const`:

Meyers, Scott, *Effective C++,* 2nd ed. Addison-Wesley, 1997.

Murray, Robert B., *C++ Strategies and Tactics.* Addison-Wesley, 1993.

Stroustrup, Bjarne, *The C++ Programming Language,* 3rd ed. Addison-Wesley, 1997.

Here is a great resource for C++-style casting:

Meyers, Scott, *More Effective C++.* Addison-Wesley, 1995.

TEMPLATES

In This Chapter

- The Search for Generic Code
- Templates
- Drawbacks
- When to Use Templates
- Template Specialization (Advanced)

S ometimes we find ourselves writing the same code over and over. Perhaps the code is not something that can be put in a function and called repeatedly because it requires different classes and data types, not just different data. *Templates* are a new concept in C++ that addresses this issue. Using templates, we can write generic code that does not depend on specific data types, and to later reuse that code in different parts of our program with different classes.

4.1 THE SEARCH FOR GENERIC CODE

Before we dive into a detailed explanation of templates, let us take the time to understand the need for generic code, to see the real need for templates, and to look at a common use of templates through an example.

We will take a very simple situation that arises all the time in game programming and that you have already tackled in past projects—lists.

Lists are used everywhere in games: the game entities in the world, the scene nodes to be rendered, the meshes in a model, the actions to be performed in the future by an AI, or even the names of all the players in the game. Chances are, a full game will need many dozen different types of lists.

How do we go about implementing those lists? There are many different ways. The following sections examine some of the possibilities.

4.1.1 First Solution: List Built into the Class

The most straightforward approach is to just build the list into the class itself. After all, it is not all that difficult: just add a `next` pointer (and a `previous` pointer if it is a doubly linked list), throw in a few quick functions to insert and delete elements, and we are done.

```
class GameEntity
{
public:
    // All GameEntity functions here
    GameEntity * GetNext();
    void RemoveFromList();
    void InsertAfter(GameEntity * pEntity);
private:
    // GameEntity data
    GameEntity * m_pNext;
};
```

Is it really that simple? Not quite. Like many bad designs, the preceding code will work, but when it is put to the test on a large project, it will sink under its own weight. The first thing we need to realize is that even if we are very good programmers, we are bound to make mistakes. Almost the same code must be written for every class that needs to be part of a list. It is too easy to accidentally forget to set a pointer to NULL or to check the special case when we are removing an element from the end of the list. Failure to do any of these things (or many other small things) correctly will most likely cause the program to crash.

Even if we manage to write the code correctly the first time through, what if we need to make a change? We have written custom linked-list code in several different classes. Now we realize that we want to change our implementation to use end guards or maybe use a doubly linked list. Imagine having to go through all the classes making those changes. Even if you somehow end up not creating any bugs (unlikely), doing such a tedious and boring job is guaranteed to drive you out of your mind.

Just in case you were not already convinced of the problems with this approach, here are a few more reasons to avoid it. The different lists in the project are likely to have different interfaces. After all, other programmers probably wrote a few more lists from scratch, and they probably had different ideas on how the lists' interfaces should be. Maybe you used `Next()` in your list, but the other programmers used `GetNext()` or something even more exotic. What if you want to know how many elements are in a list? Maybe you have a `GetNumElements()` function that returns a number in constant time, but the other programmer's implementation has a function called `Count()` that iterates through all the elements in the list, counting the number of elements. This would be quite a shock if you had expected `Count()` to be a trivial function. The point is, you do not have a standard interface to iterate through lists, and you never quite know which functions to call and how they are implemented.

As a consequence, you also cannot have common functions that work on any linked list. With a standard linked list, it would be possible to have a set of functions to sort the elements in a list, move sections of a list around, or look for duplicate elements. With separate implementations, each list would only have the functions it absolutely needs, and new functions would have to be written as the need arises for each type of list—which leads to even more code duplication and general waste of time.

4.1.2 Second Solution: Using Macros

We can solve most of the issues described in the previous section with the use of preprocessor macros. We can create a set of macros that make adding linked-list functionality to our classes a snap. We would simply create two macros; to use them, all we have to do is add `LIST_DECL` `(MyClassName)` to the header file and `LIST_IMPL(MyClassName)` to the .cpp file.

```cpp
// In GameEntity.h
class GameEntity
{
public:
    // All GameEntity functions here
    LIST_DECL(GameEntity);
private:
    // GameEntity data
};

// In GameEntity.cpp
LIST_IMPL(GameEntity);
```

All the lists in our program will now use a unified interface, so we know what to expect when we are manipulating the code. Also, if we ever need to make changes to the list implementation, we can just change the macro, and all our classes will immediately get the latest list implementation.

Unfortunately, this solution introduces a few more problems of its own. Preprocessor macros are notorious for being difficult to develop, maintain, and especially debug. Their code is expanded in place by the preprocessor, so when the compiler comes along and attempts to compile that section of code, it does not look any different than any code we wrote by hand. Any compiler errors will be flagged as happening in the line that contains the macro, with no information of where exactly in the macro they happened. This can make debugging long macros very tiresome.

If that were the only drawback of this approach, we might be able to overlook a bit of discomfort when debugging macros for the ideal solution. There are still two fundamental problems with this approach that run deeper than any macro can fix.

The first problem is that we still cannot write a function that will act on any type of list. We have managed to standardize our list interface across all the classes, but there is still no type-safe way of dealing with all the different class types that implement a list. We will address this problem with the next solution (inheritance).

The second problem is one that we are not going to examine right away, so this is more of a heads up on what is coming. So far, we have successfully added the list functionality to our classes. Now, it is very easy to keep all the game entities in a list. But what if the same entity needs to be in more than one list at a time? For example, the `Player` class might want to keep a list of entities in the field of view so it can then pick the best one to target. Do we need to add a second list to every entity? What if we want the entity to be in more than two lists at once? Or in a tree? Clearly, we cannot add all those possible data structures to the class itself. Instead, we can make the list a separate class and completely remove the list implementation from our classes. We will see that in more detail in the fourth solution.

4.1.3 Third Solution: Inheritance

Instead of using a macro to add list functionality to any class, we can create a base class that is a list element. It contains all the normal list data, such as `next` and `previous` pointers as well as the appropriate functions, such as `Insert()` and `Delete()`.

Any class that wants to have list functionality only has to inherit from this newly created list element class to automatically get all the benefits of the list. Even if the class already inherits from a parent class, we can use multiple inheritance and also inherit from the list class (see Figure 4.1).

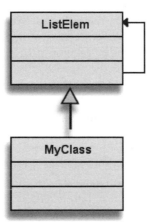

FIGURE 4.1   Any class that wants to be part of a list can inherit from `ListElem`.

Things get trickier if the parent class, in turn, also inherits from the list class; then we get the dreaded diamond of death. Even though in this case things will work as expected (your new class will be able to be in several lists at once), you will still need to deal with ambiguity and having to specify what parent list you are accessing. This is the first downside of this approach (refer to Chapter 2, "Multiple Inheritance," for details on the problems of multiple inheritance).

Unlike the solution involving macros, debugging is trivial using the inheritance approach. All the list code is just regular code, so it is possible to see it in the debugger and step into it, just like you would with any other code.

Another advantage of this approach is that we can treat list elements polymorphically. That is, because they all inherit from the base class `ListElem`, we can write functions that work on pointers and references of type `ListElem`; that approach will work for any of our lists.

This approach is almost perfect. It has the problem of multiple inheritance creeping in, but often we can live with that. The major problem it does not solve, however, is the separation of the list functionality from the class itself. As mentioned earlier, this approach does not support having an object in multiple lists, or in a list and a tree, or some other data structure. For that, we must separate the list from the elements contained in the list.

4.1.4 Fourth Solution: Container List of Void Pointers

In our quest to find the perfect solution for a linked-list implementation, we will now try to totally separate the list from its contents. We treat a list as a container for the elements we choose to add to it.

The problem is that we want to have lists of many different types of classes. We could write one list for every type of class we want to add to it, but then we would have gone full circle and ended back up with a variant of the first solution. We already saw why the first solution was not a good idea.

If all the different types of classes that needed to use lists inherited from a common parent class, we could make it so the list contained pointers to that class. In a real project, though, that is not likely to be the case. Even if we have a root class for game entities, chances are that meshes, AI commands, or players do not inherit from it. We might also want to have a list of integers, strings, or floats, and those certainly do not inherit from any common base class.

A simple solution is to just make the list deal with void pointers. Whatever gets added to the list gets cast into a void pointer; whenever that entity's pointer is retrieved from the list, we cast it back to its real class. The list code does not need to manipulate its elements in any way other than to copy them around, so it does not matter what the real type of the data we added is, as long as it is only as large as a void pointer, which is 32 bits for most current platforms (see Figure 4.2).

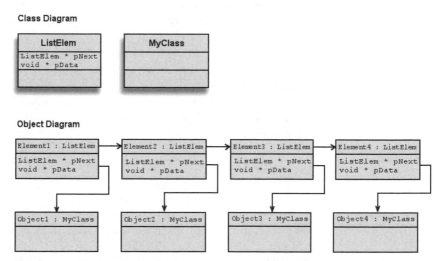

FIGURE 4.2   A list of void pointers can be used with any class.

What we are giving up with this approach is type safety. It is now up to us (that is, up to the code) to remember what type the elements in a list are. If we make a mistake, the compiler will not catch it, and we will cast an element to the wrong type. If we are lucky, this will result in a runtime crash; if luck is not on our side, it will result in bogus data and strange program behavior. Tracking down these kinds of bugs can be extremely difficult, so this is an important drawback to note.

One advantage of structuring a list this way is that we can now deal with a list class, not just with list elements. It makes much more sense to have global operations and queries done on the list itself, such as getting the total number of elements or clearing the list.

There is one more downside to this solution—not a major problem, but an annoyance nonetheless. We have totally separated the list nodes from the data they contain. That means that creating a new object and adding it to the list will result in two memory allocations: one for the object and one for the list node that points to it. When the list data was built into the object itself, as in the first solution, only one memory allocation was required. In platforms that have slow memory allocation or that have problems with memory fragmentation, the difference could be significant (see Chapter 7, "Memory Allocation," for more information and strategies for memory allocation).

To find a better solution, we need to look at C++ templates. The next few sections detail templates, revisit this particular problem, and then come up with a solution based on templates.

4.2 TEMPLATES

Templates allow us to write a piece of code without being tied to a particular class or data type. Code written in this way is said to be *generic*. Whenever we want to use this code, we instantiate the template to work with a specific class. There are two types of templates: class templates and function templates, depending on the type of code being *templatized*.

4.2.1 Class Templates

Let us start with a simple example that might not be worth implementing with templates, but illustrates the concept very nicely. Suppose we need a rectangle class in our game or tools. There are many uses for it: window coordinates, the size of some graphical user interface (GUI) component, viewport position and size, and so forth. A straightforward implementation looks something like this:

```
class Rect
{
public:
    Rect(int px1, int py1, int px2, int py2) {
        x1 = px1; y1 = py1; x2 = px2; y2 = py2; }
```

```
    int GetWidth() { return x2-x1; }
    int GetHeight() { return y2-y1; }

    int x1;
    int y1;
    int x2;
    int y2;
};
```

It is not the best class design, and it probably needs a few extra functions to be truly useful, but this code will do for now.

So far, the rectangle class has served us very well but, at some point later in the project, we find ourselves needing to use a rectangle in a different coordinate system whose coordinates vary between 0.0 and 1.0. We cannot reuse our existing class because it uses integers instead of floats, which is what we need to represent the new coordinates. We could copy and paste the code, and make a new class called RectFloat by replacing all appearances of variables of type int with ones of type float.

By now, we should realize that anything that requires copying and pasting is usually a sign of trouble, so let's avoid it. Instead, we can use templates and make it so that the rectangle class does not explicitly use integers or floats until it is instantiated.

```
template<class T>
class Rect
{
public:
    Rect(T px1, T py1, T px2, T py2) {
        x1 = px1; y1 = py1; x2 = px2; y2 = py2; }
    T GetWidth() { return x2-x1; }
    T GetHeight() { return y2-y1; }

    T x1;
    T y1;
    T x2;
    T y2;
};
```

As you can see, any occurrences of the type int have been replaced with a T instead. T is the class type the template depends on. To create a rectangle that uses integers, we use the following code:

```
Rect<int> myIntRectangle (1,10,2,20);
```

When the compiler encounters that definition, it goes through the original template, replaces all instances of `T` with `int`, and compiles the new class on the fly. Similarly, the following code does the same thing with floats:

```
Rect<float> anotherRectangle;
```

We could create rectangles of imaginary numbers or just about anything else if we had a class to represent them. The only restriction in this case is that we must be able to subtract objects of the class we use because both the `GetWidth()` and `GetHeight()` functions rely on that functionality. If we tried to instantiate a template with a class that did not support subtraction, we would get a compile-time error.

One important thing to notice is that all the template code must be visible to the compiler when it instantiates the template with a particular class. That means that we must put all the template code in the header file; otherwise it will not be visible and it will not be compiled (which will result in a link-time error). As we will see later, this has some unfortunate consequences with dependencies and compile time.

The C++ standard actually has a provision to avoid having to put the full implementation of the template in a header file. It allows the implementation of a template to reside in a .cpp file by using use the keyword `export` to make that implementation "visible" to the compiler. Such a scheme would allow us to avoid any extra dependencies when using templates. Unfortunately, virtually no commercial C++ compilers have currently implemented this feature. Hopefully, in a few years, we will see some support for this feature. For now, our only option is to clump all the implementation in the header file and live with the consequences.

4.2.2 Function Templates

Now that you understand the concept of a class template, function templates are easy. They are very similar to class templates, but they work on a function instead of on a class. The main difference is that we do not need to explicitly instantiate a function template. Instead, it is created automatically based on the type of the parameters passed to it.

Here is a very simple example. This function swaps the two values of two objects, but it is not tied to any particular class type:

```
template<class T>
void swap(T & a, T & b)
{
```

```
        T tmp(a);
        a = b;
        b = tmp;
}
```

This function works for integers, floats, strings, or any class with a copy constructor and assignment operator. The function is instantiated based on the type of the parameters passed to it, as shown in these examples:

```
int a = 5;
int b = 10;
swap(a, b);    // Integer version is instantiated

float fa = 3.1416;
float fb = 1.0;
swap(fa, fb);  // Float version is instantiated
```

Notice how both parameters to the `swap()` function are of the same type. What happens if we pass two parameters of different types? We cannot. It would result in a compile-time error. Even if one of the objects has an implicit conversion to the correct data type, such code would result in an error.

```
// The following is illegal. Compile error.
swap(a, fb);
```

4.2.3 List Example Revisited: Template Solution

Armed with our new knowledge about templates, let us again tackle the list example from earlier in this chapter. This time we will use C++ templates to come up with a much more refined solution that addresses most of the problems. As a reminder, the objective we are trying to accomplish is to write a list class with the following characteristics:

- The class can be used on a wide variety of different classes.
- All the list code is in one location and is not copied for every class type that becomes part of a list.
- All lists have a standard interface.
- The list code itself is separated from the class code.

By now you should see how templates allow us to do all those things with extreme ease. We will create a list class that is templated on the type of its elements. We will also create two different classes: one for the list object itself and one for the list nodes (the second class contains the data elements and the list pointers).

```cpp
template<class T>
class ListNode
{
public:
    ListNode(T);
    T & GetData();
    ListNode * GetNext();
private:
    T m_data;
};

template<class T>
class List
{
public:
    ListNode<T> * GetHead();
    void PushBack(T);
    //...

private:
    ListNode<T> * m_pHead;
};
```

We use this list just like any other templated class:

```cpp
List<int> listOfIntegers;
List<string> listOfStrings;
```

Now we can effortlessly create lists to hold just about any type of object or data we want, without tying those classes to the list itself. The template solution for this particular problem is by far the best of all of them.

It should be mentioned that you will hopefully never have to write such a common data structure by yourself. The C++ Standard Template Library (STL) has a large variety of data structures and algorithms you can use freely in your programs. One of the many data structures included is a list, and you can use it in the same way as the list we just created:

```cpp
std::list<int> myListOfIntegers;
```

We will have a close look at the STL in Chapter 9, "Standard Template Library: Containers," and Chapter 10, "Standard Template Library: Algorithms and Advanced Topics."

4.3 DRAWBACKS

Templates are far from being perfect. But they are the best solution for many problems we have right now. Knowing their drawbacks and trade-offs is just as important as being familiar with their syntax.

4.3.1 Complexity

The biggest problem with using templates is complexity. Compare again the code in the previous section, where we solved the list implementation with templates, to the straight list from the first solution. Which one is easier to read? Which one do you feel more capable of modifying and updating in the future?

To make things worse, even if you get past all the little brackets and references to a generic class T and other templates, templated code is notoriously difficult to debug. Granted, it is not as bad as preprocessor macros, but it comes close. A lot of debuggers get very confused when you attempt to step into a section of templated code, and some compilers produce rather incomprehensible error messages at the tiniest typing mistake.

4.3.2 Dependencies

In addition, templates have a few more issues. As mentioned earlier, all the code belonging to a template must reside in a header file so that the code is visible to the compiler when it is time to instantiate the template. The unfortunate side effect is that this arrangement increases coupling between different classes in the program. Any class that includes a template will automatically include all the header files needed by the implementation of that template. Apart from the negative architectural ramifications of extra coupling, these dependencies are noticeable in an everyday kind of way by longer compile times when only a small change was made. On a large project that makes heavy use of templates, the longer compile time becomes a significant problem because waiting several minutes for a compile to finish between minor changes is unacceptable.

Templates also cause compile times to go up independently of the tighter coupling between classes. When a template is instantiated, the compiler creates a new class and compiles it on the fly. Fortunately, this extra time is not a very large factor and goes mostly unnoticed for most projects.

4.3.3 Code Bloat

Another problem that template detractors often bring up is that of code bloat. Whenever we create a list of a new class, the compiler has to create a whole new list class on the fly. This means that all the functions are duplicated, as well as all the static member variables. The same thing happens if we use templated functions: new function code is generated for every type of parameter we pass to the function. On the whole, it is not as big an issue as it might seem. The typical size of code is very small compared to the amount of data today's games move around. You should start worrying about code bloat only when you start creating combinations of templates of templates. In such a case, you might cause a combinatorial explosion of templates, and the amount of extra code generated by the compiler will start to become noticeable in the overall size of the project.

Assuming that code bloat becomes a significant issue in your project, you could attempt to move some of the common code out of the template into a normal function that is called from the templated code. This way, the function is not repeated once for every instantiation of a template. Unfortunately, this fix is often not possible or significant enough. Unless we have huge templated functions, it is not easy to pull out any significant amount of common code.

4.3.4 Compiler Support

Finally, one thing you need to be very aware of if you decide to use templates is their level of support in your compiler and platform. Templates were finalized and added to the C++ standard only fairly recently. Even though they have been around for quite a while, they existed only as a proposed solution and did not have a firm standard. This fact shows in the lackluster template support provided in most compilers. Fortunately, most compilers have basic template support, but many fail in the more advanced features, such as partial template specialization. Compiler support is even more important if you are planning to use third-party libraries with heavy template usage.

4.4 When to Use Templates

The best bit of advice related to the use of template is the same as we gave you for inheritance: use them with caution. Be very aware of the level of expertise of your current (and future) team members, and use templates accordingly. There are few things more difficult and frustrating than untangling a badly designed mess of templates in a large project while a deadline is fast approaching. If that happens, you would probably wish for a much simpler implementation.

Remember that there is no point in using templates for the sake of using "advanced" C++ features. Templates are a tool, and it is there to make your life easier and save time. If you save a few hours now, only to cause you many lost days down the line, using templates does not look like a good deal.

That being said, there will be times when you want to apply a set of code to a variety of totally unrelated classes, and you want those classes to continue being totally independent of each other. C++ templates might be a good solution at that point, as you saw in the list example presented earlier this chapter.

Some of the best candidates for template use are container classes: data structures that contain objects of many different classes. Fortunately, a lot of those have already been written for us in the STL (see Chapter 9). However, the STL does not have available some specific containers, such as a good tree container, some special priority queue, or something else specific to your situation. Templates might be a good solution in these cases.

You might also want to look at the Boost library. Boost is a set of C++ libraries that, for the most part, make heavy use of templates and are intended to extend and complement the STL. If what you need is not in the STL, check out Boost. Only if you still have not found what you need, you might want to write a template on your own.

One good suggestion is to try to write any template code in a style similar to the STL. The Boost library is a good example of this advice. Following this suggestion allows your template to be integrated much more easily with the rest of the code, makes life easier on other programmers already familiar with STL, and might even allow for some interaction with STL algorithms, iterators, or containers. Other potential candidates for templatization are manager/factory classes (classes that take care of creating and keeping track of objects), resource-loading code, singletons, and serialization of objects.

4.5 TEMPLATE SPECIALIZATION (ADVANCED)

By default, all new classes created from a template are exactly the same, but they apply to different class types. The problem with writing totally generic code is that we have very little idea of what data types the code will work on. With large objects, we definitely want to avoid copying them as much as possible, so adding a few extra pointers to avoid any copies seems like a good trade-off. On the other hand, a very small object, or even a pointer itself, can be copied around very easily; keeping several pointers around to manage a single 32-bit object seems like overkill.

Template specialization allows us to add some customization to a template for a particular class or set of classes. That way, we can provide optimizations for specific classes that we plan on using frequently, such as pointers or strings. Optimizations can be both in the form of a more efficient implementation or one that takes less memory, depending on our needs.

4.5.1 Full Template Specialization

The first type of specialization is *full template specialization*. It allows us to provide a custom version of a template for a specific class.

Let's revisit the simple template from earlier in this chapter. Recall that it provides a list implementation for any data type. Suppose that we have fleshed out its implementation to be very efficient and then used it everywhere in our game. Toward the end of the project, we realize that we have many lists of very small elements; in particular, we are using lists of game entity handles all over the place.

A game entity handle is a tiny class that just holds an integer and has no virtual functions or any type of inheritance, so an object of that class is just 32 bits. Having a whole list node allocated for every entity handle is very wasteful. Not only does a list node have two other pointers (which triples the size of the data), but because it is allocated dynamically it might have some extra overhead from the memory system, which wastes still more memory. (For details on memory allocation and possible solutions to this problem using a pool system, refer to Chapter 7.)

For now, let us improve this situation by using template specialization. We can write a custom version of the list template that stores its elements in a contiguous block of memory. Inserting and deleting elements from the middle of the list is somewhat more costly, but because the size of the game entities is so small, it is a small price to pay for cutting down memory usage by a factor of three.

The following code does not replace the previous template, but it does complement it. It also must appear after the declaration of the general template, not before that definition. Any functions the specialized template implements override the default ones from the general template.

```
template<>
class List<GameEntityHandle>
{
public:
    ListNode< GameEntityHandle > * GetHead();
    void PushBack();

private:
    GameEntityHandle * m_pData;
};
```

Of course, along with the template declaration, we must also provide an implementation for those functions that take care of managing a list of game entity elements on a contiguous block of memory. In this case, we must also provide a specialization for the list node ListNode<GameEntityHandle> so it can work in conjunction with the specialized version of the list.

4.5.2 Partial Template Specialization

What if we realized that the lists we were using were not of one class type, but of many different types that had elements in common? For example—and this is a very likely situation if we are using object-oriented design and polymorphism—suppose most of our lists contain pointers to different types of objects. Pointers are small, probably the same size as a game entity object, so they would also benefit from a specialized list implementation. For this situation, we use the second type of specialization, which is *partial template specialization*. The following code uses partial template specialization to create a template for a list of pointers of any type:

```
template<class T>
class List<T *>
{
public:
    ListNode<T *> * GetHead();
    void PushBack();

private:
    T * m_pData;
};
```

Whenever we instantiate a new type of list, the specific template is chosen based on the classes we are using to instantiate the template.

```
// Normal templated list is used
List<Matrix4x4> matrixList;

// Fully-specialized list, because it stores GameEntityHandles
List<GameEntityHandle> handleList;

// Partially-specialized list, because it stores pointers
List<Matrix4x4 *> matrixPtrList;
```

4.6 Conclusion

In this chapter, we introduced the concept of templates. Templates allow us to write code that does not depend on specific data types. The compiler takes care of instantiating templates at compile time as they are needed in our programs. Templates come in two flavors: class templates, which apply to whole classes, and function templates, which apply to individual functions. The major advantages of templates are listed here:

- We don't duplicate code in different places.
- We have type safety.
- We are not forced to inherit from a common base class.

However, templates are not without drawbacks:

- Code becomes more complex and difficult to maintain and debug.
- Extra dependencies are included, and compile times are increased.
- Code size might increase.
- Compiler support is not totally available.

Knowing the tradeoffs of templates and when to use them is a very important aspect of C++ game development. Finally, we covered the concept of template specialization, which allows us to customize parts of a template for a specific class or set of classes. We can use this feature to write more optimized versions of a template for specific data types.

SUGGESTED READING

The following sources are some gentle introductions to templates as well as discussions on their use:

Murray, Robert B., *C++ Strategies and Tactics*. Addison-Wesley, 1993.
Stroustrup, Bjarne, *The C++ Programming Language,* 3rd ed. Addison-Wesley, 1997.

More in-depth coverage of templates can be found in this resource:

Vandevoorde, David, and Nicolai M. Josuttis, *C++ Templates: The Complete Guide*. Addison-Wesley, 2003.

The following resource has some very advanced and mind-stretching uses of templates:

Alexandrescu, Andrei, *Modern C++ Design*. Addison-Wesley, 2001.

5

EXCEPTION HANDLING

In This Chapter

- Dealing with Errors
- Using Exceptions
- Exception-Safe Code
- Cost Analysis
- When to Use Exceptions

C++ introduces a new technique for dealing with errors: *exception handling*. Exception handling allows us to write robust, simple code that deals correctly with any errors or unexpected situations. This chapter covers the reasons to use exceptions, how to use exceptions effectively in our programs, and the tradeoffs involved in their use, especially with respect to how they affect performance. We will finish by making some specific recommendations on the use of exceptions in game programming.

5.1 DEALING WITH ERRORS

From the very beginning of the history of computers, programmers have had to deal with errors. There has never been an ideal solution, and typically we either spend too much time and effort worrying about errors, or we ignore them altogether. This section illustrates the alternatives that are available when dealing with errors and introduces the concept of C++ exceptions.

5.1.1 Ignore Them!

The first strategy when dealing with errors is to ignore them. It may sound ridiculous, but that is how most programs deal with errors—or at least the great majority of them. Sure, we all check whether opening a file was successful or not, but who checks the `return` value from `printf`?

A lot of programs can get by fine this way. As long as nothing unexpected happens, everything will go well. However, as soon as things take a turn for the worse, the program is likely to crash. What if there is not enough memory? What if the desktop display is set to 8-bit color depth? What if there is no more disk space, or if the user pulls the CD-ROM out while the game is loading?

Ignoring errors might be a fine way of handling them in quick and dirty tools, or maybe even for internal development tools (depending on the internal standards of quality that your company expects). But this is clearly not the way we want to handle things in the programs we sell to users, so we need to look for alternative solutions.

5.1.2 Use Error Codes

We could use the time-honored approach of returning error codes from functions. Every function that could fail returns an error code, or at least a boolean, indicating whether the function was successful or not. The calling code checks that `return` value and handles any failed calls correctly.

In theory, this approach works just fine. In practice, it falls short when applied to a full project. First of all, it leads to really ugly code that becomes difficult to maintain. A function that could have been a really simple two-statement function now becomes an ugly, thirty-line mess of tangled `if-then-else` statements. And it is not just that it is ugly (which it is), but most importantly, it is now difficult to discern what the function is really doing. The error-handling code obfuscates the real purpose of the function.

The following code loads a mesh from a data stream. The top function does not do any form of error checking; the second one does. Which function is more readable?

```
void Mesh::Load(Stream stream)
{
    ParseHeader(stream);
    ParseFlags(stream);
```

```
        ParseVertices(stream);
        ParseFaces(stream);
}


int Mesh::Load(Stream stream)
{
    int errCode = OK;
    errCode = ParseHeader(stream);
    if (errCode != OK)
    {
        FreeHeader();
        return errCode;
    }
    errCode = ParseFlags(stream);
    if (errCode != OK)
    {
        FreeHeader();
        return errCode;
    }
    errCode = ParseVertices(stream);
    if (errCode != OK)
    {
        FreeHeader();
        FreeVertices();
        return errCode;
    }
    errCode = ParseFaces(stream);
    if (errCode != OK)
    {
        FreeHeader();
        FreeVertces();
        FreeFaces();
        return errCode;
    }
    return errCode;
}
```

The source code speaks for itself. But we are not letting error codes get off the hook that easily. There are still some major problems with every function returning error codes. Checking error codes is not only ugly and cumbersome, it is also wasteful. If every function we call has `if` statements surrounding it, the overall effect could be felt in the game as a marked decrease in performance.

Then there are the logical problems of where the error codes are kept. Are they one huge file that everybody includes, or does each subsystem have its own set of codes? How can they be converted from the numerical code to a human-readable string? There has to be a better way.

5.1.3 Blow Up (with Asserts)

One legitimate way of handling errors is to throw up our hands and surrender—except that instead of letting the computer crash by itself, we will stop it by using the assert() function (or a customized assert() function like the one described in Chapter 19, "Crash-Proofing Your Game"). At least by stopping the program, we can report more information, such as the filename and line number of the error, and maybe a descriptive message. It is better than nothing, but it still leaves much to be desired.

5.1.4 Use setjmp() and longjmp()

Hardcore C programmers will probably be familiar with the functions setjmp() and longjmp(); setjmp() allows us to set a place in the code (along with the stack state) to be called in the future, and longjmp() restores the program to that particular location and stack state. We could supposedly handle errors by calling longjmp() every time there is some sort of error. Unfortunately, apart from being very inflexible, this approach does not mesh well with C++. The longjmp() function unwinds the stack, but it does not destroy the objects that were in the stack. So the destructor of the objects in the stack would never be called, which probably means memory leaks or resources that were not freed. If we are planning on exiting the program right away, this is probably not a big deal. However, if we intend to recover from the error and continue, it is an unacceptable solution that will cause the program to run out of resources and eventually crash.

5.1.5 Use C++ Exceptions

Now we come to C++ *exceptions*. So far, all the proposed error-handling mechanisms had major drawbacks. Before we see the exact syntax of C++ exceptions, let's look at how they are used in a general way, and why we might prefer to use them over the previous error-handling methods.

5.1.5.1 How Exceptions Work

Exceptions work as follows: whenever a program comes up against something unexpected, it can throw an exception. That will cause the execution of the program to jump to the nearest exception-handling block. If there is no exception-handling block in the function where the exception was thrown, the program unwinds the stack (correctly destroying all the objects there) and goes to the parent function looking for an exception-handling block. It continues going up through the function call stack until an exception-handling block is found, or the top is reached—at which point the default exception-handling code is triggered and the execution of the program stops.

We can do anything we want in an exception-handling block. We can report the error, try to fix the problem, or even ignore it. We can also do different things, depending on what caused the exception (for example, we probably want to treat a corrupt file differently than a division by zero). After the exception-handling block has been executed, program execution resumes as normal from this point on, *not* from where the exception was thrown.

5.1.5.2 Advantages

The first advantage of exception handling is that it does not result in messy code. A loading function that uses exception handling could look just like the previous example that had no error checking at all. Clean code is easier to understand and easier to maintain; it is more than just aesthetically nicer.

Exceptions are flexible. We can handle different types of errors in different ways. Sometimes we will want to recover; at other times, we will want to terminate the program just as assert() did.

Exceptions also make it a lot easier to pass information about the nature of the error to layers of code higher up. Usually, if something goes wrong deep in the bowels of the file IO code, we want to report that error all the way up the chain of caller functions so we can display an error message to the user in our GUI. To do that using return codes, every single function along the way must be prepared to return failure codes that are passed from below. With exception handling, the error automatically propagates up to the nearest try-catch block, and the exception object can contain much more meaningful information than just a single error code.

There was one situation we did not even mention when talking about return codes: constructors. A constructor returns no values, so it makes life very difficult if our own error-reporting mechanism is based on returning error codes. We could set some flag on the object, marking it as failed, but then the calling code would have to check it before it did anything with the object. Alternatively, we could avoid doing anything that could fail inside a constructor, but that would limit its usefulness. A very common idiom is *resource acquisition on initialization*, which relies on objects fully initializing themselves when they are created, instead of having a separate step. That allows us to always treat objects as correctly initialized, instead of having to constantly check.

Incidentally, destructors are in the same situation; however, because the object is being destroyed, it usually does not matter as much whether or not something failed. Nobody should be able to touch the object after it is destroyed, anyway. Still, we might want to at least report that something went wrong while the object was being destroyed.

You can probably imagine where all this is leading: exceptions let us report errors that occur inside a constructor. We will see exactly how this is accomplished in a moment.

Finally—and this is a relatively minor point—exceptions avoid the need for a large error code table that has to be maintained project wide. There is also no need to convert between error codes and human-readable error messages. Often, exceptions themselves contain the error-description strings, which makes debugging much easier.

5.2 USING EXCEPTIONS

In the previous section, we were treated to a nice preview of what we will get when using exceptions. Yes, they also have their drawbacks, which we will see later. For now, let's see how to use exceptions in our own programs.

5.2.1 Overview

The syntax to use exceptions in C++ is very easy. Whenever the code needs to throw an exception, it uses the keyword throw. Control is passed to the nearest exception-handling block, which is indicated by the keyword catch. The catch block must be found immediately after a try block, which surrounds the code that might throw an exception. Here is a very simple code snippet that throws an exception and handles it:

```
void f()
{
    printf ("Start function f.\n");
    throw 1;
    printf ("End function f.\n");
}

main()
{
    printf ("Start main.\n");
    try
```

```
        {
            printf ("About to call f.\n");
            f();
            printf ("After calling f.\n");
        }
        catch (...)
        {
            printf ("Handling exception.\n");
        }
        printf ("Ending main.\n");
    }
```

The output from this program looks like this:

```
Start main.
About to call f.
Start function f.
Handling exception.
Ending main.
```

Notice that as soon as the exception is thrown, the rest of function
f() is skipped, as well as the rest of the code inside the try block. Execution resumes inside the catch block and then continues as normal.

5.2.2 Throwing Exceptions

As we saw in the previous section, the throw keyword takes an identifier
that it uses as the exception to throw. It turns out that C++ is extremely
flexible, and it lets us throw an object of any type as an exception.

In the previous example, we just did throw 1 because we did not really care what type of exception we were throwing; the important part
was just to throw an exception. Most of the time, we want to be more explicit about our exceptions. If we have different parts of the code throwing exceptions for different reasons, how are we going to know what the
cause of the exception was when we catch it?

To solve that problem, we can create our own exception objects that
contain all the information we need. We can throw those exception objects whenever we have an exception, and they will be passed to the
catch statement. Here is a simple exception class:

```
class MyException
{
public:
    MyException(const char * pTxt) : pReason(pTxt){};
```

```
            const char * pReason;
     };
```

To use it, we just throw an exception with an object of that type. The following code attempts to read vertex data from a stream and throws an exception if it cannot read enough data because the file is too short:

```
void Mesh::ParseVertices(Stream stream)
{
    for (int i=0; i<m_numVerts; ++i)
    {
        VertexData data;
        int nRead = stream.Read(data, sizeof(VertexData));
        if (nRead < sizeof(VertexData)
            throw MyException("File too short");
        Vertex vertex(data);
        m_verts.push_back(vertex);
    }
}
```

We will see in a moment how the object we created is passed to the `catch` statement. This object can then be used to do different things based on its contents.

If our program has many different reasons for throwing exceptions, we might want to create different types of exceptions for different categories. For example, we could have a category of exceptions related to file IO, another category for graphics hardware, another one for math functions, and so on. This organization is particularly useful if we want to handle exceptions of one type differently than exceptions of another type. For example, graphics hardware-related exceptions are probably going to be a lot more serious than file-related exceptions.

To accomplish this, we can create a hierarchy of exception classes. By arranging them in a hierarchy, not only do we get to share some common implementation, we can also take advantage of the hierarchy organization when we process the exceptions in the `catch` statement. A possible exception hierarchy is shown in Figure 5.1.

C++ already has a set of standard exceptions organized in a hierarchy for different general types. Some of the broad types are `logic_error` and `runtime_error`, while some of the more specific exception types are `out_of_range`, `bad_alloc`, or `overflow_error`. Some of the functions in the standard C++ library throw these types of exceptions, so you might want to be prepared to deal with them correctly.

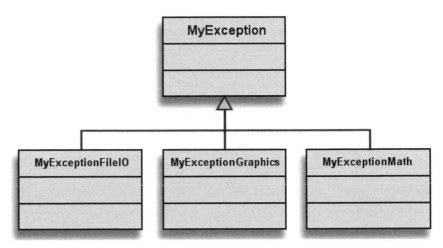

FIGURE 5.1   An exception hierarchy.

5.2.3 Catching Exceptions

So far, we have only seen one form of catching exceptions: using the `catch` statement. This statement means that we want to catch all exceptions, regardless of what type they really are.

5.2.3.1 Catching One Type

Normally, it is far more useful to catch specific types of exceptions. We can do this by using a slightly different form of the `catch` statement that takes a specific exception type as a parameter. The following code demonstrates how to catch a file IO exception in our mesh-loading code:

```
void Mesh::Load(const char * filename)
{
    try
    {
        Stream stream(filename);
        Load(stream);
    }
    catch (MyExceptionFileIO & e)
    {
        // Do something with the exception here
    }
}
```

Because we suspected that creating a new stream from a filename or loading the mesh from the stream could cause an exception, we surrounded that code with a `try` statement and followed it with a `catch` statement. If an exception of the type `ExceptionFileIO` is thrown in the code inside the `try` block, our handler will catch it and deal with it.

5.2.3.2 Catching Multiple Types

When our code throws an exception, but it is of a different type than the preceding code is set up to handle, our handler will not deal with it, so the exception will continue propagating up the function call chain until it finds an adequate handler or reaches the top of the chain. At that point, the exception will call the predefined `terminate()` function, which stops the execution of the program.

We would prefer to handle other types of exceptions in this function instead of allowing the program to crash. We can add multiple `catch` blocks, each accepting a different type of exception, almost as if it were a `switch` statement. Let's improve the preceding example to deal with possible math exceptions:

```
void Mesh::Load(const char * filename)
{
    try
    {
        Stream stream(filename);
        Load(stream);
    }
    catch (MyExceptionFileIO & e)
    {
        // Do something with the exception here
    }
    catch (MyExceptionMath & e)
    {
        // Deal with it here.
    }
}
```

This approach has the potential to become really cumbersome if we have to write one `catch` statement for every type of exception we want to handle. We could easily have dozens of different exceptions, making the writing of error-handling code very tedious, which was one of the things we were trying to avoid in the first place.

Remember how we organized our exceptions in a hierarchical manner? Now we can really take advantage of that organization. A `catch` statement handles exceptions of the type indicated in its parameter *or any type derived from it*. This means that if we do not need to be more explicit, we can write a handler for exceptions of the type MyException, and it will handle all its derived types as well.

Going back to the previous example, it turns out we were not so much concerned with catching the math exceptions, but we just wanted to make sure there were no exceptions getting out of the Load() function. We can accomplish this goal in a much better way by using the base class of our exception hierarchy as the parameter for the catch statement.

```cpp
void Mesh::Load(const char * filename)
{
    try
    {
        Stream stream(filename);
        Load(stream);
    }
    catch (MyExceptionFileIO & e)
    {
        // Do something with the exception here
    }
    catch (MyException & e)
    {
        // An exception that was not file IO-related was
           thrown.
        // Deal with it here.
    }
}
```

The order in which the catch statements appear is important. They are processed from top to bottom, and as soon as one is found that can be used for the current exception, the rest are ignored.

If we wanted to make our Load() function totally bomb-proof and make sure that absolutely no exceptions get out, we could also attempt to catch all other types of exceptions—even the ones that are not derived from our exception base class—by adding another catch statement at the end.

```cpp
void Mesh::Load(const char * filename)
{
    try
    {
        Stream stream(filename);
        Load(stream);
    }
```

```
        catch (MyExceptionFileIO & e)
        {
            // Do something with the exception here
        }
        catch (MyException & e)
        {
            // An exception that was not file IO related
            // was thrown. Deal with it here.
        }
        catch (...)
        {
            // All other exceptions get handled here
        }
    }
```

5.2.3.3 Rethrowing an Exception

So far, when we catch an exception, we have assumed we handled it correctly and that program execution can continue as usual. It is also possible that we caught an exception, tried to solve the problem, and were not able to handle it correctly. So, we would like other parts of the program to deal with it. Or maybe we caught an exception, looked at it in more detail, and decided it was not something we wanted to deal with.

Whenever an exception handler decides it does not want to fully handle an exception, it can *rethrow* it. To do that, the exception handler just needs to use the keyword throw, without any parameters, from within the catch block, and it will automatically throw the same exception to let the next try-catch block deal with it.

For example, the following code processes only those exceptions caused by corrupt data. All other exceptions, including all other file IO exceptions, are handled by other parts of the program.

```
    void Mesh::Load(Stream stream)
    {
        try
        {
            ParseHeader(stream);
            ParseFlags(stream);
            ParseVertices(stream);
            ParseFaces(stream);
        }
        catch (MyExceptionFileIO & e)
        {
            if (e.IsDataCorrupt())
```

```
                    {
                        // Handle corrupt data here
                    }
                    else
                    {
                        throw;     // Throw the same exception again so it
                                   // can be handled somewhere else
                    }
                }
            }
```

5.3 EXCEPTION-SAFE CODE

Using exceptions in our programs is more than knowing how to call `throw` or how to set up a `try-catch` block. To use exceptions effectively, we must write code that works correctly in the face of exceptions, without leaking memory or stranding resources.

5.3.1 Resource Acquisition

The term *resources*, in the context of C++, refers to anything the code acquires but then has to explicitly release so it can be used by the rest of the system. Resources can be in the form of memory, file handles, or things we traditionally call *resources* in game development, such as textures, geometry, sounds, and so forth.

5.3.1.1 The Problem

The problem this section addresses is: after a resource has been acquired, if there is an error, how can we release that resource? This is not a new problem. We have to struggle with it no matter what type of error-handling system we are using. Using exceptions just makes it much more noticeable because there are no easy hacks around it.

The following illustrates the problem in the simplest way. The function is supposed to create a new texture from a file. It opens the file, gets the texture's dimensions, allocates the texture, and reads the data into it. So far, it does no error checking at all:

```
            Texture * CreateTexture(const char * filename)
            {
                FILE * fin = fopen(filename, "rb");
                TextureHeader info;
                ReadTextureHeader(fin, info);
```

```
        Texture * pTexture = new Texture(info.width, info.height,
                                            info.colorDepth);
        ReadTextureData(fin, pTexture);
        fclose(fin);
    }
```

We will try several approaches with this function in this section, so let's have a closer look at it. How many resources are acquired in this function? We do not know exactly what the functions `ReadTextureHeader()` and `ReadTextureData()` do, but assuming they do not acquire any resources of their own, the `CreateTexture()` function gets two resources. One is the file handle, and the other is the texture object created in the middle of the function. Of these two resources, only the file handle is released. The texture is supposed to be passed on to the function that called `Create Texture()`.

5.3.1.2 Return Codes

How would the previous function look if we used `return` codes for error handling? It would look something like this:

```
Texture * CreateTexture(const char * filename)
{
    FILE * fin = fopen(filename, "rb");
    if (fin == NULL)
        return NULL;

    TextureHeader info;
    if (!ReadTextureHeader(fin, info))
    {
        fclose(fin);
        return NULL;
    }
    Texture * pTexture = new Texture(info.width, info.height,
                                        info.colorDepth);
    if (pTexture == NULL)
    {
        fclose(fin);
        return NULL;
    }
    if (!ReadTextureData(fin, pTexture))
    {
        delete pTexture;
        fclose(fin);
```

```
            return NULL;
        }

        fclose(fin);
        return pTexture;
    }
```

As you can see, there is duplicate code all over the place, and adding new steps to the function makes it very error prone. If we can get past our reluctance to use goto statements, we could make the code a little cleaner:

```
    Texture * CreateTexture(const char * filename)
    {
        bool bSuccess = false;
        Texture * pTexture = NULL;
        TextureHeader info;
        FILE * fin = fopen(filename, "rb");
        if (fin == NULL)
            goto cleanup;
        if (!ReadTextureHeader(fin, info))
            goto cleanup;
        pTexture = new Texture(info.width, info.height,
                              info.colorDepth);
        if (pTexture == NULL)
            goto cleanup;
        if (!ReadTextureData(fin, pTexture))
            goto cleanup;
        bSuccess = true;

cleanup:
        if (!bSuccess)
        {
            delete pTexture;
            pTexture = NULL;
        }
        fclose(fin);
        return pTexture;
    }
```

This code is a little better, but only slightly. At least the use of goto is limited to skipping to the end of the function, so it is still reasonably readable.

5.3.1.3 Exceptions

When we use exceptions, we get the `goto` jump for free if there is an error, and the code is not cluttered with error checks.

```
Texture * CreateTexture(const char * filename)
{
    FILE * fin = NULL;
    Texture * pTexture = NULL;
    try
    {
        fin = fopen(filename, "rb");
        TextureHeader info;
        ReadTextureHeader(fin, info);
        pTexture = new Texture(info.width, info.height,
                                info.colorDepth);
        ReadTextureData(fin, pTexture);
    }
    catch(...)
    {
        delete pTexture;
        pTexture = NULL;
    }
    fclose(fin);
    return pTexture;
}
```

This is certainly the cleanest of all the options so far. Still, it would be great if there were an even simpler way. Also, what if we wanted to actually let the exception go up to the calling function? Then the only reason to set up the `try-catch` block would be to release the resources we acquired, and we would have to rethrow the exception again.

5.3.1.4 Resource Acquisition Is Initialization

A much cleaner approach is to use the *resource acquisition is initialization* idea. When an exception is thrown and the current function is exited, all the objects created during the function are destroyed. In this case, the object `info` of type `TextureHeader` is destroyed correctly because it was in the stack, but the variables `fin` and `pTexture` are just pointers, so they do not really have a destructor. What we would really like is for their destructors to release the resources they are holding.

For the case of the file handle, we could create a simple class that wraps the file handling. Whenever the object is constructed, it opens the file; whenever it is destroyed, it closes the file. Now we just have to create an object of that type on the stack, and the file resource is released as soon as the object falls out of scope.

For the other resource, the texture pointer, we can apply an easier solution to all pointers: the `auto_ptr` class. The `auto_ptr` class, which is part of the standard C++ library, is similar to the class we used with a file handle, but it applies to pointers instead of files. Whenever the `auto_ptr` object is destroyed, the pointer it holds is deleted. Apart from that, it can be dereferenced and used just like a regular pointer. This is how our example would look using the new classes to release resources automatically:

```
auto_ptr<Texture> CreateTexture(const char * filename)
{
    FilePtr fin (filename, "rb");
    TextureHeader info;
    ReadTextureHeader(fin, info);
    auto_ptr<Texture> pTexture = new Texture(info.width,
                                            info.height,
                                            info.colorDepth);

    ReadTextureData(fin, pTexture);
    return pTexture;
}
```

This is much better. Notice how now we do not do any exception handling in this function, and instead let the calling function deal with it. All the resources have been released correctly, though.

There are other alternatives to `auto_ptr`, some of which might be more appropriate to your specific situation, depending on whether you want shared ownership, reference counting, or a variety of other options. The Boost library offers several different smart pointers that could be used instead of `auto_ptr`.

Also, it is worth noting that we could have used the same technique in the case where we were handling errors using return codes. Doing that would definitely improve the clarity of the code, allow us to return right away, and be confident that all the resources would be correctly released.

5.3.2 Constructors

Constructors have always been different. As mentioned earlier, constructors do not have a `return` value, so it becomes impossible to return error codes that indicate something has failed.

Exceptions work well with constructors because they do not rely on any `return` codes. However, they present some unique challenges. Consider the following:

```
class Bitmap
{
public:
    Bitmap(int width, int height)
    {
        m_pData = new(width*height);
        // ...
    }
    ~Bitmap() { delete m_pData; }
private:
    byte * m_pData;
};
```

This `Bitmap` class is very straightforward. Whenever an object is constructed, it allocates enough memory to store a bitmap of the specified size; and whenever it is destroyed, the memory is released. So far, the code looks good.

What happens if an exception is thrown in the constructor after the memory in `m_pData` is allocated? The stack unwinds, and the execution is transferred to the nearest `try-catch` block, just like it did before. But what happens to the memory we just allocated? It will be leaked because it is a resource we did not release.

The reason for the memory leak is that the destructor for the object is not called. After all, because the constructor failed by throwing an exception, it makes no sense to call the destructor. However, the objects that were created so far in the constructor will be destroyed. But because we were using a dumb (that is, not a "smart" or a "normal") pointer, even though the pointer is destroyed, the memory it points to is still allocated.

A way to write the same constructor in an exception-safe manner is to use `auto_ptr` again so that the memory is freed as soon as the `auto_ptr` object is destroyed. As a side benefit, we do not need to free the memory in the destructor; that action happens automatically for us:

```
class Bitmap
{
public:
    Bitmap(int width, int height) :
        m_pData(new(width*height))
    {
        // ...
    }
private:
    auto_ptr<byte> m_pData;
};
```

5.3.3 Destructors

Destructors are not as problematic as constructors, as far as exceptions go. After all, we are destroying an object, so it is not like anybody is going to try to access the object after we are done with it.

The only rule we need to keep in mind is that a destructor is not allowed to throw an exception if the destructor was called in response to another exception. That is, an exception was thrown somewhere, and as part of the stack unwinding, the object's destructor was called. If the destructor were to throw an exception at that point, what should the system do? Ignore the older one and deal with this one? Queue them? Instead, C++ disallows that situation. And, if it ever *does* happen, the function `terminate()` is called, stopping the execution of the program.

If you are worried about that situation, you can always wrap calls that potentially throw exceptions in your destructors in a `try-catch` block that catches all exceptions and either ignores them or deals with them in some fashion.

5.4 COST ANALYSIS

The specifics of the implementation of exceptions are left totally up to the compiler writers, so there is no way to talk in absolutes about the performance cost of exception handling. On the other hand, it is a very important aspect of the implementation, especially for game programming. As with other topics, take the information in this section as a general rule of what you might expect, but measure what the results are in your platform, or look at a disassembled version of the code involved in your exception-handling setup.

First of all, we need to differentiate between two totally different situations: the situation in which no exceptions are thrown, and the situation in which an exception is thrown.

When an exception is thrown, all sorts of things happen: the program searches for the nearest exception-handling block; it unwinds the stack, destroying objects in the process; and then it transfers execution to the `catch` statement. Is that operation slow? Yes. Do we care? Absolutely not.

Exceptions should be exactly that—exceptional. Exceptions are not used to indicate whether a unit gets killed or not, they are used to let us know we just ran out of memory, or maybe that the DVD was removed. Those are truly exceptional circumstances that should either never happen or happen very rarely. We really do not care if the process of throwing and catching an exception is slow. Chances are we are going to temporarily stop the game and tell the user about the problem anyway, so we can certainly afford to spend 100 ms unwinding the stack.

What we really care about is whether performance is affected when no exceptions are thrown. Another interesting question is whether the use of exception handling requires more memory. It turns out those two questions are tied together.

The compiler implements exception handling in one of two main ways. The first and simplest way requires very little extra memory, but it imposes a slight performance overhead every time a `try-catch` statement is reached. The second way has virtually no performance overhead, but it might require a significant amount of memory to efficiently deal with exceptions. The worst part is that you have no control over which implementation is used, other than changing compilers. So if that is a concern to you, refer to the compiler's documentation to find out which implementation it uses.

The other important aspect of implementation to consider is the frequency of `try-catch` statements and what the alternatives are. If `try-catch` statements appear infrequently in the code, or appear only in situations where performance is not as crucial, such as during resource loading, then any performance overhead might go totally unnoticed. On the other hand, if the `try-catch` statements are executed several thousand times per frame, they might add up to a more noticeable performance hit.

When evaluating the performance of exception handling, we also must think about the alternatives. We cannot compare it to code that does no error checking at all. If you can live without error checking, then don't waste your time with exception handling. Most commercial tools and games require some level of robustness, so we are forced to deal with errors in some way. A small overhead for setting up the stack unwinding might seem very reasonable when compared to a function with dozens of nested `if` statements.

On the other hand, if your compiler implements the version of exception handling that trades memory for speed, the drawback might be more than you can afford, especially in some game consoles with very limited system memory. Run some quick experiments before you commit to either using or ignoring exceptions.

5.5 WHEN TO USE EXCEPTIONS

By this point, we know how to use exception handling, what changes it demands in our code, and how much it costs us. The question remaining is: when should we use exceptions? Or even, should we use exceptions at all?

First, it is important to reiterate a previous point: exceptions should be exceptional. Never lose sight of that truth. Avoid the temptation to use the new toy for everyday uses. A good rule to follow is to use exceptions only where errors could happen but are never expected. When exceptions occur, they might require the user's attention. Some situations where exception handling is a good idea are: data file corruption, hardware failing to operate correctly, defective media, or even a sudden disconnection from the network. We should have some way to deal with those situations, but they will hopefully never happen during normal use.

What that means is that exception handling is no substitute for returning error codes from functions. There are many circumstances where return codes are the best solution. For example, if we attempt to open a file with a previous position of the game saved, it is quite likely that the filename was misspelled. Attempting to open the file and returning an error code if it does not exist is a perfectly valid approach. Sometimes you might also want to perform an operation and then check whether it was successful or not. Clearly, a failure in that case is not an unexpected result, so error codes would be a much better, simpler solution.

Both approaches can coexist peacefully, with each applied to circumstances where it is the best solution. It is important to carefully document which error-handling method different parts of the program use. We do not want other programmers putting `try-catch` blocks around functions we wrote that return error codes.

So far, the argument seems to be to use exceptions sparingly for things such as development tools, but is it a good idea to use exceptions inside our game? What if it is a console game? The answer is probably *yes* in both cases. As long as exceptions are used rarely and indicate truly exceptional situations, they can save a lot of effort when debugging the code.

5.6 CONCLUSION

Before our introduction to exceptions, we saw what the alternatives were for handling errors in our programs: we could ignore them, return error codes, or use the C-centric `setjmp()` and `longjmp()` functions. All these alternatives had major drawbacks.

Exceptions can be used to report errors in a very clean way. They do not require us to fill our code with `if` statements, and they are also foolproof because they cannot be easily ignored (unlike `return` codes). Unfortunately, writing exception-safe code is not a trivial matter, especially in the case of constructors.

We then saw how different exception-handling implementations can have very different performance and memory requirements. However, if exceptions are used sparingly for situations in which errors are possible but not expected, the overhead they introduce should be negligible to the point where it is worth considering using them in the game code itself.

SUGGESTED READING

There is a fair amount of literature out there dealing with exceptions. These are some great references, which include some very sound advice on appropriate situations to use exception handling as well as some discussions on writing exception-safe code.

Dattatri, Kayshav, *C++ Effective Object-Oriented Software Construction*. Prentice Hall, 2000.

Murray, Robert B., *C++ Strategies and Tactics*. Addison-Wesley, 1993.

Stroustrup, Bjarne, *The C++ Programming Language*, 3rd ed. Addison-Wesley, 1997.

Sutter, Herb, *Exceptional C++*. Addison-Wesley, 2000.

The Boost library has several types of smart pointers that can be used effectively with exception handling.

C++ Boost Smart Pointer Library. Available online at *http://www.boost.org/libs/smart_ptr/index.htm*.

II

TAPPING THE POWER OF C++

All the right ingredients are there: compelling gameplay, breathtaking visuals, and an outstanding soundtrack. Now the game will stand or fall based on how well it runs. If it is a clunker running at five frames per second, it will be a beautiful clunker, but it will not be very popular. If the game bogs down after 10 minutes of play because of memory leaks, a lot of angry customers are going to be returning your game.

Internal development tools are not exempt from efficiency requirements, either. If loading the level editor takes a minute, or if scrolling through the tree of entities in the world is sluggish and unresponsive, the productivity of the designers and the final product quality will definitely suffer.

C++ is a complex programming language. There are two sides to that: with that complexity, we can accomplish things other languages can only dream of; on the flip side, it has a fairly steep (and long) learning curve, and a large potential for programming errors. With great power comes great responsibility.

Part II of this book deals with the nuts and bolts of C++: how to avoid common performance pitfalls and what things to do to speed up the program, how to deal with memory management efficiently, and how to use high-level data structures and algorithms easily and effectively.

6

PERFORMANCE

In This Chapter

- Performance and Optimizations
- Function Types
- Inlining
- More Function Overhead
- Avoiding Copies
- Constructors and Destructors
- Data Caches and Memory Alignment (Advanced)

Some people claim that C++ is just too complicated. You might even be starting to fall into that category after having read the previous chapters. There is no denying that C++ is a very complex language. Fortunately, however, the language is also extremely powerful and flexible; once mastered, it provides all the tools necessary to engineer a state-of-the-art game engine.

In this chapter, we examine some of the most common performance pitfalls and how to use C++ effectively to avoid them. Specifically, we look at the different types of function calls and the overhead involved with each of them, and how to minimize their impact in our programs. We also go in detail about some of the hidden costs of C++—things that happen behind your back without being explicit in the source code, such as generation of temporaries or the cost of constructors and destructors.

Understanding what is happening behind the scenes and keeping a few rules in mind make it possible to tame the complexity of C++ and walk away with all the performance benefits it provides.

6.1 PERFORMANCE AND OPTIMIZATIONS

Performance is not everything. This observation might seem surprising in a chapter dedicated exclusively to performance, but it is true. At some point, we have all become focused on a tiny section of a program, trying to make it faster by pulling every trick in the book. It can be an exhilarating experience to wring out all the performance the hardware can provide, and then some. At times, such persistence might be necessary, but more often than not, it is wasted effort. Figure 6.1 illustrates the profile of a typical PC game that makes good use of an accelerated graphics card.

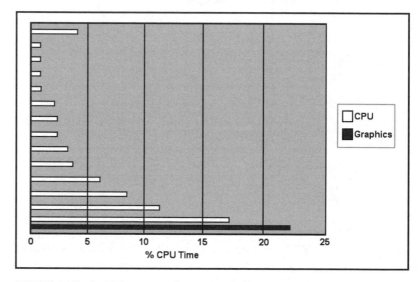

FIGURE 6.1   Typical PC game performance profile.

There are several interesting things in that profile. First of all, a large amount of the time is spent in the graphics card. All the C++ optimizations in the world are not going to make the graphics card any faster. Instead, we need to look at other ways of making graphics more efficient, such as rearranging the vertex data, reducing the number of state changes, or using better-designed shaders.

On the CPU side, there are some interesting patterns: 90% of the code execution time is spent on about 10–12 different functions. If we heavily optimize a function outside those top functions and make it twice as fast, we will not even notice the frame rate increase. It would be completely wasted effort.

What is worse, even if we optimize one of those top 10 functions, we might not get any improvement because the CPU might just spend more time waiting for the graphics card to be done. In the future, as we see more specialized hardware for different tasks, maximizing parallelism will become even more important. This situation is already true for most game consoles because they have several specialized chips in addition to the main CPU.

As if this picture were not grim enough, let's consider some of the dangers of optimization with a hypothetical example. Programmer Pete decides it is time to speed up the AI pathfinding function, so he spends a whole day pulling every trick in the book to speed things up and sweats over every cycle. At the end of the day, Pete times his improvements and notices he has gotten a 20% performance boost in the pathfinding functions. Very proud of himself, he does the programmer victory dance, pats himself on the back, checks the code in, and goes home for some well-deserved rest.

The next morning, Programmer Pete runs the full build of the game and notices that it is not appreciably faster. When he looks at the frame rate, he sees that it is indeed running faster: about 2% faster. This is not surprising because the AI pathfinding was 10% of the CPU usage; so the overall improvement was not as dramatic as he might have hoped. But any small improvement is desirable, so Pete moves on to something else.

A week later, Programmer Pete is asked to add pathfinding for flying units. What he had implemented so far was only for land-based units. This should be no problem, he thinks. He pulls out the optimized code he worked so hard on last week and realizes that it is impossible to cleanly add flying units. It is so tightly optimized that it is completely inflexible. Not only that, but Pete is afraid to touch it at all because it is very hard to understand what exactly is going on. Making any changes could break all the pathfinding, and the project has a milestone just a few days away!

The story probably ends with Programmer Pete undoing all his clever optimizations, putting the old code back, and adding the flying unit support. Sadly, that is the *happy* ending. The alternative ending is that Pete stubbornly hacks in flying-unit support (spending three precious days to do so), and then it never works right and crashes half the time, leading to the missed milestone and eventual cancellation of the project. The moral of the story is that optimizing at the wrong moment—or thinking too much about optimizations from the very beginning—causes more problems than it solves.

Nobody denies that performance is important, though. As a matter of fact, it is much more important in games than in most other types of software development. It just needs to be dealt with carefully and at the right time. Performance should be addressed in two distinct phases: during program development and at the end of development.

6.1.1 During Program Development

During program development, the primary aim is to avoid doing something grossly inefficient. We should not be too concerned about exact cycle counts, hand-tuned assembly language, or cache interactions. We are only trying to avoid doing things that will unnecessarily slow everything down. This chapter addresses many issues that come up during the development phase.

It is not always easy to decide what to optimize and what to leave for later. A lot of that depends on experience, team expertise, and individual abilities. A good rule of thumb is that if you are in doubt as to whether or not to incorporate a particular optimization *now*, then leave it out.

Also during this phase, it is important to keep rough algorithmic performance in mind. Do not be too concerned about whether or not a search is optimal. At the same time, however, avoid searching a large list for the same element a hundred times during a frame. Instead, cache that result and reuse it whenever you need it. Or, if you know your game is going to have many units and objects in the world at once, avoid traversing the whole list of game objects to search for elements; use a spatial database for fast spatial queries instead.

6.1.2 At the End of Development

The end phase does not just refer to when we are getting the game ready to ship. It can be at the end of the development of a particular subsystem (for example, the graphics renderer), or when we have decided that enough is enough, and we are not going to tweak the pathfinding algorithms anymore.

At this point, we can pull some of the more esoteric optimizations. We will be trading readability and maintainability for faster performance. If we want to reuse this code in a future project, we should think long and hard about what we do to it. If the code is very well encapsulated, maybe optimizing it heavily would be fine. Otherwise, we should go easy and carefully document all the optimizations in the code itself for future reference. There is nothing more frustrating than digging up some code you wrote a while ago that is so cleverly optimized that it runs blazingly fast, but you have no idea what it does.

Keep in mind that optimizations at the end phase usually are not going to result in major performance improvements. The big gains come from decisions we made in the previous phase, during development: the choice of algorithms, avoiding unnecessary computations, and so forth. Optimizing the code itself will get us a few percentages of improvement here and there for the overall program performance—maybe even a total boost of 10% to 15% in performance; but do not expect much more than that.

That said, what is the point of this chapter, then? This is not a chapter about bit-twiddling or replacing C++ with assembly code. It is also not about choosing the best algorithms to solve the problem at hand or about avoiding doing duplicate or unnecessary work. It is about avoiding potentially expensive operations in everyday C++ usage—things to keep in mind both when you are designing a piece of code and when you are implementing it.

6.2 FUNCTION TYPES

Function calls are something we have used in many programming languages, and we have come to expect a certain overhead for each function call. There are two reasons to bring it up here:

- In addition to normal function calls, C++ introduces class member function calls, class static function calls, and virtual function calls. Knowing what the costs are of each of them helps improve the performance of the program.
- C++ encourages a more object-oriented approach, which typically involves more function calls than a procedural program. So function call overhead might be more noticeable than in a straight C program.

In C++, function calls fall into one of four categories: *global functions*, *class static functions*, *nonvirtual member functions*, and *virtual member functions*. There are also two distinct cases of virtual members from a performance perspective: virtual functions under single inheritance and virtual functions under multiple inheritance.

6.2.1 Global Functions

Global functions are the same types of function calls we encountered in C. For example:

```
int iHitPoints = GetHitPoints (gameUnit);
```

This type of function amounts to a call to a specific memory location that is computed at link time. So the only overhead comes from the actual jump to a different memory location and its effects on the code cache and CPU pipeline. In most modern platforms, the cost is fairly negligible. It is possible to set up situations where the overhead of global function calls starts becoming noticeable, but these situations are fairly unlikely to happen during real development, especially with some judicious *inlining* (which is the topic of the next section, so hang in there). Because global functions are the simplest and fastest type of function, we use them as our baseline to analyze and compare the other types of function calls.

Usually, a good rule to follow is to forget about performance overhead and make a new function call anytime it makes sense to do so. Getting in the habit of using functions liberally has many benefits that totally outweigh any minor performance drawbacks. Using functions in this way:

• Encourages a solution to be implemented in smaller substeps.
• Produces more readable code because each function has only one objective, making its purpose easily understood just by reading the function name.
• Results in more maintainable code because it is possible to replace or fix just one of the many functions that went into solving a larger problem.
• Encourages reuse because many problems might require some of the same substeps in their solutions.

The main drawback of using a large number of functions is that it might be difficult to follow the flow of the execution of the program, particularly if calls happen across multiple files. Having a good tool, such as an Integrated Development Environment (IDE) or source code browser, to navigate the code can be very helpful in those situations. If at some point the performance of the function calls slows noticeably in some particularly sensitive section of code, it is always very easy to merge several functions together and eliminate most of the performance overhead.

6.2.2 Class Static Functions

Class static functions are similar to global functions except that their scope is limited to a particular class. They are different than member functions because they are not associated with objects of that class, just the class itself.

Class static function calls are treated by the compiler in the same way as global function calls. They just have a slightly different appearance in the code because their scope parameter indicates the class to which they belong:

```
// Class static function
int iNumUnits = GameUnit::GetNumUnits();
```

The exact same comments apply as for normal static functions with respect to performance and use. The only thing that class static functions provide is a way to organize a group of related functions under one class, which helps us, the programmers, understand the code better.

6.2.3 Nonvirtual Member Functions

Member functions are functions associated with particular objects. Here, we consider only member functions that are not marked as virtual.

```
GameUnit gameUnit;
int iHitPoints = gameUnit.GetHitPoints();
```

This type of function call is similar to the previous two types. As before, the address of the function to call is determined at link time because the type of the object it is called from is also known at compile time (but that changes in the case of virtual functions).

The only difference is that member functions refer to a particular object. This is implemented under the hood by having a hidden this parameter that points to the object being called. Internally, the preceding function call is converted to something like this:

```
GameUnit gameUnit;
int iHitPoints = __GameUnitClass__GetHitPoints( &gameUnit );
```

The extra underscores (__) are just a way for the compiler to rename member functions in order to know the class to which they belong. This conversion is referred to as *name mangling* and is usually much less attractive than the example just given.

What is the extra performance cost of a nonvitrtual member function call compared to a global function call? The cost is only the extra parameter passing. Most of the time, this amounts to no difference at all, so feel free to use member functions to your heart's content. We look in more detail at the performance of parameter passing later in this chapter.

6.2.4 Virtual Functions Under Single Inheritance

Virtual member functions have the potential to be the most expensive. (For detailed explanations of how virtual functions are implemented, both in single and multiple inheritance, refer to Chapter 1, "Inheritance," and Chapter 2, "Multiple Inheritance.") Normally, virtual function calls occur when we invoke methods on polymorphic objects. Continuing with the previous example of the GameUnit class, we now have a reference of the type GameUnit, but remember that it can point to a derived class. RunAI() is a virtual member function declared in the GameUnit class itself.

```
GameUnit * pGameUnit = new SomeGameUnit;
pGameUnit->RunAI();
```

In this case, calling `RunAI()` triggers the virtual mechanism and incurs some extra overhead of dereferencing the vtable (see Chapter 1). The equivalent code shows how the compiler interprets the preceding call:

```
GameUnit * pGameUnit = new SomeGameUnit;
(pGameUnit->vptr[3])(pGameUnit);
```

In this particular case, `RunAI()` is the third virtual function in the vtable, so the compiler invokes it by accessing the vtable and calling the function in the first slot by doing `this->vptr[3]()`. Notice how an extra parameter gets passed in, pointing to the object the function is acting on, just like with nonvirtual member functions.

The cost of this extra dereferencing varies from platform to platform. Until it becomes an issue by being called thousands of times per frame, it is probably not worth losing much sleep over. As we saw in Chapter 1, if you truly need the functionality of a virtual function, that is about as fast as it is going to get.

Actually, that last statement is not precisely true. Any type of virtual function mechanism is going to require some indirection before making the function call, but what can make the difference is where that indirection happens. Using C++ inheritance, the indirection happens by indexing into the vtable for the class of the object we are making that call on. There is only one vtable per class, and it can be stored anywhere in memory, possibly even far from the object itself. That means that the vtable access could cause a data cache miss, especially if we are calling virtual functions for many different classes and we are on a platform with a small data cache. This problem is compounded if the platform we are working on has slow memory access whenever there is a cache miss, as is the case with some game consoles. In a situation like this, it might be slightly faster to have a custom method in which each object stores its own table of function pointers. This is one of those classic memory-space tradeoffs, but it can make a difference in some very specific circumstances.

A particularly frustrating aspect of the performance hit, which is caused by vtable cache misses, is that it is extremely difficult to narrow down. The overall slowness shows up in unexpected places in a profiler, and apparently simple loops seem to take much longer than they should. Making a few changes simply moves the performance hot spots around. If you run into a similar situation and are making extensive use of virtual function calls, you might want to look into this possibility.

Something you might be wondering about is the effect of hierarchy size on virtual function call performance. Does a very deep hierarchy mean worse performance? In the case of single inheritance, fortunately the answer is no. Each class has its own vtable; it does not matter how it was derived.

Finally, there is one situation under which virtual function calls do not cost any more than a normal static function call. That happens whenever a virtual function is invoked directly on the object, not through a pointer or a reference. C++ supports the concept of polymorphism only on references, not on objects themselves; so if we make a call to a member function of an object, the compiler can resolve the final address during compilation, bypassing all the virtual function mechanisms at runtime.

In the following example, even though `RunAI()` is a virtual function, it is invoked just like any nonvirtual member function because it is applied on the object directly:

```
GameUnit gameUnit;
gameUnit.RunAI();
```

On the other hand, the following code shows the same function being called through a pointer to the object. Because the compiler has no way of knowing the true type of the object at runtime, the function call goes through the virtual function lookup.

```
GameUnit * pGameUnit;
pGameUnit->RunAI();
```

6.2.5 Virtual Functions Under Multiple Inheritance

In Chapter 2, we saw how multiple inheritance was implemented— specifically, how the vtable of a class that used multiple inheritance was created by appending the vtables of its parent classes. When it comes time for a virtual function call, the compiler indexes into the vtable, just as it does in the case of single inheritance. What is unique about multiple inheritance is that, depending on the parent from which we inherited that virtual function, the vtable pointer might have to be offset to point to the correct section. That offsetting incurs a relatively minor performance cost.

Everything else is the same as for single inheritance, even the cache misses caused by the vtable lookup. Even though the vtable is constructed from its parents' vtables, it is still in one contiguous location in memory.

A class that makes extensive use of multiple inheritance, especially near the bottom of a large hierarchy tree, could have a very large vtable, because it might inherit a large number of functions from all its parents. This makes the data cache misses when calling many different virtual functions in the same object somewhat worse, because the vtable is so large that it might result in more cache misses and slower overall performance.

6.3 INLINING

Function *inlining* is a technique that can greatly reduce function over-head in some specific cases. To use it effectively, we must learn how it works and under what situations it is beneficial.

6.3.1 The Need for Inlining

Consider the following code:

```
class GameUnit
{
public:
    bool IsActive() const;
    // ....
private:
    bool m_bActive;
};

bool GameUnit::IsActive() const
{
    return m_bActive;
}

// .....

if ( gameUnit.IsActive() )
{
    // ....
}
```

To evaluate the `if` statement, we must first make a function call to `GameUnit::IsActive()`, with all the regular costs involved in a member function call. As we saw in the previous section, those costs are fairly small. However, the function itself is trivial, so it feels like a waste to have to do all that work for so little payoff. Besides, if we need to call that function several thousand times per frame, that extra overhead starts adding up and eating into the frame rate.

We could make `m_bActive` a public variable and access it directly. That will certainly avoid any extra performance costs. Unfortunately, that solution causes more trouble than it is worth in the long run. Some compelling reasons not to have public member variables are the difficulty involved in changing the class implementation when other parts of the code are accessing variables directly, the difficulty of keeping track of how and when certain variables are accessed, and the impossibility of restricting certain variables to read-only access.

Another, even larger, practical problem with using public member variables is what to do when the function does something other than return a member variable. What if the `IsActive()` function from our example were defined this way:

```
bool IsActive() const { return m_bAlive && m_bRunning };
```

Then things start getting ugly. If we get rid of the function and let other parts of the code access the variables directly, it means we have to expose both `m_bAlive` and `m_bRunning`. Whenever any part of the code wants to check whether a game unit is active or not, it has to check both variables. What if later on we decide that `IsActive()` should be like this instead:

```
bool IsActive() const { return (m_bAlive && m_bRunning) ||
                                m_bSelected };
```

Imagine the nightmare of updating all your code everywhere. We should look at other alternatives.

6.3.2 Inline Functions

Instead, we can use *inline* functions. Inlining has the exact same performance results as accessing the variables directly, with none of the drawbacks. All we have to do is flag a function with the keyword `inline`, and the compiler takes care of removing the function call and embedding its contents directly into the calling code. Inlining the previous example would look like this:

```
class GameUnit
{
public:
    bool IsActive() const;
    // ....
private:
    bool m_bActive;
};

inline bool GameUnit::IsActive() const
{
    return m_bActive;
}
```

```
// .....

if ( gameUnit.IsActive() )
{
    // ....
}
```

The function call still looks the same, but internally the compiler substitutes the function call with the body of the function itself, like this:

```
if ( gameUnit.m_bActive )
{
    // ....
}
```

All the costs associated with function calls totally disappear. For small, frequently called functions, inlining them can be a huge performance boost. This is particularly true of functions whose performance cost is so small that it is comparable to the function call overhead itself.

Using inlining is very straightforward, but there are a few ways it can trip you up. The first way is that for a function to be inlined, it must be defined in the header file. This is because the compiler only "sees" the header files we have told it to include for the file it is compiling. If it is going to substitute the body of the function in the calling code, it has to have access to it, and it is not smart enough to open the .cpp file by itself.

There are two ways to declare a function inline and provide its definition in the header file. The definition can be provided right after the declaration, like this:

```
class GameUnit
{
    inline bool IsActive() const { return m_bActive };
    // ....
};
```

Alternatively, the definition can be provided after the function declaration. This tends to look neater and is better for functions longer than a single line of code.

```
class GameUnit
{
    bool IsActive() const;
    // ....
};
```

```
inline bool GameUnit::IsActive() const
{
    return m_bActive;
}
```

Be aware that some compilers refuse to inline functions unless the `inline` keyword appears both in the declaration and definition of the function. If you are dealing with one of those compilers, you might want to get in the habit of putting the `inline` keyword in both locations.

The second potential trip-up is that there is no guarantee a function will actually be inlined. The `inline` keyword is nothing more than a hint for the compiler. In the end, the compiler decides whether to inline it or not. Usually, the simpler the function, the more likely it will be inlined. When the function becomes longer, contains calls to other functions, or has complex loops or operations, chances are the compiler will refuse to inline it. You cannot even rely on the inlining behavior being consistent across different platforms because different compilers have different rules about inlining.

It would be nice to get a warning or an error if a function marked as inline does not get inlined. Unfortunately, we have no such luck. Most compilers silently ignore the `inline` keyword if they cannot comply with it. The ways you can tell if an inline worked is by noticing the improved performance or by looking at the disassembly of the generated code. This is not the most convenient way, but it might be worth the effort to verify that some particularly crucial section of the code is indeed being inlined.

6.3.3 When to Use Inline

So, why not use inlining all the time? Ironically, that could easily degrade the game's performance instead of improving it. As if that weren't bad enough, there are other reasons why indiscriminate inlining can be problematic.

At first, the idea of inlining every function sounds good. After all, it means we can get rid of all the function call overhead. The first problem is that the size of the executable would skyrocket out of control because every part of the code that calls a function would duplicate that function's code. Apart from consuming more memory, this approach results in very poor use of the code cache, resulting in constant cache thrashing and significantly lowering the program's performance.

The other main reason why indiscriminate inlining is a bad idea has to do with the location of the function definition. We saw earlier that for a function to be inlined, its definition must be present in the header file. This means that `include` statements that could otherwise be in the .cpp file must be moved to the .h file, which results in longer compile times.

This might not be a big deal for just a handful of files. But if done on a consistent basis across a project with thousands of source files, it can exponentially increase compile times (see Chapter 18, "Dealing with Large Projects," for more information).

What is the best way to use `inline`, then? Start by avoiding the use of inlining while you are developing code; then, when that code is mostly complete, profile the program and see whether any small functions appear toward the top of the most-called functions. Those will be great candidates to inline, and you should see immediate performance improvements as a result.

There will be times when we know right from the beginning that a function should be inlined. For example, some of the functions in a `Point` class, where the operations are almost trivial and the performance is critical, might be perfect targets for inlining. Go ahead and inline those functions right away; just do not get in the habit of inlining everything.

Die-hard C programmers often ask, "What is the difference between inline functions and macros?" After all, the preprocessor always expands a macro, unlike an inline function, which is left to the mercy of the compiler. The main advantage of inlining is that it still provides the same amount of type checking as a normal function, while a macro has no type checking whatsoever. That is quite important for catching potential errors right away at compile time. Inline functions are also easier to debug and step into in the debugger, and they also mesh a lot better with classes because they can be part of a class and access all its private and protected members, while a macro has no intrinsic knowledge about classes at all.

That said, there might come a time when we are sure that inlining a function would result in a net performance gain, but the compiler steadfastly refuses to inline it. In that case, we can fall back on the use of a simple macro with the contents of the function we were trying to inline. It might not be pretty, but at least the macro is not going to refuse to do its job.

6.4 More Function Overhead

The overhead introduced by functions does not end with the actual function call. The parameters we pass to them and their `return` values can greatly affect the performance of a function.

6.4.1 Function Parameters

The most important thing to remember when dealing with function parameters is to never pass a large object by value. By *large* we mean an object that requires more than a handful of bytes of allocation when created.

When such an object is passed as a parameter by value, a temporary copy of the object is created, which is potentially a very expensive operation. (We deal with temporaries later in this chapter.) Unless we are really confident about the small size of an object, we should always pass objects by reference.

The following function takes a matrix and updates the bounding volumes for that node. This code works just fine, but it is slower than it should be:

```
// Slow version of the function
void SceneNode::UpdateBV (Matrix mat)
{
    m_BV.Rotate (mat);
    // ...
}
```

Instead, we could rewrite the function to take a reference, which gives us the same functionality, but much better performance:

```
// Much faster version of the same function
void SceneNode::UpdateBV ( const Matrix & mat )
{
    m_BV.Rotate (mat);
    // ...
}
```

Notice that not only did we change the matrix to a reference, we also made it into a const reference. The reason for this is that the function is not supposed to change the matrix object passed to it. Specifying the reference to be constant enforces that restriction at compile time, so any attempts to modify it result in a compile error. We saw this concept in detail in Chapter 3, "Constness, References, and a Few Loose Ends."

Very small objects or basic data types do not have to be passed by reference. It can depend on the platform, but with most current hardware, a reference or a pointer is 32 bits. There is usually no reason to pass anything of that size or smaller by reference, unless it has particularly expensive constructors or destructors.

Assuming that all the parameters are basic data types or that we are passing larger objects by reference, is there a penalty for passing many parameters to a function? The answer is usually yes, but the penalty is fairly small, and the specifics depend on the platform and compiler.

Usually, compilers try to put as many parameters as possible into CPU registers so they can be accessed directly in the called function. Some

CPUs have a large number of registers, so this is usually not a limiting factor. However, in other architectures such as PCs, it is possible to fit only so many parameters before we run out of unused registers. In this case, the rest are put on the stack. Doing so means copying them to the stack memory location and retrieving them from the called function when they are needed. This is by no means a large overhead (as long as the objects are passed by reference), and the stack is in the data cache because it is used so frequently, so this is usually not something that causes performance to degrade significantly.

However, the most important lesson to be learned from parameter passing does not involve performance; rather, it involves people. A computer does not care how many parameters we pass to a function. As we saw, the computer simply puts them in the stack when they do not fit in registers. People are not as fortunate, and there are only so many things we can juggle in our minds at once. As a rule of thumb, if you ever find yourself writing a function that takes more than five to seven parameters, you should really consider whether there is another, better way of writing it. You will be glad you did it when that part of the program needs to be changed or debugged in a few months. Chances are, we can encapsulate some data into a new class or structure and make the program a lot clearer. It will even be a tiny bit faster. For once, clarity and performance are not at odds with each other, so there is no reason not to do it.

6.4.2 Return Values

Returning a basic data type, such as an integer or a float, is usually a free operation. Again, this depends on the platform, compiler, and calling convention, but typically, the return value is copied to a register and checked by the calling code.

References and pointers are usually treated the same way. So, as long as we need to return objects that already exist somewhere in the code, references to existing objects are one of the most efficient ways to go. Just remember to never return a reference or pointer to an object that was created on the stack because it will not be there when the function returns. Fortunately, most compilers can detect this situation at compile time and issue a warning. The following code makes good use of returning references, especially if the function is marked as inline:

```
const Matrix & SceneNode::GetMatrix () const
{
    return m_matrix;
}
```

But what about when we need to return an object that does not exist already? Then we have three options:

- Return a copy of the object.
- Create an object outside the function, pass it as a non-const reference, and fill it inside the function.
- Dynamically allocate the object inside the called function and return a pointer to it.

The third option is always very efficient as far as `return` values are concerned, but it has several major drawbacks. The main problem is that it dynamically allocates an object. That in itself is not a bad thing, but it can be a serious drawback in a performance-intensive function. Also, if done very frequently, it can seriously affect the memory heap, leading to fragmentation and loss of performance. There are ways to avoid this situation, as we see in Chapter 7, "Memory Allocation."

Another major problem is that the third option, as it stands, is not a very safe solution. It requires the function to dynamically allocate the object and return a pointer to it to the caller, and it is then up to the caller to deal with the object correctly (for example, free it, store it, or whatever). This can become a serious maintenance headache later on.

The cleanest and simplest option is the first one. Unfortunately, the second option can be much more efficient. If both solutions were just as fast, returning a copy of the object would make things more consistent. That way we could always return all the objects directly from a function, independent of their size. As it is, we do different things depending on the internal implementation of the class we are calling, which is less than ideal from a software-engineering point of view. Sometimes we have to make small concessions to get big performance gains.

This is how the `GetMatrix()` function would look if we did not have a matrix already in the `SceneNode` object and had to return it from the function:

```
void SceneNode::GetMatrix (Matrix & matrix) const
{
    // This object has a rotation object, but not a matrix,
    // so we need to fill the one that gets passed in.
    m_rotation.ToMatrix (matrix);
}
```

If it returned a copy of the matrix, we might incur an extra copy and a performance penalty:

```
// This code is potentially much slower
Matrix SceneNode::GetMatrix () const
{
    return m_rotation.GetMatrix();
}
```

This second version is cleaner looking and more consistent with returning objects by reference, but it is potentially slower because of what the compiler does with it. A good optimizing compiler internally converts the second version into something that looks like the first version. So, we still get the cleanest syntax, but also the best performance. That optimization is called *return value optimization* (RVO). Check your compiler's documentation to find out whether or not it supports RVO. RVO is a fairly common optimization these days, so chances are it is supported.

There are two types of `return` value optimizations: named and unnamed. The easiest one for compilers to implement is the unnamed one, which we saw in the previous example. The `return` value is just a temporary (that is, it is an unnamed variable), and the compiler creates and assigns it directly into the object that gets the `return` value from the function.

Named return value optimization is a bit trickier for the compiler to support. It works just like the unnamed return value optimization, but with an actual named variable, not just a temporary. For this optimization to work, all `return` paths of the function must return the same value. The following is a function where the compiler could apply named return value optimization:

```
Matrix SceneNode::GetTransformedMatrix () const
{
    Matrix mat = m_matrix;
    if (m_pParent != NULL)
    {
        mat.Concatenate(m_pParent->GetMatrix());
    }
    return mat;
}
```

As usual when dealing with optimizations, you should also take into consideration how efficient the function has to be. If we are talking about returning a `Point3d` object (which would be just three floats), and the function is hardly ever called, then returning a copy of the object is a perfectly good approach. If the function gets called in an inner loop many times per frame, unless we know for a fact that our compiler performs the return value optimization, then it is worth the extra inconvenience of passing in a non-const reference to be filled in by the function in order to save a few precious CPU cycles.

6.4.3 Empty Functions

At first it might seem an odd thing to talk about the performance of completely empty, useless functions. Why would anybody write such functions? Surprisingly, they are not as uncommon as we might expect.

Sometimes development teams have a set of templates that create the code for a new class from scratch. In that template, a function might be declared and implemented with an empty body for convenience and to save some typing later on. At other times, a macro is used to give a class certain behavior, and it too might contain empty functions.

Does the compiler get rid of the empty functions? As usual, it depends. Sometimes the compiler does get rid of them, but that is often not the case. Typically, unless the empty function is inlined, the compiler has no way to know it is empty and leaves it untouched. Any calls to that function go through all the motions of putting the parameters in registers and the stack, dereferencing the vtable if it is a virtual function, calling its address, and returning. All of that for nothing!

The obvious advice is this: do not do it. There is usually no good reason to have empty functions. If we are creating a skeleton class for someone to fill in later, we should consider using pure virtual functions. That way we set up the interface, and by flagging the functions as pure virtual, we force the programmers who flesh out the class to create an implementation for those particular functions.

Another common mistake is to provide almost-empty functions in a class hierarchy, whose only function is to call the equivalent parent class function (which in turn is empty, except for a call to its parent's class, all the way to the root). The mechanics of virtual functions already do that for us by calling the closest implemented function from a parent class if that function has not been overridden. Virtual functions also do it much more efficiently, avoiding a whole chain of calls every time a virtual function is called. Not only that, but adding those functions everywhere makes it much more difficult to change the interface of that function at a later time, because doing so involves going into every single class file and changing the source code within.

6.5 Avoiding Copies

Do not copy objects unless you have to. This might sound obvious, but it crops up surprisingly often. Things are not helped by the fact that C++

tends to copy objects behind your back as soon as you are not paying close attention.

Unlike in C, the consequences for copying an object can be quite unexpected. Creating a new object from an existing one calls its copy constructor, which often calls the copy constructors for the objects it contains, and so on down the line. All of a sudden, copying that object does not seem like such a great idea.

6.5.1 Arguments

The first thing to do to address this problem is to use const references when passing objects to and from functions whenever we can. That way, the syntax is the same as for passing an object by value, but we avoid any performance hits for extra copies. For example, we want to avoid declaring a function like this:

```
bool SetActiveCamera (Camera camera);
```

Instead, we want to declare it like this:

```
bool SetActiveCamera (const Camera & camera);
```

The const part is not necessary to avoid the extra copy; it is simply there to indicate that the camera object we passed in should not be modified by the SetActiveCamera() function.

6.5.2 Temporaries

The next thing to do is to watch out for *temporaries*. Temporaries are objects created by the compiler without any explicit instructions in the code to do so. These can be hard to catch unless you are familiar with the rules for creating temporaries. Also, because the creation of temporaries can happen extremely often, it has the potential to dramatically affect the overall game performance.

We have already seen a place where a temporary is generated under the hood: the passing of arguments by value. Nowhere in the code is there an explicit copy of the object being made, yet one is silently created.

A fairly common and hard-to-catch type of temporary is the one caused by type mismatch. Consider the following piece of code:

```
void SetRotation (const Rotation & rot);

float fDegrees = 90.0f;
SetRotation (fDegrees); // Rotate unit 90 degrees
```

Everything looks fine, and the code compiles and works as expected. But what is happening under the hood? After all, the SetRotation() function does not take a float as a parameter. Looking closely at the Rotation class, we notice some of its constructors:

```
class Rotation
{
public:
    Rotation ();
    Rotation (float fHeading, float fPitch = 0.0f,
            float fRoll = 0.0f);
    // ....
};
```

Things start becoming clearer. The compiler is trying to be helpful. Because it detected that we are passing a float to a function that takes a Rotation reference, and it knows that it is possible to create a Rotation object from a float, it went ahead and did that for us. That is a perfect example of a hidden temporary.

This is one of those features that is rarely helpful in game development. It might come in handy and save a bit of typing in a few specific cases, but most of the time it just gets in the way. Chances are the caller of that function did not want to pay the associated cost with creating an extra Rotation object. Maybe if the code had been more explicit about the costs, the programmer could have chosen a different, cheaper function instead.

6.5.3 Being Explicit

Fortunately, C++ provides a feature to disable those type conversions. We can flag certain constructors as explicit. If we did that with the Rotation class from the preceding example, it would look like this:

```
class Rotation
{
public:
    Rotation ();
    explicit Rotation (float fHeading, float fPitch = 0.0f,
                    float fRoll = 0.0f);
    // ....
};
```

This means that calling `SetRotation()` with a `float` results in a compile-time error. If we still want to go ahead and construct a `Rotation` object, we can do it explicitly like this:

```
float fDegrees = 90.0f;
SetRotation (Rotation(fDegrees)); // Rotate unit 90 degrees
```

The resulting code is going to be exactly like the first version, but this time the temporary is explicit in the code. Anybody reading over this section of code is aware of the object that is being constructed and passed along.

6.5.4 Disallowing Copies

In game development, we usually have many classes that aren't meant to be copied. This is different than other types of software development where the flexibility provided by copying objects outweighs the possible performance implications. For these types of objects, we would like to be warned right away if anybody tries to copy them, including the compiler in the case of temporary objects. A very useful technique for these classes is to provide a private declaration for a copy constructor and an assignment operator, but not provide a definition. That results in perfectly legal C++ code that compiles and runs correctly. However, as soon as anybody tries to copy an object of that type, it results in a compile (or link) error. That way, the code that attempted the copy can be changed right away.

For example, if we have a geometry mesh that we do not want easily copied around because that requires some expensive object creation (probably a smart decision), the code might look like this:

```
class GeomMesh
{
public:
    // ....
private:
    // Private copy constructor and assignment op to avoid
        copies
    GeomMesh ( const GeomMesh & mesh );
    GeomMesh & operator= ( const GeomMesh & mesh );
};
```

This is an invaluable technique for catching potential performance drains early on. The beautiful thing about it is that having those functions declared does not incur any extra cost, so it is a perfectly safe solution. It is so useful that you might want to consider putting it in all your classes by default. If you later decide you need to create a class with a real copy constructor and assignment operator, make them public and provide the appropriate implementation, or comment them out all together and use the default C++ copy constructor and assignment operator.

6.5.5 Allowing Copies

Sometimes we need to copy objects around. There's nothing wrong with that as long as we're aware of the performance implications. The smaller and simpler the object it is, the safer it is to copy it around. A *simpler* object is one that contains fewer non-basic data types than another object. Still, we might be concerned with the potential for unwanted temporaries that happen without us knowing it if we just create a normal copy constructor and assignment operator.

A good alternative that still provides us the ability to copy an object is to create copy functions by hand. Usually, we want to have two separate functions: `Clone()`, which just makes a new instance of the same object, and `Copy()`, which copies the contents.

```
class GeomMesh
{
public:
    // ....
    GeomMesh & Clone () const;
    void Copy ( const GeomMesh & mesh );
private:
    // Private copy constructor and assignment op to avoid
    // copies
    GeomMesh ( const GeomMesh & mesh );
    GeomMesh & operator= ( const GeomMesh & mesh );
};

GeomMesh & GeomMesh::Clone () const
{
    GeomMesh * pMesh = new GeomMesh();
    pMesh->Copy (*this);
    return *pMesh;
}

void GeomMesh::Copy (const GeomMesh & mesh)
{
    // Do the actual copying here
}
```

```
// To use it we just call Clone
GeomMesh * pNewMesh = pMesh->Clone();
```

Finally, keep in mind that there are times when it is perfectly fine to leave the default copy constructor and assignment operator accessible. Plain structures are perfect candidates for this architecture, as well as very simple, basic classes such as vectors or points.

6.5.6 Operator Overloading

Operator overloading is one of those C++ features that people tend to either love or hate. There are good reasons for both dispositions, but we shall consider neither in this section. The point is to highlight one of the potential dangers of a specific type of operator overloading.

The type of operator overloading that has some potential performance implications is one that returns an object of the type it operated on, usually binary operators. For example, operator+() is one of those operators. Consider the following code:

```
Vector3d velocity = oldVelocity + frameIncrement;
Vector3d propulsion = ComputePropulsion();
Vector3d finalVelocity = velocity + propulsion;
```

Vector3d clearly has the operator+() function overloaded to add two 3D vectors. The code looks clean and straightforward. Unfortunately, there is a hidden temporary in the last line. So operator+() is probably implemented like this:

```
const Vector3d operator+ (const Vector3d & v1,
                          const Vector3d & v2)
{
    return Vector3d (v1.x+v2.x, v1.y+v2.y, v1.z+v2.z);
}
```

Notice that the return type of the operator is not a reference or a pointer, but an object itself. That means that the compiler first creates a temporary object, loads it with the result of the function, and then copies it into the variable finalVelocity.

In this case, it might not be a big deal. After all, the Vector3d class is probably fairly lightweight, and copying it a few times is not going to slow things down much. That might be true, but the class might be copied more often than is apparent. What if that code were executed to update the particles in a particle-effect system? Then it would probably get executed many thousands of times per frame, which might begin to make a difference. Also, `operator+()` might be defined for other heavier classes such as a matrix, rotation, or game object.

The good news is that there is a way around it that still allows us to use operator overloading without incurring any extra performance overhead. The solution is to replace binary operators of the form `operator+()` with unary operators of the form `operator+=()`. The latter type of operator acts directly on the object on which it was invoked, so there is no extra copying of temporaries. Here is the definition of `operator +=()`:

```
Vector3d & Vector3d::operator+= (const Vector3d & v)
{
    x += v.x; y += v.y; z += v.z;
    return *this;
}
```

Notice how we are not copying any objects; we are just returning a reference to the object on which the function acted (by dereferencing the `this` pointer). The code that uses it would then look like this:

```
Vector3d velocity = oldVelocity + frameIncrement;
Vector3d propulsion = ComputePropulsion();
Vector3d finalVelocity = velocity;
finalVelocity += propulsion;
```

Even better, it might look like this:

```
Vector3d velocity = oldVelocity + frameIncrement;
velocity += ComputePropulsion();
```

It is possible for the compiler to optimize out some of the temporaries generated when using binary operators, which is a very similar process to return value optimization. In that case, the performance of binary and unary operators might be similar. If you prefer to use binary operators, check to verify what optimizations the compiler is doing so you do not get a surprise later on in the project.

6.6 CONSTRUCTORS AND DESTRUCTORS

Constructors and their counterparts, destructors, are extremely useful features of C++. They take care of initializing or destroying objects automatically, which greatly simplifies the code and reduces potential for bugs.

However, like all automatic procedures, sometimes they might do things you do not want, you do not expect, or that you simply do not remember. As with many other C++ features, having a good understanding of what is going on underneath will help you avoid major performance hits.

As a quick review, consider the classes with the inheritance chain shown in Figure 6.2.

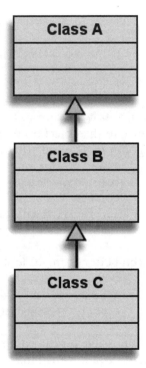

FIGURE 6.2 Simple class hierarchy with single inheritance.

This is a simplified version of the sequence of calls when an object of type C gets created:

1. The new() function gets called to allocate memory for the object.
2. The constructor for A gets called.
3. The constructor for B gets called.
4. The constructor for C gets called.

In addition to each constructor being called, if class A, B, or C contains any objects, then their constructors and all their parents' constructors are also called. The destruction sequence is similar, but in reverse:

1. The destructor for C gets called.
2. The destructor for B gets called.
3. The destructor for A gets called.
4. Memory is freed by calling the delete() function.

Again, any objects contained in those classes are destroyed in turn. What this means is that constructors and destructors have the potential to be very expensive by triggering a long chain of function calls. It is up to us to be aware of the cost associated with each object and to avoid creating them many times in performance-critical sections.

However, C++ was created with performance in mind, and one of the overriding design goals of the language is that we should pay for only the things we want to use. For example, notice that member variables in an object are not automatically initialized to some default value when the object is created; it is up to us to set them to some appropriate value if we care. Sometimes that is an annoyance, but it is the price we pay for performance. This arrangement allows the compiler to avoid generating a constructor (or destructor) altogether if there is no need for one.

There is a constructor or destructor call only if we explicitly create one, or if the object contains other objects that have a constructor or destructor themselves. Also, if a class belongs to some inheritance chain, and the class itself does not have a constructor, that constructor call is skipped completely during object creation, and the constructor for its child is called instead. The same principle applies for destructors.

However, constructors and destructors are extremely useful. Avoid unnecessary ones in performance-critical classes, but do not get rid of them when you need them. If they are doing useful work that must be done, we would probably not get any performance improvement by using an initialization function for the same task.

One simple approach to reduce the call overhead of constructors and destructors is to inline them. Constructors and destructors are like any other function in many aspects, and inlining them works beautifully. Be aware, though, that only very simple ones will be inlined, and if they are part of an inheritance chain, most compilers will have a really hard time trying to inline them. Also, in the case of destructors, any class that has a destructor and is part of an inheritance chain should have a virtual destructor, which makes inlining of the destructor very difficult or even impossible.

Another technique to reduce the overhead of constructors is to use initialization lists. One of the typical functions of a constructor is to set member variables to some default values, or perhaps to the values that were passed as parameters to the constructor. This is the way it would be done in any normal function:

```
// Inefficient SceneNode's default constructor
SceneNode::SceneNode ()
{
    m_strName = "Scene node";
    m_position = g_worldOrigin;
    m_rotMatrix.SetUnit ();
}
```

This code clearly works, but it is also inefficient in the case of a constructor. A better way of doing it is to use *initialization lists*, a feature available only in the constructor. Initialization lists allow us to call the constructor for each member object with specific parameters. Doing so avoids wasting a call to the default constructor for an object and then changing its state again.

In the preceding example, the variable m_strName is of the type string. Before the first line of that constructor is executed, m_strName is initialized to an empty string, maybe even causing some dynamic memory allocations. Then as soon as the first line of the constructor is executed, it is replaced with a different string. Clearly, whatever was done as part of the string's default constructor was wasted time. The same thing applies to the point m_position and the matrix m_rotMatrix. A more efficient way of writing the preceding constructor is as follows:

```
// Better SceneNode's default constructor
SceneNode::SceneNode () :
    m_strName("Scene node"),
    m_position(g_worldOrigin),
    m_rotMatrix(Matrix::Unit)
{}
```

In this case, all the initialization happens only once as the objects are constructed and initialized. Notice that the code assumes that this particular matrix class has a constructor that will generate a unit matrix (probably not a bad idea). This is not always going to be the case, though; sometimes there is work that must be done in the constructor that cannot be done as part of the initialization list because it cannot be performed as a constructor call for the object being initialized. In that case, the best thing is to leave the object completely uninitialized in the initialization list and then initialize it in the constructor body.

In the preceding example, imagine that the Matrix class cannot be set to a unit Matrix through its constructor. Then, the next best thing to do is to prevent it from doing any work in its constructor, and then set it to a unit Matrix by hand:

```
// SceneNode's default constructor
SceneNode::SceneNode ( void ) :
    m_strName("Scene node"),
    m_position(g_worldOrigin)
{
    m_rotMatrix.SetUnit();
}
```

By not calling any specific constructor on the `Matrix` object, the default constructor is called automatically. Hopefully, the default constructor for that `Matrix` class does nothing and leaves all the values uninitialized. Having default constructors that avoid doing expensive initializations can sometimes be very useful for high-performance classes that get created frequently.

Finally, even when the constructor cannot be made any faster, it might still be possible to make the overall program faster: do not call the constructor unless you absolutely have to. This may sound simple, but for programmers coming from many years of straight C, it can take some getting used to. All it requires is to delay the declaration of the object until it is actually needed. Consider the following code:

```
void GameAI::UpdateState ()
{
    AIState nextState;

    if ( IsIdle() )
    {
        nextState = GetNextAIState();
        // ...
    }
    else
    {
        ExecuteCurrentState();
    }
}
```

Unless `AIState` is a trivial object, its default constructor and its destructor will get executed every time the function is called. Considering that this function is probably called once per frame for every game AI in the world, the cost quickly becomes very noticeable. To make things worse, most of the time the AIs will probably not be idle, so the `nextState` local variable is not used the majority of the time. To avoid paying for its costs when we are not using it, we just need to defer the declaration of the variable until we need it:

```
void GameAI::UpdateState ()
{
    if ( IsIdle() )
    {
        AIState nextState = GetNextAIState();
        // ...
    }
    else
    {
        ExecuteCurrentState();
    }
}
```

Even if `AIState` were just a structure without any constructors, it would still be better to declare it right before it is used. `AIState` might change over time and become an expensive object, and because there is no drawback to delaying its declaration as much as possible, we might as well do it right from the beginning. Additionally, not only is the new version of the code faster, it is easier to read because the type of the variable is declared near where it is used. You might want to consider getting in the habit of declaring all your local variables that way, even simple data types such as `int` or `float`.

6.7 Data Caches and Memory Alignment (Advanced)

Memory alignment can play a crucial role in most modern hardware architectures. CPU speeds keep getting faster and faster, but memory speeds are not increasing at the same rate. This means that the gap between what a CPU can theoretically do and what it does when paired up with slower memory is increasing. This pattern is not likely to change any time soon, so it is a problem we will have to keep dealing with in the foreseeable future.

Ideally, we would like our CPU to be always running at maximum capacity, without being slowed down by memory at all. That is what *memory caches* do. A memory cache is a small but very fast memory, much faster than the main memory for the system, where recently used data and code is stored. This works because most programs do not access data and code uniformly. The rough rule of thumb is that a program spends 90% of its time in 10% of the code; this is called the *principle of locality*.

Some architectures have more than one cache level, each of them of increasing size and lower speed. This arrangement is called a *memory hierarchy*, and it helps keep the CPU running as fast as possible under most normal usage.

Caches are often divided into *data caches* and *code caches*. Here we will concentrate only on data caches because those are the ones we have more control over and are the ones that can net us some significant performance gains.

Caches, by definition, are small, so they cannot hold all the data the CPU needs to use during program execution. The ideal case is when the CPU needs to use some data that is already in the cache; then the data can be read right away, and the CPU does not have to wait long. On the other hand, whenever some data is needed that is not in the cache, a *cache miss* occurs, and the CPU has to wait for several cycles while the data is fetched from the slower main memory. The faster the CPU and the slower the main memory, the more cycles it has to wait, causing all the programs to halt until the data is retrieved. We want to avoid this situation as much as possible.

As an example, consider the following situation: a three-gigahertz CPU is humming along at full speed. Whenever it fetches some data from the fastest cache, it takes just one CPU cycle. All of a sudden, it needs a piece of data that is not in any of the caches, so it has to wait for a full main memory access.

With some of the fastest memory available today, it takes six memory cycles to fetch a cache line from main memory. However, even with memory buses running at 512 MHz, the CPU still has to wait about 36 CPU cycles. Using faster processors or slower memory makes things even worse. So, code that looks like just an innocent access to a variable can cause a major stall and be 36 times slower than another part of the code that looks exactly the same, but which can find its data in the cache. Fortunately, we can adapt our program to be as cache-friendly as possible and minimize the number of cache misses.

6.7.1 Memory Access Patterns

The first technique we can apply is to change our access pattern to the program's data. Take, for example, the updating of all game entities for one frame. Normally, we want to give each entity the opportunity to update its state and run any logic it needs to run.

A very cache-unfriendly way of doing it would be to randomly traverse all the entities after we figure out which ones need to execute, then, as a second step, execute all those entities, and finally do another pass over all the entities again. In this scenario, the first step consisted of traversing all entities. Because we have a few thousand game entities, there is no way they can fit in the lowest-level cache; so it is normal that every time we come to a new entity, we cause a cache miss. There is nothing we can do about that. However, what makes this approach very inefficient is that we then make a second and a third pass over all the entities. This means that we are going to incur a second and third cache miss for every entity again.

A much better approach is to do everything we need to do to each entity in one pass. That way we cause a cache miss, we do all the updating and anything else on that entity, and we move on to the next one. The difference in performance between the two approaches can be huge.

Be careful with this technique, however. It is one of those optimization techniques that requires a major organizational change. This is not a matter of rewriting a small loop in assembly; this could potentially require that we rethink our algorithms and change the sequence of events inside our game loop. We might also sacrifice some encapsulation and clarity for performance; but that is a common tradeoff for a lot of optimizations.

The best approach is to avoid doing multiple passes over large sets of data when one pass can suffice. However, we should also not obsess about memory access patterns until later on in the project. It is much more important to get the code working correctly, and to have it clear and easy to change, than to have some very efficient but incorrect and flaky code. Later in the project, if some loop shows up as being particularly slow, and you suspect multiple cache misses, it is probably worth looking into restructuring how the code accesses memory in order to improve performance.

6.7.2 Object Size

One thing we did not mention when talking about memory caches is the granularity of the data in a cache. Caches are typically organized in *cache lines*, which are the smallest units of memory that can be cached in and out independently. They will clearly vary from architecture to architecture, so you should find out what they are for your target platform. In the case of most PCs, a cache line is 32 bytes.

What this means is that if we ever need to fetch a single byte that is not in the cache, we are also going to get the corresponding 32 bytes for that cache line for free. This has some important implications for our code.

First of all, for objects we expect to have hundreds or thousands of, and that must be processed extremely efficiently, we would like to keep their sizes at 32 bytes; if the objects must be larger, keep their size to a multiple of 32 bytes. That way, accessing any part of the object uses up only one or two cache lines.

A perfect example of an object that fits this description is a particle in a particle system. We expect to deal with thousands of particles, and we need to touch and update every single one of them in every frame. If we manage to squeeze a particle into 32 bytes, we might obtain much better performance than if its size were 100 bytes.

6.7.3 Member Variable Location

In addition to size, the location of the most accessed elements is also important. A data cache knows nothing of C++ objects; it knows only about the addresses of the memory we have requested and cache line sizes. That means that even if our particle objects were 100 bytes in size, as long as we update only their first 32 bytes, we should cause only one cache hit per particle. So in cases like that, it is definitely worthwhile to rearrange the member variables of a class so that the most commonly used ones are at the top.

Also, remember that an object that has virtual functions has a vtable, which is usually a pointer at the very beginning of the object. If we make any virtual function calls, we must access the vtable pointer, which brings the first 32 bytes of the object into the cache. That is one of the reasons why we want to put the frequently accessed variables at the top and not in some other place in the object.

Member variables are ordered in memory in the exact same order they are specified in the class declaration, so to move a particular variable toward the top, just declare it before the other member variables.

6.7.4 Memory Alignment

If a cache line is 32 bytes, as we have been assuming so far, it does not pull in just any 32 bytes from memory. Those 32 bytes must be aligned on a 32-byte boundary address. This means that the beginning of each cache line always maps to an address that is a multiple of 32 bytes. As an example, if we request the contents at memory location 0xC00024, the cache line will be filled with the data from 0xC00020 to 0xC0003F.

Again, this has very important implications for how we lay out our objects. Imagine the following disastrous situation. We have 1,000 particle objects to update this frame, and each object is 32 bytes. This sounds like an ideal situation for our data cache. Every time we access an object, we should just have one cache miss because each object fits nicely in one cache line.

Here is the big problem: the particle objects have been allocated in memory carelessly, so they are not guaranteed to start in a 32-byte boundary. What does that mean for us from a performance point of view?

If a 32-byte object is not aligned on a 32-byte boundary, accessing all its variables causes *two* cache misses and takes up two full cache lines. So even though the object size has not changed, because of its alignment in memory, it becomes twice as expensive.

Sometimes compilers try to align things correctly for us, but we might have to turn on specific compiler options dealing with memory alignment. Otherwise, dynamic memory allocations might only be four-byte aligned, with potentially terrible performance consequences. Memory alignment of dynamic memory allocations is something we also must be aware of if we end up using our own memory allocation strategy, as described in Chapter 7, "Memory Allocation."

When objects are allocated in the stack, we have even less control over their alignment. They are usually added to the top of the stack without any consideration as to whether they start at a 32-byte boundary or not. Dynamic allocation is a better alternative for objects for which we want to guarantee certain alignment.

Memory alignment also influences the ideal size of an object. An object that is 40 bytes in size (which sounds like a nice, round number) could cause a total disaster if we create an array of them. Unless the compiler intercedes and pads the objects for us, the beginning of each object is not at a 32-byte boundary, causing more cache misses than necessary. In a situation like this, we might want to pad our own objects to become a multiple of 32 bytes, so that whenever they are allocated in contiguous memory, they are all aligned on a 32-byte boundary.

Memory alignment is a crucial aspect of high-performance programming. Every time we look into data cache optimizations, we should verify that the alignment of our objects is optimal.

6.8 CONCLUSION

In this chapter, we have seen some of the most common C++ performance issues and have presented ways to incur those performance hits only when absolutely necessary, or even how to bypass them completely. First we saw all the different types of function calls that C++ offers, what the performance implications of each type are, and when each should be used. Then we saw how to minimize the overhead of small functions by using the inlining optimization. We also examined other aspects of function overhead, such as parameter passing and return values.

We then saw some situations under which C++ silently creates temporary objects that might cost us some performance without us ever being aware of it. We examined the role of constructors and destructors and their potential performance implications. Finally, we covered an important topic for high-performance games: the effects of the data cache and what we can do in our program to be as cache-friendly as possible.

SUGGESTED READING

There is a large amount of material written about C++ performance. These books cover some aspects of C++ performance in detail, such as when temporaries are generated, the constructor call sequence, and the effects of different function calls.

Bulka, Dov, and David Mayhew, *Efficient C++*. Addison-Wesley, 2000.
Isensee, Pete, "C++ Optimization Strategies and Techniques." Available online at *http://www.tantalon.com/pete/cppopt/main.htm*.
Meyers, Scott, *More Effective C++*. Addison-Wesley, 1995.
Meyers, Scott, *Effective C++*, 2nd ed. Addison-Wesley, 1997.
Pedriana, Paul, "High Performance Game Programming in C++." Conference Proceedings, 1998 Game Developers Conference.

Here are some specific references on return value optimization:

Lippman, Stanley B., and Josee Lajoie, *C++ Primer*, 3rd ed. Addison-Wesley, 1998.
Lippman, Stanley B., *Inside the C++ Object Model*. Addison-Wesley, 1996.
Meyers, Scott, *More Effective C++*. Addison-Wesley, 1995.

The following is a great, in-depth book about computer architecture, with a superb section on data caches and memory hierarchies:

Hennessy, John L., and David A. Patterson, *Computer Architecture: A Quantitative Approach*, 2nd ed. Morgan Kaufmann, 1996.

7

MEMORY ALLOCATION

In This Chapter

- The Stack
- The Heap
- Static Allocation
- Dynamic Allocation
- Custom Memory Manager
- Memory Pools
- In Case of Emergency . . .

M ost C++ programs need to create new objects and allocate memory during program execution. Applications have the choice of stack-based allocation or heap-based allocation. Each type of allocation has its own characteristics of how objects can be allocated and what their lifetimes are.

As normal application developers, that is all we need to know. As developers of high-performance games or high-load servers, we need to pay much more attention to the problem of allocation. This chapter deals with the performance problems associated with heap allocation and suggests some possible solutions and tricks often used in games to alleviate those problems.

We will see how, by giving up some flexibility, we can restrict ourselves to static allocations and bypass all the associated problems with dynamic allocation. We will also see how to make effective use of full dynamic memory allocation at runtime and still be able to keep a good idea of what memory is allocated. Finally, we will see how memory pools can help us use dynamic memory allocation with minimal runtime cost and avoid most of the inherent problems of the heap.

7.1 THE STACK

When programs need to create new objects during program execution, if these objects are only going to be used temporarily in a limited scope, sometimes it is enough to create them on the *stack*. The arguments passed to a function, or the variables declared locally within a function, are all created on the stack.

The stack is a pretty nice place: things are always added at the bottom (or top, if your particular implementation grows upward), and they are always removed in the opposite order they were added. Because the stack has a limited size, trying to push too many objects onto it will result in a stack overflow exception or some other error. Fortunately, we have control over the size of the stack when we compile our program, and we can always increase it if stack use is heavy and we run out of room. The return memory address of the current function is also stored on the stack, so if some of the memory there were to get corrupted or overwritten, our program would be left stranded, not knowing how to go back. Other than that, there really are not many things that can go wrong with the stack.

Figure 7.1 shows an image of the stack before any allocations (a) and after a lot of allocations and deallocations (b).

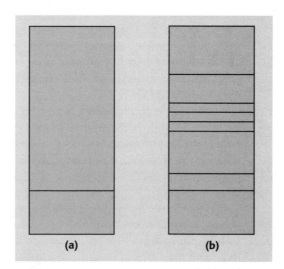

FIGURE 7.1 Image of the stack **(a)** before any allocations and **(b)** after a lot of allocations and deallocations.

Unfortunately, the stack often does not meet our needs. When we need to create a new object, but its use is not temporary or limited in scope, we need to allocate it in a different way. This is done in the *heap*. Memory is allocated in the heap through the use of `new` or `malloc`, and removed from it through their respective calls, `delete` and `free`.

7.2 THE HEAP

Although the stack is a very orderly place, the *heap* can be an extremely chaotic one. It is the Wild West of memory allocations: there are no rules, and you can probably get away with just about anything. The heap is the source of many recurring problems: memory leaks, dangling pointers, memory fragmentation, and so forth. Figure 7.2 shows the heap before and after a lot of allocations and deallocations occur. Notice how, unlike the stack, the free space has become very fragmented.

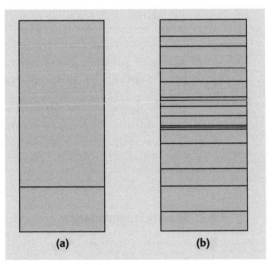

FIGURE 7.2   Image of the heap **(a)** before any allocations and **(b)** after a lot of allocations and deallocations.

7.2.1 Allocation Performance

The main performance problem of heap allocation boils down to the time it takes from the moment the memory has been requested to the time when the correct amount of memory is returned. The exact amount of time it takes is completely platform dependent, and it can even vary wildly from request to request.

Before you are ready to dismiss this problem as not much of an issue, consider the following example. Our game is humming along at a nice, solid 60 frames per second. That means that, at most, we are spending 16.7 ms per frame, including input handling, AI, physics update, collision detection, network update, and graphics rendering. Imagine that, in some frames, we are requesting up to 500 memory allocations. For all those allocations to take under one ms (six percent of our frame time), they must each be completed in an average of 0.002 ms. This is quite speedy; clearly, allocations must happen blazingly fast or else we cannot use them in our games.

Even if your game is not locked into a particular frame rate, you cannot afford to have a frame take a long time to display while some memory allocation is going on because minimum frame rates are often more important than average or peak frame rates as far as the user's experience is concerned.

The time taken by a single memory allocation request is typically highly variable. Most memory system implementations do some searching through tables and lists of memory blocks, and sometimes do some additional types of work such as compacting when a request comes in. Often, single requests can take a few milliseconds by themselves—clearly not an acceptable situation for performance-sensitive games. If we run out of physical RAM in a system with *virtual memory*, then the cost of allocation skyrockets up to hundreds of milliseconds or more while the virtual memory system is swapping out memory to the hard drive.

Dynamic memory allocation is not likely to get much better with faster CPUs, either. As hardware improves, CPUs increase in speed, but chances are we will have more memory available, making heap management even more difficult. This continues to be a problem in the foreseeable future.

7.2.2 Memory Fragmentation

Another, more subtle problem with the heap is *memory fragmentation*. Because of the nature of the heap, memory sections are allocated and freed in an apparently random order, certainly not in the nice first-in, last-out order of the stack. That allocation pattern leads to memory fragmentation.

Before any memory allocation takes place, the heap is a pristine place with just one big block of contiguous free memory. No matter what allocation size we request (as long as it is under the memory total), it is almost trivial to allocate. As more memory is allocated and freed, things start looking a bit uglier. Blocks of memory of wildly differing sizes are allocated and freed in almost random order. After a while, the large, contiguous memory block has been shredded to pieces, and while there might be a large percentage of free memory, it is all scattered in small pieces.

Eventually, we might request an allocation for a single block of memory, and the allocation will fail, not because there is not enough free memory, but because there is no single block large enough to hold it. Because of the nature of memory fragmentation, there is no easy way to predict when this will happen, so it could cause one of those really hard-to-track-down bugs that are almost impossible to reproduce.

A *virtual addressing* system can greatly reduce this problem. Virtual addressing is an extra level of indirection offered by the operating system or the memory allocation libraries, usually relying on hardware features to make its performance cost almost free. The way it works is by using a virtual address instead of the physical address of the memory for a particular memory location. Physical memory is divided into equal-sized blocks (four kilobytes, for example), and each block can be given a different virtual address. That virtual address goes into a table that translates it into the corresponding physical address. All this is done transparently to the user of the memory allocation functions. The key point is that, under such a scheme, two separate memory blocks in completely different parts of the physical memory could be made to map to two contiguous blocks in the virtual address space (see Figure 7.3). Thus, one of the major problems with memory fragmentation has almost disappeared because we can always piece together a larger memory block from several scattered ones.

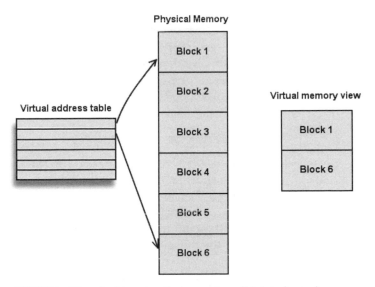

FIGURE 7.3   Virtual addressing that maps two disjoint physical memory blocks into one consecutive virtual address block.

As with any indirection system, virtual memory addressing introduces a bit of overhead. This overhead usually does not amount to much, but as memory gets more fragmented, the algorithm to find and collect unused blocks has to do more work, leading to some of the extreme performance problems mentioned in the previous section. All in all, the advantages of having virtual addressing more than make up for the small performance overhead they introduce. Besides, as we will see later in this chapter, we can always take more control over memory allocation where it matters, bypassing all expensive allocation operations caused by virtual addressing.

Both the PC and the Xbox have virtual addressing as part of their standard OS and libraries. In the PC, it is taken a step further, and when memory is tight, some of the least-recently used memory blocks are saved to the hard drive to make room for new allocations. This is called a *virtual memory* system. Needless to say, that is usually not an acceptable situation for games because it causes major slowdowns in the game while memory is being read from or written to the disk.

It is possible to build such an addressing scheme in a platform that does not support it natively, but it is a fairly involved task and is not as fast without hardware support. The allocation and translation part is relatively straightforward; the real issue is in creating a translation scheme for mapping memory pointers and addresses between the virtual and physical spaces. Such a change is very pervasive across all the source code. Because there is no way to automatically translate pointers every time they are about to be used, we would either need to call some sort of `Translate()` function directly, or we would need a special pointer class that does it automatically. Neither of these solutions is particularly encouraging. The problem is even worse when we use some third-party source code or library because it does not use our pointer-translation scheme.

7.2.3 Other Problems

In addition to the problems described in the preceding sections, the heap is a source of other nonperformance-related problems that can plague projects from the start. They are mentioned here because some of the techniques we employ later on to tame the heap can also solve (or at least help with) these problems.

Two of the most common heap problems are *dangling pointers* and (its flip side) *memory leaks*. Dangling pointers are pointers that refer to a memory location that has changed since the pointer was last assigned and is therefore no longer valid. This can happen when multiple pointers are pointing to the same place in memory, and that location is freed without updating them all. If an attempt is made to dereference that pointer, two things can happen:

- If we are lucky, an access violation exception is raised and the program either catches it or crashes. An access violation occurs if the location pointed to by the dangling pointer is either still unallocated or was allocated by a different process. The best thing about this option is that it is caught right away and is relatively easy to track down and fix.
- If we are not lucky, the memory location pointed to by that pointer is reallocated at a later time by the program for a different use. Trying to read from it returns meaningless data—and even worse, trying to write to it overwrites and trashes an apparently unrelated part of our own game. This is called a *memory overrun*, and it is one of the hardest bugs to track down.

Virtual addressing improves this problem a bit because the range of virtual addresses is usually much larger than the range of physical addresses; the likelihood of the virtual address pointed to by the dangling pointer being reused is quite small. Most of the time, under a virtual addressing mode, accessing a dangling pointer results in an immediate exception.

Memory leaks are exactly the opposite: they are memory chunks that the program allocated and then "forgot" about without giving them back to the system. The consequences of this are fairly obvious: memory consumption continues to increase as the program executes, fragmentation increases, and eventually memory can run out or force the system to page memory out to disk if a virtual memory system is implemented (with the consequent slowdown that it causes). We have all seen games that start slowing down after half an hour of play and eventually crawl to a halt, forcing us to exit and restart to be able to continue playing at normal speed. That behavior is a telltale sign of rampant memory leaks.

One thing we sometimes want to do, especially when tracking down one of these problems, is to get an accurate report on the status of the memory. We usually want to see the differences in the heap between two points in the execution of the program, or we simply want to see a map of all the allocated memory.

Sometimes we just want more information about a memory block: what section of the code created it, when was it created, the size of the block, and so forth. Finally, a very useful feature is to be able to do a dump of memory—not to display the raw allocations, but to give a higher-level overview: how much memory is allocated in textures, how much in geometry, or how much in pathfinding data. These types of reports can be invaluable for tuning the memory consumption of game levels (which is much more important on consoles than on the PC), as well as tracking down memory-related bugs.

7.3 STATIC ALLOCATION

One of the oldest solutions to all dynamic memory allocation problems is to avoid them altogether. A program could be designed so it never uses new and delete (or malloc and free), and relies exclusively on statically allocated objects or objects created on the stack. These are some examples of static allocation:

```
// Create a fixed number of AI path nodes
#define MAX_PATHNODES    4096
AIPathNode s_PathNodes[MAX_PATHNODES];

// Create a fixed-size buffer for geometry
// 8 MB
#define GEOMSIZE         (8*1024*1024)
byte * s_GeomBuffer[GEOMSIZE];
```

This approach has some definite advantages. Clearly, dynamic allocation performance is not an issue because it never happens. Also, because everything is statically allocated by the compiler and nothing changes during the execution of the game, neither memory fragmentation nor the potential to run out of memory is an issue.

Another advantage of static initialization is that it is very straightforward to keep track of where memory goes and how much each type of data takes. We explicitly decide how large each array and buffer is at compile time, and we know they will never grow; just glancing at the source code is enough to know the memory distribution. In the preceding example, it is clear that we are reserving 8 MB for geometry, and 4,096 times the size of a path node of pathfinding memory.

7.3.1 Advantages and Disadvantages of Static Allocation

So far, all the advantages listed address the main problems we set out to solve in this chapter. Does that mean that static allocation is the answer we were looking for? It might be, under some very specific circumstances, but it probably is not.

The first major drawback of static allocation is wasted memory. We are forced ahead of time to decide how much memory is dedicated to each aspect of the game, and that memory is allocated all at once. That means that for a game with a lot of things happening on the screen that change over time, we are wasting large amounts of memory. Think of all the explosions, particle effects, enemies, network messages, projectiles in the air, temporary search paths, and so forth. All these things must be created ahead of time; with dynamic memory allocation, only the ones we currently need are allocated, and we allocate more only as we require them. It is unlikely we would ever need as much memory at once as we do with static allocation.

It is important to note that it is not enough to decide ahead of time how many objects of a whole hierarchy branch we want allocated. We must decide exactly how many we need *of each individual class type*. For example, if we have a game object hierarchy from which other, more concrete object types derive (for example, enemies, players, projectiles, triggers, and so on), it is not enough to say that we will have 500 game objects. Instead, we must decide exactly how many enemies we need, how many projectiles, and so on. The more detailed the class hierarchy, the more difficult this exercise becomes—and the more wasteful of memory it becomes. On the other hand, having a complex inheritance hierarchy is probably not the best of designs, so it is not such a bad thing that static allocation discourages this approach.

One apparent advantage of static allocation is that it seems to reduce the chances of dangling pointers because the memory referred to by a pointer is never freed. It is very possible, though, to have the contents of that memory become invalid (for example, after a projectile explodes and its object is marked invalid), at which point the pointer is still valid but accesses meaningless data. That is an even more difficult bug to track down than a dangling pointer to an invalid memory location because using the dangling pointer would most likely result in an immediate access violation exception with dynamic memory allocation. But under the static scheme, the program silently continues to run with bad data, possibly crashing at a later point.

Finally, one of the disadvantages of static allocation is that objects must be prepared to be statically initialized, with all associated consequences. When dealing with dynamic allocation of objects, it is a good practice to make sure the object gets fully initialized when it is first constructed, and that it gets correctly shut down when it is destroyed. With static allocation, objects are constructed ahead of time but are not initialized until some time later. That means we need to add extra logic to all our objects to correctly initialize and shut down multiple times without ever being freed.

In addition, we need to be extremely careful with any initialization done in the constructor. We plan to create static arrays of those objects, and, as you may recall, static initialization is a sticky issue with C++; in short, you have very little control over the order in which things become initialized. So we cannot rely on our pathfinding data being ready when the enemy objects are initialized or the effects system being ready when the special effects objects are created. As a matter of fact, in a situation like this, it is probably best to leave all initializations until later and not do anything in the constructor other than set default values and mark the object as uninitialized.

7.3.2 When to Use Static Allocation

The question is still open: when is static allocation preferable to dynamic allocation? The answer is, it depends on the circumstances.

A good piece of advice is to use static initialization only when there is no other easy way around it. If the platform you are using has extreme penalties for any type of dynamic memory allocation, then it would be a good idea to use only static allocation. Also, if your game is a mostly static world with the player running around, it might be advantageous to statically allocate everything you need. However, games are moving in the direction of increasing interactivity, not less, which makes static allocation more difficult. Players nowadays expect to interact with any part of their environment—to pick up things, to destroy things, to move things, to create new things. Dynamic memory allocation is a better fit for that type of environment.

How about mixing the two approaches? Objects that do not change during the course of the game (if there are any) are created statically, and everything else is created dynamically. The combination is not as attractive as it seems. In a way, it seems to introduce the worst problems from each world instead of the best. By having some objects created dynamically, we have to deal with all the performance and fragmentation problems that come along with it. But also, by allocating some objects statically, we must make sure our objects have a separate initialization and shutdown pass, mixing two fairly incompatible architectures and programming mentalities. Then, unless the free process is automated, there is the danger of forgetting whether an object was statically or dynamically allocated, releasing it the wrong way, and causing even more havoc.

Instead of mixing the two allocation styles, one of the best approaches is to adopt dynamic memory allocation exclusively, follow the advice in the rest of this chapter, and use *memory pools* extensively for performance-sensitive allocations. We learn about memory pools later in this chapter.

7.4 DYNAMIC ALLOCATION

When static allocation is not enough, we need to turn to the flexibility offered by dynamic allocation. As usual, understanding exactly what goes on during dynamic memory allocation is the key to finding efficient solutions that allow us to use dynamic memory allocation at runtime with very few drawbacks.

7.4.1 Call Chain

Before we start customizing the memory system, we must understand what exactly happens as a result of a memory-allocation request.

1. Everything starts with an innocent-looking object creation in the code.

```
SpecialEffect * pEffect = new SpecialEffect();
```

2. The compiler internally substitutes that call with two separate calls: one to allocate the correct amount of memory and one to call the constructor of the SpecialEffect class.

```
SpecialEffect * pEffect = __new (sizeof(SpecialEffect));
pEffect->SpecialEffect();
```

3. The global operator new must then allocate the amount of requested memory. In most of the standard implementations, the global operator new simply calls the malloc function.

```
void * operator new (unsigned int uiSize)
{
    return malloc(uiSize);
}
```

The call sequence does not end there; malloc is not an atomic operation. Instead, it calls platform-specific memory-allocation functions to allocate the correct amount from the heap. Often, this can result in several more calls and expensive algorithms that search for the appropriate free block to use.

Global operator delete follows a similar sequence, but it calls the destructor and free instead of the constructor and malloc. Fortunately, the amount of work needed to return memory to the heap is usually much less than the work done allocating it, so we will not look at it in detail.

7.4.2 Global Operators New and Delete

With the call chain in mind, we can now override the global operators new and delete to suit our purposes better. We don't want to change the allocation policy yet, so we continue calling malloc and free. However, we also add some extra logic to allow us to keep track of what system the allocated memory belongs to. Later on, we will add more parameters to give us finer control over memory allocation.

To specify our memory-allocation preferences, we will create a heap class. For now, this heap does not correspond to a fixed amount of memory or even to a set of contiguous memory. It is just a way for us to logically group some memory allocations together. To start, all the heap class needs is a name:

```
class Heap
{
```

```
public:
    Heap (const char * name);
    const char * GetName() const;
private:
    char m_name[NAMELENGTH];
};
```

Now we are ready to provide our first version of the global `new` and `delete` operators.

```
void * operator new (size_t size, Heap * pHeap);
void operator delete (void * pMem);
```

In addition, we will need one version of `operator new` that does not take a heap parameter. That way, all the code that does not explicitly pass a heap can still work correctly. Because there is only one `operator delete`, it always needs to correctly free the memory allocated by any of the different `operator new` functions. In effect, that means that if we create any `operator new`, we must override all of them *and* the `operator delete`.

```
void * operator new (size_t size)
{
    return operator new (size,
                        HeapFactory::GetDefaultHeap() );
}
```

Before we look at how `operator new` is implemented, let's see how it is used. To call our special version of `operator new`, we explicitly pass a heap reference as a parameter to the `new` call:

```
GameEntity * pEntity = new (pGameEntityHeap) GameEntity();
```

Admittedly, it does not look like the cleanest and most unobtrusive plan, but this will improve. Our implementation of `operator new` is going to start very simply. For now, all we want is to keep the association between the heap it was allocated from and the allocated memory itself. Notice that the `delete` operator takes only a parameter as a pointer; somehow we need to get from a pointer to the information it points to.

For now, we allocate a little bit more memory than was requested—enough to fit a header for each memory allocation with the information we need. For simplicity, this header contains just a pointer to the correct heap.

```
struct AllocHeader
{
    Heap * pHeap;
    int    iSize;
};
```

The functions operator new and operator delete look something like this now:

```
void * operator new (size_t size, Heap * pHeap)
{
    size_t iRequestedBytes = size + sizeof(AllocHeader);
    char * pMem = (char *)malloc(iRequestedBytes);
    AllocHeader * pHeader = (AllocHeader *)pMem;
    pHeader->pHeap = pHeap;
    pHeader->nSize = size;
    pHeap->AddAllocation (size);

    void * pStartMemBlock = pMem + sizeof(AllocHeader);
    return pStartMemBlock;
}

void operator delete (void * pMem)
{
    AllocHeader * pHeader = (AllocHeader *)
                ((char *)pMem – sizeof(AllocHeader));
    pHeader->pHeap->RemoveAllocation (pHeader->nSize);
    free(pHeader);
}
```

These two functions are doing the bare minimum to get the job done. There are a lot of things they should do to comprise a robust memory manager. Some of the lacking features are error checking, detection of memory overruns, and correct memory alignment. We will add those later; for now, we should be happy to have a good starting point.

Even with those limitations, the two functions are already quite useful. At any point in time, we could traverse all the heaps and print their names, number of allocations per heap, amount of memory allocated in each heap, peak memory usage, and so forth. We also have enough information to detect memory leaks during the execution of the program. We will see that implemented later on.

So far, we have been purposefully ignoring the close relatives of operator new and operator delete: operator new[] and operator delete[]. Their job is to allocate and free memory for a whole *array* of objects. For the moment, we can just treat them like their non-array counterparts and call operator new and operator delete from them.

Even though this system starts being useful, it is still quite cumbersome to have to explicitly pass the heap to every allocation we care about. Overriding the class-specific new and delete operators automates this task and finally makes it useful enough to use in our game and tools.

7.4.3 Class-Specific Operators New and Delete

So far we have ignored another step in the dynamic-allocation call chain: the class-specific operator new and operator delete. When a class overrides those operators, the call to new calls the class-specific function instead of calling the global operator new. These functions can do any bookkeeping and then allocate the memory themselves, or call the global operators new or malloc directly.

We can use the class-specific operator new to automate some of the complexities of our memory-management scheme. Because we usually want to put all objects from a certain class in a particular heap, we can have the class operator new deal with calling the global operator new with the extra parameters.

```
void * GameObject::operator new (size_t size)
{
    return ::operator new(size, s_pHeap);
}
```

Now every time an object of the class GameObject is created with new, it is automatically added to the correct heap. That starts to make things easier. What exactly do we need to add to each class to support such functionality? We need to add an operator new, an operator delete, and a heap static member variable to each class.

```
// GameObject.h
class GameObject
{
public:
    // All the normal declarations...

    static void * operator new(size_t size);
    static void operator delete(void * p, size_t size);
```

```
private:
    static Heap * s_pHeap;
};

// GameObject.cpp
Heap * GameObject::s_pHeap = NULL;

void * GameObject::operator new(size_t size)
{
    if (s_pHeap==NULL)
    {
        s_pHeap = HeapFactory::CreateHeap("Game object");
    }
    return ::operator new(size, s_pHeap);
}

void GameObject::operator delete(void * p, size_t size)
{
    ::operator delete(p);
}
```

By the fifth time we add those same functions to a class, we realize that there has to be an easier way instead of doing all that error-prone typing. And there is. We can easily provide the same functionality with two macros, or even with templates if you really must. Here, we show the simpler macro version. The class example just shown now looks like this:

```
// GameObject.h
class GameObject
{
    // Body of the declaration
private:
    DECLARE_HEAP;
};

// GameObject.cpp
DEFINE_HEAP(GameObject, "Game objects");
```

One important observation: any derived classes from a class that has custom new and delete operators use their parents' operators unless they have their own. In our case, if a class GameObjectTrigger inherited from GameObject, it also automatically uses GameObject's heap.

Now it is finally very simple to hook up new classes to our memory-management system, and it is probably worthwhile to apply this technique to all the most important classes in our game. An object could also do *raw memory allocation* from the heap during execution. A raw memory allocation is caused by allocating a certain number of bytes straight from memory—not by allocating new objects. If this is the case, the allocation can be redirected to point to that object class's heap to keep better tabs on memory use.

```
char * pScratchSpace;
pScratchSpace = new (s_pLocalHeap) char[1024];
```

At this point, we have the basis for a simple but fully functional memory-management system. We can keep track of how much memory is used by each class or each major class type at any time during the game execution. We also have access to some other useful statistics, such as peak memory consumption. With a few more features, the system will be ready for use in a commercial game.

7.5 CUSTOM MEMORY MANAGER

ON THE CD

The time has come to put all the concepts from the past two sections together and build a fully functional memory manager. The source code for this system is on the CD-ROM, located in the \Chapter 07.MemoryMgr\ folder (the Visual Studio workspace for the project is MemoryMgr.dsw), and you can refer to it for the details. In this section, we cover some interesting features omitted from the descriptions in the past two sections, as well as add a few new useful features and describe how they are implemented.

7.5.1 Error Checking

To make the memory manager truly appropriate for use in commercial software, we must consider the possibility of error and misuse. The memory manager described in the past two sections had no provision for errors. If we accidentally passed the wrong pointer to delete, the operator would try to interpret it as a valid memory pointer and try to delete it anyway.

The first thing we want to do is make sure that the memory we are about to free was allocated through our memory manager. The way operator new and delete are implemented, this should always be the case; but, there is the possibility of another library allocating the memory, or perhaps some part of the code is calling malloc directly. In addition, this check catches any stray pointers that are referring to other parts of memory, as well as problems with memory corruption (where allocated memory was later overwritten by something else).

To accomplish our goals, we can add a unique signature to our allocation header:

```
struct AllocHeader
{
    int     iSignature;
    int     iSize;
    Heap * pHeap;
};
```

Of course, there is no unique number we can add, nor even any combination of numbers. There is always the possibility that somebody will allocate memory with that exact same number, but the possibility of this occurring at exactly the place we are looking at is pretty slim. Depending on our comfort level, we can add more than one integer at the cost of higher overhead; however, one should be enough for this example and for most purposes.

What should that unique number be? Anything that is not a common occurrence. For example, using the number 0 is not a good idea; it happens too often in real programs. Same thing with 0xFFFFFFFF, common assembly opcodes, or addresses to virtual memory. Just typing any random hexadecimal number is usually good enough. Purely for its amusement value, one of the old favorites is 0xDEADCODE. Our implementation for operator delete and new looks like this:

```
void * operator new (size_t size, Heap * pHeap)
{
    size_t iRequestedBytes = size + sizeof(AllocHeader);
    char * pMem = (char *)malloc (iRequestedBytes);
    AllocHeader * pHeader = (AllocHeader *)pMem;
    pHeader->iSignature = MEMSYSTEM_SIGNATURE;
    pHeader->pHeap = pHeap;
    pHeader->iSize = size;

    pHeap->AddAllocation (size);

    void * pStartMemBlock = pMem + sizeof(AllocHeader);
    return pStartMemBlock;
}

void operator delete (void * pMem)
{
```

```
        AllocHeader * pHeader =
                (AllocHeader *)((char *)pMem -
                                sizeof(AllocHeader));
        assert (pHeader->nSignature == MEMSYSTEM_SIGNATURE);
        pHeader->pHeap->RemoveAllocation(pHeader->iSize);
        free (pHeader);
}
```

One common mistake when dealing with dynamically allocated memory, especially in the form of an array, is to write past the end of the allocated block. To check for this situation, we can add a guard number at the end of the allocated memory. Just a simple magic number will do for now. Additionally, we can save the size of the allocated memory block to double-check against it when we attempt to free the memory.

```
void * operator new (size_t size, Heap * pHeap)
{
    size_t iRequestedBytes = size +
            sizeof(AllocHeader) + sizeof(int);
    char * pMem = (char *)malloc (iRequestedBytes);
    AllocHeader * pHeader = (AllocHeader *)pMem;
    pHeader->nSignature = MEMSYSTEM_SIGNATURE;
    pHeader->pHeap = pHeap;
    pHeader->iSize = size;

    void * pStartMemBlock = pMem + sizeof(AllocHeader);
    int * pEndMarker = (int*)(pStartMemBlock + size);
    *pEndMarker = MEMSYSTEM_ENDMARKER;

    pHeap->AddAllocation (size);

    return pStartMemBlock;
}

void operator delete ( void * pMemBlock )
{
    AllocHeader * pHeader =
            (AllocHeader *)((char *)pMemBlock -
                            sizeof(AllocHeader));
    assert (pHeader->nSignature == MEMSYSTEM_SIGNATURE);
    int * pEndMarker = (int*)(pMemBlock + size);
    assert (*pEndMarker == MEMSYSTEM_ENDMARKER);
```

```
    pHeader->pHeap->RemoveAllocation(pHeader->iSize);
    free (pHeader);
}
```

Finally, as another safeguard, a good strategy is to fill the memory we are about to free with a fairly distinctive bit pattern. That way, if we accidentally overwrite any part of memory, we can immediately see that it was caused by attempting to free a pointer. As an added advantage, if that pattern is also the opcode for an instruction indicating a halt of program execution, our program automatically stops if it ever tries to run in a section that was supposed to have been freed.

By now, we have added a fair amount of overhead: memory overhead with our expanding allocation header and end marker as well as performance overhead with the operations we do while allocating or freeing the memory. Because the original purpose of creating our memory manager was to get better performance out of it, we do not seem to be heading in the right direction. Fortunately, most of what we are doing here is enabled only for debug builds. As we see in a later section, most of the overhead we are introducing does not appear in retail builds.

7.5.2 Walking the Heap

Sometimes it is necessary to iterate through all the allocations in one heap to check for consistency, to gather more information, to defragment a heap, or simply to print a detailed heap status for debugging purposes. The point is that walking the heap is not something we can do with what we have so far. We must add some extra information to our allocation header.

```
struct AllocHeader
{
    int          iSignature;
    int          iSize;
    Heap *       pHeap;
    AllocHeader * pNext;
    AllocHeader * pPrev;
};
```

We have added the pNext and pPrev fields, which point to the next and previous allocations done in this heap. Under different circumstances, it would have been better to use an STL list, but this is such a low-level system that it is preferable to do it this way to avoid any extra memory allocations.

Operators `new` and `delete` take care of correctly updating the list pointer for each allocation and each free call. Because we are maintaining a doubly linked list, the performance overhead for maintaining the list is trivial. Now it is finally possible to start with the first allocation of the heap and walk through all the allocations in order.

7.5.3 Bookmarks and Leaks

One of the pleasures of having your own custom memory manager is the fact that you can do anything with it that you need to. Tracking down memory leaks comes up very often, so let's modify our memory manager to support this task.

The concept of finding memory leaks is simple: at one point in time, we take a bookmark of the memory status; later on, we take another bookmark and report all memory allocations that were present the second time but not the first time. Surprisingly, the implementation is almost trivial.

All we have to do is keep an allocation count. Every time we have a new allocation, we increase the allocation counter and mark that allocation with its corresponding number. In this example, let's assume that we will never have more than 2^{32} allocations. If that is a problem, we need to keep 64 bits for the allocation count or devise a scheme to wrap around. In either case, it is reasonably easy to implement. Our allocation header now looks like this:

```
struct AllocHeader
{
    int          iSignature;
    int          iAllocNum;
    int          iSize;
    Heap *       pHeap;
    AllocHeader * pNext;
    AllocHeader * pPrev;
};
```

Operator `new` is just like before except that it fills in the `iAllocNum` field. Next, we create a trivial function, `GetMemoryBookmark()`. All it does is return our current allocation number.

```
int GetMemoryBookmark ()
{
    return s_iNextAllocNum;
}
```

Finally, the function that does a bit more work is `ReportMemoryLeaks()`. It takes two memory bookmarks as parameters and reports all memory allocations that are still active that happened between those two bookmarks. It is implemented simply by traversing all allocations in all heaps, looking for allocations that have a number between the two bookmarks. Yes, it is potentially very slow to traverse all allocations in all heaps, but this is a luxury we can permit ourselves this time because this function is used purely for debugging, and we do not really care how fast it executes. The memory leak-reporting function is shown here in pseudo-code form:

```
void ReportMemoryLeaks (int iBookmark1, int iBookmark2)
{
    for (each heap)
    {
        for (each allocation)
        {
            if (pAllocation->iAllocNum >= iBookmark1 &&
                pAllocation->nAllocNum < iBookmark2)
            {
                // Print info about pAllocation
                // Print its alloc number, heap, size...
            }
        }
    }
}
```

7.5.4 Hierarchical Heaps

One aspect of heaps that we left out earlier is their hierarchical arrangement. This might seem like a cosmetic change, but it comes in very useful during the development of a large program.

Heaps tend to proliferate. What starts out as a heap for all graphics memory quickly becomes 15 different heaps: one for vertex information, another for index lists, another for shaders, another for textures, materials, meshes, and so forth. Before we realize it, our game is using hundreds of heaps, and trying to find relevant information becomes a slow, tiresome process. Besides, sometimes we just want the big picture, such as when the art lead asks, "How much memory is our graphics data taking as a whole?"

Here is where hierarchical heaps come in. There is nothing inherently different about them: they are just regular heaps, like we have seen so far, but they are arranged in a tree shape. Every heap has a parent and potentially many children. The only difference is that each heap keeps statistics on both itself and itself combined with all its children.

For example, earlier we might have had the memory heap report shown in Table 7.1.

Table 7.1 Nonhierarchical Memory Heap Report

HEAP	MEMORY	PEAK	INST
Vertices	15346	16782	1895
Index lists	958	1022	1895
Textures	22029	22029	230
Materials	203	203	321

With a hierarchical heap, we instead have the report shown in Table 7.2.

Table 7.2 Hierarchical Memory Heap Report

	LOCAL			TOTAL		
HEAP	MEMORY	PEAK	INST	MEMORY	PEAK	INST
Renderer	0	0	0	38536	40036	4341
Geometry	0	0	0	16304	17804	3790
Vertices	15346	16782	1895	15346	16782	1895
Index lists	958	1022	1895	958	1022	1895
Materials	0	0	0	22232	22232	551
Material objects	203	203	321	203	203	321
Textures	22029	22029	230	22029	22029	230

From an implementation point of view, the only difference is that we need a way to indicate where in the hierarchy a heap will be created, and we need to keep track of its parent and children. There is nothing complicated in that, and it is mostly a lot of pointer handling, so refer to the source code on the CD-ROM for the details (\Chapter 07.MemoryMgr\ MemoryMgr.dsw).

ON THE CD

7.5.5 Other Types of Allocations

Unfortunately, overriding global new and delete is not the end of the story. Although overriding these operators takes care of all new and delete calls, both global and overridden ones, there are other types of dynamic memory allocation.

Direct calls to `malloc` are not intercepted by our memory manager. Neither are calls to platform-specific memory allocation functions (such as `VirtualAlloc()` or `HeapAlloc()` under Win32). In situations like these, there is no other solution than to try to fix the problem by hand.

One possibility is to create a custom version of `malloc` that takes a heap pointer and calls it instead of `malloc`. That approach works fine as long as we have access to the source code and it is not being called in many places.

Another alternative, especially if we do not have access to the original source code that is making those memory allocations, is to keep track of the allocations by hand. Before calling a function that we know performs some memory allocations out of our control, we get the total memory status, make the call, then find out how much memory was allocated; we then assign that amount to a particular heap.

```
int iMem1 = GetFreePhysicalMemory(); //Platform-specific call
// Made-up function that will use platform-specific
// memory allocation functions.
AllocateBuffers();
int iMem2 = GetFreePhysicalMemory();
pHeap->AddAllocation( iMem2-iMem1 );
```

This technique works only as long as there are not many of those calls, and as long as it is always very clear when memory is allocated and freed. If those function calls try to cache some of the allocated memory, it is impossible to keep track of memory reliably.

Some of the better-designed APIs have hooks for the memory-allocation functions. They allow you to provide an object (or a series of function pointers if they are not very C++ inclined) that is called every time the API needs to do any sort of heap memory allocation. In this case, we can create an object that calls our versions of `operator new` and `delete` with a specific heap to allocate memory, and all the memory allocated by the API is tracked in our heaps.

7.5.6 Memory System Overhead

We have added a lot of very useful features to our custom memory manager that can really help us keep tabs on memory usage and improve performance. But, there is a problem: we have added several bytes to each allocation to keep track of our information. You might think that a few bytes do not matter, but this is not true. Here is our allocation header so far:

```
struct AllocHeader
{
    int         iSignature;
    int         nAllocNum;
    int         iSize;
    Heap *        pHeap;
    AllocHeader * pNext;
    AllocHeader * pPrev;
};
```

Assuming four bytes per int and pointer, that is 24 bytes right there. As we see later, we might want to round that up to 32 bytes in some platforms to improve the memory alignment of the allocation that will be returned. In addition, there is an additional 4 byte end marker for each allocation block, so that adds up to a grand total of 36 bytes.

This would be perfectly acceptable overhead if there were only a few dynamic memory allocations and if they were mostly large blocks of allocated memory. But if that were the case, this entire chapter would be unnecessary because dynamic memory allocation performance and memory fragmentation would not be an issue. As we saw at the beginning of this chapter, however, C++ encourages a lot of small and frequent heap allocations, so our overhead very quickly becomes significant. This situation is made even worse on consoles with limited amounts of memory.

A C++ game designed to fit in 64 MB of memory can easily have 50,000 or more heap allocations in memory at once. At 36 bytes per allocation, that is 1.7 MB of overhead introduced by our system. On a 64 MB platform, this is probably not an acceptable solution.

In debug mode, things are even worse. If our implementation of the global operator new calls malloc, then we most likely have another 32 bytes of overhead that malloc adds (depending on the specific malloc implementation). That brings the total overhead to 3.2 MB.

Fortunately, we can get around it the same way malloc does. Bookkeeping information is very useful in debug mode, but there is no need for it in release mode (the executable that is actually shipped to the manufacturer). So in release mode, we do not need to keep any information at all—no allocation header and no end marker. And malloc also does not keep any extra information, so our overhead has completely disappeared.

```
void * operator new (size_t size, Heap * pHeap)
{
#ifdef _DEBUG
    // Same implementation as before
#else
    return malloc(size);
```

```
#endif
}

void operator delete (void * pMemBlock, size_t size)
{
#ifdef _DEBUG
    // Same implementation as before
#else
    free (pMemBlock);
#endif
}
```

The only drawback is that all the error checking is also gone in release mode. That means that the memory system will not immediately detect a memory overrun, or that passing an invalid pointer to be deleted will cause all sorts of bad things to happen. Whether this is acceptable or not depends on your particular situation—the type of game you are writing or the platform you are targeting. (See Chapter 19, "Crash-Proofing Your Game," for more information about that topic and what to do in release mode when errors occur.)

7.6 MEMORY POOLS

With the memory manager so far, we can have an instant representation of where memory is being spent, track down memory leaks, and avoid any unnecessary overhead. One thing we have yet to address is the performance issue. When we set out to write the memory manager, one of the main motivations was to improve performance over direct calls to new and delete. So far, we have replaced new and delete calls with malloc and free (which is probably what the libraries did in the first place), but we have not improved performance any. The solution to most allocation-performance problems is the use of *memory pools*.

Recall that the expensive part of the default implementation of heap memory allocation was finding the block of memory to return. Especially when the memory is heavily fragmented, the search algorithm might have to look through many different blocks before it can return the appropriate one.

Conceptually, a memory pool is a certain amount of pre-allocated memory used to allocate objects of one size at runtime. Whenever one of these objects is released by the program, its memory is returned to the pool rather than being freed back to the heap. This approach has several advantages:

- **No performance hit:** As soon as memory is requested from the pool, the first free pre-allocated block is returned. There are no calls to `malloc` and no searching.
- **No fragmentation:** Memory blocks are allocated once and never released, so the heap does not get fragmented as program execution progresses.
- **One large allocation:** We can pre-allocate blocks in any way we want. Typically, this is done as one large memory block from which we return small subsections. This approach has the advantage of further reducing the number of heap allocations as well as providing spatial coherence for the data being returned (which might improve performance even more by improving data cache hits).

The only disadvantage is that pools usually have some unused space (called *slack space*). As long as the pools are reasonably sized and are used only for dynamic elements, that extra space is well worth the benefits.

One added advantage of memory pools is that we can wipe all objects in a pool at once, without calling their destructors. Obviously, this should not be done carelessly, but if we make sure nobody outside the pool is referring to those objects, the pool could just wipe that memory and forget about those objects. The reason for doing this is efficiency: wiping all objects at once can be much faster than destroying each one individually. In games, it can be quite useful to either clear large chunks of memory when exiting a level or to destroy several related small objects that need to disappear at once (such as particles, pathfinding nodes, and so on).

7.6.1 Implementation

First, we create a class that represents a memory pool, and then we hook it up to our memory system. The first thing the memory class needs to know is how large the objects to be allocated from it are going to be. Because this size is not ever going to change, we will pass it in the constructor. In addition, the two fundamental operations we perform on the pool are allocating and freeing memory. Here is the first, barebones version of a memory pool class declaration:

```
class MemoryPool
{
public:
    MemoryPool (size_t iObjectSize);
    ~MemoryPool ();

    void * Alloc (size_t iSize);
    void Free (void * p, size_t iSize);
};
```

We need to come up with a scheme for managing many similarly-sized memory blocks, return one in the `Alloc()` call, and put it back to be managed when it is returned in the `Free()` call. We could pre-allocate all those memory blocks and keep a list of pointers to them, get the first one in the list in the `Alloc()` call, and return it back to the list in the `Free()` call. Conceptually, this approach is very simple and avoids doing dynamic heap allocations at runtime; however, it also has several problems. The main one is that we are increasing the memory overhead per allocation. Now an allocation requires an entry in the list of free objects. It also means that all the pre-allocated objects are allocated individually, not as a large memory block, so we also incur whatever overhead the operating system requires for multiple, small allocations.

There is a solution that solves all those problems, but it requires getting our hands a bit dirty: handling memory directly, casting memory addresses to specific data, and other unsightly things. It is well worth the trouble, though; in the end, it requires no extra overhead, and all the memory is allocated out of large, contiguous memory blocks, which is exactly what we were looking for. Besides, all that complexity is hidden under the memory pool class, so nobody using it has to know how it is implemented in order to use it correctly. As a matter of fact, when we are done, if we have done our job correctly, nobody even has to know there is a memory pool class at all.

Let us start by allocating one large memory block. We will think of that block as made up of contiguous, similarly-sized slices of memory. Each slice is exactly the size of the allocations we will be requesting from this pool (see Figure 7.4a).

At the start, before any allocations are done, all memory in the block is available; all slices can be marked as free. To do that, we create a linked list of free slices. Because the memory block has already been allocated, but we have not given any of that memory to the program, we have a lot of unused memory lying around, so we might as well put it to good use. Instead of wasting memory with a separate list, we can double up the first two double words from each slice as the `next` and `previous` pointers for a list element, and we can link all the slices in one doubly linked list (see Figure 7.4b).

The rest is simple. Anytime a new request comes to the pool class, we grab the first element in the free slice list, fix up the list, and return a pointer to that slice. Whenever memory is freed, we add that memory to the head of the free slice list. After a few allocations, the slices are out of order in the list, but it does not matter. We are not causing any memory fragmentation, and we allocate and free memory blazingly quickly (see Figure 7.4c).

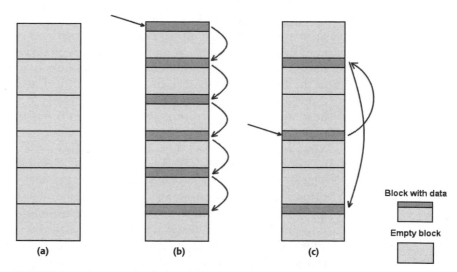

FIGURE 7.4   **(a)** A newly allocated pool object. **(b)** A pool object with the linked list connections. **(c)** A pool object after being used for a while.

The first question that comes to mind after reading how the pool class works is, "What if we need more memory?" The answer is simple. We allocate a memory block similar to the first one, and we link them together along with the rest of the free blocks.

Then the question becomes, "How big should those memory blocks be?" This is a much harder question to answer. It completely depends on the type of allocations we are performing and on the behavior of the program that uses the memory pool. On one hand, we do not want to waste a lot of space by having a really large block that is never completely used; on the other hand, we do not want to have many little memory allocations all the time.

The best course of action is to pick some default. For example, each pool creates a block that can hold 512 slices. (We do not really need a power of 2 for anything here, but it makes programmers feel better; feel free to change this value to anything you want.) After we have memory pools hooked up to our memory manager, we can report how much wasted space there is and tweak the values accordingly. We might also want make sure that the allocated blocks of memory are multiples of the memory page size or some other significant size that might make our lives easier and the allocations faster. In Win32, it makes sense to make each block a multiple of 4 KB and to allocate that memory directly, bypassing `malloc` and all its overhead.

As soon as we start dealing with memory allocation, the alignment issue comes up again. In some platforms, for best performance, the structures we access should be aligned to a specific memory boundary. In Win32, for example, it is best to align allocations to 32-byte boundaries. If we have decided to create a pool to allocate objects that are 78 bytes in size, it makes sense to create slices that are rounded up to the next 32-byte boundary—in this case, 96 bytes; that way, all the memory returned from the pool is 32-byte aligned. At least we should consider adding an option to the heap class to enforce some specific alignment. That extra wasted memory is also worth reporting through the memory manager so that we are always aware of where all the memory is going at all times.

7.6.2 Hooking It Up

Right now, the memory pool class does a lot of things, but it is still not particularly useful. It only allocates raw memory, so we cannot even allocate an object through it. Also, it is rather cumbersome to use because we need to explicitly get the pool we want and then call `Alloc()` with the number of bytes we need.

Let us improve things by hooking it up through the class-specific `operator new` and `operator delete`. To make sure all objects of a particular class use the pool for their allocation, we must create a pool static member variable and then override `operator new` and `operator delete` to use it to allocate the memory they need.

```
// MyClass.h
class MyClass
{
public:
    // All the normal declarations...

    static void * operator new(size_t size);
    static void operator delete(void * p, size_t size);

private:
    static MemoryPool * s_pPool;
};

// MyClass.cpp
MemoryPool * s_MyClass::pPool;

void * MyClass::operator new(size_t size)
{
    if (s_pPool==NULL)
    {
        s_pPool = new MemoryPool(sizeof(MyClass));
```

```
    }
    return s_pPool->Alloc(size);
}

void MyClass::operator delete(void * p, size_t size)
{
    s_pPool->Free(p, size);
}
```

Every time an object of type `MyClass` is created, it uses memory from a memory pool. This is not bad, but it is still a bit tedious to have to type all that for every class we want to have use a pool. We can clean it up a bit more by wrapping up all the common statements in a macro. Now we can write the class as follows:

```
// MyClass.h
class MyClass
{
public:
    // All the normal declarations...
    MEMPOOL_DECLARE(MyClass)
};

// MyClass.cpp
MEMPOOL_IMPLEMENT(MyClass)
```

This macro version is much neater. Just by adding those two lines, we can make any class use our memory pools.

Finally, to really integrate pools with the memory manager, each pool can contain a heap and register all its allocations through the heap. Now all the allocations, pooled or not, appear correctly in the pool display. The source code on the CD-ROM (\Chapter 07.MemoryMgr\MemoryMgr. dsw) contains the macro definition in the source code and the final version of the memory pool macros, including their integration with the memory heaps.

ON THE CD

7.6.3 Generic Pools

What if we have an inheritance hierarchy of objects, each with a slightly different size? Any class that inherits from `MyClass` will attempt to use the same memory pool object, and because its objects most likely have different sizes, it asserts as soon as you try to instantiate an object. Clearly, we cannot just inherit from it and hope that things work out.

Fortunately, it is often the case that most objects that need to be pooled are simple structures that are not intended to be inherited from. In that case, what we have seen so far will work perfectly. Some examples of objects of that type are handles, messages, and nodes of a spatial structure (such as BSP and quadtree).

On the other hand, we might have an inheritance hierarchy of game objects of varying sizes that we want to pool because they are allocated very often during program execution and are affecting performance. For this situation, we can create a generic memory pool allocation system. Instead of every class having a memory pool of its own, the memory manager can have a fixed set of memory pools—about five or six. Previously, each pool was used to allocate objects of a particular size. Here we can use them to allocate objects of that size or smaller. When a pooled memory allocation request arrives, the memory manager finds the heap with the smallest object size that still fits the request and allocates it from there.

Clearly, this scheme results in even more wasted memory, but it is sometimes worthwhile if we have many different objects that must be created at runtime. Tweaking the sizes and numbers of the generic pools is crucial to having good performance and as little wasted space as possible. In addition, it is usually not worthwhile to create heaps for allocations larger than 4 KB or so because those allocations happen infrequently during gameplay, and because operating systems are usually quite efficient at allocating large memory blocks.

Notice that generic pools can live side by side with regular pools and non-pooled memory allocations. We can choose what type of allocation behavior we want on a per-heap basis, so we should always be able to choose the best tool for the job.

7.7 In Case of Emergency . . .

You have decided to use dynamic memory allocation in your game. You implement a memory manager and a pool system, and you add them to your game engine. You get all the flexibility of dynamic allocations with almost none of the drawbacks. Unfortunately, there is one situation you must be ready to handle: running out of memory.

It is tempting to ignore it, but we have to face the facts. Unless you are extremely careful with how and when every single dynamic allocation happens, the player can probably cause a scenario in which so many dynamic allocations happen at the same time that the system runs out of memory—not a pleasant situation. There are two main strategies to deal with this likelihood: prevent memory from ever running out, or deal with it once it happens.

Perhaps the most natural way of handling these situations is to avoid running out of memory in the first place. We can accomplish this by adding some feedback on systems that require dynamic memory allocation based on the current amount of free memory. For example, the number of particles a particle system puts out could be scaled back as soon as a minimum amount of free memory is reached. If the amount of memory continues to decrease and reaches a critical point, we could stop putting out particles altogether. The game might not look as pretty, but at least it will not crash. Besides, we are counting on the large amount of allocated memory being somewhat temporary, and that it will go down in a few frames, at which point all particle emitters will go back to normal. We can set up similar feedback with the sound system, the AI calculations, or any other system that allocates dynamic memory and can be scaled back without breaking the game.

Alternatively, we could let the system run out of memory and then deal with it. That is going to be a little bit more complicated. First of all, we do not have the luxury of checking for low memory anywhere we want. We will know it when the new call fails, and we will need to handle it there.

A common strategy is to have some spare memory allocated at the beginning, perhaps 50 or 100 KB. When we run out of memory, the first thing we do is to free that spare memory we put aside. This should give us enough breathing room while we try to fix the situation.

Now we can handle the scarcity in a variety of ways. We could give up, just finish the level, and send the player back to the main menu. This is not ideal—but again, it is better than a crash. We could also try to do some digging around in the memory pools and free any memory that is not currently used, or even try to compact some of the entries in the pools to free some memory.

Independent of how you decide to handle the low-memory situation, an invaluable tool that you can add to your game is a memory stress-test mode. When in that mode, all available memory, except for a small amount, is allocated. Your game should be able to continue working in that situation. If you added a feedback mechanism to some of the systems with dynamic memory allocation, you should be able to see it kicking in and observe its consequences. If you want to make your game totally bulletproof, take over all available memory and see if the game continues to run.

7.8 Conclusion

In this chapter, we have presented the problem of memory allocation and different ways of dealing with it. One of the simplest ways is to use static memory allocation exclusively. This spares us the problems of memory fragmentation and the performance of dynamic memory allocation, but at the cost of being quite inflexible and wasting a lot of memory. Static memory allocation tends to fall short in situations with a lot of interaction in dynamic worlds.

Dynamic memory allocation is a much more flexible solution, but it comes with the cost of some added complexity. We must deal with the problems of memory fragmentation, running out of memory during the game, and the performance of the actual allocation. We presented the source code for a memory manager system that allows easy integration into existing source code to keep track of how dynamic memory is allocated and also to provide us with some debugging aids.

Finally, we saw how using memory pools can allow us to use dynamic memory allocation without performance or memory-fragmentation problems. We also saw some sample source code that can be used to easily put any class into a memory pool of its own.

Suggested Reading

The following book has several interesting insights on overriding `new` and `delete` operators:

Meyers, Scott, *Effective C++*, 2nd ed. Addison-Wesley, 1998.

Here are some good articles on dynamic memory allocation:

Hixon, Brian, et al., "Play by Play: Effective Memory Management." *Game Developer Magazine*, February 2002.
Johnstone, Mark S., and Paul R. Wilson, "The Memory Fragmentation Problem: Solved?" *Proceedings of the International Symposium on Memory Management*. ACM Press, 1998.
Ravenbrook. The Memory Management Reference. Available online at *http://www.memorymanagement.org/*.

The following is another interesting article covering memory pools, but with an emphasis on a small memory footprint:

Saladino, Michael, "The Big Squeeze: Resource Management During Your Console Port." *Game Developer Magazine*, November 1999.

A very good and detailed explanation of a custom small-object allocation system can be found in this resource:

Alexandrescu, Andrei, *Modern C++ Design*. Addison-Wesley, 2001.

Something worth a look, as a starting point, is the Boost Pool library:

C++ Boost Pool library. Available online at *http://www.boost.org/libs/pool/doc/index.html*.

8

C++ PATTERNS

In This Chapter

- What Are Patterns?
- The Singleton
- The Façade
- The Observer
- The Visitor

In this chapter, we set the stage for the increasingly advanced features of C++ that are discussed as this book progresses to the finish. We will take a break from the concrete for a moment and delve a bit into the more abstract by discussing *patterns*. By the time you finish reading this chapter, you should have a better understanding of just how evolved C++ is from straight C; you should also have an appreciation for the way the language empowers you to design code at a high and very natural level.

8.1 WHAT ARE PATTERNS?

When you learn to program for the very first time and are taking your first glance at a programming language—any language—the strange mix of symbols and word-like formations can be quite intimidating. Soon, however, you start to understand some of the syntax and symbology, as well as some of the basic functionality they afford when used appropriately. After getting comfortable with the basics, you find yourself able to think very naturally about them without explicit translation. A small statement such as "x += 1" loses its odd appearance and becomes simply the way to increment a variable.

After mastering the concepts of variables and operators, you begin to learn about control structures; when the unfamiliarity of the idea wanes, you find yourself able to speak easily with others about the nature of for loops and switch statements. Next you encounter basic structures, functions, and the more-complex features of the language. At this point, your understanding of program structure has achieved a new level, as has your ability to effortlessly "speak the language" to your peers. You become increasingly able to communicate programming ideas to other programmers. You also start to enjoy acceleration in your own evolution as a coder because the easier concepts become second nature, and the more-complicated ones are settling into your brain with increasing ease.

This is the nature of learning and mastering any system that builds complexity and sophistication on top of simpler and more atomic elements; programming is an excellent example of such a system. Object-oriented languages are particularly good examples of this kind of learning because, by their nature, they take programming to increasingly abstract levels, allowing you to wrap your understanding of lower-level concepts inside the more familiar (or more logical) structure of higher-level ones.

This is where *patterns* come in. Patterns (or *design patterns*) are abstract structures that encapsulate both the nature of problems typically encountered in program design as well as the most commonly accepted solutions for those problems. Examples of such problems include the following:

- How to achieve the equivalent of global access to a set of classes while not actually polluting the global namespace, and while maintaining proper encapsulation.
- How to write code that operates on the common features of dramatically different classes while providing a single well-organized interface to the new functionality.
- How to allow objects of different classes to maintain references to each other without risking the perils of dangling pointers and other out-of-scope problems.

This chapter focuses on four very common patterns that are particularly useful in game development. These patterns are chosen because just about every system in a game can benefit from their use. In fact, you might already be using them without realizing it. The upside to this possibility is that your code might already be organized in ways that are commonly regarded as ideal. The downside is that, being unaware you are using these patterns, you haven't yet learned to add these concepts to your vocabulary. This prevents you from communicating programming ideas at your full potential and keeps you from taking your own under-standing of code design to the next level.

But, don't worry. By the end of this chapter, you will have a solid un-derstanding of the following important patterns:

- The Singleton
- The Façade
- The Observer
- The Visitor

Each of these patterns is described in the sections that follow. The discussion is kept fairly basic to allow easy digestion of the concepts. However, you are encouraged to consult the resources in the "Suggested Reading" section at the end of the chapter to learn more about the details of each pattern that bear consideration when you implement them in your projects.

8.2 THE SINGLETON

The first pattern we will look at is the Singleton. As the name implies, a Singleton is a class for which there is (at most) only one instance. The general purpose of a Singleton is to provide a central location for a set of functionality that is globally accessible to the rest of the code. In line with typical C++ philosophy, the Singleton encapsulates this logic and pro-vides access to it through a typical well-defined protective interface like those we've seen in previous chapters.

Another feature of the Singleton is that the lone instance itself is also protected from external dabbling. As we will see shortly, the only way to create the instance is through the public interface of the class itself—but not the constructor! Before getting into the details of creation, however, we will first take a look at an example of a system that is a perfect candi-date for implementation as a Singleton.

8.2.1 Example: File Manager

Just about every game has a system for finding, opening, closing, and mod-ifying files. Such a system is appropriately referred to as the *file manager*, and typically there is only one such system in the game because, unlike the files themselves, there just isn't a need for more than one manager. Hope-fully by now you can imagine that the file manager would be implemented as a class, perhaps something like the following:

```cpp
class FileManager
{
public:
```

```
        FileManager();
        ~FileManager(); // why not virtual?
        bool FileExists(const char* strName) const;
        File* OpenFile(const char* strName, eFileOpenMode mode);
        bool  CloseFile(File* pFile);
        // Etc…
protected:
        // Internal stuff here…
};
```

To use the file manager, you would first create one:

```
    FileManager fileManager;
```

And then you could make use of the newly created instance:

```
    File* pFP = FileManager.OpenFile("ObjectData.xml",
    eReadOnly);
```

Although this code works fine, there are a few problems with this approach, particularly with large projects. The first is that there is nothing preventing the creation of multiple file managers. Because file management is usually not bound to the specifics of any particular class or system, it really doesn't make sense for there to be several file managers; it's just a waste of space. More significantly, file operations usually involve a few specific hardware resources, and in multithreaded games, having multiple file managers blindly reading and writing to those resources is just asking for a lot of headaches.

What you really want is a single manager that is solely responsible for accessing those resources, so that you can add whatever thread-safe code you need in a single place and rest assured that everything is nicely—safely—encapsulated. Now, you might be thinking, "Okay already! So I'll just create one instance!" Well, maybe *you* would, but you can't guarantee that someone else won't create a second instance. Even if you did manage to create only a single instance, you still have the problem of access. Where does that single instance of the file manager go? Hopefully you are turned off by the idea of having it just sitting around in global space. Maybe you can think of other ideas, but let's just skip to the best one: make the file manager a Singleton.

8.2.2 Singleton Implementation

Now that we've seen an example where the use of a Singleton makes sense, it's time to see how to implement one. We'll start with a basic class:

```
class Singleton
{
public:
    static Singleton * GetInstance()
    {
        return s_pInstance;
    }

    static void Create();
    static void Destroy();
protected:
    static Singleton * s_pInstance;
    Singleton(); // hidden constructor!
};
```

Here is the implementation:

```
// Initialize the lone instance to NULL
Singleton* Singleton::s_pInstance = NULL;

// Create()
static void Singleton::Create()
{
    if (!s_pInstance)
    {
        s_pInstance = new Singleton;
    }
}

// Destroy()
static void Singleton::Destroy()
{
    delete s_pInstance;
    s_pInstance = NULL;
}
```

Note the use of an explicit `Create()` and `Destroy()` method. It is possible to hide the creation of the single instance inside `GetInstance()` by "lazy creating" that instance when the first access to it is made. However, because it is generally cleaner to have an external object explicitly create and destroy our Singletons, we'll use the implementation presented. Continuing the file-manager example, we can now realize it as a Singleton and create a single instance of it at startup:

```
FileManager::Create();
```

And we can access the functionality as before:

```
FileManager::GetInstance()->OpenFile("ObjectData.xml",
eReadOnly);
```

Finally, when we are done with the single instance at program shut-down, we destroy it:

```
FileManager::Destroy();
```

8.3 THE FAÇADE

The next pattern we'll look at is the *Façade.* As the name implies, a façade is a "false front"—a cover to something that is hidden from view. In programming, a Façade typically appears as an interface to a collection of (possibly only loosely related) systems or classes. It essentially acts as a wrapper that unifies the various interfaces of these systems into a less complex and more accessible one.

For example, consider the class structure illustrated in Figure 8.1. Notice how the class in system A is coupled to several classes in system B. In such an arrangement, there is effectively no encapsulation in system B because class A1 must know about classes B1, B2, and B3. If system B were to change in some non-superficial way, it's likely that class A1 would have to be updated each time such a change occurred.

Imagine that system B is the graphics engine, and system A is a client of B, perhaps the pre-action user interface. The various classes in the graphics engine may include a texture manager, a renderer, a font manager, and a 2D overlay manager. If the UI has to display a text message on the screen in some nice artistic format, it's likely to have to interact with all four of these classes just to accomplish what amounts to a single task:

```
Texture* pTexture =
GfxTextureMgr::GetTexture("CoolTexture.tif");

Font* pFont = FontMgr::GetFont("UberRoman.fnt");

Overlay2d* pMessageBox =
OverlayManager::CreateOverlay(pTexture,
        pFont, "Hello World!");

GfxRenderer::AddScreenElement(pMessageBox);
```

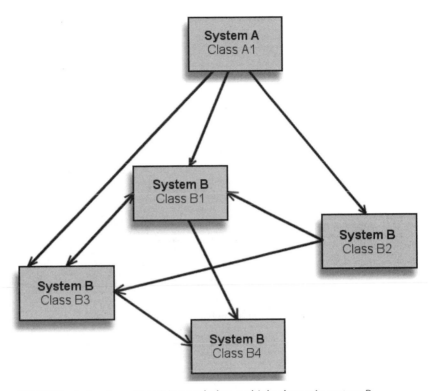

FIGURE 8.1   A class in system A is coupled to multiple classes in system B.

By introducing a Façade to system B, we can effect the encapsulation of that system and provide an interface that serves the needs of system A more directly. Figure 8.2 illustrates this concept. Notice that the introduction of the system B Façade allows system A to interact with a single class.

Continuing with our graphics example, the user interface can now make a single call to accomplish the task of getting a message box on the screen:

```
// GraphicsInterface is our new façade that hides the
// functionality of the graphics system
GraphicsInterface::DisplayMsgBox("CoolTexture.tif",
                                 "UberRoman.fnt",
                                 "Hello World!");
```

Behind the scenes, `GraphicsInterface` might internally make the same sub-system calls that the user interface explicitly made before. Then

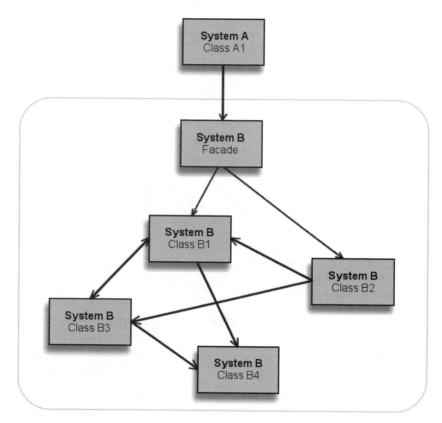

FIGURE 8.2   A Façade for system B effectively encapsulates that system and provides a single entry point for clients that make use of it.

again, it might not, and in fact the implementation of `DisplayMsgBox()` might change dramatically over the course of development. By using a Façade, however, the changes that occur to the graphics system remain hidden from everything external to it, and so the single call made by the UI remains intact even as the graphics system undergoes restructuring. As shown in Figure 8.3, the growing complexity of system B (graphics) need not ever be revealed to any other external user of system B.

This graphics example is very simple and probably somewhat obvious, and if you have written a graphics system from scratch, you very likely implemented a common interface to the underlying functionality without realizing that you were essentially creating a Façade. But there are more interesting and useful examples of Façades, discussed next.

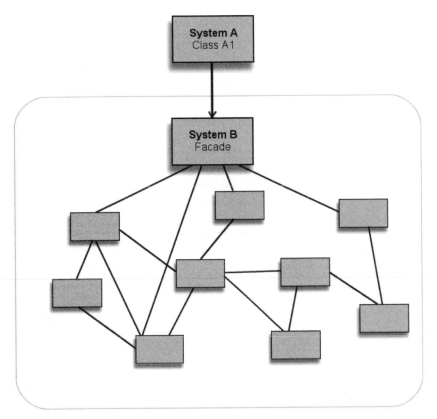

FIGURE 8.3   Because system B provides a Façade interface, it is free to change—even dramatically—over the course of development without affecting users of the system.

8.3.1 The "Under Construction" Façade

Generally speaking, if you are at the start of a project and have to write the technical design for a system, you will do your best to consider all the requirements of the users of your system. In doing so, you will have on paper a description of the classes you intend to write, the interface to those classes, the overall system structure, and so on.

Hopefully, you will have enough time to create an excellent design for your system up front. However, the reality is that there often isn't enough time for a thorough design. Time crunches occur at all stages of the project, and sometimes you have to just get things done as fast as possible. If others on the development team are waiting on your system to become available, the urgency of your task increases significantly because now you are holding them back and preventing them from getting their jobs done.

In this situation, there is often pressure to adhere strictly to policy and continue the practice of completing a design before implementing the system. However, in most cases, this is a huge waste of precious time. It's true that the clients of your system rely on a stable interface to work with so that they don't have to rewrite the code that uses the interface. However, they might also be unable to write the internals of their own systems because *their* system design may be contingent on a variety of factors such as the efficiency of your system or the types of supported features.

The problem here is one of dependency, of course, and by holding clients of your system back, you reduce a large portion of the project to serial operation when it could be developing in parallel. In other words, if only you could just get some of your basic functionality up and running quickly, others could get back to work on their own systems.

The solution is to create a temporary interface—a Façade—that allows access to the features of your system while it's under construction. Even if the interface to the system is likely to change dramatically, at least you allow others on the team to resume work on their own parts of the project. In spite of the fact that they might have to respond to changes in your system interface numerous times, the net gain of allowing progress to be made on the internals of their systems far outweighs the cost they incur when adjusting to changes in your interface. The advantages of this are further illustrated in the next example.

8.3.2 The "Refactoring" Façade

Here's another use of the façade that you might find similar to the construction Façade. The next time you find yourself in the need to "refactor" an entire system in your project, consider using a *refactoring Façade* as a way of partitioning the "good" code you want to keep from the "bad" code you want to rework. Typically during the reworking of a system, you'll want to make numerous changes to the various class interfaces, a task that represents potentially substantial changes to the system interface as a whole.

Imagine, for example, that you've inherited a shabby old particle system and have been tasked with making it work again with the rest of the "new code" in the game. The old system might be devoid of features that are expected in a modern one, or at least simply doesn't support everything required by the game design. The various classes in the old system must be rewritten (or "refactored," if your boss is in on the discussion), new classes have to be added, and old ones tossed out. Of course, doing so brings whatever existing functionality there is offline, which might bring the work of others who depend on the particle system to a halt. You have two choices.

The first option is to start ripping into the old system, temporarily breaking all particle emissions in the game. The resulting downtime of the system could potentially effect just about everyone on the team, from the graphics programmers who need to keep an eye on particle budgets, to artists who might be testing different textures, to level designers who have to keep their levels in working order. Even if you think you can rework the system quickly, the odds are good that you will experience unexpected delays in getting things back to working order. Often, one of the most damaging things you can do to a project is taking existing functionality that management or the publisher is used to seeing working and disabling it for a while. The tendency of those who don't understand the need to re-work an engine is to believe that the project has regressed. You would be wise to have as many of the features of the game ready to show at any time to assuage the ever-increasing anxiety of those who pay the bills.

So consider the second option: set up a temporary Façade that provides an interface both to the old functionality that is to be kept and the new functionality that is to be implemented. Most likely you already know what features are to be present in the new system (because you interact with the designers on a regular basis, right?), so this temporary Façade interface almost writes itself. The next step is to use the Façade as a wrapper for the old functionality you'll be keeping. This step allows that existing functionality to remain alive while the system is getting ripped apart and reworked. As new system features come online, pipe them through the Façade.

After the refactoring Façade is in place (which should not take long at all), you will be free to work on the internals of the new system while everyone else blissfully enjoys the uninterrupted availability of all those pretty particles.

By the time you've completed the system, you most likely will discover that the Façade has in fact turned into a robust manager for the particle system (especially if you plan it that way to begin with). But if not, you can quickly remove the Façade and expose the complete, newly written interface without bringing the system down for more than a few hours.

8.4 THE OBSERVER

One of the most common (and difficult to track down) problems encountered during game development occurs when one object (ObjectA) that is referenced by another object (ObjectB) goes out of scope without any form of notification being sent to the second object. If ObjectB later decides to reference ObjectA, an exception is thrown (if you're lucky) because that reference is no longer valid. The code in Listing 8.1 illustrates the problem.

LISTING 8.1   Two Classes Exhibiting the "Has-a" Relationship

```
// A tiny class
class ObjectA
{
public:
    // Constructor, etc. goes here
    void DoSomethingCool();
};

// Another tiny class that has an instance of ThingA
class ObjectB
{
public:
    ObjectB(ObjectA* pA) : m_pObjectA(pA) {}
    void Update()
    {
        if (m_pObjectA != NULL)
            m_pObjectA->DoSomething();
    }

protected:
    ObjectA* m_pObjectA; // We own an ObjectA
};

// Create an ObjectA
ObjectA* pA = new ObjectA();

// Create an ObjectB, passing in pA
ObjectB* pB = new ObjectB(pA);

// Update B
pB->Update(); // works fine!

// Destroy A
delete pA;

// Now B's update will fail miserably
pB->Update(); // uh-oh…
```

The reason the second call to pB->Update() fails is because the memory location that m_pObjectA points to is no longer valid: it was deleted.

One solution to this problem is to have ObjectA know about ObjectB. Then, on destruction, ObjectA can notify ObjectB that it is about to be destroyed, allowing ObjectB to gracefully handle the deletion of memory (see Listing 8.2).

LISTING 8.2   Adding Destruction Notification Helps Prevent Dangling Pointers

```
// ObjectB now has a notify method
class ObjectB
{
public:
    // Everything else here, and…
    void NotifyObjectADestruction()
    {
        // Since we know m_pObjectA is about to be
        // destroyed, go ahead and set the pointer to NULL
        m_pObjectA = NULL;
    }
};

// ObjectA now knows about the ObjectB that owns it
class ObjectA
{
public:
    // Everything else here, and…
    ~ObjectA()
    {
        m_pOwner->NotifyObjectADestruction();
    }
    void SetOwner(ObjectB* pOwner);

protected:
    ObjectB* m_pOwner;
};
```

Notice how the destructor of ObjectA tells its owner that it is about to be destroyed. ObjectB sets the pointer to NULL and on subsequent updates does not try to call DoSomethingCool() because the check for NULL protects against the invalid memory access. This basic idea works fine in principle, but we can do a bit better.

Now imagine that we want ObjectB to do something more interesting that depends on the state of ObjectA. If the state of ObjectA changes, we'll want ObjectB to somehow know about the change and respond. Let's further complicate things by introducing two new objects of completely different classes, ObjectC and ObjectD, each of which also needs to know about changes in ObjectA. Our simple owner scheme no longer works, and in fact the relationship between ObjectA and Objects B, C, and D has evolved—there really isn't a sense of ownership anymore. We simply want the latter objects to be able to witness changes in ObjectA for some arbitrary purpose.

The solution is the Observer pattern. An *observer* is an object that relies on being able to observe changes in another object called the *subject*. The subject can have any number of observers, and when the subject changes, it notifies all of its observers of the change. The base classes shown in Listing 8.3 set the scene.

LISTING 8.3   The Basic Observer and Subject

```
// Base Observer class
class Observer
{
public:
    virtual ~Observer();
    virtual void Update() = 0; // An abstract base class
    void SetSubject(Subject* pSub);

protected:
    Subject* m_pSubject;
};

// Base Subject class
class Subject
{
public:
    virtual ~Subject()
    {
        std::list<Observer>::iterator iter;
        for (iter = m_observers.begin();
            iter != m_observers.end(); iter++)
        {
            // tell our observers we're outa here
            (*iter)->SetSubject(NULL);
        }
    }
    virtual void AddObserver(Observer* pObserver)
    {
        m_observers.push_back(pObserver);
    }
```

```
    virtual void UpdateObservers()
    {
        std::list<Observer>::iterator iter;
        for (iter = m_observers.begin();
            iter != m_observers.end(); iter++)
        {
            (*iter)->Update();
        }
    }
protected:
    std::list<Observer*> m_observers;
};
```

The base `Observer` class is pretty simple: it knows about a subject that
it is to observe. The `Subject` class has a bit more going on. It has a list of
observers and a way of telling those observers of some change in its state
by using the `UpdateObservers()` method. Additionally, the subject "notifies" the observers when it dies by setting the observers' subject pointer to
`NULL`. (Note that this is just one of many different ways to handle such an
event.)

Let's take a look at a concrete example of the Observer pattern in action. Imagine that you want to implement a rocket launcher in your
game. After firing the weapon, a rocket is emitted that will have a particle effect, a dynamic light, and a sound that plays for the duration of the
rocket's flight. Each of these three effects should update according to the
state of the rocket, and should cease to update after the rocket collides
with something and is removed from the world. Using the base classes
from Listing 8.3, we can create subclasses that make use of the benefits of
the observer pattern (see Listing 8.4).

LISTING 8.4   The Observer Pattern Applied

```
// Our basic rocket
class Rocket : public Subject
{
public:
    Rocket();
    float GetSpeed();
    float GetFuel();
    void Update(float fDeltaT)
    {
        // Do some interesting update stuff
        // ...
```

```
            // Tell our observers to update as well
            UpdateObservers();
        }
};

// A particle class that is attached to rockets
class RocketFlames : public ParticleSystem, public Observer
{
public:
    RocketFlames(Rocket* pRocket)
    {
        m_pRocket = pRocket;
        pRocket->AddObserver(this);
    }
    virtual void Update()
    {
        // Do some cool fiery flickering effect based on the
        // rocket's remaining fuel
        float fFuelRemaining = m_pRocket->GetFuel();
        // …
    }
protected:
    Rocket* m_pRocket;
};

// A dynamic light that is attached to rockets
class RocketLight: public DynamicLight, public Observer
{
public:
    RocketLight (Rocket* pRocket)
    {
        m_pRocket = pRocket;
        pRocket->AddObserver(this);
    }
    virtual void Update()
    {
        // Adjust brightness and color according to the
            rocket's remaining fuel
        float fFuelRemaining = m_pRocket->GetFuel();
        // …
    }
protected:
    Rocket* m_pRocket;
};
```

```
// A sound effect that is attached to rockets
class RocketWhistle: public Sound3D, public Observer
{
public:
    RocketWhistle (Rocket* pRocket)
    {
        m_pRocket = pRocket;
        pRocket->AddObserver(this);
    }
    virtual void Update()
    {
        // Adjust pitch according to rocket speed
        float fSpeed = m_pRocket->GetSpeed();
        // …
    }
protected:
    Rocket* m_pRocket;
};
```

Using the classes shown in Listing 8.4 (filled in with a bit more detail, of course), we can create rockets and attach several kinds of effects to them that will automatically update as the rocket updates, and will automatically get notified when the rocket is destroyed. With our current implementation, the observers would gracefully handle the destruction of the rocket, although they would continue to persist in the world. We would probably want to have each of the effects destroy itself, or notify a manager that's responsible for destruction. Either way is simple to implement and serves our purpose equally well.

8.5 THE VISITOR

One of the most irritating tasks a game programmer can face is implementing some particular functionality and then having to duplicate the code in multiple places. Typically, this occurs when the classes involved are completely unrelated in the class structure but have similar features on which the new functionality is to operate.

A classic example of this has to do with position-relative queries to be performed on placed objects of different types. Some examples of such queries are listed here:

- Finding all enemies within a certain distance to the player
- Finding all health packs that are beyond a certain distance from the player

- Counting the number of items that are within the vision cone of an AI
- Locating all teleportation points that are below the player
- Enumerating the set of all navigation points (waypoints) that are within a certain distance of at least one enemy
- Finding all dynamic lights in the player's view
- Finding the five nearest 3D sounds to the player

The list goes on an on, and each of these needs can be realized in just about every system in the game, including AI, graphics, sound, triggers, and so on. To make things worse, at times the positional queries can be combined to be pretty specific. Take, for example, a complex trigger that uses a within-range proximity check combined with an out-of-range check combined with an in-cone check . . . if you haven't seen something like this, count yourself lucky.

If you *have* seen something like this, you might have also been unfortunate enough to see an implementation like the following:

```
// A basic waypoint
class Waypoint
{
public:
    // Waypointy stuff here
    // Get location
    const Vector3D& GetLocation();
};


// A basic 3d sound, that happens to have similar properties
// as waypoints, but is otherwise completely unrelated
class Sound3D
{
public:
    // Sound stuff here
    // Get position
    const SoundPosition& GetPos();
};


// And now a spawnpoint...
class SpawnPoint
{
public:
    // SpawnPoint stuff here
    // Get position — this time it's 2D!
    const Vector2D& GetSpawnLocation();
};
```

Notice how each of these classes has a similar public accessor for a location, but the type of the location object is different (that is, `Vector3D` is different than `Vector2D`, and so on), and the names of the accessors are different. Because of these differences, you will probably see something like the following in the code:

```
// A waypoint manager that can do waypoint-specific
// positional queries
class WaypointManager
{
public:
    Waypoint* FindNearestWaypoint(const Vector3D& pos);
    Waypoint* FindNearestWaypointInRange(const Vector3D& pos,
            float fInnerRange);
    Waypoint* FindNearestWaypointOutsideRange(float
            fOuterRange);
    WaypointList&  FindWaypointsInCone(const Vector3D& pos,
            const Vector3D& dir):
    // etc., etc., etc.
};
```

Looking further in the code, you might find in a completely different subproject that the `LightManager` does similar things with lights, or the `AIManager` does similar things with the AI agents, or the `SoundManager` with sounds.

If you are at the beginning of a project, you could avoid this reproduction headache by subclassing waypoints, lights, sounds, and anything else from some common base class that has a position and orientation. However, many times you'll encounter this issue well into a project, when it's too late and too risky to make such substantial interface changes.

The answer is the Visitor pattern. Visitors allow you to effectively extend a collection of (typically unrelated) classes without actually touching the class interfaces. Usually, Visitors are used in this manner to create a new set of functions that operate on the different class interfaces to access similar information within each class. In this case, each of our hypothetical classes (waypoints, lights, AIs, and so on) has a position (and probably an orientation), and we'd like to be able to write a set of positional queries one time that can operate on objects of any of these classes.

There are two main components to the implementation of the visitor class:

1. For every class we want to visit, a parallel visitor class is written to provide the visitation mechanism. Alternatively, we can have one visitor for each category of common functionality we want to implement that operates across a set of different classes.

2. Each class to be visited has a single method added to its interface, `AcceptVisitor()`, which allows a visitor to access its public interface.

Returning to our example of positional queries, let's take a look at a simple class used to visit objects of various types that each has a position represented in some way:

```
class PositionedObjectVisitor
{
public:
    PositionedObjectVisitor ();
    virtual ~ PositionedObjectVisitor ();

    // Explicit visit methods for each object type to be
        visited
    virtual void VisitWaypoint(Waypoint* pWaypoint);
    virtual void VisitSound3D(Sound3D* pSound);
    virtual void VisitSpawnPoint(SpawnPoint* pSpawnPoint);
};
```

As required by the second "rule," each of the classes to be visited must have an `AcceptVisitor()` method:

```
void Waypoint::AcceptVisitor(PositionedObjectVisitor & viz)
{
    viz.VisitWaypoint(this);
}

void Sound3D::AcceptVisitor(PositionedObjectVisitor & viz)
{
    viz.VisitSound3D(this);
}

void SpawnPoint::AcceptVisitor(PositionedObjectVisitor & viz)
{
    viz.VisitSpawnPoint(this);
}
```

The corresponding visit methods are shown next:

```
void PositionedObjectVisitor::VisitWaypoint(Waypoint*
pWaypoint)
{
```

```
    const Vector3D& waypointPos = pWaypoint->GetLocation();
    // Do interesting things with the waypoint position
}

void PositionedObjectVisitor::VisitSound3D(Sound3D* pSound)
{
    const SoundPosition& soundPos = pSound->GetPos();
    // Do interesting things with the sound position
}

void PositionedObjectVisitor::VisitSpawnPoint(SpawnPoint*
                                              pSpawnPoint)
{
    const Vector2D& spawnPos = pSpawnPoint-
    >GetSpawnLocation();
    // Do interesting things with the spawn point location
}
```

Now that we have a visitor for positioned objects and have added an AcceptVisitor() method to each object we intend to visit, we can add all that position-related functionality to our visitor class. If we have public access to some container of each of the types of objects we need to visit, then our visitor can iterate across the containers and collect whatever information it needs during visitation—while maintaining a running tabulation of information such as the nearest waypoint found so far. Each of our position-related queries can operate this way, and we can even combine the different object types to find, for example, the nearest waypoint *or* spawn point to a given location.

8.6 Conclusion

The patterns discussed in this chapter are but a few of the many that appear in the literature, although they do represent four of the most common ones encountered in game development. The Singleton is perhaps the most familiar, and is often used for creating lone instances of resource managers that must be globally accessible. The Façade is an excellent pattern to use when you need to expose the functionality of a system in flux without shutting that system down and preventing its users from getting their jobs done. The Observer pattern provides a mechanism for allowing objects to automatically update themselves when other objects they depend on change in some way. Finally, the Visitor pattern allows you to extend the functionality of a class or set of classes while minimally invading their interfaces.

Numerous details of each pattern were omitted for brevity in the discussion in this chapter. These details might be of concern to you depending on the particular needs of your project. You are encouraged to investigate the resources in the "Suggested Reading" section to determine the specific pros and cons of each pattern discussed here, as well as the many others at your disposal.

SUGGESTED READING

The following resources provide considerable discussion and detail on a wide variety of patterns you might find useful in your game projects. In this chapter, we attempted to give a brief overview of four patterns while ignoring some of the finer points on theory and implementation. You are encouraged to investigate the following resources to discover the issues you might encounter when patterns are not implemented correctly given the nuances of a particular problem.

Gamma, Erich, et. al., *Design Patterns*. Addison-Wesley, 1995.
Meyers, Scott, *More Effective C++: 35 New Ways to Improve Your Programs and Designs*. Addison-Wesley Professional, 1995.

9

STANDARD TEMPLATE LIBRARY: CONTAINERS

In This Chapter

- STL Overview
- To STL or Not to STL?
- Sequence Containers
- Associative Containers
- Container Adaptors

This chapter is not intended to teach you all you need to know about the C++ Standard Template Library (STL). Dedicated books on the topic would be necessary for that, and fortunately, other people have already written them. If you have not used the STL before, check out some of the introductory STL books listed at the end of the chapter and then come back.

This chapter and the next concentrate on how to use STL effectively for game development or for any situation that requires high-performance programming. You are expected to know basic concepts, such as the difference between a `vector` and a `list`, and how to use an iterator to traverse all the elements in a container. That should be enough to get you through this chapter, although the more hands-on experience you have had with the STL, the more you will understand the problems we are trying to solve, and the more you will appreciate the solutions.

In this chapter, we first ask ourselves whether or not we should use the STL in our projects. Then we examine each major type of container in detail to become familiar with its performance and memory trade-offs, which are crucial during game development. Chapter 10, "Standard Template Library: Algorithms and Advanced Topics," deals with algorithms and advanced topics such as custom allocators.

9.1 STL Overview

This is a quick refresher on the basic STL concepts. If you have never used the STL, it would be best if you read some of the introductory resources listed under "Suggested Reading" at the end of this chapter and try to get some hands-on experience. Also, you should have some rudimentary understanding of templates to get the most out of this chapter (see Chapter 4, "Templates," for a review of that topic). This section is more of a quick brush-up to get us all on the same wavelength.

The C++ Standard Template Library is a collection of classes providing *containers* to store data in different structures, *iterators* to access the elements in containers, and *algorithms* to perform operations on containers. All the classes are generic through the use of templates, so they can be adapted for use with any of our own classes.

There are several different types of containers, each with different operations and memory and performance characteristics. Choosing the right one for the job is a crucial step. The main two types are *sequence containers*, in which the elements are stored in a specific order, and *associative containers*, in which the order of the elements is not preserved.

```
// Adding three elements to a vector of integers
vector<int> entityUID;
entityUID.push_back(entity1.GetUID());
entityUID.push_back(entity2.GetUID());
entityUID.push_back(entity3.GetUID());
```

Iterators allow us to access the different elements in a container. All containers have two very important functions that return two different iterators: begin() returns an iterator to the first element, and end() returns an iterator past the last element. Notice that end() does not return an iterator to the last element, but to the one *past* it. This is a very important convention throughout STL. Most functions that specify a range of elements require us to pass the iterator to the first element and past the last element in the range. This might seem odd at first, but it makes things a lot simpler when we are iterating through all the elements in a container or implementing an algorithm.

After we have an iterator to a part of the container, it is possible to use it as a starting point to get to nearby elements. It is always possible to at least access the next element from a given iterator. Not all iterators have the same amount of functionality implemented, but sometimes it is possible to get the previous element, or even a random element, depending on the type of iterator:

```
// Traverse the vector of UIDs
vector<int>::iterator it;
for (it = entityUID.begin(); it != entityUID.end(); ++it)
{
    int UID = *it;
    // Do something with the UID
}
```

The STL provides a set of standard algorithms that can be applied to containers and iterators. They are all rather basic algorithms that are usually combined to obtain the results we are looking for in our code. There are algorithms to find elements in a container, copy them, reverse them, sort them, and so forth. As with all the STL code, the algorithms have been highly optimized, and they typically use the best available implementation instead of a more straightforward, slower one.

```
// Reverse the entire vector of UIDs
reverse (entityUID.begin(), entityUID.end());
```

All the classes and functions provided by the STL are wrapped up inside the namespace std. That means that you must prefix all the STL names with std:: or add a using namespace std statement to the top of the .cpp file where you will be using them.

9.2 TO STL OR NOT TO STL?

When embarking on a new project, programmers should ask themselves whether or not they should use STL. You might think you know the answer to that question, given that this book has two whole chapters dedicated to it, but let's look at STL one point at a time and try to come up with a reasonable answer. If you have used STL before and are a convert, feel free to skip this section and dive right into the meat of the chapter.

9.2.1 Code Reuse

One of the biggest arguments in favor of using the STL is obvious: it is a large body of code that has already been written for you. People have implemented several different types of containers and algorithms, debugged them, ported them to your platform, and made it available either for free or for a reasonable amount of money.

Most of the code available is for the truly basic building blocks of any game or tool, such as lists, hash tables, sort algorithms, and searches. Do you really want to spend time writing those from scratch? Because the STL is mostly made out of templates and templatized functions, it is possible to integrate them seamlessly with your code base. You do not have to change all your list elements to inherit from some base class, or make any other intrusive changes; the code is a straight drop-in.

The code base has been debugged for several years, and many projects all around the world have used it to good effect, including other game projects. In other words, it is a solid piece of code. If you have problems with anything in particular, chances are somebody had the same problems already, and there is a solution for it. The active online community can be a great resource for trying to work around any glitches you might find.

You also get all the source code along with it. Unfortunately, that is not as useful as it might sound, because the source code is nearly unintelligible to the casual reader. It is a tangled nest of highly customized and optimized template code, full of `includes` and `defines`. Do not expect a neat little function that shows how a vector works. Instead, you are treated to several implementations, depending on your platform and current configuration, all templatized and using preprocessor macros. Hitting the books or browsing through online discussion forums is often a better approach than wading through thousands of lines of code to solve a particular problem. Making your own changes is an even more daunting proposal. But if worse comes to worst, you can always go to the source and find out exactly how something is implemented.

Another advantage that cannot be ignored is that a good deal of the rest of the world is using STL. New hires can get up to speed faster if they do not have to learn a different internal set of classes for things such as lists or sorting. Also, some libraries might become available that are designed to interface effortlessly with STL.

9.2.2 Performance

Now we get to the issue that burns in most programmers' minds: performance. Game programmers are particularly concerned about performance, perhaps obsessively so. Does STL deliver the goods when it comes to performance?

The short answer is a resounding yes. Remember that STL has been improved by hundreds of users over the years. Some very smart people have taken it upon themselves to tweak every ounce of performance they can from particular containers or algorithms for each platform—all transparently for you.

If you have a hard time believing that such generic and elegant code can compete with your homemade programs, fire up your compiler and give it a try. Usually, you find that STL outperforms a quick implementation by a huge margin, and it is usually no slower than your best effort after spending days or weeks tweaking and optimizing the code.

That said, it *is* possible to beat STL performance. Usually, this entails either deeper knowledge of the data you are manipulating or specific hardware platform knowledge that STL does not have (maybe because the port to your specific platform is rather new and has not had time to mature and become faster). How many times are you going to need that extra bit of performance? Usually not often, and perhaps not during the whole course of a project. If the time ever comes, then you can replace a particularly slow part of the code with your own homemade functions. Until then, STL results in a more robust, faster program than you can achieve without it.

One thing to take into account is how truly empowering STL can be. Having a whole set of fundamental data structures and algorithms at your fingertips is quite an experience. With STL, the basic elements of a problem are not pointers and memory buffers, but nodes in a list or entries in a set. Solving problems becomes a lot more natural, and better solutions are usually found.

For those of you still concerned about performance, keep this in mind: working with STL often results in much more efficient algorithms because of the ease of using advanced data structures and algorithms. The same solution implemented at a lower level is often done with a simpler, much less efficient algorithm just because it was the easier one to write. With STL, we can take a bunch of elements, throw them in a hash table, and search them later on in constant time. Without STL, a lot of programmers might simply put them in a fixed-size array, search for them in linear time, and keep their fingers crossed that we never add more elements than the maximum size of the array.

Although STL can offer superb performance, it can also be the source of major slowdowns if it is not used properly. With the added complexity comes added responsibility on the part of the programmer. Something as simple as choosing the wrong data structure for the operations we want to perform in it can be a performance killer. More subtle problems include dynamic memory allocation for a particular container, or even extra copies introduced by copying elements. To use STL effectively, especially in a performance-sensitive environment such as games, it is important to understand what is going on underneath the hood and to choose the right tool for the right job.

9.2.3 Drawbacks

So is there anything bad about STL? Are there reasons we should not choose it for all our games and tools? Unfortunately, there are a few.

The most notable drawback is that debugging sometimes becomes quite hard. You can pretty much forget about stepping into some of the container operations or algorithms. The STL's heavy use of templates makes it very difficult (or impossible) for the compiler to facilitate good interactive debugging and useful breakpoints. But that is not so bad; after all, the code has supposedly already been debugged, and we should not have to get our hands dirty with it. The main issue is in just viewing the contents of the containers we have created. It is often impossible to see what an iterator is pointing to, or simply to see all the elements in a vector. It is possible, but it certainly takes some coercing of the debugger to do it.

The error messages generated by the compiler when using STL are not something we want to deal with often, either. They are usually long, multiline cryptic messages, often pointing to places that are not even in the code we wrote, just because we mistyped the class in a container we are using. It definitely takes some experience and patience to parse those messages correctly, and find the (usually trivial) bug that was causing them.

The last major drawback is memory allocation. STL is intended for a general computing environment with large amounts of memory and not much of a penalty for memory allocation. Although that is most often the case when we are developing tools, it is not always the case on our target game platform, especially consoles. Fortunately, it is possible to provide custom memory allocators to specific containers, which allows us to control how and when memory is allocated. We cover allocators in more detail toward the end of this chapter. Integrating STL into our own memory management also requires some extra work, either by providing more allocators or by altering some of the global memory-allocation functions to use our memory system. Fortunately, development can start on a game without the need to do either of those things up front. Only after development is well underway is it necessary to deal with some of the lower-level memory issues.

Overall, there is absolutely no reason not to use STL in all your tools. You should also really consider using STL in your game code, and decide to roll your own functions only if STL simply cannot do the job. Many PC and console games have already shipped that take full advantage of all the power STL has to offer.

9.3 SEQUENCE CONTAINERS

Sequence containers are so called because their distinguishing characteristic is that they store their elements in a specific order. Because the elements are in a specific sequence, it is possible to insert and remove elements at particular points in that sequence (for example, at the beginning, the end, or anywhere in the middle).

9.3.1 Vector

Perhaps the simplest and one of the most commonly used containers is the *vector*. Elements can be added or deleted anywhere in the sequence, although with different performance characteristics—depending on their specific position—as we will see in a moment. A vector provides bi-directional iterators. That is, we can access any element forward or backward from a given iterator. In addition, a vector's elements can be accessed in random order, just like a plain C array:

```
vector<int> entityUID;
// Fill it up
if (entityUID[5] == UID) // do stuff…
```

Apart from its similarity to an array, there is no hard limit to the number of elements that can be added to a vector. When working with an array, the normal technique is to try to guess the maximum number of elements we will ever need at once and allocate an array of that size. Whenever we attempt to add one more element to the array, we first check that we are not exceeding its maximum size. If the array is already full, in the best case we get an error, and hopefully the program can deal with it correctly. In the worst case, the program tries to add the element anyway, causing memory corruption or a page fault, and an immediate crash. Using vectors instead of arrays makes all these problems disappear.

9.3.1.1 Typical Implementation

Vectors hold all their elements contiguously in one large block of memory. That block of memory usually has some spare room for future elements. Each element is copied at the right offset, without adding any pointers or additional data (other than some padding, depending on the platform). Because all the elements in a vector are of the same type and consequently of the same size, the location of a vector can be calculated from its index in the sequence and its size.

In addition to the block of memory that holds the element, a vector has a small header with a pointer to the beginning of the elements and some other information, such as the current number of elements and the size of the currently allocated memory block. Figure 9.1 shows a typical implementation of a vector container.

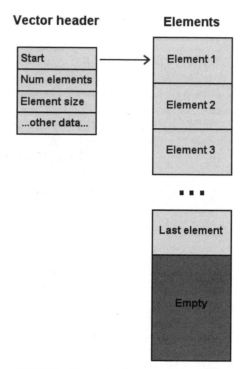

FIGURE 9.1   Vector implementation.

9.3.1.2 Performance

Inserting or deleting elements at the end of the vector is very efficient, as is true with an array. The STL documentation guarantees a performance cost of O(1). All that it tells us is that the insertion time does not depend on the size of the array. But how fast is it, really? Constant-time insertion is not of much use if it takes 30 ms to insert an element. Fortunately, it is as blazingly fast as it can be, and the only cost involved is in copying the element in place.

However, inserting or deleting elements anywhere else, other than at the end, becomes a more expensive operation because it requires copying all the elements from the insertion point until the end and shifting them up or down by one. That is not to say that it is not possible to insert or delete elements in the middle of the sequence. The vector class is prepared for that; it is simply not the most efficient of all containers for that particular operation.

Also, inserting elements at the end of a vector might cause the allocated memory block to run out of memory. This causes some reallocation and copying of all the elements, as we see in the following "Memory Usage" section. With some care, this can be completely avoided in loops that require high performance, so it should not be a consideration when looking at the overall performance of a vector.

A vector might still be the best container to use if our program adds or deletes elements from different positions very infrequently, or if the number of elements in the sequence is very small.

Traversal of all the elements in the container is as fast as it is going to get. A well-written traversal loop on a vector is just as efficient as the same traversal on an array.

```
vector<int>::iterator it;
for(it=entityUID.begin(); it!=entityUID.end(); ++it)
{
    int UID = *it;
    // Do something with the UID
}
```

9.3.1.3 Memory Usage

As we saw earlier, vectors hold all their elements in one large block of memory. That memory block has to be large enough to hold all its current elements, with some extra room for future elements. As more elements are added, there is less extra space, until at some point a new element cannot fit in that memory block anymore. At this point, the vector allocates a larger memory block, copies all its current elements to the new block, adds the new element, and deletes the previous memory block. Usually, this new memory block is twice the size of the previous one. This arrangement gives the vector a lot of room for expansion without the need for allocating new memory very frequently, or allocating too much memory and wasting space.

Notice that there is no mention of shrinking. A vector never gets any smaller by itself. So if at some point it grows to be really large, and then most of the elements are removed, there will be some unused allocated memory.

The astute reader might have already noticed something a bit disquieting in the previous paragraphs. Whenever the vector reaches its size limit, new memory is allocated, and all its elements are copied over to the new location. So what happens if we have a pointer to some element when that happens? We are totally out of luck. A vector makes no guarantees about the validity of pointers or even iterators after an insertion. The same situation arises if we delete or insert an element into the middle of the sequence and have to shift all the remaining elements up or down by one. If we need to refer to specific elements, even after those operations, we should keep their indices and access them through the operator[] function.

Allocating a new memory block and copying all the elements in the sequence to the new location might not be cheap, either. The more elements we have and the more expensive they are to copy, the worse off we are. Is this something we have to worry about? Yes, it probably is. Fortunately there are a few things we can do to alleviate the problem.

First is to pre-allocate enough entries in the vector to avoid doing a lot of allocations. Remember that every time the vector runs out of memory, it doubles in size. So if it starts with 16 elements, it allocates 32, then 64, then 128, and so on. If we know we are going to need at least 800 elements, we can expect at least six allocations (and copies). We can bypass that by pre-allocating 1,024 elements through the reserve() function. But reserve() does not change the number of elements in the vector (as resize() does), it just changes how much memory is allocated for the whole vector and its future elements.

Vectors might often be filled with a lot of values that are used during a computation and then discarded. If this happens frequently, it means that we are constantly allocating and freeing the vector (possibly multiple times if we are not using reserve()). A good solution in this case is to keep that vector static and clear all its elements before each use. Clearing the elements does not free any memory; it marks the vector as empty and calls the destructor for each element (assuming there is a destructor to call).

One really handy characteristic of a vector is that all its elements are stored sequentially in memory; that is, there is just one block of memory allocated, and all the elements are located next to each other as part of that block. Several good things come out of that arrangement. First of all, traversing all the elements results in good data-cache consistency. This is more important for some platforms than others; but, in extreme cases involving thousands of elements, it is probably noticeable, even on a PC. The second advantage of the sequential arrangement is that the contents of a vector can be passed straight to a function that takes a pointer to an array of elements as a parameter. This simple optimization can be done to interface with functions that do not use STL. For example, a pointer to the contents of a vector could be passed to a 3D API function as an array with vertex data. Beware: use this trick carefully, and make sure that the function itself does not try to add or delete elements from the array, or the vector will get out of synch with its contents.

9.3.1.4 Recommendation

Use vectors everywhere you can, given their performance characteristics. More specifically, you can use them almost everywhere you would normally use a *static* array. There is almost no reason to use arrays anymore, so use vectors instead unless memory is so tight that you cannot afford the extra few bytes a vector requires. This applies even in cases where the maximum number of elements is known ahead of time. Using vectors everywhere gives you a bit of extra flexibility, it does not require you to keep track of the number of elements separately, and it uses the same interface as all other vectors in the game.

Vectors have a lot of ideal properties for high-performance programming, so you should always start by considering whether a vector is appropriate for a given application and move to other, more complex, containers only if the vector is not sufficient. Situations that come up during game development that could be best implemented using vectors include:

- The list of all the weapons the player can cycle through
- The list of all the players currently in the game
- Some pre-allocated buffers to receive network traffic
- A list of vertices with simplified geometries for collision detection
- The list of children in a tree node (if the children are reasonably static or there are only a few children)
- The list of all animations a game entity can play
- The list of all components a game entity holds
- The list of points along a path for camera movement or AI path calculations

Finally, Table 9.1 summarizes the efficiency of some key vector class operations.

Table 9.1   Vector Summary

Insert/delete element at the back	O(1)
Insert/delete element at the front	O(N)
Insert/delete element in the middle	O(N)
Memory allocation?	Rarely, only to grow
Traversal performance	Fastest (like C array)
Sequential memory access	Yes
Iterator invalidation	After an insertion or deletion
Memory overhead	12–16 bytes total

9.3.2 Deque

For those readers who are not familiar with the data structure *deque*, it is pronounced "deck," and it stands for "double-ended queue."

A deque is almost identical to a vector, but with slightly different performance characteristics. Like a vector, it provides random access to any of its elements, and it is also possible to insert and delete elements from anywhere in the sequence, although at different costs. What makes a deque unique is that it provides fast insertion and deletion at the beginning as well as at the end of the sequence.

9.3.2.1 Typical Implementation

A deque is similar to a vector in that it keeps all its elements in large memory blocks. However, the main difference is that it has several memory blocks, not just one. As more elements are added (to the back or the front), a new block is allocated, and the new elements are added there. Unlike vectors, there is no need to copy existing elements to the new block because the old memory block is still valid.

To keep track of those memory blocks, a deque has several pointers to each of them. As the number of memory blocks increases, more pointers are stored. (You can think of this list as a vector of pointers to the memory blocks.) The rest of the deque header is made up of bookkeeping information: number of elements, pointer to the first element in the sequence, pointer to the last element, and so forth. Figure 9.2 shows a typical implementation for a deque container.

9.3.2.2 Performance

As with a vector, inserting or deleting an element at the back of the sequence is a very fast operation (O(1)). Also, just like a vector, inserting or deleting an element from the middle of the sequence is a slower (O(N)) operation.

However, as mentioned earlier, the main difference between a deque and a vector is that inserting or deleting an element at the beginning of the sequence is just as fast as doing it at the back. This makes deques perfect data structures for implementing FIFO (First In, First Out) structures, such as queues.

A deque usually keeps its elements in several memory blocks instead of just one as a vector does. Within each of those blocks, elements are arranged sequentially in memory, so the benefits of cache consistency still apply to that block. However, when accessing an element in a different memory block, performance degrades a bit. Even so, because those

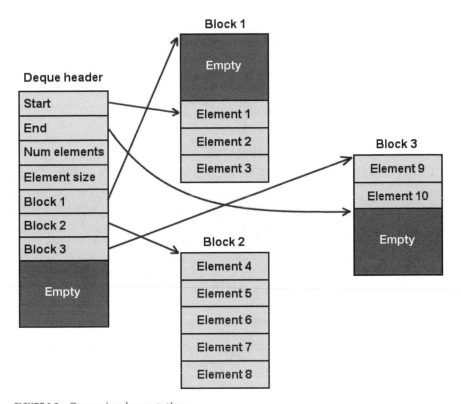

FIGURE 9.2   Deque implementation.

blocks are relatively large, the traversal of all the elements in a deque is not much slower than it is in a vector. The rest of the operations are usually either a bit slower than or just as fast as with a vector.

9.3.2.3 Memory Usage

Memory allocations happen periodically during normal use of a deque. Clearly, if we keep adding elements to a deque, new memory blocks are needed and allocated. Similarly, removing elements eventually causes some memory blocks to be freed.

The less intuitive part is that even if the number of elements stays relatively constant, a deque continues to cause memory allocations. If objects are added at the back and removed from the front, new blocks are added at the back, and old, empty blocks are removed from the front. In a way, we can imagine the deque as "sliding" along in memory, even if it always stays the same size.

Because of the dynamic nature of a deque, there is no equivalent to a `reserve()` function to pre-allocate memory for a fixed number of elements.

The last important thing to know about a deque is that it might allocate a large initial memory block. In some implementations, that initial block might be as large as 4,096 bytes, so keep this in mind if you must create many deques simultaneously.

9.3.2.4 Recommendation

Because of the lack of control over its memory allocation and the unpredictable allocation pattern, a deque might not be a good container for environments with tight memory budgets or expensive memory allocation. If you are dealing with a small number of elements, a vector is probably a better choice, even when paying the extra copying penalty every time an element at the front is removed. Otherwise, you might want to consider a list, possibly with a custom allocator.

The uses of a deque are not as numerous as those of a vector in game development. Even so, here are some situations that arise in game development where a deque might be a good choice:

- A queue to store game messages that must be processed in FIFO order
- A queue to traverse an object hierarchy in a breadth-first manner

Finally, Table 9.2 summarizes the efficiency of some key deque class operations.

Table 9.2   Deque Summary

Insert/delete element at the back	O(1)
Insert/delete element at the front	O(1)
Insert/delete element in the middle	O(N)
Memory allocation?	Periodically, during normal usage
Traversal performance	Almost as fast as a vector
Sequential memory access	Almost; several sequential blocks
Iterator invalidation	After an insertion or deletion
Memory overhead	Header of 16+ bytes; initial memory block could be 4 KB

9.3.3 List

The *list* container is another sequence container, but it has very different characteristics from vectors and deques. A list provides bi-directional iterators, which means that given the iterator to a certain element in the list, we can access the next or the previous element. However, it does not provide random access to its elements like the previous two containers we have seen. Any algorithms that require random access cannot be applied to a list. What we lose in flexibility, we gain in performance and convenience for certain operations. As we can with a vector or a deque, we can insert and delete elements from any position, as long as we have an iterator referring to that position.

9.3.3.1 Typical Implementation

A list is implemented as a doubly linked list of elements. The main departure from vectors and deques is that the elements, instead of being lumped together in a large memory block, are individually allocated as nodes in that list. Each node also contains a previous pointer and a next pointer.

The list also has the usual header information, with a pointer to the first element, the last one, and possibly some other information. A typical implementation of a list container is shown in Figure 9.3.

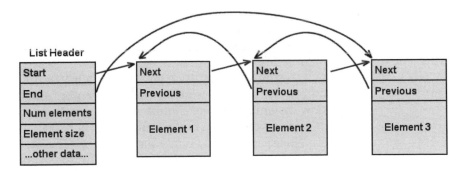

FIGURE 9.3   List implementation.

9.3.3.2 Performance

As you might have guessed, the big advantage of a list is that it does not have a performance penalty for inserting or deleting elements in the middle of the sequence. Any insertions or deletions, anywhere, are all constant time because all they require is fixing up some pointers. Of course, we must have an iterator referring to the location where we want to perform our operation, and getting there might not be constant time.

Traversal of the elements in the sequence is much slower than with a vector. To traverse the sequence, the program must read the pointer at each node and access a different location somewhere else in memory, which causes poor data-cache consistency. This results in a significantly slower traversal, possibly an order of magnitude slower than with a vector. Do not panic, though. Keep in mind that the traversal time is usually not the largest performance drain; even if it is greatly increased, it might not be very noticeable. As usual, it depends on your particular application.

Any operations that involve rearranging the elements in a sequence (such as sorting) are probably very efficient when using a list because there is no need to copy the elements to a new location, just fix their pointers. The larger and more expensive it is to copy the elements of the sequence, the more gains we get by using a list.

9.3.3.3 Memory Usage

A list is totally different from the other sequence containers. The other containers allocate large blocks of memory and try to copy as many elements as possible in them. A list allocates a small amount of memory for each element, and that small block of memory becomes a node in the list.

The advantages are that we do not disturb the nearby elements when we insert or delete one in the middle of the sequence. It also means that iterators and pointers to elements are preserved, even in the presence of insertions and deletions. These facts make many algorithms very convenient to implement.

The drawbacks of such an arrangement are that almost every operation causes a memory allocation. This can be a big hit in platforms with slow dynamic memory allocation, but it can be easily alleviated with a bit of work by creating a custom allocator.

Nodes are not laid out sequentially in memory. They are dynamically allocated at different times during execution, so they could be scattered all over memory. That could cause some severe performance penalties caused by bad data-cache consistency. Fortunately, we can improve the cache consistency through the use of a custom allocator, as described in Chapter 7. So not only does the custom allocator avoid the constant allocation of dynamic memory, it also improves performance by making the nodes more likely to be near each other. But the allocator does not make this issue go away completely, and in the worst cases, even with a custom allocator, there could be almost no spatial coherence.

Another drawback of a list is the extra memory consumption. A list node typically requires an extra 8–12 bytes per node. This might not be an issue for PC platforms, but the extra memory consumption can add up to a significant amount in consoles with limited memory if we have a lot of very small nodes.

9.3.3.4 Recommendation

Lists are a well-rounded, general sequence container. It would be very tempting to use them exclusively and forget about vectors and deques. However, their poor performance when iterating through their elements and the constant memory allocations make them poor candidates for high-performance situations. It is best to consider lists only when we have determined that vectors and deques are not well-suited for the problem at hand.

Interestingly, even though it is not part of the standard, several STL implementations provide a different sequence container: slist. It is just like the list, but it is implemented as a single-linked list with the usual tradeoffs: there is less memory per node (no need for a back pointer) and slightly less pointer management. With an slist, it is impossible to move back from a node, so the iterators provided by slist are only forward iterators. Additionally, slist can have some unexpected performance characteristics because some operations rely on accessing previous elements (for example, deleting an element in the sequence). It is best to use slist only if the minor memory savings are very important. Otherwise, a normal list is a better all-around choice.

A few of the many uses for lists during game development are listed here:

- A list of all game entities, with many insertions and deletions throughout the course of the game
- A list of possible objectives evaluated by the AI, from which some will be chosen and removed
- A list of all meshes that we want to render in this frame, to be sorted by material and render state

Finally, Table 9.3 summarizes the efficiency of some key list class operations.

Table 9.3   List Summary

Insert/delete element at the back	O(1)
Insert/delete element at the front	O(1)
Insert/delete element in the middle	O(1)
Memory allocation?	With every insertion or deletion
Traversal performance	Much slower than a vector
Sequential memory access	No
Iterator invalidation	Never
Memory overhead	8–12 bytes plus 8–12 bytes per element

9.4 ASSOCIATIVE CONTAINERS

Sequence containers preserve the relative positions in which the elements are inserted and deleted from the table. Associative containers forego that characteristic and instead focus on finding a single element within the containers as quickly as possible.

Finding a particular object in a sequence container usually requires O(N) time because we have to look at every single element in the sequence. In the case of a vector or a deque, if the elements are already sorted, it is possible to find an element in O(ln N) time by using a binary search because those containers provide fast random access to any element. However, to take advantage of this speed, we must keep the sequences sorted in a particular order, which is not necessarily what we want, and which is rather expensive to maintain as new elements are added and old elements deleted.

Associative containers provide us with either O(ln N) or even O(1) time to find specific elements. Usually, elements are keyed off some particular data for fast lookup through the data; sometimes the elements themselves are their own keys.

9.4.1 Set and Multiset

A *set* provides a container that is very similar to a mathematical set: it contains some objects, without saying anything about their order. An object simply is or is not in a set.

It should be possible to check whether two objects added to a set are not equal. In particular, they should have the `operator<` ("less-than") defined, or we should provide a function as part of the template to compare the equality of two of the objects.

New objects are added by calling `insert()` and are removed by calling `erase()`. To find whether a particular element is present in the set, we call the function `find()`, which finds the element in O(ln N) time. The template declaration for a set is shown here:

```
set<Key, Compare, Alloc>
```

`Key` is the type of the element we want the set to contain, and `Compare` is a functor used to compare the elements as they are inserted. (Don't worry if you are unfamiliar with functors, we'll cover them in detail in the next chapter.) We will see how the last parameter, `Alloc`, works in Chapter 10. As usual, not all parameters are necessary, and the template provides a default allocator and a default comparison function. Specifically, it attempts to use the `operator<` on the elements themselves, so you need to provide a comparison functor only if the elements do not have an `operator<` already defined, or if you want to do some different type of sorting.

```
set<int> objectives;
objectives.insert(getObjectiveUID());
//...

if (objectives.find(objectiveUID) != objectives.end())
{
    // That objective was completed. Do something
}
```

The set container keeps only one instance of each similar object. So inserting the same object multiple times does not change the set. A *multiset*, on the other hand, keeps multiple copies of the same object if it was inserted multiple times. A multiset also has some extra functions to deal with, having multiple elements such as count(), which returns how many of a particular element there are in the container.

A set can be the perfect container for taking some data and removing all redundant entities. We can just throw all the entities in a set and read them back. This approach is much more efficient than doing an $O(N^2)$ pass through the list, looking for duplicates, especially as the number of elements grows larger.

We can also use the fact that we can pass our own comparison function to create more-interesting applications. Imagine that we have a set of points in 3D space, and we want to collapse all points within a certain distance of each other. One quick solution is to create an equality function to compare two points, but to consider two points equal only if they are within a minimum distance of each other. We can then create a set of points that uses that equality function, throw all the points in, and then read them back out:

```
struct PointNearbyLess
{
    bool operator()(const Point3d & pt1,
                    const Point3d & pt2) const
    {
        float fDist = ::Distance(pt1, pt2);
        return (fDist > POINT_COMPARE_THRESHOLD);
    }
};

typedef set<Point3d, PointNearbyLess> PointCollapseSet;
PointCollapseSet pointSet;
// Insert points in pointSet...
```

Notice that we did not actually create an equality function, but rather an inequality function—or more specifically, a "less than" function. This is because STL uses the "less than" comparison rather than equality in its set implementation. Actually, STL often checks for equality of two elements, not by applying `operator==`, but rather by using this approach:

```
!(k1 < k2) && !(k2 < k1)
```

Therefore we write "less than" functions very often when working with STL.

Sets and multisets are called *sorted associative containers* because in addition to being associative containers, they store the elements in a certain order (based on the comparison function). That means that in addition to being able to find any element quickly, we can iterate through all the elements in that given order. Not all associative containers have this property.

9.4.1.1 Typical Implementation

As the containers get more complex, implementations from STL version to STL version vary more. What is described here is just a typical implementation that we can use as a basis for our discussion about performance and memory usage. If you are using an obscure STL implementation or a strange target platform, you might want to check the source code to verify that things are implemented in roughly this way.

Sets and multisets are usually implemented as a balanced binary tree to facilitate O(ln N) searches of its elements. Each element is in its own node, as in the case of a list, but now they are arranged in the form of a binary tree, and they are ordered based on the comparison function provided with the template. A possible implementation of a set container is shown in Figure 9.4.

9.4.1.2 Performance

The strength of a set is that we can very quickly find out whether or not an element exists in the set. How quickly is very quickly? A set is usually implemented as a balanced binary tree, so it usually requires on the order of O(ln N) comparisons. We also must take into account how expensive the comparisons actually are. Comparing two integers is very straightforward, but comparing two large matrices or strings can be much more time consuming.

Clearly, sets pay off whenever there are a lot of elements in the set. We can use them for convenience even with a very small number of elements, but in that case a vector and a simple linear search could be just as fast.

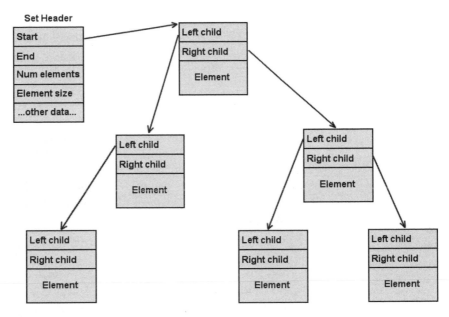

FIGURE 9.4   Set implementation.

Another alternative, especially if the contents of the set do not change frequently, is to store the elements in a vector, sort them, and then use binary searches every time we want to find out whether or not an element is already present. All the cost associated with the initial filling and sorting of the vector can be quickly amortized if it is frequently queried but its contents never change.

Inserting new elements in a set requires knowing whether more elements of that type already exist, so it is at least as expensive as a normal search through the elements, which is O(ln N). In addition, the insertion might cause some small rearrangements of the tree to keep it balanced. Most implementations try to minimize the insertion cost by using red-black trees or some other well-known algorithm to keep the tree balanced, so the extra cost should not be very noticeable.

Traversing through all the elements in a set is a matter of following pointers, as in the case of a list. There might also be a slight extra cost because the elements are arranged in a tree, but the overall performance should be very similar to a list.

9.4.1.3 Memory Usage

If the exact memory usage of a container is of prime importance to you, then associative containers might not be the best choice. Because they are implemented as balanced binary trees, every insertion requires the allocation of a new node, and removing an element causes its node to be deleted. Fortunately, rearranging the tree to keep it balanced does not cause any extra allocations.

9.4.1.4 Recommendation

Sets and multisets are not the type of containers we need everyday. But whenever we have any application that needs to cull out all redundant instances of all items, sets are a very good solution to the problem. (Depending on your specific situation, a *map*, which is described in the next section, might also be a good solution.) Some of the frequent uses of a set are to do the following:

- Keep a set of collision normals so we do not process the same one multiple times.
- Keep a set of objects that we are reading from disk. Those objects are read in date order (older to newer), and newer objects can override older ones. Putting them in a set as we read them automatically checks whether they already exist and overrides the old ones.

Finally, Table 9.4 summarizes the efficiency of some key set and multiset class operations.

Table 9.4   Set and Multiset Summary

Insert/delete elements	O(ln N)
Find an element	O(ln N)
Memory allocation	With every insertion or deletion
Traversal performance	A bit slower than a list
Sequential memory access	No
Iterator invalidation	Never
Memory overhead	8–12 bytes plus 8–12 bytes per element

9.4.2 Map and Multimap

Maps are another type of associative container, so their primary objective is to provide very quick search operations for particular elements. They are very similar to sets, but with an added twist. In the case of sets, the elements themselves are the keys used to sort and search the elements of the set. In the case of a map, there are two separate pieces of data: the element and the *key*, which is used to search in the map.

Alternatively, you can think of a map as an array, but instead of using integers to index into it, you can use any type of data. Conveniently, maps provide a custom `operator[]` that allows us to use the array syntax to access its elements. The specific template declaration for a map is given here:

```
map<Key, Data, Compare, Alloc>
```

Here, `Key` is the data type used for the map keys, `Data` is the data type for the actual elements, and `Compare` is a functor used to compare and sort the keys as they are inserted into the map.

The difference between maps and multimaps is easy to guess. It is the same as between sets and multisets: a map can have only one of a particular key, but a multimap can have multiples of the same key. Notice that the difference applies only to the keys and not to the elements themselves. It is certainly possible to have multiple copies of the same element with different keys in a plain map.

The applications of a map are many, but one that comes up frequently is the quick lookup between some arbitrary number and a piece of data. Consider, for example, an architecture in which each game entity in the world has a unique ID, and those IDs are 16-bit numbers, so the range is between 0 and 65,536. We definitely want to have a way to go from ID to the entity with which it corresponds.

One possibility is to traverse all entities, checking the ID for each one until we find the one we are looking for, or until we run out of entities. Considering that there will probably be many game entities, and that this is something that will happen many times per frame, this approach quickly breaks down and becomes way too expensive.

A different approach is to create an array (or a vector) of pointers with $2^{16} = 65,536$ elements. Every time a game entity is created, we fill the element in the array with an index corresponding to its ID, with the pointer to that entity. Going from IDs to entities is a piece of cake because we need to look up only the correct array element. The problem is that the array takes a fair amount of memory. If pointers are 32 bits, the array itself takes 256 KB, independently of how many objects there are in the game world. And this might seem wasteful already, but things get worse. Maybe 256 KB does not sound like much, but game-entity IDs are not necessarily limited to 16 bits. It is more likely that they will be 32 bits or more. An array large enough to hold that many pointers would need 16 GB. That amount of memory should sound a lot scarier than 256 KB. Clearly, we need a different approach.

Maps are the perfect solution. We can create a map with the key as an integer and the elements as pointers to game entities. We can still access the map with the same syntax as the array in order to get the entity pointer, and the operation is relatively efficient. What is more important, we use only as much memory as the entities we add to the world.

Maps and multimaps are also sorted associative containers, so it is possible to traverse all the elements in a map in the order in which they are stored. As in the case of sets and multisets, that order is not the order in which they were inserted, but the order resulting from applying the Compare functor to the keys.

9.4.2.1 Typical Implementation

Maps and multimaps are implemented just like sets, using balanced binary trees. The only difference is that the keys to access and sort the elements are different objects, instead of being the elements themselves.

9.4.2.2 Performance

The performance of maps and multimaps is the same as for sets and multisets, except that all comparisons are done on the keys, not on the elements. If you have large or expensive elements and very simple keys, this can be a significant advantage. On the other hand, if you have more complicated key types, such as strings or other complex objects, comparing two of those keys is slower and slows down the overall search.

A couple of words of warning about operator[] defined for a map. On the surface, it looks like a very convenient notation to access map elements, just like with a vector or an array. The first thing we need to realize is that if we choose to use it, operator[] is not as fast on a map as it is on a vector. Even though it gives us the illusion of constant-time random access to any element, it still needs to find the element in O(ln N) time, underneath.

The next interesting bit about operator[] is what happens when we try to access an element that does not already exist. If we are writing to an element that does not exist, then the new element gets added to the map with the key we used to access the map.

```
// A new entry is added to the map as we would expect
map<int, string> playerName;
playerName[0] = game.GetLocalPlayerName();
```

However, what happens if we are attempting to read an element with a key that does not already exist? Surprisingly, the result is that a default element is added for that key, and its value is returned.

```
// Try to get the name of player 0, even though there is
// no such player. A new player gets added!
map<int, string> playerName;
const string & playerName = playerName[0];
// Now playerName[0] == ""
```

So if you are just trying to find out whether an element is already in the map, you should use the `find()` function, which returns an iterator to that element if found, or an iterator to `.end()` if it was not found.

Finally, if we want to add a new element to a map, it is slightly more efficient to use the `insert()` function rather than the `operator[]`. This is because using `operator[]` usually causes several temporary copies of the key-element pair to be created and copied before they are finally inserted in the map. When calling `insert()` directly, we are creating those copies explicitly, and there is as little copying as possible involved. However, when updating the contents of an existing element, using `operator[]` ends up being slightly more efficient than calling `insert()` again with the same key to override the existing element.

9.4.2.3 Memory Usage

Maps have a very similar memory usage pattern to sets, so the same comments about many memory allocations and hard-to-predict behavior apply.

9.4.2.4 Recommendation

Maps are often used as fast dictionaries when we need to go from a handle, a unique ID, or a string to a certain object. They can also be thought of as arrays that can be indexed by types other than integers, including complex data types, such as strings or other more complicated objects.

Maps are a useful concept, but hashed maps (see the next section, "Hashes") provide the same functionality with better performance. Consider using hashed maps when dealing with a lot of elements unless your STL implementation does not provide them, or you have very tight memory requirements.

Some applications of maps are listed here:

- Maintaining a dictionary of unique IDs to their corresponding game entities. Maps allow the game to avoid using pointers to entities, which can disappear at any time.
- Translation between strings and integers: for example, translating between player names and their respective IDs.

Finally, Table 9.5 summarizes the efficiency of some key map and multimap class operations.

Table 9.5   Map and Multimap Summary

Insert/delete elements	O(ln N)
Find an element	O(ln N)
Memory allocation?	With every insertion or deletion
Traversal performance	A bit slower than a list
Sequential memory access	No
Iterator invalidation	Never
Memory overhead	8–12 bytes plus 8–12 bytes per element

9.4.3 Hashes

One type of associative container did not make it in the standard but is available under several STL implementations. It is not just one container, but rather a whole family of them: the *hashed associative containers*.

The hash family of containers consists of *hash_set*, *hash_multiset*, *hash_map*, and *hash_multimap*. As you can probably guess, those containers are very similar to set, multiset, map, and multimap. They are so similar, in fact, that they do not look any different from the user's point of view. The only difference is in how they are implemented and the performance and memory consequences they have.

All the associative containers we have seen so far are implemented as some sort of balanced binary tree. This organization allows reasonably fast access to any element in the containers, which is the primary goal of associative containers. In this case, "reasonably fast" means O(ln N), but many times we can do better.

Hashed containers have the same rules as their corresponding binary tree containers, but they are implemented with hash tables. That means that given the right keys and the right hash table size, finding an element can be as fast as O(1). Unfortunately, it means that if things are not set up correctly, performance can be as bad as O(N), in which case the balanced trees are faster.

Fortunately for most cases, performance of a hashed container is very close to O(1). It is a bit like quick sort: theoretically it could be pretty slow, but for most random sequences, it is usually the fastest sort algorithm. The template declaration for a hash_map looks a bit more complicated than for a plain map:

```
hash_map<Key, Data, HashFnc, EqualKey, Alloc>
```

Key and Data are the same as with a map: the data type of the keys and the elements the container will hold. HashFnc is a functor that takes a reference to a key and returns a hash key of type size_t. This is the function that does the actual hashing, and the container just takes care of inserting elements in the right position based on their hash value. EqualKey is another parameter that is different from a map. Unlike a map, the hash table does not care whether two keys are smaller than each other; it just cares about whether they are exactly equal, and that is what this function does. By default, hash_map tries to use operator== on the keys.

The template declaration for hash_set and hash_multiset is the same except that it does not have a Data parameter because the Key doubles as both key and data.

9.4.3.1 Typical Implementation

Hashed containers are implemented as a traditional hash table. There is a set of buckets (usually allocated contiguously in memory, just as with a vector), each holding a pointer to a linked list of elements that belong to that bucket.

Adding new elements is a matter of running the key through the hash function, which then points to the correct bucket and inserts the element into the list. The actual order of the elements in the list is not important.

Finding an element follows a similar process, but instead of adding an element, once we find the bucket where that element should be, the whole list is traversed to find the element we want. Ideally, that list should be as short as possible, and should have only one element. Figure 9.5 shows a typical implementation of a hashed associative container.

9.4.3.2 Performance

We already talked about the performance of hashed associative containers because, after all, performance is their main distinguishing characteristic from the other associative containers. As we saw, in the ideal case, finding an element in the hashed container is a very fast, O(1) operation. However, as with any hash table, things can go wrong. The hash function takes care of generating an internal hash key from the key of the element we are inserting. The overall performance of the container completely depends on how well this function performs. A good hashing function generates a good spread of keys and avoids having many elements in the same hash bucket.

Hash header

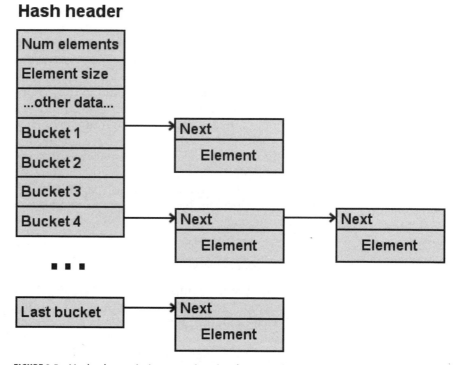

FIGURE 9.5   Hashed associative container implementation.

However, it is possible that a very particular set of keys can all map to just a few hash buckets, slowing down the performance of most operations linear to the number of objects O(N). Fortunately, most of the time, the default hash function provided with the hash templates is enough, especially if your hash keys are simple integers or strings.

9.4.3.3 Memory Usage

What about memory usage? Not surprisingly, hashed containers allocate and free dynamic memory quite often. Elements are still node based, just as they are with the sorted associative containers; so inserting a new element requires allocating new memory, and removing an element frees memory.

In addition to the nodes themselves, hashed containers also allocate all the buckets. The buckets themselves should be pretty small, but keep in mind that you most likely have about one bucket per element, possibly more. If the elements in the hash table are also small, then the buckets could make the total memory consumption double or triple. For larger elements, the memory overhead introduced by the buckets is not as large a percentage.

Interestingly, hashed containers have some functions to deal with buckets directly. The function `bucket_count()` returns how many buckets are currently allocated, and `resize()` works just as it does with a `vector`, but it sets the number of buckets instead of the number of elements. That way, if you know you need a minimum number of elements in the hash table, you can `resize()` it to the right number of elements and avoid extra allocations and copies of buckets while the hash table is growing.

9.4.3.4 Recommendation

For a large number of elements and with a good hash key, hashed containers can be much faster than sorted associative containers. The only drawbacks are that hashed containers do not keep the elements in any particular order, and they can take more memory. If you want maximum performance, if you can live with those restrictions, and if you are reasonably sure you can come up with a good hash key, then hashed associative containers are the perfect tool.

If performance is not a top priority, then using a sorted associative container might be a less risky move. With a sorted associative container, we do not have to worry about strange data distribution that might cause really bad runtime performance; also, it is part of the STL standard, which makes it easier to port to different platforms.

Because performance is often crucial in games, hashed containers are used more often than regular sorted associative containers. Some of the situations in which a hashed associative container is useful are listed here:

- Maintaining a dictionary of unique IDs to their corresponding game entities. This allows the game to avoid using pointers to entities, which can disappear at any time. It is the same example we presented for the case of a map, but because this is often a query that is done many times per frame, it is worth using a hashed container to achieve the best possible performance.
- Performing a fast lookup between class unique IDs and class information. This can be used to implement a very efficient RTTI system (see Chapter 15, "Runtime Type Information").

Finally, Table 9.6 summarizes the efficiency of some key hashed container class operations.

Table 9.6   Hashed Associative Containers Summary

Insert/delete elements	O(1) – O(N)
Find an element	O(1) – O(N)
Memory allocation	With every insertion or deletion
Traversal performance	A bit slower than a list
Sequential memory access	No
Iterator invalidation	Never
Memory overhead	Very implementation dependent; easily 8–16 bytes per element for a well-distributed hash table

9.5 CONTAINER ADAPTORS

So far, we have seen all the containers provided in STL. Some of them were expected, such as vector (which is nothing more than a resizable array), list, and set. Some of them were not as well known, such as deque or multimap. But what happened to some of the other, very basic data structures? Does the STL provide a stack or a plain queue?

Let's think about the operations necessary to support a stack. All that is required is to push elements at the top of the stack, and remove them from the top. Any of the sequential containers can do that. So a stack would be a more limited container than any of them.

If the STL implementation had provided a stack container, how should that stack be implemented? Should it be like a vector—when it grows past a certain size, should it reallocate memory and grow? Or should it be more like a list, where every element is a node? Or maybe a deque, and use page-based allocations? All those possible implementations are valid, and we might need different versions of the stack for different applications.

So instead of just giving us one stack implementation, the STL provides *adaptors*. Adaptors give an existing container a new, more restrictive interface without adding any functionality of their own.

Why provide an adaptor to restrict what we can do with a container? It seems like we do not need an adaptor at all. If we want to treat a vector just like a stack, we can do so by ourselves in the code. In fact, this is true. There are two mains reasons for using a container adaptor:

- By declaring a data structure as a stack, we make very clear to everybody reading the code what we intend to do with it and what rules it will follow. It conveys more information than just using a vector.

- In addition of telling other programmers what we intend to do with that data structure, we are also telling the compiler, which does not let us sneak by a single operation that does not belong to the stack interface. If we had used a vector, it would be too easy to accidentally peek at the second item on the stack, which would break the rules we set for that data structure.

9.5.1 Stack

The simplest type of container adaptor is the *stack*. As we just saw, the main operations we can do on the stack are to add and remove elements from the top, as well as to see what the top element is.

Because the stack is more restrictive than any of the sequence containers, it can be used on any of them. Clearly, the performance and memory characteristics of the stack are the same as for the container it uses. By default, a stack is implemented using a deque. The following code implements a game event system in which the last event added must be resolved first:

```
// Create a stack using a deque for game events
stack<GameEvent> eventStack;
eventStack.push(currentEvent);
//...
// Resolve all events in the stack
while (!eventStack.empty())
{
    GameEvent & event = eventStack.top();
    event.Process();
    eventStack.pop();
}
```

If we decided that the underlying deque implementation was not good enough for our purposes, and we would rather use a vector, the only necessary change is in the definition of the eventStack variable:

```
// Create a stack using a vector
stack< vector<GameEvent> > eventStack;
```

9.5.2 Queue

The *queue* is another very popular data structure that is apparently missing from the STL containers. Again, like the stack, the queue is simply a restricted version of a container. In this case, the only operations allowed are adding elements at the back and removing elements from the front. We cannot add, remove, or even access other elements in the sequence.

By default, a queue uses a deque for its implementation, but it is also possible to use a list. Surprisingly, it is not possible to use a vector, even if we are fully aware that the performance of removing elements from the front is not particularly good. This is because vectors do not have a `push_front()` function, which is required by the queue adaptor.

```
// By default the queue is using a deque
queue<Message> messages;
messages.push(getNetworkMessage());
//...
// Process all messages in the order they were received
while (!messages.empty())
{
    const Message & msg = messages.front();
    process(msg);
    messages.pop();
}
```

To use the same code implemented as a list, we can declare the queue to use a list container:

```
// Now the queue is using a list
queue< list<Message> > messages;
```

9.5.3 Priority Queue

A *priority queue* is very similar to a plain queue: elements can be added only at the back and removed only from the front. The difference is that with a priority queue, the element that is ready to be removed from the front is always the one with highest priority, not the one that was inserted first.

Unlike other container adaptors, the priority_queue adaptor adds a bit of functionality. Whenever elements are added to the container, they are sorted based on the priority function. This is something we could have easily done ourselves; so in a way, the priority queue does not add anything new. It just wraps some higher-level functionality into the adaptor.

By default, the priority queue uses a vector as its underlying representation. It can also be used with a deque, but not with a list because it requires random-order access to elements for efficient insertion of sorted elements.

Also by default, the comparison between elements, which is what determines the priority of an element, is done by using less<Type>. If we want a different comparison function for our priority, or if our elements do not have an operator< defined, then we must provide our own comparison function.

The following code snippet shows a priority queue whose priority is based on distance. Something like this can be used often in a game, such as when we want to prioritize the sounds we hear from the camera or the lights that affect an object, or even the game entities that an AI entity has to process to decide what to do next.

```
struct EntityPos
{
    EntityPos(uint nUID, const Point3d & pos);
    uint    iUID;
    Point3d pos;
};
template<typename T>
class CloserToCamera
{
public:
    bool operator()(const T & p1, const T & p2) const;
};

bool CloserToCamera<typename T>::operator()(const T & p1,
                                            const T & p2)
                                            const
{
    const Point3d & campos = GetCurrentCamera.GetPosition();
    Vector3d camToP1 = p1 – campos;
    Vector3d camToP2 = p2 – campos;
    return (camToP1.length() < camToP2.length());
}

priority_queue<EntityPos, CloserToCamera<EntityPos> >
entities;
// Fill all the entities we might want to consider
entities.push(EntityPos(iUID,pos));
//...
// Now process entities in order of distance to the camera
// until we run out of time, or maybe a fixed number of them
while ( WeShouldContinue() )
{
```

```
        uint iUID = *(entities.top()).iUID;
        entities.pop();
        // Do something with that entity
    }
```

9.6 Conclusion

In this chapter, we have seen that there is very little reason not to use the STL in your development, both for your development tools and for the game code itself. However, you have to be very aware of all the performance and memory implications when using different containers. Some containers are wholly inappropriate to use for certain tasks, and there might even be some really low-level code that should not use STL containers at all. There are two major types of containers: sequence containers and associative containers.

Sequence containers allow the user to specify the order in which the elements are stored. They all allow insertions and deletions from any part of the sequence, but with very different performance characteristics. The sequence containers are:

- *vector:* Similar to a resizable array. Elements are stored sequentially in a memory block that is resized whenever there is need for more memory. Inserting or deleting elements anywhere else other than the end is usually slow.
- *deque:* Similar to a vector, but it allows very efficient insertion and deletion from the front as well as the back. It is implemented by allocating several memory pages, and elements are stored sequentially in each of those pages.
- *list:* A list allows very efficient insertion and deletion from anywhere in the sequence at the cost of extra memory per element and more memory allocations. Elements are not stored sequentially in memory, which causes more data-cache misses when traversing large lists.

Associative containers provide fast searches for a particular element. As a tradeoff, associative containers maintain elements in their own order, instead of in the order specified by the user.

There are two flavors of associative containers: sorted associative containers and hashed associative containers. Each of the four types of associative containers is available in both flavors.

Sorted associative containers are typically implemented as balanced binary trees. Elements are actually stored in the order used by the container. Access to elements is guaranteed to be logarithmic time (O(ln N)).

Hashed associative containers are implemented as a hashed table. As a consequence, elements are not stored in any particular order. Access to any element can be as fast as constant time, but the worst case is a painfully slow linear time (O(N)). The associative containers are best summarized with a chart, as show in Table 9.7.

Table 9.7   Associative Containers

CONTAINER	CAN HAVE MULTIPLE INSTANCES OF THE SAME ELEMENT?	THE KEY IS THE ELEMENT ITSELF?	IMPLEMENTED AS A HASH TABLE?
set	no	yes	no
multiset	yes	yes	no
map	no	no	no
multimap	yes	no	no
hash_set	no	yes	yes
hash_multiset	yes	yes	yes
hash_map	no	no	yes
hash_multimap	yes	no	yes

In addition to the different containers, the STL provides container adaptors. They present a new interface on top of an existing container and are used to implement other popular data structures. The three container adaptors present in the STL are stack, queue, and priority_queue.

SUGGESTED READING

These are some introductory books about the STL. Some of them go into quite a bit of detail, but they all start from scratch.

Austern, Matthew H., *Generic Programming and the STL*. Addison-Wesley, 1999.
Josuttis, Nicolai M., *The C++ Standard Library*. Addison-Wesley, 1999.
Musser, David R., and Atul Saini, *STL Tutorial and Reference Guide*. Addison-Wesley, 1996.

Meyers' is one of the few STL books that deals with the ins and outs of actually using the STL in your programs effectively. After you are done with this chapter, and if you are hungry for more nitty-gritty details, it is highly recommended.

Meyers, Scott, *Effective STL.* Addison-Wesley, 2001.

For everyday work, it is handy to have some good STL references, especially online:

SGI's STL reference, includes hashes and other nonstandard containers. Available online at *http://www.sgi.com/tech/stl/*.

CHAPTER

10

STANDARD TEMPLATE LIBRARY: ALGORITHMS AND ADVANCED TOPICS

In This Chapter

- Function Objects
- Algorithms
- Strings
- Allocators (Advanced)
- When STL Is Not Enough (Advanced)

Chapter 9, "Standard Template Library: Containers," covered the basics of STL: the containers. Even if you decide to use only containers in your programs, the STL would already be worthwhile. You get a set of highly varied data structures that are optimized and thoroughly debugged.

However, there is more to the STL than just containers. This chapter covers the different types of premade algorithms that can be used on containers, the string class, and even some advanced topics that can be very useful for game development, such as writing custom allocators and keeping track of STL memory.

10.1 FUNCTION OBJECTS (FUNCTORS)

Before we dive into the details of algorithms, we need to quickly cover *function objects* (or *functors*). We actually saw them briefly last chapter, but they become a lot more relevant as soon as we start talking about algorithms.

10.1.1 Function Pointers

Let's take as an example a situation that is similar to how we used function pointers in Chapter 9. Imagine that we have a container and we need to determine how the elements will be sorted. If we want total flexibility in how we sort the elements, it is clear that we need to write a function that takes two elements and determines which one is "larger" than the other. So what is the best way to pass this function to our container code?

Traditionally, this would have been done with a function pointer. The following code illustrates the point by creating a comparison function that compares two numbers based on their absolute values. Then a function pointer is created that can be passed around to other functions.

```
bool LessAbsoluteValue (float a, float b)
{
    return (fabs(a) < fabs(b));
}


bool (*mycomparison)(float, float);
mycomparsion = &LessAbsoluteValue;

// Now we can pass mycomparison to any function that takes
// function pointers of that type.
```

Function pointers might look ugly and messy, especially when you start piling up the parentheses and pass them as function parameters. For example, here is the declaration of a possible function that sorts a vector of floats, given any comparison function, and takes a pointer to the comparison function as an argument:

```
void sort (bool(*cmpfunc)(float, float), vector<float>);
```

We usually get around the messy code—and most important, the difficulty in parsing function parameters quickly—by using a typedef on the function pointer type.

```
typedef bool (*ComparisonFunct)(float, float);
ComparisonFunct mycomparison = &LessAbsoluteValue;

void sort (ComparisonFunct, vector<int>);
```

This code is a bit better. So far, we have been assuming we know the type of the elements we want to sort. If we want to make this function work on any type of element, we should use templates. The syntax for a templated function pointer becomes even uglier, and to make things worse, C++ does not allow templated `typedefs`. To get around that, people wrap the `typedef` inside a templated class, which gets the job done at the expense of more code and more complexity.

10.1.2 Functors

It is no surprise that the STL chose a different route. Passing functions to containers and algorithms is something done extensively throughout the STL, so it is important that passing functions be as simple and clear as possible.

The STL solution is to use function objects, also known as functors. A functor is anything that can be called as a function. Typically, functors are objects that have `operator()` implemented, but a function pointer or even a function itself can be considered a functor, and therefore can be used with STL.

```
class EvenNumbersFirst
{
public:
    bool operator()(int a, int b) const
    {
        return (fabs(a) < fabs(b));
    }
};
```

If we need to make the same function work for different data types, we can treat it just like any other template. In this particular case, the only data types it works for are ones that are acceptable parameters to the function `fabs()`, so it is rather limiting:

```
template <typename T>
class EvenNumbersFirst
{
public:
    bool operator()(T a, T b) const
    {
        return (fabs(a) < fabs(b));
    }
};
```

Using this new, templated function with the STL's own `sort()` function is now easy. In this case, we specify that we want the comparison function to work on floats.

```
sort(sequence.begin(), sequence.end(),
        EvenNumbersFirst<float>);
```

Apart from the pure convenience of passing them as arguments, functors have several other advantages. The first is convenience. A functor is an object, and therefore it can also contain some member variables or other helper functions. If the function we are encapsulating in a functor is complex and would benefit either from some associated data or some extra functions, they can all be made part of the same functor.

For example, imagine that our function needs some reference number that it will use in all its calculations. This number can be made a member variable and used every time it is needed. If we are using several instances of the same functor simultaneously, each can have its own unique reference number. Accomplishing the same thing with function pointers usually requires a global static variable, or a stack of them, and the function would have to be aware of the existence of other similar functions, which can make the program unnecessarily complex.

The other advantage of functors is performance. When using a function pointer, there is no way the compiler can do anything smart about the call. It has to wait until the last second and make the appropriate call at runtime. These types of functions are often very small and are called very often, so the overhead can be significant.

When we use functors in conjunction with a templated class or templated function, we are telling the compiler what specific function we want to call. That way, the compiler can optimize the code and can often inline the function with the templated code. For small, often-called functions, this can be a significant performance improvement.

10.1.3 Functor Adaptors

One situation that comes up often is when we want to pass a function that is already a member function of a particular class. We cannot just pass a pointer to it (remember that member functions take a "hidden" parameter that is a pointer to the object they are acting on), so it appears that the only solution is to create a wrapper functor class that just calls the function we want. This approach would do the job, but it is more work than it should be for something so simple. Fortunately, the STL provides us with *functor adaptors*.

Functor adaptors are templates that let us use existing member functions as functors, and they can be used in any place where we could use a functor. Obviously, the function called should have the same number and type of parameters that the calling code expects, just like with any functor. Functor adaptors come in three flavors:

- `mem_fun:` Works on member functions through a pointer
- `mem_fun_ref:` Works on member functions through an object or a reference
- `ptr_fun:` Works on global functions through a function pointer

As an example, imagine that we are trying to sort some elements again, but this time they are objects, not just integers. Specifically, they are scene nodes, and we are trying to sort them to minimize render state changes and render them as fast as possible. If there were a global function that compared two scene nodes to which one should be rendered first, we could just pass a function pointer into the sort function and be done with it. But what if the sort function were a member function of the scene nodes themselves? This is the right time to use a functor adaptor:

```
vector<SceneNode *> nodes;
//...
sort(nodes.begin(), nodes.end(),
     mem_fun(&SceneNode::RenderFirst));
```

Notice that we used `mem_fun` because the container had pointers to objects. If we had actually stored `SceneNode` objects directly in the vector, then we would have used `mem_fun_ref`, instead.

Strictly speaking, `ptr_fun` is not necessary most of the time. In addition to binding the functions to a functor, the functor adaptors also do some extra work behind the scenes by defining a few `typedefs` that are used by some algorithms. If you try to pass a function pointer directly to one of those algorithms, you get a syntax error, which can be fixed by using the `ptr_fun` adaptor.

10.2 ALGORITHMS

A large portion of the STL is made up of *algorithms*: templated functions of common operations that are performed on containers. Because the functions themselves are templated, they can work with any data type, and because they work on existing containers, they know how to traverse them and modify them.

There are four broad categories of algorithms, depending on their behavior. The breakdown is a bit arbitrary, but it is better than listing hundreds of unclassified functions. Besides, if you know what you are looking for, it is very easy to zero in on the appropriate algorithm based on these categories.

Many algorithms take two iterators to the same container as parameters. The first iterator points to the first element in the sequence to which we want to apply the algorithm, and the second iterator points (as is the custom with STL) to one element past the end of the sequence to which we want to apply the algorithm.

Several algorithms require that a value be passed as a parameter, and they use that value to perform some operation on the container, such as to search for it, replace it with something else, or count it. Most of those algorithms have a variant of the same function that takes a *predicate* instead of a value. A predicate is a function that returns true or false, and it is usually implemented as a functor. The predicate versions of the algorithm functions give us more flexibility in operating on a whole range of elements determined by the predicate, instead of matching only one element. The version of the algorithm that takes a predicate is usually named like the original version with _if appended to the name, so it is very clear at a glance which function is used, instead of relying on polymorphic function calls.

This section lists the STL algorithms used most often in games and gives some examples of specific situations in which they could be applied. For a comprehensive list and description of all the algorithms, refer to one of the STL references listed in "Suggested Reading" at the end of this chapter.

10.2.1 Nonmutating Algorithms

Nonmutating algorithms, as the name implies, work on a container but do not modify its contents in any way. For example, searching for an item or counting the number of items are nonmutating algorithms.

10.2.1.1 Find

Probably the most common nonmutating algorithm is find. It iterates through all the items in a sequence (between the two iterators we pass as arguments) and looks for a specific item.

The find algorithm has a linear time performance because it does not assume anything in particular about the container it accessed, and so looks through every element until it finds the one we are looking for. Associative containers offer better performance for finding specific elements; in this case, you should use the member function find() instead of the standalone algorithm, which takes into account how the associative container is organized and searches the element in O(ln N) time, instead.

The find() algorithm should be used when you need to search for an element in a sequence container that is not ordered. You should do this only infrequently, or with a small number of elements to avoid needless performance degradation. For example, we could search through the player list or through the different personalities the local player has set up, but we should probably avoid using this algorithm to search for a particular game entity in the world.

```
list<string> PlayerNames;
//...
// Make sure the player name is not taken for this session
if (find(PlayerNames.begin(), PlayerNames.end(),
    wantedName) == PlayerNames.end() )
{
    // Name was taken, do something
}
```

There is a predicate version of this algorithm, called find_if. It looks for an element in the sequence that makes the predicate true. For example, the following code looks through a list of game entity IDs for those with a value less than 10,000 (possibly because IDs under that range are reserved for other purposes).

```
class LessThan10K
{
public:
    bool operator(int x) const { return x < 10000; }
};

vector<int> GameUIDs;
//...
vector<int>::iterator it;
it = find(GameUIDs.begin(), GameUIDs.end(), LessThan10K());
if (it != GameUIDs.end())
{
    // We found at least one
}
```

10.2.1.2 For_each

The for_each algorithm simply executes a particular function on each element of a sequence. As you would expect, the range of the sequence is passed through two iterators, and the function is passed through a functor.

As an example, let's take a very common situation in game programming. Our task is to call the Update() function of all our game entities for a particular frame. Running Update() gives the entities the chance to run the AI, update their position, start new animations, and so forth. The most natural way we can think of to accomplish this is to set up a for loop:

```
// EntityContainer is a typedef for the specific container
// of the game entities.
EntityContainer::iterator it;
for (it=entities.begin(); it!=entities.end(); ++it)
{
    GameEntity & entity = *it;
    entity.Update();
}
```

Now, we can accomplish the same thing using the `for_each` algorithm:

```
void Update (GameEntity & entity)
{
    entity.Update();
}


for_each (entities.begin(), entities.end(), Update);
```

This second example is only marginally clearer because it does not use a loop, but it requires us to create a whole new function. The reason for the new `Update()` function is that, as previously discussed, we cannot pass member functions directly as functors. Fortunately, we can get around that by using the `mem_fun_ref` adaptor. Now our new code looks like this:

```
for_each (entities.begin(), entities.end(),
    mem_fun_ref(&GameEntity::Update) );
```

That is better, but is it really that much better than our original plain `for` loop? Frankly, no. They are largely equivalent, and the `for` loop might have an edge in that more people can understand it without any problems, but `for_each` is more concise and a bit less error prone. Your choice comes down mostly to personal preference.

However, `for_each` has one extra advantage that might be of particular interest to game developers: performance. It is possible for the algorithm `for_each` to take advantage of the underlying implementation of the container it is applied to and perform a faster traversal than is possible with a plain `for` loop with iterators. The possible performance boost is highly dependent on the specific container and the STL implementation. If you are interested in that extra bit of performance, you should do some timings on your target platform. One thing is certain: `for_each` is never going to be any slower than any loop you can write by hand.

10.2.1.3 Count

If you just want to know how many elements are in the container, you use the member function `size()`. This algorithm does not just count all the elements, it counts all the elements that match a particular value.

Imagine we have a vector of game entity UIDs (unique IDs), and as entities are removed, we set their entries to 0 instead of just removing them. Every so often we want to count how many entries are set to 0. Yes, we can do this with another `for` loop, but the algorithm `count` is the perfect tool:

```
int iNumZeros = count(UIDs.begin(), UIDs.end(), 0);
```

Probably, a more useful version of `count` is its predicate variant: `count_if`. Instead of counting the number of elements with a particular value, we can count the number of elements that make the predicate true. The following code uses `count_if` to count the number of enemy units within a certain distance of the player. We can then use such a value to change the music tempo or to flash some warning on the screen, alerting the player to a large number of enemies headed his way.

```
class IsEnemyNearby
{
public:
    bool operator()(const GameEntity & entity)
    {
        return (entity.IsEnemy() &&
            ::dist(player.GetPos(),entity.GetPos())<RADIUS));
    }
    static float RADIUS = 100.0f;
};

int iNearbyEnemies = count_if(entities.begin(),
                              entities.end(),
                              IsEnemyNearby());
```

Obviously, be careful with any such function that traverses all elements in a container. If the number of game entities in your world is very large, you probably want to do a fast cull of all the entities that are not roughly within distance of the player before you attempt to traverse them all.

10.2.1.4 Other Nonmutating Algorithms

The remaining nonmutating algorithms are `adjacent_find`, `mismatch`, `equal`, and `search`. They are not used as often as the ones we saw in the preceding sections, but it is still worth knowing them and keeping them in mind for when they are the best tools for the job at hand. Refer to the "Suggested Reading" at the end of this chapter for references to a full description of each of them.

10.2.2 Mutating Algorithms

Mutating algorithms work on a container and change its contents. They do not include sorting algorithms, which are a different type of STL algorithm. Mutating algorithms can be used to copy values, reverse the order of some elements, change their order, and so on.

10.2.2.1 Copy

The copy algorithm copies all the elements in a range specified by two iterators to another range, possibly in a different container. If we just want to copy all elements in a container to another container of the same type, the easiest way is to simply copy the whole container, like this:

```
vector<int> highScores;
//...
vector<int> newScores = highScores; // Copies all the scores
```

The copy algorithm comes in handy when we need to copy only a specific range, or when we want to copy across different types of containers.

```
// Only copy the first 10 scores (assume there are at
// least 10)
list<int> newScores;
copy(highScores.begin(), highScores.begin()+10,
    newScores.begin());
```

Notice that copy takes only three iterators. The first two denote the start and end of the source range to copy from, and the third denotes the start of the range to copy to. There is no need to specify the end of the destination range because the number of elements is already determined by the first two iterators.

As long as certain conditions are met, copy works with overlapping ranges. Elements are copied one at a time; as long as the beginning of the destination range does not overlap the source range, everything works as expected.

If you need to copy between two overlapping ranges, where the first element of the destination is part of the source range, use the variant `copy_backward`, which starts from the end of the sequence, avoiding the overlapping problem.

10.2.2.2 Swap_ranges

The algorithm `swap_ranges` is similar to copy. It takes the same parameters to specify the same ranges, but instead of copying one range into another, it just swaps the elements of the two ranges.

10.2.2.3 Remove

We finally come to one of the most useful and least intuitive algorithms in the STL. You can imagine that the following call perhaps removes all the elements that have the given value in that range:

```
remove (first, last, value);
```

Almost, but not quite. The `remove` call does not actually remove any elements. Instead, it puts all those elements that match `value` at the end of the sequence and returns a new iterator, `newlast`, such that there are no elements equal to `value` in the range `first` to `newlast`. This is an important point, so let's go through a simple example:

```
vector<int> test;
test.push_back(3);
test.push_back(1);
test.push_back(4);
test.push_back(1);
test.push_back(5);
test.push_back(3);
test.push_back(1);
test.push_back(8);

remove(test.begin(), test.end(), 1);
```

The call to `remove` returns `test.begin()+5` because it removed three elements from the sequence, and now all the elements between `test.begin()` and `test.begin()+4` are guaranteed not to be equal to 1. Specifically, the first five elements of the sequence are now 3, 4, 5, 3, and 8. What about the remaining three elements? Are they the three 1s we removed? The standard says that they are undefined, so they could be anything. In practice, they are usually the same elements that were in the original sequence; they just have not been modified, but they are most definitely *not* the elements that were removed.

So once again, remove does not remove anything from the container; the number of elements is the same. Its name is somewhat misleading, but there is no other name that better expresses what the algorithm does.

What if we really wanted to remove those elements from the container? Then we should call the erase function in the container, which actually takes care of totally eliminating a range of elements from the container. In the preceding example, to reduce the container to just the elements that are not equal to the value we pass, we would write code such as this:

```
vector<int> newEnd = remove(test.begin(), test.end(), 1);
test.erase(newEnd, test.end());
```

After we get comfortable with this idea, we can put it all in one line. This is the way you see it used most often:

```
test.erase(remove(test.begin(), test.end(), 1), test.end());
```

As you can probably imagine, the remove algorithm has a predicate variant called remove_if, which matches not only a value, but also the functor evaluated at each element.

10.2.2.4 Ordering Algorithms

There is a whole set of mutable algorithms whose only function is to change the order of the elements in a sequence. Again, these are not sorting algorithms (see "Sorting Algorithms" later in this chapter). Ordering algorithms include the following:

- **reverse(first, last):** Reversing all the elements in a sequence, it puts the first one at the end, the second one second to last, and so forth.
- **rotate(first, middle, last):** It rotates all elements in a range. Another way to think of it is as a shift with wraparound. The elements in that range are shifted until the middle element is at the first position, and any elements that were shifted out one way are added in from the opposite end.
- **random_shuffle(first, last):** It shuffles all the elements in the given range. The possibilities for games are quite obvious—not just for card games, but every time we need to randomize a set of events ahead of time and have to make sure the events are all used (as opposed to just picking one at random every time).

10.2.2.5 Other Mutating Algorithms

There are a fair number of mutating algorithms, some more useful than others. Algorithms that are not specifically covered in this chapter include `transform`, `replace`, `fill`, `generate`, `unique`, and `partition`. Several of those algorithms have slight variations. Again, refer to a comprehensive STL reference for all the details.

10.2.3 Sorting Algorithms

Sorting is an important operation in game programming. It happens more often than we think. From a simple sort of the players on the scoreboard based on the number of points they scored, to the sorting of possible threats for an AI unit, to the sorting of meshes to minimize state changes before passing them to the renderer—sorting functions are important tasks. The STL has a whole range of algorithms to help us with sorting, although the main workhorse is the `sort` algorithm, itself.

Before the STL was developed, our only choice was using `qsort` from the standard C library or rolling our own sort functions. The standard C `qsort` ended up being a very efficient implementation most of the time, but with a rather ugly and type-unsafe syntax that required function pointers to take void pointers.

At the core of all sorting functions is the generic algorithm `sort`. It sorts all the elements in a range by applying `operator<` to compare them or using a functor passed as an argument. The `sort` algorithm is implemented by using `quicksort`, which results in an average sort time of $O(N \ln N)$, but could be as bad as $O(N^2)$ in some situations.

Because `sort` requires random access to any of the elements, it can be used only with containers that provide random access (such as vector, heap, or a custom container with that property). The following code snippet sorts a vector of player pointers, based on their high score:

```
class HigherScore
{
public:
    bool operator()(const Player & p1,
                    const Player & p2) const
    {
        return (p1.GetScore() > p2.GetScore());
    }
};

vector<const Player *> players;
sort(players.begin(), players.end(), HigherScore());
```

An important characteristic of the `sort` algorithm is that it is not *stable*. This means that two elements with the same sort order might end up in different relative positions with respect to each other after the sort. This is usually not an issue for most situations in game development, but it is important to be aware of in case it becomes a requirement at some point.

If a stable sort is required, we should use the `stable_sort` algorithm. It has the same interface as `sort`, but it guarantees that the sort will be stable. Unlike `sort`, it runs slower, in $O(N (\ln N)^2)$ time, so use it only when a stable sort is really necessary.

Sometimes we have a really large number of elements, but all we care about is the sort order for the top X elements. In that case, we can use `partial_sort`, which does exactly that: it sorts the top X elements, puts them at the beginning of the sequence, and leaves the rest of the sequence in an unspecified order. The performance of `partial_sort` is $O(N \ln X)$, which is much better than the regular `sort` algorithm when we want to sort only a small number of top elements.

The STL offers several other sorting-related algorithms, such as merging ordered sequences, determining whether a sequence is ordered, and working with heaps.

10.2.4 Generalized Numerical Algorithms

Finally, the STL offers a small set of numerical algorithms that operate on containers. These algorithms do not frequently come up in game development, but they could come in handy one day, so it might be worth knowing how to use them.

- `accumulate(first, last, init):` Performs a sum of all the elements in the specified range. The initial value is set to `init`. By default, it performs the sum of the elements, but it can perform any binary operation we pass as a functor.
- `partial_sum(first, last, output):` Computes the partial sum of a range and stores it in a separate container. A partial sum is defined as the sequence of numbers created by adding all the elements up to the nth element for each of the output elements. As with `accumulate`, we can also provide our own binary operator to replace the default addition.
- `adjacent_difference(first, last, output):` Calculates the difference between adjacent pairs of elements and stores them in the sequence pointed to by `output`. As usual, we can pass any binary operator to replace the subtraction.
- `inner_product(first1, last2, first2, init):` At first, this might seem like something very useful for game development. After all, the inner product is the same thing as the dot product, which we use con-

stantly in code, from camera movement to plotting paths for the AI, to lighting equations. Unfortunately, it is not as useful as it might seem. Most of the dot products in game development are done on specialized vector classes, not on generalized STL containers. Still, the algorithm does exactly that: it performs the inner product of two different ranges. It is also possible to pass custom functors to replace the default addition and multiplication with other operations.

Some STL implementations offer additional algorithms not covered in the standard. If cross-platform portability is not a big issue for you (or if your STL implementation is available in all your target platforms), you might want to investigate which extensions they provide and whether they fit your needs.

10.3 STRINGS

The STL also offers a class that has been long-needed in C++: the string class. In this section, we see why strings are useful and how to use them effectively.

10.3.1 No Strings Attached

Unlike most languages, C and C++ do not have a native concept of a string. Instead they have to make do with arrays of characters and conventions, like marking the end of a string with a NULL character. Unfortunately, working with arrays of characters is very inconvenient.

Arrays have to be created large enough to hold the intended string. When the string changes dynamically, this can create a real problem: how large is "large enough"? For example, a function that retrieves the full path for a file and copies it into an array that we pass as a parameter requires that the array be large enough to hold the whole string. To achieve this, each operating system comes up with some maximum constants, such as MAX_DIR_PATH, that set an upper limit in the length of a file path.

```
char path[MAX_FILE_PATH];
GetFilePath(filename, path);
```

This same situation happens often. When we get the contents from a Web page, we do not know how large that Web page is before we start downloading it. So all sorts of convoluted functions have been devised to make sure the functions work with fixed-size character arrays.

To make things even worse, character arrays are very error prone. The only way to know where the string ends is by setting the last character to NULL, or simply 0. This means that the number of characters allocated in the array is always at least one more than the length of the string itself. This leads to a lot of fudging around with +1 and -1 in the code to convert between length and array size.

And what happens when somebody gets confused by a +1 in the code, or simply tries to read or write past the end of the array? All sorts of things can happen, depending on the platform and depending on how lucky we are. If we are fortunate, the program crashes right away, as soon as we try to access anything past the end of the array. Then we can immediately fix the problem and prevent any future headaches. If we are not so lucky, the program continues to work as usual, and every so often it causes weird crashes or subtle bugs—the kind that don't repeat themselves and are impossible to track down. These bugs are the feared buffer overruns. If we accidentally write past the end of an array, but that memory location was used by some other part of our program, nothing crashes, but we will have corrupted some potentially crucial data. Maybe it will be just corrupted graphics, maybe the AI will act weird, or maybe the program will crash once in a blue moon. It gets worse, though. Every time we make a change, the strange behavior also changes, or even temporarily disappears. Even something such as adding a simple printf to track down the problem can cause the problem itself to change. This is without a doubt one of the most frustrating and time-consuming bugs a programmer can encounter. Anything we can do to avoid it is a big bonus.

What about performance? If char arrays are so painful to work with, at least they must be very efficient. Unfortunately, this is not the case. Getting the length of a character array requires counting all its characters until we hit the NULL character, so it is not particularly fast. Concatenating two strings usually requires allocating new memory and copying both strings to a different location unless somebody had the forethought of creating one of the arrays large enough. They are not even that good at saving memory because arrays are often larger than the strings they need to hold in order to avoid running out of space.

10.3.2 The String Class

C++ had the chance to fix this sorry state and introduced the string class in the STL. Strings address all the major problems of the character arrays:

- Strings grow larger (transparently) when needed, so our program never runs out of space or produces buffer overruns when writing to them.

- We do not have to worry about the size of the allocated memory versus the length of the string.

In addition, the `string` class provides a lot of functions that were previously available through the C library for string manipulation. The advantage is that this time we can treat strings as objects, and the syntax is a lot cleaner and more self-evident.

```
string text1 = "This is an example string";
string text2 = text1;        // We can copy them
string text3 = text1 + text2; // Append them
if ( text3 == text2 )        // Compare them
    //...
```

But how well does `string` mesh with C-style `char` arrays? Pretty well. The people who designed the `string` class clearly had that in mind, so we can easily go from a string to a character array by using the c_str function on the `string` class. The returned character pointer can be used like any `char` array.

```
string text = "Yada, yada, yada...";
char oldstyle[256];
strcpy (oldstyle, text.c_str());
```

One thing to note is that `c_str` returns a `const  char` pointer. That constness should never be cast away because doing so would allow other parts of the program to modify the contents of the string without the string's knowledge. If you need to go from a `char` array to a string, then you should create a new one or assign the contents of the array to an existing string. This approach causes the contents of the character array to be copied, but it is the safest way.

One operation that was not mentioned in this discussion is how to write to the string—not just add another string, which is easy to do by splitting and concatenating the string. Writing an integer, float, or some other data type is a bit more complicated. If we were using `char` arrays, we would use the handy `sprintf()` function and freely write to it.

```
char txt[256]; // Let's hope it's large enough!
sprintf(txt, "Player %d wins with %d points and
            an accuracy of %.2f.",
            player.GetNumber(), player.GetScore(),
            player.GetAccuracy());
```

C++ purists might cringe, but even though `sprintf()` might be type-unsafe and a bit ugly, it gets the job done. To accomplish the same with a string, we are encouraged to use *streams*.

```
ostringstream oss;
oss << "Player " << player.GetNumber() << "wins with" <<
        player.GetScore() << "points and an accuracy of " <<
        player.GetAccuracy();
string txt = oss.str();
```

This version is type-safe, and it is supposed to accomplish the same thing. Unfortunately, specifying the exact formatting is not as straightforward, so in the previous example we left out that we want to display only two digits after the decimal point in the player's accuracy.

The most important drawback is that it requires that we buy into the whole stream paradigm for doing input and output. This is fine, and there are many advantages to streams, but not everybody is ready to take that step. Strings without streams are a bit crippled when it comes to writing to them.

An alternative is to write to a character array like we did before, and then convert the existing array to a string. This approach is not the most elegant solution, and it causes the extra performance hit for converting from an array to a string, but it works.

Fortunately, the Boost library provides an alternative: the Format library. The Format library gives us the ability to format the contents of a string in a more direct way by using a format string. There are several variations, but one of the types of format strings supported is the `printf` style, which a lot of programmers are already familiar with. We can finally write to strings directly like we used to do with character arrays, with the only difference being that now we use percent signs to separate the arguments instead of commas.

```
string txt = boost::io::str(
        format( "Player %d wins with %d points and
                an accuracy of %.2f." %
                player.GetNumber() %
                player.GetScore() %
                player.GetAccuracy() ));
```

By now you might be wondering why the `string` class is part of the STL. From all we have seen so far, it does not look like a template. Actually it is. The class `string` is just a `typedef` for a template:

```
typedef basic_string<char> string;
```

The template is `basic_string`, and it can work with characters or with any other type of element. For example, another useful string type is one that contains wide characters (`wchar_t`), which is very useful for localizing our game in different parts of the world where they use different character sets than ours. There is also a `typedef` for that type of string, called `wstring` for wide-character string.

Technically speaking, a string is just another container, like a vector or a list. However, because it is typically used for completely different purposes, we consider it a separate type of template for the purposes of this book.

10.3.3 Performance

If you are used to dealing with `char` pointers for passing strings, you might need to adjust to using `string`. When working with `char` pointers, to pass the text as a parameter to a function, we pass only the character pointer itself. That is a very efficient operation because only the pointer is copied. With strings, things are a bit different; we have to be careful how we pass them as parameters. If we just pass the string by value, we create a copy of the string object and its contents, which could be very wasteful of memory and performance. To avoid that, we should pass strings by reference most of the time and probably by `const` reference, unless we want the function to modify the contents of the string.

The same thing applies to returning a string from a function. If we assign the value returned by the function to a `const` reference, we avoid making any extra copies. Otherwise the contents of the string are copied if we try to assign the string to a new string. The following code illustrates both cases:

```
// Bad code! We are making two copies of the contents
// of the string!
void SetHighScore(string name);

string playerName = player.GetName();
SetHighScore(playerName);

// Much better version. No copies involved.
void SetHighScore(const string & name);

const string & playerName = player.GetName();
SetHighScore(playerName);
```

Another common performance penalty was already mentioned in the previous section: every conversion of a character array into a string involves allocating a new buffer and copying all the characters to the string. This might not be necessary if the original array was not going to change, but most implementations go ahead and copy the contents of the array anyway. It becomes more of a problem when a code base uses both character arrays and strings. Fortunately, converting from a string to a character array is completely free.

Even if we are using only strings, using *string literals* as a function argument also usually causes its contents to be copied into the string objects. For example:

```
void SetPlayerName(const string & name);

// Will usually cause a new string buffer to be created and
// the contents of the literal to be copied to it, passed
// to the function, and then discarded. Pretty wasteful!
SetPlayerName("Player1");
```

On the other hand, we should not have many string literals hard-coded in the game. Most of that type of data should be read from resources created by the artists and designers. Things like text, especially, should come from an outside source to make localization easier.

Actually, it might turn out that there is not much of a performance penalty for passing strings by value in your particular STL implementation. Remember, for good or bad, there is a huge amount of variation between STL implementations, even though they all adhere to the standard. So it is possible that your implementation is using reference counting and copy-on-write (CoW). Unfortunately, even though reference counting makes copying strings much more efficient, it has its own share of problems that can lead to totally unexpected results. This is especially true in multithreaded environments. If your string implementation uses reference counting, you might want to disable that feature, switch to another STL implementation, or consider one of the alternatives presented toward the end of this section.

10.3.4 Memory

Memory usage can be a concern if you are using many strings in an environment that is very tight in memory. Every string is allocated with a bit of extra padding so that concatenation operations are quite efficient without requiring the string to be reallocated and copied. Unfortunately, if you have no plans to ever increase the size of the string, that extra space is just wasted. Exactly how much space is allocated for padding is implementation dependent, but it is usually around 16 or 32 bytes—not enough to worry about under normal circumstances, but it adds up if you are using thousands of strings.

To make things more interesting, some STL implementations also use a memory-pooling scheme. That means that allocating several strings does not necessarily cause many memory allocations, but it also means that freeing some strings does not necessarily free all the memory they were using. This is an advantage most of the time because it allows for much faster string-creation operations. On the other hand, if you were already tight in memory, this scheme makes things worse, particularly if at some point during program execution (during level loading, perhaps), your string use spikes up considerably and then goes back to normal. At that point, the amount of memory reserved for strings is much larger than necessary.

In addition, each string has a fixed overhead. Depending on the implementation, the overhead can be anywhere from 4 to 16 bytes. Those extra bytes are used to keep track of bookkeeping information, such as the start address and length of the string.

10.3.5 Alternatives

If the `string` class does not suit your needs, before you revert to using `char *` again, there are a few alternatives. The classes `rope`, `vector<char>`, and `CString` are worth considering.

10.3.5.1 Rope

The first alternative to the `string` class is the `rope` class. It is not part of the standard, but it is provided by several implementations. Like the `string` class, it is really a templated class, so it is possible to specify what type of elements you want to work with and to specify an allocator: `rope<type, alloc>`.

The `rope` class is intended to work with very large strings as a unit. It accomplishes this by storing the string data in several memory blocks instead of just a single consecutive one. In particular, assignment, concatenation, and substring operations are much faster for large strings. On the other hand, doing single-character operations on a `rope` is much more expensive. Also, converting a `rope` to a character array is a much more expensive operation than it was with the `string` class.

Clearly the `rope` class is not going to completely substitute for the `string` class. But, it might be worth considering for very specific circumstances.

10.3.5.2 Vector<char>

A string is little more than a sequence container for characters, so why not use `vector<char>`? We are already familiar with its syntax, its performance, and its memory-use characteristics, so it seems like a good candidate.

There is no explicit call to convert to character arrays; but with a few tricks, you can get a pointer to the sequential memory block where the characters are stored. As long as all your operations maintain a NULL character to indicate the end of the string, everything should work fine.

The best thing about vector<char> is that you know there is no reference counting or CoW going on under the hood, so the integrity of your text data is guaranteed. Sometimes this is the best alternative for people who want to avoid their own string implementation but do not want to switch STL versions.

The main drawback of this approach is its lack of many string-specific functions, such as replacement or substring operations. It is possible to implement all of them in terms of more basic STL algorithms and vector functions, but you have to write them yourself, and you will end up with a different syntax than what people are used to for the string class.

10.3.5.3 CString

The Microsoft Foundation Classes (MFC) introduced the CString class to solve all the problems of manipulating char * arrays. The CString class evolved along a very different path than the STL string class and is not compatible with the STL, but to its credit, it was created many years before the string class saw the light of day.

CString is not template based because there was no decent support for templates when it was created, but it does everything you could ever need from a string class. If anything, it does a little too much, and it has often been criticized for its kitchen-sink approach and bloated interface.

The most common complaint about CString is that it is tied to MFC and the Windows platform. That is not totally true because there are some implementations available that let you use it without bringing in a single MFC header file or library, but they are still dependent on the Win32 API. That alone might rule it out for your application if you are targeting anything other than Windows-based platforms.

Even if you are using only Windows, unless you are tied to a large body of code that uses CString extensively, there is almost no reason not to switch to the standard and portable STL string class.

10.4 ALLOCATORS (ADVANCED)

There might come a time when the STL memory allocation strategy is just not enough. That could be for many different reasons. Maybe the constant allocation and freeing of memory when dealing with node-based containers is fragmenting memory or causing major performance hiccups. Maybe we need to keep better track of where memory is going, as we saw in Chapter 7, "Memory Allocation." Maybe we need to keep elements of a container allocated contiguously in memory to improve data-cache consistency. Maybe we want to create some elements temporarily on the stack and then release them without any penalties. If that time arrives, the answer lies in using custom allocators.

On the other hand, you should not automatically assume that the STL memory allocation is *not* going to be good enough. Depending on your platform and your requirements, you may never need to change your allocation strategy. If so, you can count yourself lucky. In any case, it is a good idea to peruse this section, just to be aware of potential problems and how to go about solving them if you ever need to write your own custom allocators.

At its core, a custom allocator is simply an object that allocates and frees memory when requested. This might not sound all that different from overriding new and delete in a class, but that is not the case. Unfortunately there is quite a bit of baggage that comes along with allocators, and things are made even worse by compilers' lack of language features or specific workarounds.

In practice, allocators are implemented slightly differently in different platforms, so a full, working allocator is not provided on the CD-ROM. Instead, the best way to write a custom allocator is to start with the default allocator of your STL implementation and change the specific parts related to the new memory-allocation strategy.

As an example, let's create an allocator that uses our own memory heaps, like the ones described in Chapter 7, to keep better track of where memory is being allocated. Every time there is an allocation, we want to call the new version of operator new with the correct heap.

So we dig out the standard STL allocator, copy it somewhere else, and attempt to modify its allocation and deallocation functions to call our overridden new and delete operators. This might be an initial attempt:

```
template<typename T>
MyHeapAllocator
{
public:
    pointer allocate(size_type iNumObjects,
                    const void * hint = 0)
    {
        return static_cast<pointer>
        (new(iNumObjects*sizeof(T),
                                pHeap));
    }
    void deallocate(pointer p, size_type iNumObjects)
    {
```

```
            delete(p, iNumObjects*sizeof(T));
        }
        //...
    };
```

There is a slight problem here. How do we pass `pHeap` into the operator? Ideally, we would like the allocator to keep a pointer to the heap we want to use and pass it to `new` every time there is an allocation. Here comes the first quirk of STL allocators: allocators should not have any per-object state. So we cannot keep a pointer to the heap. To get around that, we need to create a quick wrapper class around our heap and use that class as a parameter into the allocator template. Here is a new attempt at writing the allocator:

```
class HeapGraphics
{
public:
    static void * allocate(size_t iNumBytes)
    {
        return new(iNumBytes, s_pGraphicsHeap);
    }
    static void deallocate(void * p, size_t iNumBytes)
    {
        delete(p, iNumBytes);
    }
};

template<typename T, typename Heap>
MyHeapAllocator
{
public:
    pointer allocate(size_type iNumObjects,
                    const void * hint = 0)
    {
        return static_cast<pointer>(Heap::allocate(
                    iNumObjects*sizeof(T), pHeap));
    }
    void deallocate(pointer p, size_type iNumObjects)
    {
        Heap::deallocate (p, iNumObjects*sizeof(T));
    }
    //...
};
```

This new version respects all the rules of allocators and allows us to allocate all memory from our own heap. The only drawback is that we need to create one wrapper class for every heap we want to use, which can be a nuisance. As has been mentioned, though, STL allocators are not perfect.

The actual workings of the insides of allocators are a bit more involved, but from a user's point of view, this is all you need to know to get up and running at writing your own custom allocators. Refer to some of the sources listed in "Suggested Reading" at the end of this chapter for some interesting coverage of allocators.

10.5 WHEN STL IS NOT ENOUGH (ADVANCED)

Ironically, after spending two entire chapters discussing how STL can be a real benefit to your game project, we are going to wrap it up by discussing alternatives. Let's be very clear about one thing: STL is a great starting point. There is very little reason not to use it to get things up and running. If used carefully, as explained in this chapter and in Chapter 9, you will be on your way to shipping a game or creating tools with some solid data structures and slick algorithms without the need to implement them from scratch. The less time you spend on trivial work, the more time you can spend improving gameplay, researching new techniques, or even taking a break. And if you are developing for the PC, then that is probably all you will have to worry about.

However, there might come a time when the STL is just not good enough, particularly if you are developing for a console with much more limited resources than a PC. The most common reason to look beyond STL is its lack of fine control over memory allocation. Maybe you already fiddled with the nontrivial task of creating custom allocators, and you are still not satisfied with the memory allocation patterns of STL containers. Maybe you want to reliably release the memory in a vector, or you want more control over the block sizes of a deque. Hopefully this is motivated by something you saw that was interfering with your game. Do not just assume that more control over memory is a good thing; if it is not detracting from the game in any way, then do not waste your time. Look for alternatives only if it is slowing down your game at crucial moments, or if your game is using more memory than you think it should.

Another of the common complaints about STL, and templates in general, is code bloat. Some compilers are more prone to this than others, but it is possible for the same template to be created over and over for use in different classes, causing a large growth in the final executable size.

Finally, another reason for looking at alternatives to STL that we have not yet considered is the increase it causes in compile times. Do not forget that STL is made out of templates, and templates are nothing more than code that is generated at compile time, so that is more work for the compiler. The more work the compiler has to do, the longer the compile step takes. The longer the turnaround time from making a trivial change to getting the game up and running, the more costly and cumbersome development becomes. If this situation arises and you suspect that it is being caused by overuse of STL, then it might be time to consider an alternative. However, first make sure that STL is really the cause. A lot of project developers are careless about their physical structures and how header files are included (see Chapter 18, "Dealing with Large Projects," for some possible explanations for slow compilations).

So what should we do about these situations? Is there a better library out there? Unfortunately, not yet. Probably the best thing to do is to provide your own custom containers.

It might come as a bit of a shock to get a recommendation for writing your own containers after hearing all about the virtues of STL; but given the circumstances, it is probably the best solution. Just do not totally give up on STL and start writing your own container classes without carefully examining the need to do so.

Have a look at your code base. Think about what parts of STL you use most often or which ones give you trouble. Chances are that 90% of your STL use is limited to a couple of containers—maybe vectors, some sort of maps, and possibly strings. That does not mean you are not using STL for the rest, but these are probably the bread and butter of your everyday STL usage.

A good approach, then, is to replace only those containers that are used often, or the ones with which you are having trouble. You can continue using the rest of the STL normally in your code; you do not need to give it up completely. For example, you could create your own version of vector and call it `myvector` or `array` or whatever you want. It can have an interface that is very similar to the STL vector: you still have `push_back`, `clear`, `resize`, and `reserve`. But you can also add new functions that let you more carefully control how memory is allocated and freed. You can also provide custom versions of your containers to fit your needs. For example, you could provide a bare-bones vector that has minimal overhead, so you can use it in each of the thousands of game entities in your world.

You can also provide iterators to access your container, and if you are careful about how those iterators are implemented, you might still be able to use a good part of the STL algorithms on your own container. So in a way, you are not totally replacing STL; you are augmenting it, and you can use pieces of it even with your new containers.

Again, this is not a task to be undertaken lightly. Do not underestimate the amount of effort require to make a robust, solid container that fits your needs and is more efficient than the STL version. Take your time when deciding if you really need it and what exactly needs to be different. Until then, continue using STL, and maybe the time to replace it will never come.

10.6 Conclusion

In this chapter, we saw the other half of the STL. We started with one of the building blocks of STL: functors, which are a more flexible way of passing functions around than just using function pointers. Then we covered the four types of algorithms the STL provides:

- Nonmutable algorithms, which work on a sequence of elements but do not change their contents. They are used to find elements, count them, iterate through them, and so forth.
- Mutable algorithms, which modify the elements in a sequence, but without sorting them. They are used to copy ranges of elements, remove them, or alter their order.
- Sorting algorithms, which order a sequence of elements and perform other related tasks.
- Numerical algorithms, which are just a few algorithms that perform numerical computations on the elements in a range.

Next, we saw the STL `string` class and its companion, the `wstring` class for wide characters. They have a few minor quirks, but they make life a lot simpler when dealing with text strings, and they are a better solution than using `char *` most of the time.

Finally, we briefly covered how to deal with the STL when we need more than the STL offers by default. We first saw how to write custom allocators for our containers and what we can expect to get out of doing so, and then we saw the circumstances under which it might make sense to write our own versions of containers instead of using the ones in STL.

Suggested Reading

The following book has great all-around tips. Specific to this chapter, it has some very good advice on functors, a discussion about strings and `vector<char>`, and a section about STL algorithms:

Meyers, Scott, *Effective STL*. Addison-Wesley, 2001.

Following are some excellent books on general algorithms. You will find that many of the STL's algorithms are explained in detail in these texts, including how the algorithms are implemented and what the consequences of their use are. Incidentally, you will also find good descriptions of most data structures used in the STL containers.

Cormen, Thomas H., et al., *Introduction to Algorithms.* McGraw-Hill, 1990.

Knuth, Donald E., *The Art of Computer Programming,* 3rd ed. Addison-Wesley, 1997.

Here are some good resources about string classes, their implementation, and related libraries:

C++ Boost Format library. Available online at *http://www.boost. org/libs/format/index.htm.*

Strings in SGI STL. Available online at *http://www.sgi.com/tech/stl/ string_discussion.html.*

Allocators are a tricky subject. There are not a lot of references out there, possibly because they are so platform dependent. Yet here are some good starting sources:

Josuttis, Nicolai M., *The C++ Standard Library.* Addison-Wesley, 1999.

Josuttis, Nicolai M., User-Defined Allocator. Available online at *http://www.josuttis.com/cppcode/allocator.html.*

Meyers, Scott, *Effective STL.* Addison-Wesley, 2001.

Treglia, Dante, et al., *Game Programming Gems 3.* Charles River Media, 2002.

Again, here is a great overall STL reference:

SGI's Standard Template Library Programmer's Guide. Available online at *http://www.sgi.com/tech/stl/.*

11

BEYOND STL: CUSTOM STRUCTURES AND ALGORITHMS

In This Chapter

- Case Study: Graphs
- Graphs in C++
- Putting Our Graphs to Work
- "Smart" Graphs
- Graphs: Not Just for Pathfinding

Now that we've taken a look at the C++ Standard Template Library (STL) in the previous two chapters, you might be wondering about how to create your own containers, data structures, and algorithms effectively in C++. This chapter shows you how to do just that while still maintaining good performance and well-organized program structure.

11.1 CASE STUDY: GRAPHS

For our discussion in this chapter, we'll take a quick look at *graphs* and a few algorithms typically associated with them. Don't worry—this chapter is not a discourse on algorithm analysis or complexity theory. Graphs happen to be extremely useful structures in game programming, and they make excellent examples of how to use C++ effectively.

11.1.1 Structural Overview

As a quick refresher, a basic graph is shown in Figure 11.1.

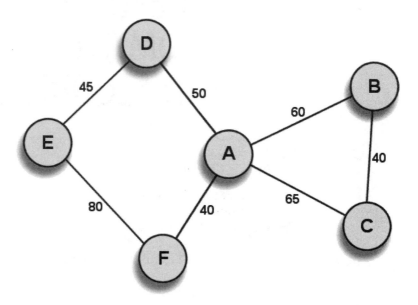

FIGURE 11.1 A basic graph with six vertices and seven edges.

The main components of a graph are its *vertices* (also known as nodes) and its *edges* (or links). The vertices conceptually represent abstract locations in some space of interest, and the edges represent connections between those locations. For example, the vertices of a graph can represent cities in our game world, and the edges represent roads that connect the cities. In this case, the graph as a whole serves as a map that shows the physical locations and relationships between cities and the different paths that can be used to travel between them. Figure 11.2 shows the same graph realized as the map for a hypothetical game world set in the land of Dor.

Notice in Figure 11.2 that the roadways have labels indicating the distance in miles between the cities they connect. In general, an edge in a graph typically has a *cost* associated with traversing that edge from one vertex to the other. Here, the distances between cities represent those costs. The edge costs in a graph help drive decisions about the relationships between vertices. In our map example, the distances associated with each edge can help us figure out the shortest route from Eldor to Aldor. We can determine that the route through Doldor is shorter than the route through Faldor simply by summing the costs associated with the roads between those cities.

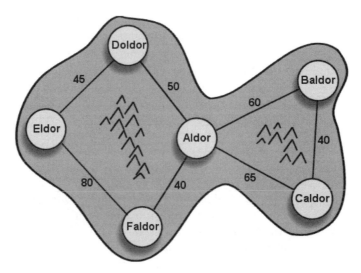

FIGURE 11.2 The basic graph transformed into a map of the hypothetical world of Dor.

11.1.2 The Bigger Picture

One of the most important skills in game programming (and programming in general) is identifying structure in the problems we face and determining how best to represent those problems in code. This is a skill that develops over time with experience, but it can be accelerated by explicit study and practice. This chapter uses the graph example as a way of illustrating the power of targeted problem solving in resolving the issues we face as game developers.

11.1.3 On the Subject of Cost

The map scenario given in Figure 11.2 is an example of a *pathfinding* problem. The basic issue of a pathfinding problem in games is determining the shortest route from one place to another. More generally, the problem deals with finding the route with the *least cost*. The distinction is important; *distance* is a concrete concept that applies to only a small number of problems associated with, for example, maps in a game. However, the idea of *cost* is abstract; if we keep the difference in mind, we can write code that allow us to solve a much broader range of problems using structures and techniques we already know well.

Imagine, for example, that civil war has erupted in Doldor. As a result, all travel to and from Doldor has become very dangerous. The design consequence of this event might be that we want to discourage players and AI units from using Doldor as a waypoint to other destinations, and encourage them to use alternative routes instead. One way of accomplishing this is to add some explicit rules in the code about traveling to Doldor, but there is a much better way. We can simply increase the costs of edges that are *adjacent* (that is, connected) to Doldor, which drives up the total cost of any path that includes Doldor. As a result, any unit that might have, for example, sought to travel from Baldor to Eldor through Doldor (the shortest route by distance) now goes through Faldor instead.

But how do we accomplish this increase in edge costs? Because we are currently using the distance between cities as the cost, it might seem that somehow we need to change the distances between Doldor and both Eldor and Aldor. Of course, we can't move the city (historically, that just doesn't happen very often), and there really isn't a clear way to change the distances any other way. The solution is to extend the nature of the information stored in the edge costs to include both distance and some representation of *danger*. Thus, the cost of traveling from one city to another can now be expressed as the sum of the actual distance plus some danger factor. Figure 11.3 shows an updated view of Dor that considers danger in the edge costs:

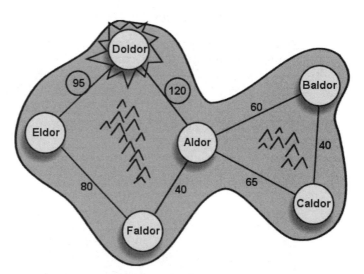

FIGURE 11.3   The game world adjusted to reflect dangers along the roadways near Doldor.

11.1.4 Edge Costs and Gameplay

A pathfinding algorithm that operates on edge costs (and not specifically distances) automatically works correctly without having to explicitly address the changes to the meaning of the edge costs. We'll get to the details of a simple pathfinding algorithm soon, but the point at the moment is to illustrate how a variety of concepts can be supported by a system constructed with flexibility in mind. To that end, here are some other examples of modifying edge costs in a graph for a variety of pathfinding-specific game play effects:

- **Movement rates.** In the real world, the distance between destinations is usually a function of how far away the destination is and how fast you can move while trying to get there. This concept shows up a lot in games. For example, racing games often have speed hints for the AI drivers that help them know to slow down for turns. Ambient traffic in urban environments usually obeys posted speed limits and other traffic laws as part of the overall realism. In these and many other cases, the cost of travel can be greatly affected by the speed at which units can move—legally or otherwise. Any unit that has to navigate under these conditions can benefit greatly from an explicit representation of speed indicators in the underlying navigation graph.

- **Terrain types.** The type of terrain can alter the difficulty of traveling across different kinds of terrain. For example, although the distance from Doldor to Aldor may be only 50 miles, perhaps those 50 miles are along a soggy, treacherous trail in an area composed entirely of swampland. We can express this cost as a function of distance and travel difficulty by assigning a difficulty value to the swamp terrain type. If we arbitrarily choose a difficulty of 10, then we can express the cost of traveling from Doldor to Aldor as 50 * 10 = 500. Similar difficulty assignments to the other roads (edges) in the map based on terrain type could completely change the pathfinding problem for units that are affected by differences in the travel environment.

- **Tolls.** Tolls associate a financial cost for traveling along a path in addition to the distance. A path that requires the player to travel over the famed troll's bridge, for example, might carry a high total cost if the troll is particularly greedy, even if the distance to the next stop is very short. The idea of a toll can be generalized as a representation of *resource costs* associated with movement along a given path. For example, a magical path could require mana expenditure during a player's movement through it, or a tunnel passage containing a lava pool could require the "expenditure" of health in order to get to the other side.

- **Operational travel delays.** Operational delays are a more complicated class of cost that can be associated with a graph. Examples include points at which an AI must wait for the arrival of an elevator before it can proceed, or a player that is subject to a travel schedule for an in-game transportation system. In these cases, representing edge costs is a bit more involved because the cost is often associated with the behavior of other objects in the game. Some sort of mechanism tying those objects to the navigation graph is required—a concept that is discussed later in this chapter.

There are countless other ways to represent edge costs in graphs that are used in games. Hopefully, by the time you finish reading this chapter, you will have many ideas for how graphs can be used effectively to solve your own particular programming needs. More importantly, you'll be able to think of the problems you encounter during game development as candidates for well-structured representation in code. You'll also learn to seek elegant solutions that allow the basic problem to be expanded in myriad ways without requiring code refactoring or hacking.

Now we will take a look at implementing what we've learned about graphs in C++.

11.2 GRAPHS IN C++

The most basic graph consists simply of a collection of vertices, each of which knows about the other vertices to which it connects, called its *neighbors*. We can implement the vertices with a very simple class:

```
class GraphVertex
{
public:
    GraphVertex ();
    virtual ~GraphVertex ();
    void AddEdge(GraphVertex * pNeighbor)
    {
        m_neighbors.push_back(pNeighbor);
    }

protected:
    std::vector<GraphVertex*> m_neighbors;
};
```

Now that we have a vertex, we can define a basic graph class as well:

```
class BasicGraph
{
public:
    BasicGraph();
    virtual ~BasicGraph();
protected:
    std::vector<GraphVertex*> m_Verts;
};
```

Of course, the preceding classes don't do very much yet. For example, the interface leaves out a few necessary things. At the very least, we should provide accessors for the members in each class, an interface for adding vertices to the graph, accessing individual vertices, and so on. You might also think that the GraphVertex class is missing a location variable (because we've been talking so much about positions and distances). But as we'll see later in this chapter, a graph can represent many different kinds of connection systems; for many of these systems, the concept of a physical location has no meaning. As a result, we'll need to keep the basic graph as simple as possible, and instead use inheritance to create new types of graphs that do rely on physically positioned vertices and edges based on distance and other costs.

Graphs used for representing pathfinding information are aptly named *navigation graphs*. The vertices—or nodes—in a navigation graph generally have, at the very least, a physical location that places them somewhere in the game world. A basic implementation of a *navigation node* (also appropriately named) is shown here:

```
class NavigationNode : public GraphVertex
{
public:
    NavigationNode();
    NavigationNode(const Vector2d& pos);
    virtual ~NavigationNode();

    // Provide access to this node's location in the world
    const Vector2d& GetPos() const    { return m_pos; }
    void SetPos(const Vector2d& pos)  { m_pos = pos;  }

protected:
    Vector2d m_pos; // world location
};
```

Observe that the nodes in our navigation graph have implicit edge costs that are simply the distances between adjacent nodes as determined from their explicit positions. Although we could provide a GetEdgeCost() accessor (or something similar), we're going to take our graph class to a whole new level very soon and give it some real power.

11.3 PUTTING OUR GRAPHS TO WORK

Now that we have our basic graph classes, it's time to make use of them. Because we have been discussing pathfinding, we begin with an algorithm that illustrates how we can use graphs to find the shortest route between two navigation nodes. Our algorithm of choice is a variation of the *uniform-cost search* (UCS). UCS is not necessarily the best algorithm for finding the shortest path between two vertices in a graph, but it is easy to understand and implement. It is also versatile in that it is easily modified to accommodate many different representations of graphs, vertices, edges, and costs, as we will see later.

The goal of all pathfinding algorithms is to find a path of *lowest total cost* from a start vertex (the source) to an end vertex (the goal), and the UCS algorithm is no different. UCS works by examining the children (that is, the neighbors) of the start node, and adding them to a *priority queue* to be examined further. In this case, the "priority" is the lowest path cost from the start node. This means that the first child to be examined is the one that is "closest" to the start node in terms of the cost of the edges leading to that child. After examining all the start node's children, each of the children's children is examined, and so on. The result is something like a ripple effect that originates at the start node and expands outward to the rest of the graph. Eventually, the goal node is reached, and with a bit of careful record keeping, the shortest path to that node is determined.

A complete implementation of the UCS algorithm is given later. For now, we simply illustrate its operation on the map of Dor. Imagine that we seek to find the shortest route from Baldor to Eldor. Thus, Baldor is the start node in the search, and Eldor is the goal node. At the start of UCS, Baldor is added to the priority queue with a cost of 0 (because it's the start of the search and therefore has no cost to get to itself). Figure 11.4 illustrates the start of the search. Note that Baldor is highlighted in

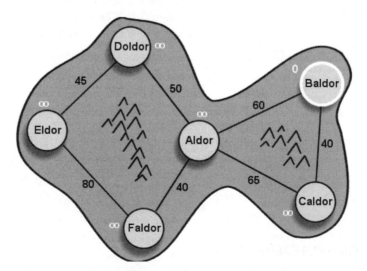

FIGURE 11.4   In determining the best path from Baldor to Eldor, the search begins with Baldor being added to the priority queue and assigned a cost value of 0.

white to indicate that it currently exists in the queue. Shown in white is the current path cost for Baldor, which remains 0. The path costs for all other nodes are also shown in white and are initialized to infinity to indicate those nodes have not yet been "discovered."

The next step in the process is to add all children of Baldor to the queue, and assign them costs based on their distance from the start node. Because the start node is Baldor itself, the costs for these nodes is simply the cost associated with the edge that connects them to Baldor. When all the children of Baldor have been added to the queue, Baldor itself is removed, indicating that the algorithm is finished considering that node for the rest of the search. Figure 11.5 illustrates the situation after Aldor and Caldor have been added to the queue. Again, notice that both these nodes are highlighted in white to indicate their presence in the queue, while Baldor is no longer highlighted because it has been removed. Also given are the current path costs for the two new nodes (60 and 40, respectively). Notice the additional features present in Figure 11.5: thick white arrows indicating the children of Baldor that have just been examined for the first time, and thin black arrows pointing from Aldor and Caldor back to Baldor. These black arrows are important: they indicate the *predecessors* of Aldor and Caldor. In this case, Baldor is the predecessor of both nodes, which means that it came before the other nodes in the search. Tracking predecessors is an important part of the algorithm, as we'll see later.

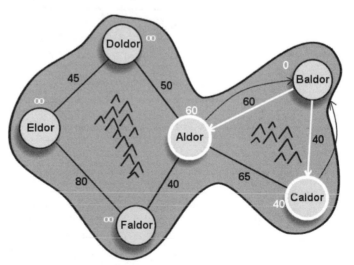

FIGURE 11.5   The children of Baldor have been added to the search queue, while Baldor itself has been removed. Thin black arrows leading from Aldor and Caldor indicate that Baldor is the predecessor of both nodes.

Now we come to the real meat of the algorithm. Both Aldor and Caldor are in the queue, but only one can be considered next. Because we have chosen to store them in a priority queue, with priorities based on the lowest total path cost, the only option is to look at Caldor next because its path cost is the lower, at 40. Figure 11.6 shows the situation after Caldor is chosen for examination. Caldor has two neighbors, Baldor and Aldor. Technically, both are considered for addition into the queue. However, in this case, neither node is added for a few different reasons. First, Aldor is already in the queue and therefore doesn't need to be added again. Second, Baldor is the predecessor of Caldor, and the algorithm doesn't allow a path to go from one node to another and then back to the first node.

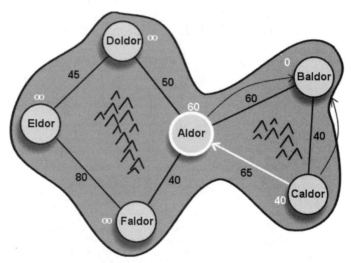

FIGURE 11.6   The search continues from Caldor because it has the lowest path cost from the start node. However, the search quickly ends because no path through Caldor is shorter than the paths that already exist through its neighbors.

But there's a more elegant reason why neither node is added back into the queue, and it has to do with path costs. Imagine a path leading from Baldor to Caldor and back to Baldor. Such a path would have a total cost of 80—a long way to travel just to get back to where we started. Also, we've already determined in the last step that Aldor is just 60 miles from Baldor. A path to Aldor through Caldor would add an additional 65 miles. In both cases, neither neighbor of Caldor can be visited in the search at this point because both of them already have shorter paths from the start node. The rule in play, then, is that as the search proceeds through the graph, only vertices whose path cost can be *lower* than their current value are added to the search queue. It's this important feature of the algorithm that makes UCS run very efficiently without wasting time searching paths that can't be the shortest one to the goal.

Because the algorithm fails to update any paths coming from Caldor, the search at Caldor ends with its removal from the queue with no additional search nodes added. This leaves only one node in the queue: Aldor. Now the children of Aldor are added to the queue with the usual updates, as shown in Figure 11.7.

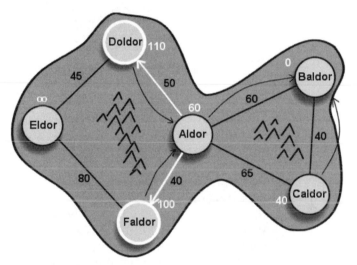

FIGURE 11.7   The neighbors of Aldor are added to the search queue, each receiving updated cost information that reflects the total cost of travel from the start node.

Notice that the costs associated with the children of Aldor (Doldor and Faldor), reflect the *total* path cost from the start node, not just the cost from Aldor. And as before, the predecessors of these new nodes are updated as well, while Aldor itself is removed from the queue.

The next step is to once again select the node in the queue with the least total path cost, which this time is Faldor. Figure 11.8 shows the situation after Faldor is examined:

Because one of the neighbors of Faldor is the goal node, Eldor, you might think that the search is over. In fact, it isn't, because while Eldor is the goal, the algorithm doesn't yet know that the path through Faldor is

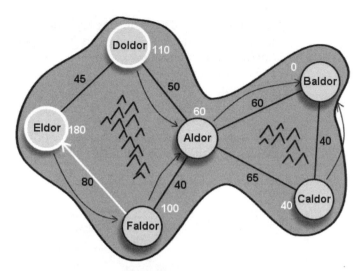

FIGURE 11.8   The search has reached Faldor.

the shortest path. Why? Because even as Eldor is added to the queue, there is still another node with a lower total path cost: Doldor. Thus, the algorithm continues in spite of the fact that the goal node was found. Notice how Eldor is treated like every other node in the search, including the setting of its predecessor.

After Faldor's children have been added to the queue, it is removed. As mentioned, Doldor remains as the lowest-cost node. When Doldor's children are examined, Eldor is "re-discovered," and this time something new happens in the algorithm. The current shortest path to Eldor has a total cost of 180. However, when examined from Doldor, an even shorter path is discovered with a total cost of 155. As a result, Eldor's cost is changed because it can be made lower than it previously was. Also, the predecessor of Eldor is changed from Faldor to Doldor because Doldor is the node through which the shortest path has reached Eldor. The algorithm next considers the only node left in the queue, which is Eldor, and determines that no additional nodes need to be considered. The final result is illustrated in Figure 11.9.

At this point, we've found the shortest path from Baldor to Eldor. However, we don't actually know what it is—at least not in the code. Fortunately, we still have the predecessor information for the nodes. When the algorithm completes, the chain of predecessors can be traversed to reconstruct the shortest path, starting from the goal node. So, starting from Eldor, we see its predecessor is Doldor, then Aldor, then Baldor. Reversing this chain we get the final path, as shown in Figure 11.10:

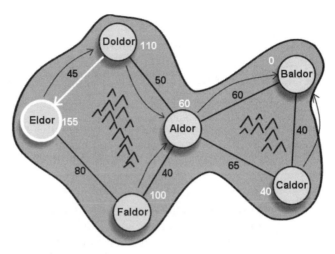

FIGURE 11.9   After Doldor is considered, an even shorter route to Eldor is discovered. This discovery is reflected in the updated path cost for Eldor, as well as a change of predecessor from Faldor to Doldor.

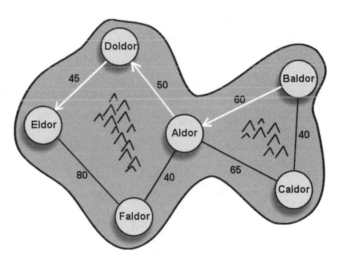

FIGURE 11.10   After the search completes, the chain of predecessors is traversed from the goal node (Eldor) back to the start node (Baldor). The resulting list of nodes is reversed, giving the final best path from start to goal.

11.4 "SMART" GRAPHS

Now that we've taken a look at how graphs serve our basic pathfinding needs, we'll move on to considerably more sophisticated graphs that extend the uses of pathfinding in our games.

11.4.1 Living on the Edge

Up to this point, we've treated the edges in our graphs as implicit costs, existing only as the distance between connected vertices, while giving our vertices more formal structure. You might be wondering if there is anything more interesting we can do with our edges, and the answer is a definite yes.

The edges of a graph provide outstanding opportunities to embed information in our game levels in a data-driven manner. For example, consider the problem of keeping AI-controlled vehicles driving correctly in the lanes of an urban road system. If our game design is complex enough, we might have rules about HOV (High Occupancy Vehicle lane) restrictions, emergency vehicles, pedestrian crossings, a variety of traffic signals, and so on. Rather than relying on our AIs to programmatically analyze the world and figure out where they can and cannot go, we can make things much easier on ourselves by embedding this type of information in the graphs that represent the roadways.

Consider the simple street intersection depicted in Figure 11.11.

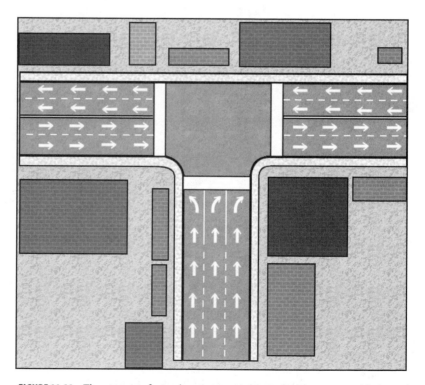

FIGURE 11.11 The streets of an urban area represented with more sophisticated edges that provide lane information, including usage, direction, and transitions to other lanes.

In the figure, quite a bit of information is apparent to those familiar with everyday urban driving, including the following:

- A variable number of travel lanes along each road segment
- Direction of movement within each lane
- Lane termination at an intersection
- A mix of one-way and two-way traffic entering/exiting the intersection
- Rules about crossing dashed lines and double-yellow lines
- Rules about turning from one lane into another
- Rules about when lane changes are legal or illegal
- Lanes dedicated to vehicle traffic only
- Lanes dedicated to pedestrian traffic only (sidewalks)
- Locations of pedestrian crosswalks

All this information can be stored in the graph structure, particularly in the edges, which typically provide the most information about a navigation system in terms of how it is to be used. Storing these kinds of information greatly reduces the amount of work we have to do when creating missions or AI behaviors, because we've essentially provided most of the cues for decision-making in the data structures on which those decisions are to operate. By putting decision-driving gameplay information in our graphs, we make them "smart" in the same sense that terrain and other objects are typically said to be smart.

Taking another look at the list of information present in our graph, notice that the items in it represent *static* aspects of the graph—that is, characteristics of the roadway system that do not change after the level is loaded. Of course, a vast amount of other static information can be stored as well, but we can do even better than that. In addition to these properties, a wide variety of *dynamic* elements can be tracked during runtime within the edges of our graph, including the following:

- A list of the vehicles or pedestrians currently occupying a given road segment
- A persistent, statistical tracking of traffic flow through all lanes, intersections, crosswalks, and sidewalks according to actor type
- The number of times a particular AI agent makes use of a given lane or roadway
- A list of items of particular importance to the current mission
- A list of actors that are currently allowed to use a given pathway
- Specialized movement requirements based on actor types (for example, crawling or running in the case of pedestrians, or reverse driving or two-wheel maneuvers in the case of vehicles)

All this information can also be contained within the elements of the underlying roadway graph. This allows a variety of disparate components in the code to access information about the roadways from a single location for a variety of very different reasons, including these:

- The obvious: detailed pathfinding information for the AIs in the game
- Directional cues to the player using a 3D HUD (Heads-up Display) that indicates turns, speeds, and so on
- Automated mission generation based on events occurring in or around the road system
- Location-balanced spawn-point generation for multiplayer games to prevent spawn camping
- Map overlays for informative UI elements before and during the action

At this point, it might appear that we are using our graphs just as containers of information to be used by other objects in the game. To some extent, this is always the case; the graphs *are* convenient store-houses of information related to traffic flow, navigation, and so on. However, the real power of our graphs comes into play when we use various algorithms that make use of all this information to enrich our gameplay.

11.4.2 Upgrading, C++ Style

To give the edges in our graphs real power, we need to treat them as objects just like the vertices. By now, you should already know what this means: graph edges become their own class. By elevating the edges to the level of a full-blown class, we get to enjoy the benefits of encapsulation, polymorphism, and everything else that gives C++ its power. Without further ado, let's introduce a class for our graph edges:

```
class GraphEdge
{
public:
    GraphEdge();
    virtual ~GraphEdge();
    GraphVertex* GetTail() const    { return m_pTail;     }
    GraphVertex* GetHead() const    { return m_pHead;     }
    void SetTail(GraphVertex* pVert) { m_pTail = pVert;    }
    void SetHead(GraphVertex* pVert) { m_pHead = pVert;    }
    virtual float GetCost() const   { return m_fBaseCost; }

protected:
    GraphVertex* m_pTail;
    GraphVertex* m_pHead;
    float m_fBaseCost;
};
```

A quick note about graph edges: an edge typically is associated with two vertices. In *undirected* graphs, there is no notion of direction with the edges; that is, the edge is considered to be a "two-way" connection in the sense that both vertices can be reached from the other along the edge. Our map of Dor is an example of an undirected graph. In *directed* graphs, edges can be "one-way" in that there is a sense of direction from one vertex to the other. In this case, the vertex from which the edge originates is often called the *tail*, and the vertex to which the edge connects is called the *head* (as in the head of an arrow). An example of a directed graph is given in Figure 11.12, later in this chapter.

With our discussion of edge directions out of the way, notice that the `GraphEdge` class is pretty straightforward. We assume directed graphs, and as such have both a tail and a head vertex associated with the edge, as well as a cost. Note that we can still represent undirected graphs using directed edges simply by giving two edges that point in opposite directions for every edge in the graph. For simple gameplay purposes, this detail can be overkill, and we can instead just add a flag to the edge indicating that it is a two-way edge. For the more sophisticated representations discussed in this chapter, it's essential that edges be distinct. Either way, we now have a base class for our edges that we can use in our graphs.

Now we can update the vertex class to make use of the edges:

```
class GraphVertex
{
public:
    GraphVertex();
    virtual ~GraphVertex();

    void AddEdge(GraphEdge* pEdge);
    std::vector<GraphEdge*>& GetEdges();
    int GetIndex() const;
    void SetIndex(int iIndex);
protected:
    std::vector<GraphEdge*> m_edges;
    int m_iIndex;
};
```

Now, instead of keeping an explicit vector of neighbors, the vertices of the graphs keep a vector of edges from which the neighbors can be found. Note also the addition of an optional index into the parent graph's vector of vertices. Although we could exclude the index, it is very useful for debugging and other purposes, so we will leave it in for now.

With both our nodes and edges updated, it's obvious that our basic graph class needs an overhaul as well. But let's not mess around: it's time to put the real power of C++ behind our graphs, and that means incorporating what we've learned in previous chapters into a much-improved and considerably more-flexible class. A new graph class is presented in Listing 11.1, with detailed discussion to follow.

LISTING 11.1 Definition of Our Upgraded Graph Class

```
//————————————
// The Graph class
//————————————
template <class VERTEX, class EDGE>
class Graph
{
public:
    // Constructor
    Graph()
    {
        // Allocate some room for some vertices and edges
        m_verts.reserve(100);
        m_edges.reserve(100);
    }

    // Destructor
    virtual ~Graph()
    {
        // Destroy our vertices and edges
        std::vector<VERTEX*>::iterator vertIter;
        for (vertIter = m_verts.begin();
             vertIter != m_verts.end(); vertIter++)
            delete (*vertIter);

        std::vector<EDGE*>::iterator edgeIter;
        for (edgeIter = m_edges.begin();
             edgeIter != m_edges.end(); edgeIter++)
            delete (*edgeIter);

        m_verts.clear();
        m_edges.clear();
    }

    // Access to the graph contents
    VERTEX* GetVertex(int iIndex) {return m_verts[iIndex];}
    EDGE* GetEdge(int iIndex)     { return m_edges[iIndex];}

    // Add a new vertex to the graph
    void AddVertex(VERTEX* pVert)
    {
```

```
        pVert->SetIndex((int)(m_verts.size()));
        m_verts.push_back(pVert);
    }

    // Create an edge between the two vertices
    bool CreateEdge(VERTEX* pTail, VERTEX* pHead,
                    bool bTwoWay = true);


    // An efficient pathfinding algorithm
    float ComputeBestPath(VERTEX* pStart,
                          VERTEX* pGoal,
                          float (*fpCostFunc)(EDGE*),
                          std::vector<VERTEX*>& path );

protected:
    // Our basic contents
    std::vector<VERTEX*> m_verts;
    std::vector<EDGE*>   m_edges;

    // Pathfinding helper method
    void InitializePathSearch();
};

//————————————————-
// Implementation of CreateEdge()
//————————————————-
template <class VERTEX, class EDGE>
void Graph<VERTEX, EDGE>::CreateEdge(VERTEX* pTail, VERTEX*
                                      pHead, bool bTwoWay)
{
    // Create an edge from the first vertex to the second
    EDGE* pEdge = new EDGE;
    pEdge->SetTail(pTail);
    pEdge->SetHead(pHead);
    pTail->AddEdge(pEdge);

    // If the edge is marked as two way, then create a new
    // edge going the other direction
    if (bTwoWay)
    {
```

```
                    EDGE* pEdge2 = new EDGE;
                    pEdge2->SetTail(pHead);
                    pEdge2->SetHead(pTail);
                    pHead->AddEdge(pEdge2);
            }
    }
```

Now we will examine the source code in detail, covering every aspect of C++ features that are incorporated. First, we begin with the declaration of the class:

```
template <class VERTEX, class EDGE>
class Graph
{ …
```

By now you should be familiar with the template syntax, but if this is new to you, refer to Chapter 4, "Templates." Our upgraded `Graph` class is a templated class, which gives it the primary source of its power and flexibility. Note that the class operates on both a `VERTEX` type and an `EDGE` type, which allows us to generate custom graphs with a mix of structural interpretations.

Templatizing our graph also allows us to build graphs around classes that don't inherit from our own `GraphVertex` and `GraphEdge` classes—a very useful feature on projects for which you want to wrap graph-based functionality around existing classes you didn't write. For our purposes in this discussion, we will use the classes we defined earlier, so creating a graph to solve our pathfinding example is as simple as this:

```
// Create a graph for basic navigation purposes
Graph<NavigationNode, GraphEdge> graph;
```

Next we define the constructor for the graph class, which simply reserves some storage for the graph's vertices and edges. (Refer to Chapter 9, "Standard Template Library: Containers," for a discussion of vectors and their efficient use.)

```
// Constructor
Graph()
{
    // Allocate some room for some vertices and edges
    m_verts.reserve(100);
    m_edges.reserve(100);
}
```

After the constructor comes the destructor. The main purpose of the graph class destructor is to destroy the memory that was created to store the vertices and edges. Notice that each container is iterated across, with every element explicitly deleted. We can't just clear the vectors because the allocated memory stored within them would be lost. After the elements in each container have been properly deleted however, the vectors can be cleared; the graph has correctly returned all the memory it used to the system.

```
// Destructor
virtual ~Graph()
{
    // Destroy our vertices and edges
    std::vector<VERTEX*>::iterator vertIter;
    for (vertIter = m_verts.begin();
        vertIter != m_verts.end(); vertIter++)
        delete (*vertIter);

    std::vector<EDGE*>::iterator edgeIter;
    for (edgeIter = m_edges.begin();
        edgeIter != m_edges.end(); edgeIter++)
        delete (*edgeIter);

    m_verts.clear();
    m_edges.clear();
}
```

The Graph class interface also provides access to the graph contents—edges and vertices. This access allows code external to the graph to alter the structure. This read/write access is indicated by the lack of the const keyword in the declaration. If read-only access were desired, additional const accessors could be added as necessary.

```
// Access to the graph contents
VERTEX* GetVertex(int iIndex) { return m_verts[iIndex]; }
EDGE* GetEdge(int iIndex)     { return m_edges[iIndex]; }
```

Now things get a bit more interesting. The graph class interface includes a public method to add a vertex, as shown next. In addition to adding the vertex (which is assumed to have been created externally to the graph), the index of the vertex is set according to the number of existing vertices in the graph. As mentioned previously, this index is used for a variety of debugging purposes, although it isn't strictly necessary.

```
// Add a new vertex to the graph
void AddVertex(VERTEX* pVert)
{
    pVert->SetIndex((int)(m_verts.size()));
    m_verts.push_back(pVert);
}
```

Vertices are not very interesting without links to other vertices, so we also need the ability to explicitly create edges between vertices, as shown in the following fragment. Notice the optional parameter bTwoWay. By default, the edge is assumed to be bi-directional, as with edges in undirected graphs. Passing `false` to the method allows unidirectional edges. Of course, our graph allows a mix of both types using the same method:

```
// Create an edge between the two vertices
bool CreateEdge(VERTEX* pTail, VERTEX* pHead,
                bool bTwoWay = true);
```

Finally, the public interface provides our highly anticipated pathfinding method:

```
// An efficient pathfinding algorithm
float ComputeBestPath(VERTEX* pStart,
                      VERTEX* pGoal,
                      float (*fpCostFunc)(EDGE*),
                      std::vector<VERTEX*>& path );
```

There is quite a bit going on in this function declaration. The details are handled in the next section, but for now just notice that ComputeBest-Path() takes as its arguments the following:

- A *start* vertex, indicating the origin of the search
- A *goal* vertex, indicating the destination of the search
- A *cost* function, used to evaluate the cost of traveling a particular edge
- A *path container*, which holds the best path generated by the algorithm's completion

Our class declaration closes with the protected section, which simply declares the containers for storing vertices and edges, as well as an internal pathfinding utility method (discussed in the next section). Refer to Chapter 1, "Inheritance," if you are unfamiliar with the protected keyword and its implications.

```
protected:
    // Our basic contents
```

```
        std::vector<VERTEX*> m_verts;
        std::vector<EDGE*>   m_edges;

        // Pathfinding helper method
        void InitializePathSearch();
    };
```

A brief note about the public interface: a number of additional items were left out to simplify the discussion, which are normally present in a usable graph class. These include methods for removing vertices and edges as well as other utilities.

After the class declaration, we have the implementation of the `CreateEdge()` method. Notice again the use of templates in defining this method; don't allow yourself to get tripped up by the syntax in your own code.

```
template <class VERTEX, class EDGE>
void Graph<VERTEX, EDGE>::CreateEdge(VERTEX* pTail, VERTEX*
pHead, bool bTwoWay)
{
    // Create an edge from the first vertex to the second
    EDGE* pEdge = new EDGE;
    pEdge->SetTail(pTail);
    pEdge->SetHead(pHead);
    pTail->AddEdge(pEdge);

    // If the edge is marked as two way, then create a new
    // edge going the other direction
    if (bTwoWay)
    {
        EDGE* pEdge2 = new EDGE;
        pEdge2->SetTail(pHead);
        pEdge2->SetHead(pTail);
        pHead->AddEdge(pEdge2);
    }
}
```

The implementation of `CreateEdge()` is pretty simple. A new object of type EDGE is created, and its tail and head are set to the vertices that were passed in to the method with the assumption that the first vertex is the tail, and the second is the head. If the bTwoWay flag were set to false, this ordering would represent the direction of the edge. Otherwise the edge is bi-directional, and so the ordering doesn't really matter. By default, the edge is bi-directional, and so a new edge is created in the reverse direction (that is, from head to tail). As previously mentioned, it isn't strictly necessary to implement bidirectionality this way; you could instead simply use a single edge that is marked as "two way." However, by keeping the edges in each direction distinct, we set ourselves up for some powerful graph magic and manipulation, as discussed later.

11.4.3 Pathfinding Implementation

With the discussion of the class interface behind us, we can now focus on the real meat of the Graph class: the pathfinding algorithm. As before, we present the complete implementation, and then get into the detailed discussion. First, however, we need a slightly enhanced GraphVertex class that is ready for pathfinding:

```
class GraphVertex
{
public:

    // . . . Everything from before, and:

    // Cost used during path searching
    void SetPathSearchCost(float fCost);
    float GetPathSearchCost() const;

    // Predecessor used during the search
    void SetPredecessor(GraphVertex* pPred)
    GraphVertex* GetPredecessor() const

protected:
    //. . . Everything from before, and:
    float m_fPathSearchCost;
    GraphVertex* m_pPredecessor;
};
```

There are just two new things in our GraphVertex class: a path cost and a predecessor. (Both of these were explained in the example pathfinding problem in the land of Dor.) You might wonder why these new items need to be in the GraphVertex class when they aren't really part of the concept of a vertex. This is one of those times where the best solution isn't necessarily the most aesthetically pleasing. Instead of adding these members here, we could instead create a table for storing all vertex path costs, and another table for storing all vertex predecessors. But where would such tables go? We certainly don't want to pollute the global space, so that option is out. We could create these tables on the fly inside ComputeBestPath(), but that is a horrible waste of CPU cycles, as well as a potentially large source of memory fragmentation with all the constant dynamic-memory allocation.

Another option is to add these tables as members to the Graph class. In fact, this is a pretty good idea in general because it allows us to create the tables once per graph, avoiding the constant memory allocations. And it would provide a nice encapsulation. But is this the best place to encapsulate the tables? The Graph class is really not much better a home than the GraphVertex class because neither is necessarily closely associated with the specifics of pathfinding.

As will become clear in a moment, keeping the path cost and predecessor information in the GraphVertex class is a pretty clean solution. It encapsulates those items in the class that is most closely associated with that information. It also turns out to be the only reasonable way to cleanly provide access to the vertices in the manner required by the ComputeBestPath() method. Okay—enough disclaimers; it's time to get to the good stuff.

First up is the implementation of InitializePathSearch(). The purpose of this method is to prepare the vertices for the search, which it accomplishes by setting all the path costs to infinity (actually just a very large floating-point value), and by setting all the node predecessors to NULL:

```
template <class VERTEX, class EDGE>
void Graph<VERTEX, EDGE>::InitializePathSearch()
{
    std::vector<VERTEX*>::iterator iter;
    for (iter = m_verts.begin(); iter != m_verts.end();
    iter++)
    {
        (*iter)->SetPathSearchCost(FLT_MAX);
        (*iter)->SetPredecessor(NULL);
    }
}
```

And now at last we come to the pathfinding algorithm shown in Listing 11.2. Discussion follows afterwards.

LISTING 11.2 Definition of ComputeBestPath().

```
//————————————-
// Implementation of ComputeBestPath()
//————————————-
template <class VERTEX, class EDGE>
float Graph<VERTEX, EDGE>::ComputeBestPath(
    VERTEX* pStart,
    VERTEX* pGoal,
    float (*fpCostFunc)(EDGE*),
    std::vector<VERTEX*>& path )
{
    InitializePathSearch();
    priority_queue<VERTEX*, std::vector<VERTEX*>,
                    GraphVertexSearchCostComparer> fringe;

    pStart->SetPathSearchCost(0.f);

    VERTEX* pCurrentVertex = pStart;

    fringe.push(pStart);
    float fTotalCostToGoal = FLT_MAX;
    while (!fringe.empty())
    {
        std::vector<EDGE*>& edges = pCurrentVertex->GetEdges();
        std::vector<EDGE*>::iterator edgeIter;
        for (edgeIter = edges.begin();
             edgeIter != edges.end(); edgeIter++)
        {
            EDGE* pEdge = (*edgeIter);
            VERTEX* pNeighbor =
                        static_cast<VERTEX*>(pEdge->GetHead());

        // Don't consider the vertex we just came from
        if (pNeighbor == pCurrentVertex->GetPredecessor())
            continue;

        float fEdgeCost = fpCostFunc(pEdge);
        float fNewCostToThisVertex =
                pCurrentVertex->GetPathSearchCost() + fEdgeCost;
        float fCurrentCostToThisVertex =
                pNeighbor->GetPathSearchCost();
```

```
    if (fNewCostToThisVertex < fCurrentCostToThisVertex &&
        fNewCostToThisVertex < fTotalCostToGoal)
    {
        pNeighbor->SetPathSearchCost(fNewCostToThisVertex);
        pNeighbor->SetPredecessor(pCurrentVertex);

        if (pNeighbor == pGoal)
        {
            fTotalCostToGoal = fNewCostToThisVertex;
        }

        fringe.push(pNeighbor);
    }
}

    fringe.pop();
    if (!fringe.empty())
    {
        pCurrentVertex = fringe.top();
    }
}

// construct the path if we found one
if (fTotalCostToGoal < FLT_MAX)
{
    VERTEX* pPathVertex = pGoal;
    do
    {
        path.push_back(pPathVertex);
        pPathVertex =
            static_cast<VERTEX*>(pPathVertex-
            >GetPredecessor());
    } while (pPathVertex != pStart);
    path.push_back(pStart);
}
    return fTotalCostToGoal;
}
```

The ComputeBestPath() method takes four arguments, as indicated in
the parameter list:

```
template <class VERTEX, class EDGE>
float Graph<VERTEX, EDGE>::ComputeBestPath(
    VERTEX* pStart,
    VERTEX* pGoal,
    float (*fpCostFunc)(EDGE*),
    std::vector<VERTEX*>& path )
```

The role of the start and goal vertex arguments should be obvious by now. The third parameter may not be; it's a pointer to a function that takes an EDGE pointer and returns a float. This *cost function* is the key to determining shortest paths according to countless gameplay considerations. We could simply examine the value of the cost associated with an edge—the GraphEdge class does provide such a cost—but our templatized cost function provides infinitely more power; it allows us to construct our edge costs from any data we like, independent of that which is available in the edge. Before spelunking into the guts of ComputeBestPath(), let's take a look at a sample cost function that can be passed as a parameter:

```
// Cost function for GraphEdges and derived classes
float GetEdgeCost(GraphEdge* pEdge)
{
    NavigationNode* pTail =
                static_cast<NavigationNode*>(pEdge->GetTail());
    NavigationNode* pHead =
                static_cast<NavigationNode*>(pEdge->GetHead());
    const Vector2d& tailPos = pTail->GetPos();
    const Vector2d& headPos = pHead->GetPos();

    Vector2d diff = headPos;
    diff -= tailPos;
    return (diff.GetLength());
}
```

It turns out that this particular cost function isn't very interesting, but it is instructive. Given an edge, it computes the distance between the two navigation nodes that the edge connects, and returns the result as the cost. Notice that this function is specifically for the NavigationNode and GraphEdge classes we used to instantiate our templatized graph. This means that this function is useful only for those classes and their derivatives. However, this is appropriate because the point of the cost function is to provide customized logic applicable to particular types of graph elements.

That said, we certainly could create far more interesting cost functions. As long as they take a `GraphEdge` pointer as a parameter and return a `float`, these new functions can be swapped *dynamically* at runtime, even in the middle of the path search. And they could do just about anything, such as incorporating the more abstract types of cost mentioned previously in the "Edge Costs and Gameplay" section.

Returning to the `ComputeBestPath()` method, we see that the very first thing that is done is the initialization of the search. Immediately thereafter, a search queue is created using the STL priority queue:

```
priority_queue<VERTEX*, std::vector<VERTEX*>,
                GraphVertexSearchCostComparer> fringe;
```

The parameters to the queue specification are the type of object to be stored in the queue, the type of base container to be used to effect the queue, and the name of a class to be used for comparing items in the queue for sorting purposes. The first two of these parameters are fairly straightforward: we want to store `VERTEX` pointers, and we're happy to use a vector to do so. The third item might look a little nutty, so it deserves a bit of explanation.

As we saw in Chapter 10, "Standard Template Library: Algorithms and Advanced Topics," numerous algorithms (such as those used for sorting) accept a comparison function as an optional parameter. The same thing occurs here: the priority queue requires a comparison mechanism for determining the priorities of the objects it contains. Rather than providing a function, however, you can provide a small class that overloads the function-call operator. The priority queue, in making comparisons on the contained objects, uses the overloaded operator within the class as a "less-than" comparison function. Here's the implementation of the `GraphVertexSearchCostCompare` class:

```
class GraphVertexSearchCostComparer
{
    public:
    bool operator()(const GraphVertex* v1,
                    const GraphVertex* v2) const
    {
        return v1->GetPathSearchCost() >
        v2->GetPathSearchCost();
    }
};
```

Thankfully, this is a very small class, so it's easy to understand. The overloaded operator simply compares the path search cost of the two vertices, and returns true if the first is greater than the second. This is indeed what we want, because we want the priority queue to keep the lowest path cost vertex at the top of the queue, so that during the path search, the shortest known path is always examined first.

Note also that this comparison mechanism is another reason for putting the search cost in the vertices themselves. The operator accepts only objects of the type stored in the search queue, so it must operate on only those objects—or the global space, which we've already decided is undesirable.

Returning to the algorithm, we now have a search queue that stores explored vertices according to their lowest cost path from the start node. The next few lines from Listing 11.2 are shown here:

```
pStart->SetPathSearchCost(0.f);
VERTEX* pCurrentVertex = pStart;
fringe.push(pStart);
float fTotalCostToGoal = FLT_MAX;
```

The first line sets the path cost of the start node to 0 because we want to make sure the search never comes back through the start node (if it did, we'd be going in circles). The second line prepares the search by setting the start node as the current search node. The third line adds the start node to the queue; because the search operates on the contents of the queue, we need to seed this operation. The fourth line states that the cost to the goal is currently set to "infinity," which basically indicates that the goal hasn't been found yet.

The next line in Listing 11.2 is shown here:

```
while (!fringe.empty())
{ // etc.
```

This code starts the main loop of execution for the algorithm. As long as there is something in the queue, the algorithm continues to run. As a side note, the term *fringe* is often used in searches as a name for the set of nodes that haven't yet been explored but are known to exist and are subject to exploration. Thus, our queue contains the nodes that have been discovered by the search but haven't yet had their children examined.

Once inside the main loop, the algorithm starts to do the actual search:

```
std::vector<EDGE*>& edges = pCurrentVertex->GetEdges();
std::vector<EDGE*>::iterator edgeIter;
for (edgeIter = edges.begin();
     edgeIter != edges.end(); edgeIter++)
{
    EDGE* pEdge = (*edgeIter);
    VERTEX* pNeighbor =
              static_cast<VERTEX*>(pEdge->GetHead());

    // Don't consider the vertex we just came from
    if (pNeighbor == pCurrentVertex->GetPredecessor())
        continue;
```

This code sets up the iteration across the neighbors (children) of the current vertex. Before doing anything else, the neighbors are rejected if they happen to be the predecessor of the current node. Again, this arrangement prevents endless cyclical searches and causes the search to consider only those paths that continue toward the goal with as little cost as possible.

If the neighbor being examined isn't the predecessor, the algorithm then computes some costs:

```
float fEdgeCost = fpCostFunc(pEdge);
float fNewCostToThisVertex =
        pCurrentVertex->GetPathSearchCost() + fEdgeCost;
float fCurrentCostToThisVertex =
        pNeighbor->GetPathSearchCost();
```

The first cost is simply the cost of the edge between the current vertex and the neighbor. This is where the cost function comes into play. Next, the algorithm calculates the total cost of the path that has come from the current vertex to this neighbor. Finally, the current known path cost for the neighbor is gathered from the neighbor itself. Armed with this information, the algorithm can decide if any new nodes need to be added to the search queue:

```
if (fNewCostToThisVertex < fCurrentCostToThisVertex &&
    fNewCostToThisVertex < fTotalCostToGoal)
{
    pNeighbor->SetPathSearchCost(fNewCostToThisVertex);
    pNeighbor->SetPredecessor(pCurrentVertex);
```

```
if (pNeighbor == pGoal)
{
    fTotalCostToGoal = fNewCostToThisVertex;
}

fringe.push(pNeighbor);
}
```

All this logic does is see whether the path from the start node through the current node to the neighbor has a lower cost than any other path found so far to the neighbor. As an optimization, the current path cost for the neighbor is also compared against the current path cost for the goal node. Clearly, if the path to the neighbor is more costly than the cheapest known path to the goal node, then the neighbor doesn't need to be considered further.

If the costs are indeed lower, the neighbor's total path cost is updated. Also, the neighbor's predecessor is set to the current node. The algorithm then checks to see whether the neighbor happens to be the goal node and updates fTotalCostToGoal if it is.

After all the neighbors of the current node have been examined, the current node is removed from the search queue, and the next node in the queue becomes the current node:

```
fringe.pop();
if (!fringe.empty())
{
    pCurrentVertex = fringe.top();
}
```

Eventually, the outer while loop terminates, at which point either a best path from start to goal was found, or it was determined that no path was found. In the case of the latter result, the total cost to the goal is still infinity. Otherwise, we can use the predecessor information stored in the nodes to reconstruct the best path:

```
// construct the path if we found one
if (fTotalCostToGoal < FLT_MAX)
{
    VERTEX* pPathVertex = pGoal;
    do
    {
```

```
                    path.push_back(pPathVertex);
                    pPathVertex =
                        static_cast<VERTEX*>(pPathVertex
                        ->GetPredecessor());
                } while (pPathVertex != pStart);
                path.push_back(pStart);
            }
            return fTotalCostToGoal;
        }
```

Now that we've completed our examination of the pathfinding algorithm, let's take a quick look at an example of how to apply it to a graph. It's very, very easy. Assuming we've created our graph as before and have used the graph interface to add nodes and create edges, the following lines of code compute the best path from one node to another:

```
        std::vector<NavigationNode*> path;
        graph.ComputeBestPath(pStart, pGoal, GetEdgeCost, path);
```

The only item worth mentioning in this code snippet is the third parameter, which is simply the cost function we discussed earlier finally put to good use.

11.4.4 A Note About A* (Advanced)

Most readers familiar with pathfinding in games are probably wondering why there has been no mention of A*, the algorithm of choice for many game pathfinding needs. The answer is hopefully pretty clear: the intent of this chapter isn't really about teaching pathfinding. The algorithmic portion of the discussion has been kept simple so as to better serve the needs of beginners and veterans alike.

That said, the discussion on advanced graph representation brings to mind a point that should be made for those who do use A*: beware the breaking of the heuristic. A* relies on the *admissibility* of the search heuristic. In this case, the word *admissible* refers to a heuristic that does not overestimate the cost to the goal vertex. Most typical A* implementations rely on the basic straight-line distance heuristic, which is simply a measure of the distance from the current vertex to the goal vertex "as the crow flies," without regard to the actual topology of the graph.

A* works beautifully as long as the heuristic remains admissible. As soon as something happens to the heuristic that ruins its admissibility, however, the algorithm can become problematic or even completely use-less depending on how important true best-path determination is. So why would the heuristic ever stop being admissible if it was working to begin with? The most common reason is that the nature of the information stored in the graph has changed, possibly long after the A* algorithm was written.

This is a surprisingly common occurrence in games during the development cycle, and it usually happens as a result of extending the basic graph information to accommodate new design ideas *without revisiting the heuristic*. You wouldn't believe how often this happens, so let's take a look at an example.

Take another look at the map of Dor represented in Figure 11.2. Recall that the labels on the graph edges represent distances between the cities. If we use A* as our pathfinding algorithm and choose the usual straight-line distance heuristic, our pathfinding works perfectly. Now imagine that we've decided to encourage travel through Doldor, and have arbitrarily chosen to accomplish this by artificially decreasing the cost of all edges adjacent to Doldor to a measly 1.0, for gameplay reasons.

Congratulations! We've just broken A*. The reason is that the straight-line distance heuristic is no longer guaranteed to *not* overestimate the cost to the goal vertex. In fact, the way we've modified the costs, the true cost to get from Eldor to Aldor is now much less than the "cost" of that crow flying directly to Aldor. The problem is that we've changed the *nature* of the cost represented in the edges without reflecting that change in the heuristic. For A* to correctly work again, we have to make the heuristic operate on the same kinds of information that are represented by the edges costs.

It's probably pretty obvious that the situation in the preceding example is a problem; if you were the one writing the A* algorithm, you would most likely know if and when the nature of the edges changed and would be able to adjust the heuristic accordingly. The real problem comes when the nature of those edges is subject to change by others—particularly non-programmers who can add the kinds of sophistication mentioned earlier using data-driven tools that never require code changes.

The lesson to be learned is twofold:

1. Adding complexity to the structures on which A* operates requires communication between those who are responsible for the code and those who are responsible for the data that drives the pathfinding. In many cases, increases in the degree of abstraction of the information represented in a graph render heuristic-based searches problematic because it becomes very difficult to characterize the nature of the edge costs.

2. More importantly, as game programmers we must be careful about how we design systems that interface with information coming from external sources. C++ can be very seductive in the way it encourages sophisticated structures and mechanisms for operating on those structures. The more flexibility we give the users of the algorithms you write, the more likely you are to suffer subtle breakages that are hard to detect. Communication is the key to maintaining sanity in such an environment.

Readers not familiar with A*, but who are interested in pathfinding in a variety of domains, are encouraged to explore the resources listed at the end of this chapter.

11.5 GRAPHS: NOT JUST FOR PATHFINDING

So far, we have devoted a lot of time to graphs and their uses in pathfinding. This is in large part because pathfinding is by far the most common application of graphs in games; most readers are familiar with the concept, and so the examination of pathfinding makes for comfortable discussion.

In spite of that, this chapter is not really about pathfinding at all. It's about identifying structures and algorithms that match the problems we face as game programmers. In the case of graphs, you might have started to see other uses for them that are not so closely related to their familiar application to maps. But in case you haven't, the rest of this section shows how we can apply what we have learned so far to a broader range of problems.

Many of today's games have extensive user-interfaces in terms of the number of setup options and other items typically presented in a series of menus. Along with the sheer number of possible menus a player can visit, there are often different paths the user can take to get to the same menu. In a finished product, the menu system has usually been refined to the point that the UI is highly streamlined. Then again, we have witnessed plenty of games where such optimization has not occurred, and in these games, the UI is often a source of confusion and frustration.

The UI should never be an obstacle in a game. It's the first thing the player sees, and it's also something the player *must* return to constantly throughout his experience with the product. As game developers, we should endeavor to make the player's experience as enjoyable as possible—especially in the places where doing so is easy to accomplish. To that end, we should seek to use structures in the implementation of user interfaces that best fit the nature of the beast.

Most UI designs start on paper as an informal flowchart showing the transitions from one menu to another as well as the inputs required to effect those transitions. Figure 11.12 shows a typical early UI design. It should be apparent that a flowchart is a form of directed graph, with the nodes represented as menu screens and the edges representing the transitions between screens. Usually the UI moves from the concept phase of a flowchart into the implementation phase in which the UI is realized in code as a finite state machine (FSM). FSMs are also graphs, but are not very often implemented explicitly as such.

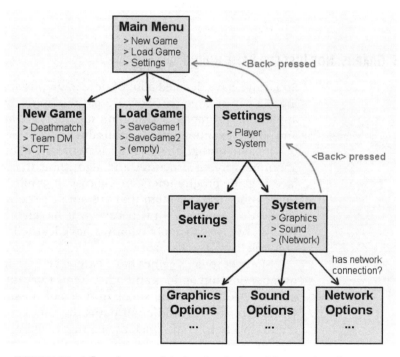

FIGURE 11.12   A flowchart used during the design of the user interface.

During the development phase of a project, it is almost certain that the UI design will change many times, usually by growing in size and complexity, but often by changes in transitions between screens. As deadlines loom and formal UI design is replaced by hurried on-the-spot changes in the code, it is very common for the UI to "break" in some way. Usually this means a screen that was previously able to return the user back to the Main Menu has somehow lost its link back up the chain.

There are numerous variations on this theme, all of which lead to unnecessary bugs and headaches for the team.

One very elegant solution to all of these problems is to implement the UI as a graph right from the beginning—or at least as an FSM that inherits from our graph classes. Doing so allows us to automate the detection of problems in the UI using the same algorithms and techniques we've already discussed. Let's take a brief look at the kinds of issues we can detect when the UI is implemented in a graph structure.

11.5.1 UI Path Optimization

Sometimes a UI is just plain cumbersome. Having to go through a dozen screens just to get the action is an unnecessary headache for the player. During development, it's very common for testers, designers, and everyone else who plays the game to discover and become numb to certain menu paths that take "too long" to get to a particular point in the UI.

Most well-designed interfaces do not suffer from this problem—at least not at the start of the project. But inevitably, the myriad rushed changes that cause UI "feature creep" when things get hectic often increase the length of the paths from startup to fun. If the underlying UI structure is maintained as a graph, we can use a searching algorithm such as *breadth-first search* (BFS) to automatically find input chains that are "too long." It's not difficult at all to set up a test script (see Chapter 14, "C++ and Scripting") that runs BFS on the UI graph starting at the Main Menu to determine how long it takes to get into the action under a variety of conditions. Similarly, the same test script can be run from every screen in the UI system to find long pathways that might be candidates for optimization. You might even be surprised to discover that a shorter path to the action (or some other goal screen) exists through a sequence of inputs you wouldn't expect.

You might be wondering about the nature of edge costs that would exist in our UI flow example, so let's consider the options. The most obvious metric for edge costs is simply the number of edges (that is, the transitions) along the path from one point in the UI to another. Clearly, a path from the Main Menu to a particular setup screen that has three intervening screens is "shorter" than a different path that has four screens. Or is it? This *edge-count* metric might be good enough, but there are other options, including these:

- **Wall-clock time.** A UI path that takes three screens to traverse could be much "longer" than a path that involves four screens if the three-screen path involves resource loading or other operations that subject the user to many seconds of system delays. Forcing the user to wait for a set of textures to load that are needed only for the screens the user is about to skip right over is never a good thing. Few people intentionally design the UI to work this way; but again, deadline-induced bugs always creep into every aspect of game development. Using a test script with the wall-clock time metric is one way to determine whether the UI just takes too long when the user proceeds down a certain path.

- **Input load.** Another very common frustration in game UIs occurs when the user is entering information on one screen, decides to go back a screen, and when he returns to the first screen discovers that all his input was wiped. Although you can blame the user, sometimes it isn't at all clear that the screen transition he's about to make is going to destroy his data. In any case, the point is that transitions (that is, edges) leading to or from a screen requiring a lot of data entry can be thought of as having a high cost in terms of the effort required by the user to get to the action.

11.5.2 Missing Return Paths

Another frustrating problem that arises in UI evolution is the loss of return paths to the Main Menu, the previous screen, or other locations the user should be able to get to easily from a given screen. Most of the time this is caused by an oversight in the implementation of the UI and not the design. In any case, bugs like these often make it into the final product because there are simply too many paths in the UI for developers to test every one.

The real point to make here is that manual testing of such things is just silly in the first place. With the UI implemented in a graph structure, you can use a searching algorithm to find the best path from a given screen to any other screen of interest to automatically determine the following for *every* screen in the UI:

- If the goal node is the previous screen, and the path cost from the current screen is something other than 1 (assuming use of the edge-count metric), then you know that there is not a way back to the previous screen.
- If the goal node is the Main Menu, and the path cost from the current screen is *greater* than the path cost from the Main Menu *to* this screen (that is, the path that got you here), then you know you haven't provided an efficient way back to the Main Menu. If you are struggling to think of an example of this, consider a situation in which the user is trying to back up the screen hierarchy to get to the Main Menu, and in doing so is forced to answer numerous "Are you sure?"

queries. Most likely the user is darn sure, by gosh. With each such query adding to the total length of the UI screen path, the potential for frustration increases, as does the opportunity for optimization.

11.5.3 Lost Menu Screens

Another common bug in UI development occurs when screens—or entire chains of screens—get completely "lost" Usually this temporary problem is discovered pretty quickly, but wouldn't it be nice to read the morning UI report and see it detected automatically? If we have a graph-based interface, it's a snap, and we have a few different options:

- The first thing we can do in our test script is to run BFS (or something similar) from the Main Menu (or any other screen chosen as the root node) in the UI graph to every other. (This is known as the *single-source shortest-path* problem.) If, for any destination screen, no path is found, then we know that the user cannot ever get to that screen.
- Another option is to use *depth-first search* (DFS) to determine the number of *connected components* in the UI graph. If the result is something other than 1, then we know we have a collection of screens that cannot be reached by some other collection of screens—something is broken.

11.6 CONCLUSION

In this chapter, we've used pathfinding to illustrate a typical problem encountered during the development of a game. By examining the nature of the problem, we were able to design our own structures and algorithms and construct a solution from those elements that can be efficiently implemented using many of the powerful features of C++.

We also looked at how we can transform the basic structures used to solve our core problem into more sophisticated and expressive structures that can be applied to a much wider range of related problems. In doing so, we empower ourselves to reuse code in unexpected ways, thereby reducing development time and automatically increasing the supported feature set for no additional cost.

This chapter focused almost entirely on graphs and a few of their applications in games. However, it is hoped that the reader will use the discussion as a starting point for learning more about the kinds of structures and algorithms that are useful during development. Although it isn't necessary to study algorithms and data structures in excruciating detail, a brief examination of the current literature on the topic reveals countless techniques that can ignite creative, effective problem solving—and allow you to write truly great code.

SUGGESTED READING

Several very good resources go into great depth on the topics we've touched on in this chapter. For a detailed look at graphs, including numerous useful algorithms and countless examples of real-world applications appropriate for games, the following text is highly recommended:

West, Douglas B., *Introduction to Graph Theory*. Prentice Hall, 2001.

The following Web ;site provides quite a bit of graph-related code you can use in your project:

The Boost Graph library. Available online at *http://www.boost.org/libs/graph/doc/*.

For a look at a precomputed method for representing pathfinding information, consider this article:

Dickheiser, Michael, "Inexpensive Precomputed Pathfinding Using a Navigation Set Hierarchy." *AI Game Programming Wisdom 2*. Charles River Media, 2003.

Finally, for a general (and very thorough) treatment of algorithms, the following texts can be invaluable:

Cormen, Thomas, et. al., *Introduction to Algorithms*, 2nd ed. The MIT Press, 2001.
Sedgewick, Robert, *Algorithms in C++*, 3rd ed. Addison-Wesley, 2002.

III

SPECIAL TECHNIQUES

There is more to putting a game together than writing some C++ code and making it run quickly. The way in which that code is put together can have important consequences for the rest of the project. Game development has some particular tasks that come up over and over in every game: creating objects, saving the state of the game, interfacing with the scripting system, writing plug-ins for tools, and so forth. Finding the most effective way of implementing each of those tasks can take many years of trial and error.

This last part of the book is intended to be a guide for specific techniques that have proven effective during the development of actual games. Often, more than one technique is presented in a chapter, along with a discussion of the merits of the different techniques. By studying these techniques, you can add them to your repertoire and use them appropriately in your project.

12

ABSTRACT INTERFACES

In This Chapter

- Abstract Interfaces
- General C++ Implementation
- Abstract Interfaces as a Barrier
- Abstract Interfaces as Class Characteristics
- All That Glitters Is Not . . .

*A*bstract interfaces are an extremely useful concept. They allow us to completely separate the implementation of a class from its interface. This suddenly opens the door for many possibilities previously out of our reach, such as swapping implementations at runtime, extending the behavior of our program after it ships, or allowing our classes to behave in different ways by implementing specific characteristics.

This chapter explains how abstract interfaces can be implemented in C++ and shows how to take advantage of them effectively in our games and tools. Chapter 13 , "Plug-Ins," presents a specific use of abstract interfaces: plug-ins.

12.1 ABSTRACT INTERFACES

The primary objective of a class is to represent a concept, encapsulating how it is implemented and sparing the irrelevant internal implementation details to its users. Ideally, only the interface describing the public functions for a class should be exposed outside of that class.

Unfortunately, C++ is not quite that clean. No doubt in part due to its C heritage, C++ exposes a lot more than just the public interface to the outside world. A C++ class is described in a header file, and any part of the program that uses that class also includes its header file. But a header file contains much more than just the class interface; it contains any other includes necessary for that header file to compile correctly, the declarations of all its protected and private functions, and the list of all its member variables, whether they are public or not. Granted, the compiler does not let any part of the program touch anything other than its public functions and member variables, but the information about implementation details can "leak" out into other parts of the program.

So why is this a big deal? Usually, this information leakage is not too much of a problem. After all, that is how C++ classes were designed from the start, and they are perfectly usable. However, sometimes we need better encapsulation. By increasing the decoupling between a class implementation and the code that uses it, we might be able to achieve any of the following things:

- We can change class implementations without having to modify any other code, just with a recompile and relink step. Imagine being able to select one of several different pathfinding implementations to test and measure, and determine which one is best for your current game, or try several spatial partitioning algorithms (octrees, quadtrees, BSP trees, and so on), just by swapping out class implementations.
- We can change class implementation at runtime. This could be particularly useful for selecting a rendering system at runtime that is based on the user's hardware or the rendering system selected from a menu.
- We can provide new implementations after the game has been released. Imagine shipping the game and then extending it by adding new units, new behaviors, or new game types, all as additional downloads. This is possible if the program is prepared to handle these extensions from the beginning. The same method can be applied to your tools (either internal or released with the game), which can be extended through plug-ins instead of being forced to release new executables (see Chapter 13 for detailed information).

An abstract interface is a particular type of organization that separates the interface and the implementation parts of a C++ class. It allows us to achieve any of the previously mentioned goals by being a little careful with how things are organized.

In addition to those specific goals, decoupling the game code from the objects it manipulates is a worthwhile goal in itself. Doing so creates cleaner, easier-to-maintain code than if objects were referenced directly. Decoupling also provides cleaner division lines between different parts of the code, which allows several programmers in the same team to work more easily together at the same time on the same code. Without that decoupling, programmers could more often be stepping on each other's toes and interfering with each other's work.

Abstract interfaces are not a new concept or a concept applied only to game development; it is a useful general programming technique. Some companies have created APIs based around the concept of abstract interfaces and even provided their own standardized abstract interface functions and macros. Microsoft's COM is one such API that relies heavily on the use of abstract interfaces. As a matter of fact, COM can do all the things we are going to develop ourselves in this chapter.

Why take the time to write our own abstract interfaces when we can just use COM? Mainly because most of the time we want the basics without any of the extra baggage. We are probably not going to be doing any remote process invocation or any of the advanced features that COM (and some of its successors, like COM+) provides. Also, abstract interfaces are such a simple concept that it is worth learning about them in isolation first. If we later realize we would rather use COM, we will have a much better understanding of how to use it effectively. Finally, a major blow against using COM is that it is platform-dependent. Nowadays, there is no single platform dominating the game market. PCs are a small part of the game market, which is currently dominated by consoles. And even among consoles, there are several totally different platforms. By creating our own platform-independent version of abstract interfaces, we can easily reuse our code on any platform we choose as long as we have a C++ compiler.

12.2 GENERAL C++ IMPLEMENTATION

An abstract interface in C++ is a class that has only pure virtual functions—no implementation, no member variables, nothing else. Recall that pure virtual functions are marked with an =0 at the end of their declaration, and that they indicate that a derived class must provide an implementation to be able to create any objects of that class. A simple abstract interface class looks like this:

```
// IAbstractInterfaceA.h
class IAbstractInterfaceA
{
public:
    virtual ~IAbstractInterface() {};
    virtual void SomeFunction() = 0;
    virtual bool IsDone() = 0;
};
```

This abstract interface does not even have a corresponding .cpp file because it has no implementation of any kind; it is simply a description of the interface. Notice that the class name was prefixed by the letter I to indicate it is an abstract interface. It is by no means necessary to use the prefix, but it is a convenient notation to remind us that the class we are dealing with is an abstract interface. To create an implementation based on that interface, we would inherit from it and provide an implementation for all its functions.

```
// MyImplementation.h
class MyImplementation : public IAbstractInterfaceA
{
public:
    virtual void SomeFunction();
    virtual bool IsDone();
};
```

Notice that the functions are not pure virtual anymore. That is because we are about to provide an implementation for them in the .cpp file:

```
// MyImplementation.cpp

void MyImplementation::SomeFunction()
{
    // ...
}

bool MyImplementation::IsDone()
{
    // ...
    return true;
}
```

Now anybody can select this class and use it in the rest of the program without worrying about what specific implementation they are using.

```
IAbstractInterfaceA * pInterface = new MyImplementation;
//...
pInterface->SomeFunction();
if (pInterface->IsDone()) // etc ...
```

This is just a general case, and so far it does not look all that useful. It almost looks like an extra layer of indirection for no reason, making our program less clear and harder to maintain. But we can put that indirection to good use, and then it will pay off. Let's look closely at some particular uses of abstract interfaces and how we can use them effectively in games. As with a lot of things, the details are the hardest part, so we describe the exact implementation and figure out how to solve a few tricky problems along the way.

12.3 ABSTRACT INTERFACES AS A BARRIER

The first, most straightforward use of abstract interfaces is simply to act as an insulation layer between the class implementation and the rest of the program. Let's look at an example.

We will create the layout for a graphics renderer. There will be two types of graphics renderers: OpenGL and Direct3D. Clearly, the graphics renderer can be extended to have any other types, depending on your platform and your program needs. Our goal is to make it so the program that uses the renderer does not have to know which one is being used and can run with either type without any modifications. In addition, we also want to be able to switch renderers at runtime.

This is a perfect application for an abstract interface. Here is the C++ source code for a possible interface for the graphics renderer:

```
// GraphicsRenderer.h
// This is the abstract interface class
class IGraphicsRenderer
{
public:
    virtual ~IGraphicsRenderer() {};
    virtual void SetWorldMatrix(const Matrix4d & mat) = 0;
    virtual void RenderMesh(const Mesh & mes) = 0;
    // ...
};
```

Those are just two representative functions. In a real situation, we would need to decide what other functions the renderer would expose in order to deal with materials, render states, shaders, lights, and so forth. Now we can provide two bare-bones implementations based on that interface: one for Direct3D (D3D) and one for OpenGL.

```
// GraphicsRendererOGL.h
#include "GraphicsRenderer.h"
#include <gl.h>
class GraphicsRendererOGL : public IGraphicsRenderer
```

```
{
public:
    virtual void SetWorldMatrix(const Matrix4d & mat);
    virtual void RenderMesh(const Mesh & mes);
    // ...
}

// GraphicsRendererD3D.h
#include "GraphicsRenderer.h"
#include <d3d.h>
class GraphicsRendererD3D : public IGraphicsRenderer
{
public:
    virtual void SetWorldMatrix(const Matrix4d & mat);
    virtual void RenderMesh(const Mesh & mes);
    // ...
}
```

The corresponding .cpp files provide the implementation for each of the functions in the abstract interface. As long as the rest of the program works only with the graphics renderer through an `IGraphicsRenderer` pointer, changing implementations is easy. We just need to create the type of renderer we want and pass a pointer to it for the program to use.

```
IGraphicsRenderer * g_pRenderer = new GraphicsRendererOGL();
// ...

// Now we don't care which renderer we're using.
g_pRenderer->SetWorldMatrix(ObjectToWorld);
g_pRenderer->RenderMesh(mesh);
```

There is nothing stopping us from changing the type of renderer at runtime either; we just create a new object and tell the system to use it instead of the old one. The only difficult part is in doing the necessary adjustments in the renderer itself to maintain the selected preferences, such as video mode, textures, and geometry. But from the abstract interface point of view, the operation is simple.

12.3.1 Headers and Factories

There is one extra beneficial side effect of the way we have organized the renderer. Notice that both `GraphicsRendererOGL.h` and `GraphicsRendererD3D.h` include one (and possibly more) platform-specific header file. This is needed because the header files of the specific implementations are filled with details about how they are implemented. They probably contain structures, enums, and macros that are specific for OpenGL or Direct3D, so the header files must be included.

If the graphics renderer had not been designed with an abstract interface, the program would be using the OpenGL or the Direct3D renderer directly, which means the rest of the program would be forced to include the platform-specific header files for each renderer. This is not necessarily a bad thing, but it has a few drawbacks:

- Those header files are usually not small. They can include other header files that in turn and have a lot of structures, classes, or macros. If every file that uses the renderer is forced to include that chain of header files, compile times are significantly degraded. An abstract interface provides both a cleaner design from a programming point of view and faster compile times. It is one of those win-win situations.
- If you are using a compiler with precompiled header support or some other way of including many header files only once, the compile times are further reduced. Unfortunately, that approach makes the next drawback even worse.
- Any code that includes the platform-specific renderer files has access to any of its contents. This fact makes it easy for unrelated parts of our program to become dependent on OpenGL or Direct3D, and we will not realize it until we try to switch to a different platform. At this point, it could cost us a lot of time and grief, and possibly a missed deadline. It can start as an innocent use of a macro that happens to be defined in `d3d.h`, then the use of a `typedef`, then calling a helper function to set up a matrix, and so on. Before we know it, our code is totally locked into one particular platform without us realizing it because we are not explicitly including the Direct3D header file in our program.

This situation is explored in more detail in Chapter 18, "Dealing with Large Projects," which deals with the physical structure of a project. However, some part of the code needs to include the implementation header files so that the code can create those objects and pass them to the rest of the program. We can restrict the header files to just one .cpp file, so it is usually not a problem.

We can take it a step further and encapsulate the implementations even more by using a *factory*. A factory is a very simple design pattern that allows the creation of related objects. In our case, it allows us to create any of the different implementations for the renderer without even needing the implementation header files.

The following code shows how the renderer can be created through our factory class. Notice that we are not dealing directly with the specific class implementations `GraphicsRendererOGL` and `GraphicsRendererD3D`, but rather we are just asking for them by name from the factory function.

```
GraphicsRendererFactory factory;
IGraphicsRenderer * g_pRenderer;

// This creates an OpenGL renderer
g_pRenderer = factory.CreateRenderer("OpenGL");

// This creates a Direct3D renderer
g_pRenderer = factory.CreateRenderer("Direct3D");
```

The actual implementation of the factory is straightforward: it checks the name that is passed to its `CreateRenderer()` function and does a `new` in the correct implementation of the renderer. Now only the factory class has to include the implementation header files for each of the renderers. The rest of the code does not need to know they even exist.

We have now totally separated the implementation from the interface. As you can imagine, such a clean break is a perfect boundary for separating that code into another library (static or dynamic). The only thing the library exposes is the abstract interface and the factory to create new implementations. Everything else can remain well hidden underneath.

12.3.2 Real-World Details

There are a few more interesting C++ implementation details worth mentioning. These are not details dealing with the concept of abstract interfaces, but purely with how they are implemented in C++ in the most effective way.

The first one is that all functions in the abstract interface are virtual. Clearly, we want to call the functions of the derived classes through a pointer to the abstract interface, which is the whole point. So we must declare all functions in the abstract interface as virtual.

In addition to being virtual, the functions are pure virtual (indicated by the =0 next to the function declaration). This means that the compiler will not let us create an object of that type until somebody has provided an implementation for that function. It is not necessary to declare them as pure virtual, but it certainly is a good reminder to implement all the functions required by the interface.

You might have noticed the appearance of the virtual destructor in the previous example, even though we did not make any comment about it. Now, did you notice something a bit strange about that destructor? For those of you who missed it, here is the destructor in the abstract interface again:

```
class IGraphicsRenderer
{
public:
    virtual ~IGraphicsRenderer() {};
    //...
};
```

The first thing to observe is that the abstract interface itself has the declaration for a destructor. And not only that, but it is a virtual destructor. The reason for making the destructor virtual is the same as for making all its other functions virtual: at some point, the program is most likely going to delete the object pointed to by the abstract interface pointer. If the destructor were not virtual, it would call the destructor for the abstract interface and leave it at that. None of the destructors of the derived classes would ever be called. By making it virtual, we ensure that we call the destructor for the specific implementation we are using.

The other interesting point is that the destructor, unlike the rest of the functions, is not pure virtual. As a matter of fact, the two curly brackets to the right of the destructor are an inline empty function body. So we are providing an empty implementation for the destructor. This has to do with keeping the compiler happy. Without it, the compiler complains about linker errors because destructors work slightly differently than normal functions.

We could have made the destructor pure virtual and provided an implementation for it like this:

```
virtual ~IGraphicsRenderer() = 0 {};
```

Or we could have made it pure virtual and hidden the empty function body in a .cpp file. All those things are functionally equivalent, but with the drawback that we force all derived classes to provide a destructor. Some of them might want to do that anyway, but some of them might not, so it is a better solution to not make it pure virtual and let the derived classes decide for themselves whether or not they need a destructor.

Finally, one question comes up often while working with this type of abstract interface. Can an abstract interface provide some partial implementation? At first this might seem an odd idea. Why would we want to provide partial implementation? After all, the whole point of an abstract interface is to separate the interface and the implementation. Unfortunately, in practice, things are not quite so clear-cut. Sometimes we want to create many different implementations of an abstract interface, but with all of them implementing a few functions in the exact same way. It would be very convenient if the abstract interface could implement them directly.

The short answer is that it is acceptable to do that in a few cases. If it is just one simple function, then it is probably fine. It is probably still a good idea to label that function as pure virtual because doing so forces the derived class to explicitly call the parent implementation and avoid some of the multiple-inheritance ambiguity.

As things get more complicated, and we want to have many different functions implemented in the interface, we need to back off and reconsider our design. The more implemented functions we add to the abstract interface, the less it becomes an abstract interface. Many of the problems we were hoping to solve come back: tighter coupling, header files leaking into the rest of the program, and so forth. A better solution is to keep the pure abstract interface, create one class that derived from it that provides all the common functionality, and then create the rest of the specific implementations deriving from that intermediate class (see Figure 12.1).

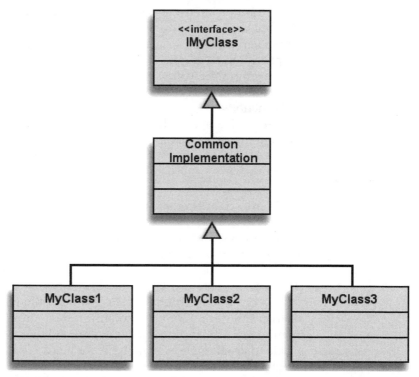

FIGURE 12.1   Providing a common implementation to many classes derived from an abstract interface.

12.4 Abstract Interfaces as Class Characteristics

In the previous section, we saw how an abstract interface could be used to totally separate interface and implementation, and allow us to switch implementations with ease. In this section, we look at a different aspect of abstract interfaces. Here we are not concerned with switching implementations, but with hiding the identity of an object behind abstract interfaces so the same code can manipulate objects of any class, even of a class that did not exist when the game shipped.

The general idea is simple: our program is not hardwired to use any objects of a specific class. Instead, every time we need to perform an operation on an object, we ask that object if it has an implementation that matches what we want to do; if so, we call the appropriate functions.

For example, consider the situation where we want to render all the objects in the world. Not all objects are renderable; some of them have purely logic functions, such as switches, counters, or flags. Using abstract interfaces, we could go through every object in the world, ask it whether it is renderable or not, and if it is, call its render function. This sounds very simple, but again, the details will be a bit tricky. (Incidentally, there are much more efficient ways of rendering the scene than checking every single object in the world, so do not take this as an example of a good architecture. We are using it as an example purely for simplicity.)

12.4.1 Implementations

Let's quickly review how we would implement the preceding render-the-objects-in-the-world example without abstract interfaces.

12.4.1.1 Hardwired Types

The first option is to hardwire the object type in the calling code and traverse all the objects in the world, checking each object for its type. Whenever we find an object of a type that we know we want to render, we call its render function. However, this approach is exactly what we are trying to avoid because it is hardwired to specific object types.

```
// Pseudo code of a render function using hardwired
// object types
void RenderWorld ()
{
    for (each object in the world)
    {
        if (object is enemy ||
            object is environment object ||
```

```
                         object is effect ||
                         object is terrain ||
                         object is sky ||
                         //... etc )
                {
                         object.Render();
                }
        }
    }
```

This approach works, but as you can see from the source code snippet, it is clumsy, error prone, and not very maintainable. Whenever we add a new object type, we must remember to also change the function that checks whether something should be rendered and add it there, not to mention all the other functions throughout the program that use the same logic to do other types of processing, such as AI, collision, and physics. It basically makes it impossible to add a new object type without changing the whole program.

12.4.1.2 Leave It Up to the Object

A better approach is to let the object itself decide whether it should be rendered. We can do that just as easily without abstract interfaces. All the object has to do is implement a function that returns a Boolean indicating whether or not it should be rendered. Then in our pass through all the game objects, we call that function and render it or not based on the result.

```
// Pseudo code of a render function asking each object
void RenderWorld ( void )
{
    for (each object in the world)
    {
        if (object.IsRenderable)
            object.Render();
    }
}
```

Clearly, this is a much neater solution than our previous one. It is still not perfect, though. The main drawback is that every object has to implement the IsRenderable() function along with all the functions that are called to render it if needed (in this case, just Render()). In itself, this approach is not a big deal, but as more characteristics like this one are added, the more functions all objects have to support, even though those functions are often empty and meaningless for a particular class because not every class needs every function. Imagine if we start adding similar functions for collision, manipulation, or movement. All the classes will be quickly cluttered up with useless functions.

Even worse, imagine that after we have dozens, maybe hundreds, of different types of objects, we decide to add one more type of characteristic, such as whether or not the object makes sounds. Now we need to modify all our existing objects and create a new function that returns whether or not it should play sounds. Certainly, this update will be easier if all the game objects inherit from a common root, but things are not always that way (or we might want only half of them to return false and the other half to return true). There is no clean way to do that with this approach.

12.4.1.3 Abstract Interfaces

An even better solution is one that allows us to implement and declare only the functions used by a particular class. That is one of the things that abstract interfaces and inheritance allow us to do. The pseudocode for the rendering function using abstract interfaces looks like this:

```
// Pseudo code of a render function using abstract
// interfaces
void RenderWorld ( void )
{
    for (each object in the world)
    {
        if (object implements Renderable interface)
        {
            IRenderable * pRend;
            pRend = object.GetInterface(IRenderable);
            pRend->Render();
        }
    }
}
```

An object that does not implement a particular interface does not need to do anything about it. As a matter of fact, it does not even need to be aware that a rendering interface exists, which is good, because it means we can extend things more easily later on.

Notice also that an object is not limited to implementing just one abstract interface. We could create a new object that implements as many abstract interfaces as we want; it just needs to inherit from each of them and implement the correct functions. Because we are inheriting from abstract interfaces, most of the potential problems of multiple inheritance are not an issue anymore. This is arguably one of the best uses of multiple inheritance in C++. Here is how an actual class that implements the `IRenderable` interface might look:

```
class IRenderable
{
public:
    bool Render() = 0;
    // ...
};

class GameEntityPhysical : public GameEntity,
                           public IRenderable
{
public:
    bool Render();
    // ...
};
```

12.4.2 Query Interface

So far, we have glossed over one major detail: how can we tell if an object implements a particular interface? One possible answer is to use `dynamic_cast`, as we did in Chapter 2, "Multiple Inheritance," to find out whether an object inherits from a particular class, and if so, to get the correct pointer to that parent class. The `dynamic_cast` works fine as long as we are willing to have runtime type information turned on in the compiler options. That is not always desirable because many times we would rather replace the standard RTTI with our own system to have better control over the memory used and the performance of the queries.

In that case, instead of relying on RTTI being enabled, it makes sense to provide a special function to determine whether objects inherit from a particular abstract interface. (This function will be different from the default custom RTTI system described in Chapter 15, "Runtime Type Information.") We are trying to do two things here. The first one we have already discussed: the function has to tell us whether an object implements a particular abstract interface. The second goal is a bit more subtle: the function has to return a pointer to the object, but the pointer must be of the type of the abstract interface.

As you might recall from our discussion on multiple inheritance in Chapter 2, an object that uses multiple inheritance has several vtables merged into one; correctly casting from one type to another requires changing the original pointer by some offset. The calling code cannot cast the pointer correctly because it does not know the type of the referenced object, so it is up to the object itself to deal with the casting. A very convenient place for doing the casting is in the same function that checks whether an interface is available.

Here is a very simple implementation of that function. It is called `QueryInterface()` because it answers the question of whether or not a particular interface is implemented by an object. If the interface is present, it returns a correctly cast pointer to that interface; otherwise it returns NULL.

```
void * GameEntityPhysical::QueryInterface(Interface
    interface) const
{
    if (interface == IRENDERABLE)
    {
        IRenderable * pRender =
        static_cast<IRenderable*>(this);
        return (void *)(pRender);
    }
    return NULL;
}
```

Notice that we first cast the `this` pointer to the type of pointer we want, and then we return it as a plain `void` pointer. Even though it looks like an unnecessary step, that casting most likely changes the actual value of the pointer. Without it, the returned value could not be safely cast to the correct interface type.

Clearly, every class that inherits from an abstract interface must implement this `QueryInterface()` function. The function must also be called by the program independently of what class it is, so it is usually best to put that function in a parent class, even if that is the only member function available.

This function also assumes that somewhere there is a list of unique identifiers for each interface. In this example, the unique identifier was `IRENDERABLE`. It is possible to use strings instead of unique numbers, but this results in poor performance at runtime, and `QueryInterface()` could end up getting called many hundreds or thousands of times per frame.

For most purposes in our own programs, a simple list of sequential numbers is plenty. If we want to let other people extend our system and add new interfaces, a method for guaranteeing the uniqueness of interface identifiers is required. Microsoft's COM system uses a system very much like this, as well as a method using unique identifiers.

If we find ourselves creating many `QueryInterface()` functions, we could easily wrap all the functionality in a few macros to make it easier to add it to new classes. When using those macros, creating a new `QueryInterface()` function is simple:

```
QUERYINTERFACE_BEGIN
    QUERYINTERFACE_ADD(IRENDERABLE,IRenderable)
QUERYINTERFACE_END
```

Adding more interfaces just requires inserting several `QUERYINTERFACE_ADD` macros after the first one. This is how the rendering function from the previous examples would use `QueryInterface()`:

```
// Render function using QueryInterface
void RenderWorld ()
{
    for (each object in the world)
    {
        void * pInterface;
        pInterface = object.QueryInterface(IRENDERABLE);
        if (pInterface != NULL)
        {
            IRenderable * pRend;
            pRend = static_cast<IRenderable*>(pInterface);
            pRend->Render();
        }
    }
}
```

12.4.3 Extending the Game

One of our goals at the beginning of this chapter was to extend the game after it has shipped. How exactly do we apply abstract interfaces to accomplish that?

The first thing we have to realize is that we might not need to change the code at all. A lot of the additions to a game after it has shipped can be done solely by adding new data files. If the game has been architected so it is mostly data driven, it should be possible to do many new things by just providing new data files: new levels, new game types, new characters, or new special powers. If you had planned on user extensibility of your game, users will have an easier time creating new content for your game if they can just add new data with the provided tools, rather than having to write C++ code.

If it becomes necessary to release new code along with the new data, sometimes the executable itself can be replaced or patched. That updated executable can be compiled with the latest classes, so using abstract interfaces for this purpose is not an absolute necessity. It does still have its share of benefits from a development point of view, simply by decoupling the game code as much as possible from the objects it manipulates.

A different approach is to release new functionality in the form of new components for the game, possibly along with new data, but no updated executable. This approach is particularly appropriate if you are making a lot of different bits of content available, and you expect the players to download only the ones in which they are interested. For example, in a tycoon-style game, you could provide hundreds of different new game units for download, each of them with some data (new graphics, animations, and sounds), along with some new code that is hidden behind abstract interfaces. The original executable can deal with these new objects as if they had been part of the original set of objects that shipped with the game.

The game normally creates game objects through a game object factory. It passes the game object type, and the function returns a game entity of the correct type:

```
GameObjecType objType = LoadObjectType();
GameEntity * pEntity = factory.CreateObject(objType);
```

The factory knows about the different object types and the classes that should be instantiated in each case. It looks something like the following:

```
GameEntity * GameObjectFactory::CreateObject(
                              GameObjectType type)
{
    switch (type)
    {
    case GAMEOBJECT_CAMERA:     return new GameCamera;
    case GAMEOBJECT_ENEMY:      return new GameEnemy;
    case GAMEOBJECT_TERRAIN:    return new GameTerrain;
    case GAMEOBJECT_PROJECTILE: return new GameProjectile;
    }
    return NULL;
}
```

The key to extending the game after shipping is to avoid having those object types hardwired in the game object factory. Instead, the factory can be extensible: it does not know anything about game object types and classes at first, and other parts of the code must register an association between a particular object type and a class to create.

Whenever the game detects any new components (Chapter 13 delves into more detail about plug-ins), those components are loaded and initialized. The first thing they do as they are initialized is to register any new game object types with the new classes that the component provides. Now, as the game attempts to load a new level that uses some of the new game objects, the factory creates them correctly, and the rest of the game treats them like any other object through their abstract interfaces.

12.5 ALL THAT GLITTERS IS NOT . . .

So far, this chapter has been expounding on the benefits of using abstract interfaces. Chapter 13 continues that trend by delving into another abstract interface application: plug-ins. However, abstract interfaces are not the be-all and end-all solution for every problem. Even though they increase decoupling between the implementation and the code that uses it—which is always something we aspire to do in our programs—they have their own set of problems. It is just as important to know when to avoid abstract interfaces as when to use them.

The first and foremost problem is the added complexity. If an abstract interface is not needed, all it does is add another layer of complexity. It makes the program more difficult to understand, maintain, and change in the future. In programming, usually the simplest approach that does everything we want is the best solution.

The second problem is closely related to the first one: code that uses abstract interfaces is more difficult to debug. If we break into the debugger while the program is running and attempt to view the elements of an object pointed to by an abstract interface pointer, chances are its contents will be empty. The debugger cannot show anything there because an abstract interface has no implementation. To see its contents, we must cast the pointer by hand to its correct type (assuming we know the object type to which it points).

The final drawback of abstract interfaces is performance. Remember that every function present in an abstract interface, by the nature of an interface, must be declared virtual. This means there will be a slight performance penalty for calling it (which is not very important), plus it can never be inlined. (This is of much greater importance for a tiny function.

Refer to Chapter 1, "Inheritance," and Chapter 6, "Performance," for the performance implications of virtual functions.)

The consequences of the last problem is that abstract interfaces must be placed carefully. The most important aspect to consider is whether it makes logical sense where the abstract interface is laid out. Then we must consider the performance implications. If the abstract interface is located at too low a level, then it will be called many times per frame, resulting in performance degradation. By moving it to a slightly higher level, we can dramatically reduce the number of calls to the interface and have no impact in the overall performance.

To continue with the example of the renderer, a bad design would be to have the abstract interface deal with individual polygons. Many hundreds of thousands of polygons—maybe even millions—are rendered every frame. Paying that extra cost every single time a polygon is rendered is wasteful. Instead, the renderer can deal with geometry at a higher level, such as meshes, and a whole group of polygons can be rendered at once with only one call to the abstract interface.

12.6 CONCLUSION

In this chapter, we have seen the concept of an abstract interface and what some of its uses are. We first learned how to create an abstract interface in C++, using a class without implementation and pure virtual functions. Specific implementations of the abstract interface inherit from the interface and provide their own implementation.

Then we saw how an abstract interface can be used as a barrier to isolate the implementation from the code that uses the interface. Doing so allows us to switch implementations on the fly much more easily, and it also provides some extra encapsulation that results in fewer physical dependencies between files.

Next we looked at abstract interfaces as characteristics a class can implement and how we can create code that does not rely on specific class types. Instead, that code checks for implemented abstract interfaces and works on them if they are found. This is the basis for being able to create new class types after the game ships without having to release a new executable.

Finally, we had a look at some of the drawbacks of abstract interfaces, and under what circumstances it is better to avoid them, or at least to be cautious with them.

SUGGESTED READING

Here is a good introduction to the concept of abstract interfaces:

Llopis, Noel, "Programming with Abstract Interfaces." *Game Programming Gems 2*. Charles River Media, 2001.

This very enlightening read on the internals of COM takes a progressive approach and develops the COM API from scratch, showing the reasoning at each step:

Rogerson, Dale, *Inside COM*. Microsoft Press, 1997.

The following book takes a detailed look at the status of component software, which is the whole idea behind writing a program as independent parts that are tied together through the use of abstract interfaces or other similar mechanisms:

Szyperski, Clemens, *Component Software: Beyond Object-Oriented Programming*. Addison-Wesley, 1999.

This excellent book covers the factory pattern, among many other fundamental patterns:

Gamma, Erich, et al., *Design Patterns*. Addison-Wesley, 1995.

PLUG-INS

In This Chapter

- The Need for Plug-Ins
- Plug-In Architecture
- Putting It All Together
- Plug-Ins in the Real World

This chapter explains the concept of *plug-ins* and how we can architect our programs to use them. You might choose to design some of your own tools so they can be extended through plug-ins, or maybe you want to simply write plug-ins for some of the popular modeling and texturing packages used in game development. In either case, this chapter gives you a firm understanding of how plug-ins are implemented and how a program should be structured to use them.

13.1 THE NEED FOR PLUG-INS

Complex tools are more than one-shot deals. People want to extend those tools, customize them, or add new functionality to fit their needs. However, putting every single possible bit of functionality in the tool is quite impossible, and it is also a bad idea. The program would quickly degenerate into an unmaintainable mess caused by the thousands of different options, not to mention that it would balloon in size and features, and become a fine piece of bloatware that nobody wants to use.

A much more flexible approach is to use plug-ins. The program provides all the core functionality, everything that most users want. The rest of the functionality can be provided through extensions, or plug-ins. The users can choose the plug-ins they want and which ones they would rather not even load. Also, by allowing a tool to be extended this way and making a small API public, users or third-party companies can create their own plug-ins to take the tool exactly where they want it to go. Sometimes we find ourselves writing plug-ins for other people's programs, and sometimes we architect our code so other people can modify our tools.

13.1.1 Plug-Ins for Other Programs

The artists at your company are very excited. They have just received Version 13.75 of their favorite modeling package. Shivering with anticipation, they install it and fire it up. It is an instant hit; it is exactly what they had been waiting for. It has countless exciting features that do everything an artist could ever want. Wait, no, it does not have *that* feature. "But we really needed *that* feature for our game! There is no way we will be able to create all the content in time without *that* feature!" the artists clamor. Fortunately, not all is lost. There are always alternatives.

One possibility is to use a different modeling program that has all the features they want. Does such a program exist? Probably not. Another option is to use several modeling programs. Hopefully, between all of them, the desired features are covered. This is quite likely, but what about cost? Modeling programs are not cheap. And what about interoperability? Can we save and load models from all of them? Then there's the question of expertise. Will the artists be able to use all the tools efficiently?

A third option is to write a tool from scratch. The tool could replace the modeling program, although it is highly unlikely we would be able to come up with a substitute for a thirteenth-generation modeling program created by a team of hundreds of people. Maybe our tool could just complement it. The artists can save their models on the full-featured modeling tool, load them in our little tool, and apply the extra features they wanted. Switching back and forth is a bit cumbersome, but it would probably work. The main issue is whether or not the artists can go back to their modeling program and continue working on their models after they have been processed by our tool. It is not always easy to make data go both ways. Will the information from our tool be overridden whenever the model is saved again in the original modeling package?

One last possibility is to extend the existing program. This option is ideal. The feature the artists want is pretty minor, so if we could only extend the modeling program, we would have the perfect solution. If it uses a plug-in architecture, we are in luck. It is probably just a matter of implementing a couple of abstract interfaces and giving the plug-in to the artists. All it takes is one afternoon's work, and you have achieved hero status among the artists.

It turns out that game companies routinely extend off-the-shelf modeling programs to export models and textures in their own formats, to tag models with extra information specific to their game, to do special filters and conversions on their textures, and even to display how a model will look when rendered with their game engine inside the modeling program. As a matter of fact, a lot of programs (not just modeling programs) are intended to be extended through user plug-ins—Web servers, Web browsers, .mp3 players, email programs, compilers, and editors.

13.1.2 Plug-Ins for Our Programs

So hero status is good, and being able to write plug-ins for other programs is very useful, but what about our own programs? Why would we want to bother to add plug-ins? We have the source code, so we can just modify the programs anytime we want, recompile them, and release them with the new functionality.

The simple answer is that the tools are easier to extend. After the plug-in architecture is in place, it is undoubtedly easier to write a new plug-in than to add basic functionality to the tool itself.

The other key point in support of using plug-ins is that the original tool is completely insulated from the contents of the plug-in. This makes it possible to have a generic tool, but add game-specific functionality to it later on without losing any generality. As an example, consider a resource-viewer program. This program allows us to browse the thousands of resources a game usually needs, such as textures, models, animations, and effects. The program might natively know about some of the basic, generic resource types, such as .tiff textures, VRML model files, and a few others. Then we can write new plug-ins to browse our game-specific resources: platform-optimized mesh files, specially compressed textures, game entity objects, and so forth.

Such a generic tool could be used to display resources from several different projects, each of them with some custom resource types. If we add that functionality in the base tool, we make the tool dependent on those projects, as well as any future projects. And even worse, what if two projects interpreted the same resource in slightly different ways? By using plug-ins, the users can choose which resources they want the tool to display. The same goes for multiplatform projects. We could display resources created for specific platforms just by having new plug-ins for them, without ever having to touch the original tool.

One final advantage of using plug-ins is that one day you might decide to release your tool to the game community so they can create new content for your game. At that point, other people might want to extend the tool in the same way we extended the off-the-shelf modeling package. Providing such power to your end-users is one sure-fire way to extend the life of your game and increase the size of the community that forms around it.

13.2 PLUG-IN ARCHITECTURE

ON THE CD

In this section, we detail how a plug-in architecture is set up, and we go over some of the most interesting parts of the implementation. The source code on the accompanying CD-ROM contains a full Win32 sample program. You can find it in the folder \Chapter 13. Plugins\, and the Visual Studio workspace is pluginsample.dsw. You might want to refer to that code for all the details.

13.2.1 IPlugin

The whole plug-in architecture revolves around the abstract interface for a plug-in. (See Chapter 12, "Abstract Interfaces," for a detailed explanation.) The abstract interface contains all the functions that the program uses to manipulate the plug-in.

As an example, let's create an interface for a set of plug-ins to export data from our tool. Here is one possible abstract interface for our plug-ins:

```
class IPluginExporter
{
public:
    virtual ~IPluginExporter () {};

    virtual bool Export(Data * pRoot) = 0;
    virtual void About() = 0;
};
```

The interface declares only the minimum set of functions necessary to interact with all the exporter plug-ins. In this case, the program interacts with the plug-ins in only two ways. The first way is by calling the Export() function and passing the appropriate data to export. Each plug-in implements that function differently and exports the same data in different formats.

The second way the program interacts with the plug-in is by calling the About() function. About() displays the plug-in's name, its build date and version information, and so forth. Having a function like this is extremely useful when dealing with plug-ins. Not only does it allow us to see what plug-ins are currently loaded, it also lets us check that the plug-ins are the correct version. Because plug-ins can be copied and updated independently of each other and the main program, being able to check their version from within the program can save the users many headaches.

In this example, all the initialization is supposed to happen in the constructor and all the shutdown in the destructor, so there are no separate initialize and shutdown functions. When possible, this is the preferred way of dealing with initialization and shutdown because it makes it impossible for an object to be successfully created but not initialized. On the other hand, if the initialization can fail (for example, if it has to access a file or allocate memory), then exception handling is needed to flag that error from a constructor (see Chapter 5, "Exception Handling").

13.2.2 Creating Specific Plug-Ins

Creating an exporter plug-in for a specific format is just a fill-in-the-blanks exercise. Here is an example:

```
class PluginExporterHTML
{
public:
    PluginExporterHTML (PluginMgr & mgr);

    // IPlugin interface functions
    virtual bool Export(Data * pRoot);
    virtual void About();

private:
    // Any functions specific to this implementation
    bool CreateHTMLFile();
    void ParseData(Data * pRoot);
    // ...
};
```

Along with the header file, we provide a .cpp file implementing those functions, and our exporter should work. There is nothing else to do. Notice that we did not have to change a single line in the original program.

Creating another plug-in to export a different format is just a matter of creating a new class that also inherits from `IPlugin` and filling in the blanks again with the new implementation:

```cpp
class PluginExporterXML
{
public:
    PluginExporterXML (PluginMgr & mgr);

    // IPlugin interface functions
    virtual bool Export(Data * pRoot);
    virtual void About();

private:
    // Any functions specific to this implementation
    // ...
};
```

13.2.3 Dealing with Multiple Types of Plug-Ins

So far we have seen how to make new plug-ins of the same type; in the previous example, they were all exporter plug-ins. Often a program needs more than one type of plug-in: one type to export data, another one to import data from different sources, another one to display new data types, or another one for user extensions. The possibilities are endless, so more than one plug-in type is clearly needed in more-complex programs.

The best way to organize several types of plug-ins is through inheritance. One abstract interface contains the interface functions common to all plug-in types, such as initialization and shutdown (assuming you have explicit functions for those tasks), and getting the plug-in name, version, and any other relevant information. In our case, the base abstract interface for all plug-ins could look like this:

```cpp
class IPlugin
{
public:
    virtual ~IPlugin () {};

    virtual const std::string & GetName() = 0;
    virtual const VersionInfo & GetVersion() = 0;
    virtual void About() = 0;
};
```

For each plug-in type, we create a new class derived from `IPlugin` that adds the new functionality for that plug-in type. Notice that these new classes are still abstract interfaces because they inherit from an abstract interface themselves and do not provide any implementation. Here are some possible classes for different plug-in types:

```
class IPluginExporter : public IPlugin
{
public:
    virtual ~IPluginExporter () {};
    virtual bool Export (Data * pRoot) = 0;
};


class IPluginImporter : public IPlugin
{
public:
    virtual ~IPluginImporter () {};
    virtual bool Import (Data * pRoot) = 0;
};


class IPluginDataViewer : public IPlugin
{
public:
    virtual ~IPluginDataViewer () {};
    virtual bool Preprocess (Data * pData) = 0;
    virtual bool View (Data * pData, HWND hwnd) = 0;
};
```

To create a specific plug-in, we need to inherit from one of these specialized types of plug-ins. Then we need to implement both the general `IPlugin` functions as well as the functions specific to that type of plug-in. The resulting inheritance tree can be seen in Figure 13.1.

13.2.4 Loading Plug-Ins

So far we have been talking about plug-ins and describing their interfaces and implementations, but we have not mentioned how they do their magic: how they get loaded at runtime. For plug-ins to get loaded at runtime, they clearly cannot be part of the program that uses them. Otherwise, as soon as the program has been compiled, we would not be able to add any new plug-ins. Instead, plug-ins need to be compiled separately and then loaded on the fly.

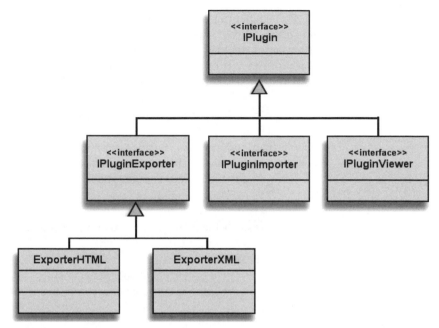

FIGURE 13.1   An inheritance tree with multiple plug-in types.

In our Win32 example, the most straightforward way of loading plug-ins on the fly is through the use of DLLs (Dynamic Link Libraries). DLLs allow us to defer linking with the code inside the libraries until run-time. Only at that point, when we explicitly load a DLL, is that code made available to the rest of the program. This sounds like a perfect match for our needs.

To create a DLL, we must specify certain settings in the compiler so that the target binary will be a dynamic-link library (.dll) and not an executable (.exe) or a static library (.lib). Depending on your compiler, you might also have a wizard that can set up a DLL project with a couple of mouse clicks.

After we have created a DLL, we must decide what functions to export. Unlike other types of libraries, a DLL requires us to explicitly flag the functions, classes, or variables we want to make available outside of the library. We want to keep the number of exports from the DLL to a minimum, just to keep things as simple as possible. Instead of exporting the plug-in class itself, we will export a global factory function that takes care of creating the actual plug-in object. The following code exports the factory function:

```
#define PLUGINDECL __declspec(dllexport)

extern "C" PLUGINDECL IPlugin * CreatePlugin(
                              PluginManager & mgr);
```

With Visual C++, the way to export a function from a DLL is to add the keyword `__declspec(dllexport)` before the function declaration, which is what `PLUGINDECL` is defined to. As we will see in a moment, we define `PLUGINDECL` instead of adding `__declspec(dllexport)` directly so that we can reuse the same header file when the DLL functions are imported instead of exported.

The other thing that might seem odd about the declaration of the factory function is the use of `extern "C"`. This keyword tells the compiler not to decorate the function name in the usual C++ way. Instead, leave it undecorated, as if it were a C function. As a result, we can look for that function later on using its normal name and not a name that has been mangled by the compiler.

Now, in addition to the actual plug-in implementation, every plug-in DLL needs to provide an implementation for the factory function. In most cases, this function is quite simple; it just creates a new plug-in of the correct type.

```
PLUGINDECL IPlugin * CreatePlugin (PluginManager & mgr)
{
    return new PluginExporterHTML(mgr);
}
```

The DLL is ready to be used as a plug-in. One convenient trick often used by tools with many different types of plug-ins (or even by tools with only one type of plug-in, just to add more safety) is to rename the file. Instead of using a generic .dll extension, they are often changed to an extension that reflects the type of plug-in they are. For example, we could give exporters .exp extensions, or importers .imp extensions. With many different plug-ins, this little trick proves quite convenient when we're trying to manage them by hand.

13.2.5 Plug-In Manager

So far we have described in detail how a plug-in is created, but we have not touched on how they are actually used. We have assumed that the program would magically load them and use them. This is the job of the plug-in manager.

The plug-in manager's only role is to deal with the plug-ins. Everything is quite straightforward, but it is a lot of bookkeeping and busy work. The objective is to make the rest of the program think that the plug-ins are just other objects; it will not know that the plug-ins were loaded dynamically.

A design decision to be made for each program that uses plug-ins is when exactly the plug-ins are going to be loaded. They could be loaded as soon as the program starts or when the user decides to load them, or maybe only individual plug-ins get loaded as the user selects them. Most programs attempt to load all the plug-ins whenever the program starts, as does the example on the CD-ROM (\Chapter 13. Plugins\pluginsample. dsw). Changing this behavior is just a matter of calling the correct plug-in manager functions at a different time.

ON THE CD

In our example, as soon as the program is loaded, the plug-in manager attempts to load all available plug-ins. It looks in a specific directory and finds all the files with matching extensions to the plug-in type with which we are dealing. This directory is usually relative to the executable and is usually something obvious because the user probably wants to add or delete plug-ins directly. In our sample code, we look in the ./plugins/ directory.

For every possible plug-in file we find, we attempt to load it as a plug-in. The first step is to load the dynamic link library:

```
HMODULE hDll = ::LoadLibrary (filename.c_str());
```

The Win32 function LoadLibrary() loads a DLL according to its filename. It returns a handle that we will need later on to free the DLL, or it returns NULL if there was an error attempting to load the DLL. At every step, we must check that the result was successful because it is possible that some other random file has the same extension as the plug-in we are looking for, or that the file might be corrupted.

Remember how we declared the CreatePlugin() function in the IPlugin header file? Here it is again, this time without leaving out the details:

```
#ifdef PLUGIN_EXPORTS
    #define PLUGINDECL __declspec(dllexport)
#else
    #define PLUGINDECL __declspec(dllimport)
#endif

extern "C" PLUGINDECL IPlugin * CreatePlugin(
                        PluginManager & mgr);
```

Now it becomes clearer that PLUGINDECL can be two different types of declarations, depending on PLUGIN_EXPORTS. Both the plug-in manager and the plug-in implementation itself need to include the Plugin.h header file, but the plug-in implementation needs to declare its function as a DLL export, and the plug-in manager needs to declare it as a DLL import. By using this little trick with the preprocessor, we can get away with using only one header file, and we avoid the maintenance headaches of having two separate header files with almost the same code. Assuming the DLL loaded correctly, the next step is that we must look for the exported factory function.

```
CREATEPLUGIN pFunc = (CREATEPLUGIN)::GetProcAddress (hDll,
                                    _T("CreatePlugin"));
```

The function GetProcAddress() looks for the specified function in the exported function list from a certain DLL. We decided to call our factory function CreatePlugin() for all the different plug-ins, so we can just look for that one function. Notice that we can look for the function by its plain name; this is because we chose to export it as extern "C", which tells the compiler not to apply the usual C++ decorations in the symbol table.

Assuming the function is found, GetProcAddress() returns a pointer to that function. Otherwise it returns NULL, and we know that we do not have the expected DLL.

The plug-in manager is finally ready to create the plug-in. We call the factory function through the function pointer we just retrieved, and we should get back a plug-in of the correct type. Of course, the plug-in manager has no idea what that type is. It is hidden behind the IPlugin abstract interface:

```
IPlugin * pPlugin = pFunc(*this);
```

We pass *this as a parameter to the factory function because it takes a reference to the plug-in manager. The plug-in needs to access the manager in order to interact with the rest of the program, as we will see in the next section. Finally, the plug-in manager keeps the pointer to the plug-in we just created in a list for the program to use whenever it is needed.

The rest of the plug-in manager functions are straightforward. We need some way for the program to enumerate the plug-ins. In our example, we just have one function that returns how many plug-ins are loaded and another function that returns the plug-in corresponding to a particular index. Things are a bit more complicated if we have multiple types of plug-ins. In that case, the program needs to query for all the exporter plug-ins, all the importer plug-ins, and so on.

There is also the need for functions to load and unload plug-ins at runtime. We at least want to unload all the plug-ins when the program exits so that all memory is freed correctly. To free a plug-in, all we do is remove it from the plug-in list, delete the actual object, and unload its DLL by calling `FreeLibrary()`. The function to unload the DLL takes as a parameter the DLL handle returned by `LoadLibrary()`, so we must make sure we keep that handle along with the plug-in pointer itself.

Another very useful feature is to be able to reload all plug-ins (or just a particular one) without having to shut down the program itself. It is particularly useful during development to be able to quickly test several iterations of a plug-in, especially if loading the main program and the data set takes a while. To do this correctly, it is not enough to just call a function to reload all plug-ins. We must be able to release a plug-in individually and then load it again at a later time. The reason is that as long as a DLL is loaded (through the function call `LoadLibrary()`), its file is locked by the operating system, which means we cannot replace it with the new version of the plug-in we have just compiled. So we must first unload the plug-in, update the DLL, and reload it again. All in all, it is usually still much faster than having to close and start the program from scratch.

13.2.6 Two-Way Communication

So far the communication between the program and the plug-in has been highly unidirectional. The program calls plug-in functions whenever it is necessary. Is it time to export a file? Call the appropriate plug-in function. Do we need to display an object for which we have a plug-in? Call the render function. Everything is working perfectly.

There are some situations in which we want our plug-in to take a more active role, such as to add buttons to the toolbar or entries to the main menu. Maybe the plug-in needs to check the status of something periodically or intercept a message before the application gets to it. To do any of those things, the program has to be structured to allow the plug-ins to have that type of access.

The cleanest way to grant the plug-in access to other parts of the program is through the plug-in manager. All plug-ins already know about the manager because we passed it as a parameter to their constructor, so we can easily extend it to become a gateway to the rest of the program.

At this point, we should decide what level of access we want the plug-in to have. The more restricted the access to the rest of the program, the less dependency between the plug-in and the program (which means that the plug-in is likely to work with updated versions of the program), but also the fewer things it can do. Giving the plug-in free reign means that it can implement anything the plug-in writer has decided, but it also means that it has a much tighter coupling with the rest of the program and more potential for errors. A good rule to follow is to use the most restrictive approach that still allows the plug-in to do all the operations it requires.

The safer and more restrictive way is to do everything through the plug-in manager. The plug-in manager anticipates the needs of all the plug-ins and has one function for every operation the plug-in will want to do. Because the plug-in manager is compiled with the rest of the program, it can have a more intimate knowledge of the different parts of the program, and the plug-in manager is less likely to cause problems than a plug-in that accesses the program directly. Also, as the program changes and new versions are made available, the plug-in manager can be changed if necessary. If the plug-ins were accessing the program directly, and there was a major architectural change, they would all become invalidated and would have to be updated and recompiled, which is exactly the situation we are trying to avoid.

In the CD-ROM sample code (\Chapter 13. Plugins\pluginsample. dsw), the plug-ins communicate with the program in a very minimal way. They are exporter plug-ins, so they do not interact with the rest of the program very much. However, they do add a menu entry under the File | Export submenu. To accomplish that, they use a couple of functions in the plug-in manager to add and remove items from the Export submenu. In that case, it is up to the plug-in manager to find a handle to the main frame, get the menu, find the correct submenu, and insert the items. Leaving that operation up to the plug-in has a lot of potential for problems because it is tightly tied to the structure of the program.

The alternative is to grant the plug-in full access to the rest of the program. The plug-in manager can return a handle to the main window, or a pointer to some of the main objects, so the plug-in can manipulate them freely. This is a much riskier approach, but it allows maximum freedom in implementation and the potential to do things unforeseen by the original program.

We can combine both approaches. A plug-in manager can provide many safe functions while allowing a "back door" to give the plug-in full access to the program if it needs it. Most plug-ins are well behaved and use the safe functions; but if somebody absolutely has to do something else, they can do so at the cost of making their plug-in more likely to break in the future.

13.3 PUTTING IT ALL TOGETHER

The source code on the CD-ROM includes an example of a plug-in-based application. It consists of three different project files for Visual Studio in the \Chapter 13. Plugins\ folder:

- **pluginsample.dsp:** This is the main MFC application. It includes the plug-in manager class. It does not do anything in itself, other than to serve as a shell to demonstrate how plug-ins are hooked up.
- **PluginA\pluginA.dsp:** This is a basic exporter plug-in. To keep things simple, instead of exporting anything, it just displays a message box when the export function is called. It also has an About dialog box that is displayed when viewing the loaded plug-ins from the application.
- **PluginB\pluginB.dsp:** Another simple exporter plug-in.

The plug-ins should be in the `./plugins/` directory relative to the application and are loaded as soon as the application starts. It is possible to unload all of them and load them again through a menu.

13.4 PLUG-INS IN THE REAL WORLD

We have seen in detail how to set up a plug-in architecture. But how do plug-ins perform in the real world?

13.4.1 Using Plug-Ins

Are plug-ins worth the complication? The answer is a resounding yes. Plug-ins are a great way of extending programs, and a lot of commercial products are designed to be extended that way. Some products take it to an extreme and provide all of their functionality through plug-ins so that the program itself is just a hollow shell, with the plug-ins doing all the useful work.

That is fine for tools, but what about games? Here, extending functionality through plug-ins is less common. Many games are designed to be extended by users, but usually in the form of new resources and new scripts instead of new code. One of the main problems with offering a full plug-in approach is that of security. After the plug-in is hooked up, it can do virtually anything to the game—or the whole computer. It could be possible for malicious code to do many unpleasant things, from sniffing passwords and private information to deleting files on the hard drive. Script code, on the other hand, is usually very restricted in the type of operations it can do, so it is a lot safer to run game scripts of unknown origin than it is to run full plug-ins.

Debugging plug-ins might at first appear as something cumbersome or difficult to do, but in reality, it turns out to be extremely easy. Most debuggers let us set breakpoints and step into source code from a loaded DLL just as you would with the executable code itself. We just need to wait for the DLLs to be loaded before we set any breakpoints. That, combined with the fact that we can reload plug-ins without having to shut down the main program, makes debugging them a very pleasant experience.

13.4.2 Drawbacks

Not all is rose-colored in the world of plug-ins, however. Communication going from the plug-in to the main program is always slightly cumbersome because it has to go through the plug-in manager (or get the correct objects or handles to access the program directly in some other way).

Plug-ins, by their dynamic nature, have difficulty dealing with global data. But because that is not a good practice anyway, removing global variables and offering Singletons and objects for accessing that data instead solves most of the problems. Along those lines, it is sometimes a bit tricky to get plug-ins to use the right GUI resources, and we might have to jump through a few hoops to make sure all works as expected.

Also, plug-ins are particularly bad at interacting with each other. Two plug-ins that depend on each other might not both be loaded at once, or they might be loaded in a different order than expected. Usually, the safest approach is to make sure plug-ins do not depend on each other.

Apart from these drawbacks, the only other potential disadvantage of plug-ins comes as a consequence of what they are trying to solve. Because plug-ins are intended to extend a program after it has been compiled, the user must install and remove plug-ins directly or through some sort of install program. There is the potential that the plug-ins might be out of date or have mismatched versions. Fortunately, plug-ins are usually intended for one program only, so at least there is no problem with different programs installing conflicting plug-in versions in the same directory, which could result in DLL havoc, as sometimes happens with shared DLLs.

A good practice is to be very careful with the versioning of plug-ins. Always make sure the user can check the version number of a plug-in, and always check for correct versions of the program or other plug-ins with which your plug-in interacts.

13.4.3 Platforms

This chapter has been entirely devoted to plug-ins running in the Win32 platform. What if we are not developing for Win32? Even if our target platform is not Win32, often our development tools run on Win32, so all the details of this chapter are relevant. Both Linux and Apple operating systems have similar mechanisms to load dynamic libraries, so you just need to change the platform-specific details.

What about game consoles? Some of them have DLL support, but some of them do not. If you are working with one that does not support DLLs, you will have to do a bit more work to achieve the same results. You might be able to use *segment loading* (a technique that allows you to load and unload specific sections of code) plus some pointer fix-ups to use dynamically loaded code. Here it really pays to export only the factory function, which is loaded and executed only once and avoids the complication of exporting the full plug-in class. After the actual plug-in objects have been created through the factory, they can be used almost as if they were normal objects.

13.5 CONCLUSION

In this chapter, we covered the extremely useful technique of plug-ins. Plug-ins allow us to extend our programs without having to modify the original source code and having to recompile everything again. We can also use them to extend other people's programs, such as off-the-shelf art tools.

We saw how we could architect our program to support the use of plug-ins, how to organize the different plug-ins, how to manage them, and how to load them on a Windows platform. Plug-ins are still possible on other platforms that do not support DLLs if we use other methods to load code dynamically. These techniques are illustrated with the sample code for a working plug-in manager that can be found on the CD-ROM (\Chapter 13. Plugins\pluginsample.dsw).

ON THE CD

Finally, we saw how plug-ins are used in the real world, and what some of their advantages and drawbacks are.

SUGGESTED READING

For such a useful technique, there is surprisingly little published material on plug-ins. Some detailed plug-in architecture descriptions can be found in the documentation for several of the major software packages intended to be extended through plug-ins, such as Autodesk's 3D Studio Max, Adobe Photoshop, and others. Scanning through the API documentation for those packages can reveal many interesting details of real-world applications of plug-ins.

What follows is a really good reference for any Windows-system programming topic. It has some excellent chapters on DLLs.

Richter, Jeffrey, *Advanced Windows*, 3rd ed. Microsoft Press, 1997.

14

C++ AND SCRIPTING

In This Chapter

- Why Use a Scripting Language?
- Architectural Considerations
- Beyond Gameplay: Other Benefits of Integrated Scripting

In a book about C++, it might seem a bit odd to include a chapter on scripting. These days, however, it's almost impossible to talk about game programming without mentioning it. Most (if not all) of the top game titles rely on a scripting language in some form. The reason is simple: the low-level power and raw speed of C++ combined with the extreme flexibility of scripting languages form a very potent development duo unmatched in its ability to deliver high-performing gameplay and data-driven creative content. This chapter deals with the important concepts behind incorporating a scripting language in your C++ project and discusses some of the key architectural considerations.

14.1 WHY USE A SCRIPTING LANGUAGE?

When some developers think of using scripting in their project, they often consider only its (somewhat historical) application to the artificial intelligence system. Others think of user-friendly design tools for mission creation. Both of these viewpoints are correct, but they are also terribly shortsighted. Scripting languages are nothing less than full-scale programming languages, which means that they are useful for just about every aspect of the game development—when used correctly.

In this section we examine the key features—good and bad—of scripting languages so that you can have a clear picture of what you're in for should you choose to incorporate one in your project. Hopefully, by the end of this discussion, you'll be convinced that adding scripting is the way to go. But, to be fair to the topic, we also present some reasons why scripting isn't feasible for your project. Reading through the good and the bad aspects presented next should help you with your decision.

14.1.1 The Bad News . . .

As with everything we encounter as developers, scripting languages have their pros and cons. All things considered, unless you are working on a system that is so resource restricted you simply can't fit a scripting system in the engine, incorporating scripting into your game is a huge win. Before that point is driven home, however, we'll take a quick look at the major downsides of scripting.

14.1.1.1 Performance

Scripting languages are notorious for being slow compared to "real" languages such as C++. When you peruse the literature, you commonly see data indicating that code written in script runs at about 1/20th the speed of code written in the mainstream compiled languages. This is caused in large part by the fact that most scripting languages execute through some form of a virtual machine.

If you've read all the chapters preceding this one (and you have, good reader, haven't you?), this statistic is probably pretty scary. After all, what's the point in learning to make the most of C++ if you are going to ruin performance by adding slow-as-snails scripted code? The question is valid, but the fear doesn't have to be. As we'll see later, a well-designed architecture allows you to have all the performance you want in the places you need it, in spite of the large number of scripts you might have running in your game.

14.1.1.2 Development Support

Another common downside to programming in scripting languages is the lack of sophisticated development tools like those we've come to know and love when working in C++. While the number of IDEs available for script development is rapidly increasing, scripting languages are still second-class citizens in the world of development. This means you are likely going to have to live without handy editing features such as auto-completion, object browsing, and so on.

More importantly, you might have to live with very limited IDE-based debugging support. As C++ programmers, being able to step through code line by line is an absolute necessity in game development. As script programmers, you sometimes must debug your code the old-fashioned way, by dumping descriptive text to standard out and reading the results post-run. As we'll see later, however, much of this headache can be mitigated by the growing collection of third-party tools, as well as the powerful built-in debugging capabilities scripting languages commonly provide.

14.1.1.3 Learning Curve

Scripting languages are *not* harder to learn than other languages. In fact, most are far easier to pick up than C++. However, a scripting language *is* a new language to most programmers, which means you do have to learn a few things you otherwise take for granted in C++. This point shouldn't be weighed too heavily, however; the real issue is simply the time required to get up to speed on something new, as with learning a new middleware API.

Beyond the basics of learning new keywords and possibly new methods of managing data, the biggest thing that trips up newcomers to a scripting language is the tendency to treat that language like C++. For example, many programmers rely heavily on the C++ compiler to catch minor syntactical errors in their code. We won't debate this practice here. But, we do recognize that it exists, and warn that most scripting languages allow you to write code that contains misspellings in variable names (for example) without letting you know you've made a mistake. Often this leads to frustration and the belief that adding scripting was all a big mistake. It isn't. You simply must give your chosen scripting language the full respect it deserves. A little time up front learning how to correctly use it prevents most of the learning-curve problems and gets you to the extremely productive phase of development faster.

14.1.1.4 Portability

The final downside worth mentioning is portability. The most popular scripting languages, such as Lua and Python, are increasingly supported on many platforms. However, not all platforms support these newer languages. And conversely, many of the languages haven't evolved enough to run platform independently. If the choice of scripting language for your project is based most heavily on platform support, you might find yourself with few options. Fortunately, the support for scripting seems to increase almost daily across all platforms, so hopefully you'll not have a problem incorporating scripting in your project. Refer to the "Suggested Reading" section at the end of this chapter for resources that can guide you in your language selection.

14.1.2 The Good News . . .

Now that we've gotten the bad news out of the way, the rest of this chapter focuses on showing you why you *should* incorporate a scripting system in your project. You should keep in mind the negatives just mentioned, but do so only to help you remain focused on the proper application of scripted structures and code. We'll get to those considerations a bit later. For now, let's get excited about scripting by taking a look at the new powers you can enjoy.

14.1.2.1 The Zen of Scripting and Programming Bliss

If you think about the very first program you wrote on your own, like many, you might recall the sheer joy of seeing magic come alive by your own hand. The first stage of a programmer's experience with code is often in a language such as BASIC. Of course, that first stage is also probably characterized by the ugliest code you've ever seen, but we'll get to that later.

In any case, it sure was terribly fun. The reason it was so much fun is because programming—and game programming in particular—is as much a creative art as it is a technical science. Art, by its very nature, is not meant to be contained, and the free-flowing creativity you experienced in your early days of programming was art gone wild, knowing no bounds, answering to no one.

One of the biggest laments we hear from today's expert programmers is regarding the loss of the "good ol' days" when programming was just sheer joy. Today's projects are highly structured and well-organized, thanks in large part to the sophistication of the languages used to implement them. All this structure and organization is a good thing—if this book is about anything, it's about how to write well-designed code.

But with all that structure, something gets lost: the freedom to *just write code*. This lack of freedom does not stem from the philosophy behind object-oriented programming, as some may claim. Nor can it be blamed on the nature of a structured architecture based on encapsulation and data hiding. Instead, it comes primarily from the hard-wired nature of compiled languages as well as the mechanisms those languages employ to protect you from yourself and other programmers who might abuse the organization of things.

Scripting languages bring back the effortlessness and instant gratification we all experienced in our early days of programming. This is especially true of those scripting languages that are run-time interpreted, because they allow you to just write code without worrying about compile times, linker errors, or the many "programmer protections" that exist heavily in the more structured languages. When you write in script, you transfer the exciting ideas you keep in your brain directly to code, without suffering any intervening protections that break the creative flow. Make no mistake—scripting requires discipline to work effectively. But when it works, it's magic. And the productivity you enjoy is unparalleled in your experience as a programmer.

14.1.2.2 Controlled Structure, Not Controlled Chaos

Some of what you have just read might paint a picture of pure chaos when working in the world of scripting languages. The truth is, it can be very easy to write absolutely horrible code when given the freedom these languages provide. However, it is also just as easy to write highly structured code, and more importantly, *to actually enjoy doing it*.

The most popular scripting languages provide little native structure by design. But they also provide tremendous power to create your own structure, allowing you to model the best aspects of the object-oriented philosophy. The language Lua, for example, has only a single native data structure—the *table*—that acts essentially as an associative array. Even with that single structure, however, the language provides mechanisms that allow you to create the equivalent of C++ classes, complete with inheritance, overloading, and numerous other features you might not expect.

Writing code in script is a balancing act: an inner struggle between self-discipline and a strong hedonistic desire to just run free through the wild west of Scriptland. Your first efforts at writing script might indeed be pretty unsightly, at least when looked at through eyes accustomed to C++ code. However, as you develop an appreciation for the power of C++ and the elegance of its structure, you also mature as a scripter and increasingly seek to mimic that structure in the scripts you write. You eventually discover that you can actually turn the free-form nature of your chosen scripting language into a more structured language that matches the elegance of C++ while still allowing you to enjoy the uninterrupted flow of ideas transformed into code.

14.1.2.3 Data-driven Architecture

One of the most compelling reasons to use scripting languages is that they inherently promote data-driven design. A script is itself data, which means that not only are the contents of the structures you create data, but the functions that operate on them are data as well.

This might be the single-most powerful aspect of scripting because it allows you a number of benefits that can't be overstated, including these:

- **Accelerated development interaction between programmers and designers.** In an engine without scripting, it's very common for the design team to request a feature and then wait for the dreaded "tomorrow's build" of the game (which often comes next week if you're particularly unlucky). This kind of latency in a deadline crunch is just plain absurd. Having much of your game logic in script allows you to experiment and brainstorm interactively with a game designer. Often, you can try out new ideas in real-time. At worst, you can alter the script and then give the designer the changes within a few hours for them to examine on their local machine.

- **Quick turnaround on new art assets.** As with designer interaction, programmers often need to interact with members of the art staff as well. The ability to sit down and drop a new asset in the game to check things out is invaluable in debugging pipeline problems, engine/tool disparities, and file format issues. An engine with a scripting system in place allows such capabilities, which greatly speeds up the process of getting great assets correctly in the game. In fact, you can design the interface to the engine such that artists can add, remove, and modify content easily on their own. This simultaneously empowers them to "debug" art problems while also freeing you to remain focused on writing great code.

- **Downloadable content.** Everyone is familiar with the concept of providing new levels, items, and missions using a downloadable content drop. Unfortunately, providing new features usually requires a formal patch. If the code is written in script, however, new functionality can be added as part of the asset drop. In fact, old code can be updated, repaired, replaced or completely removed simply by providing new scripts that modify or override the originals.

- **Community building and product longevity.** There are few things you can do to your game that will ensure longevity more than allowing the end-user to extend the product on his own. Some of the most well-respected games and gaming systems thrive because they put such power in the user's hands. Implementing the bulk of your gameplay in script allows you to open the engine up to the user (with whatever restrictions you choose to place, of course). In doing so—

assuming you have a good product on your hands to begin with—you practically ensure that your game will continue to evolve long after it is released.

Now that the sales pitch for scripting has been made, it's time to take a look at what needs to be done in your game engine to allow you to enjoy all the promised benefits. A great game based on the powerful combination of C++ and scripting begins with a well-designed architecture. The next section shows you how to make that happen.

14.2 Architectural Considerations

If the preceding discussion makes scripting sound like a dream come true, that's because for the most part it is. Transitioning from a life of development without scripting to a life with scripting is usually like seeing in color for the first time after years of black and white. The world seems awash in new possibilities you never imagined. You might even cackle with insane glee. At the very least, you'll most likely enjoy working on your project more than ever.

Having covered the pros and cons of scripting (and hopefully convincing you that adding scripting to your project is probably a very big win), we'll now take a look at the key architectural considerations. First, we present two critical points that should be kept in mind at all times:

1. C++ code is very fast, but somewhat inflexible and not easy to modify after it's packaged in the final product.
2. Script code is slow, but extremely flexible and modifiable during all stages of development *and* after the product has shipped.

14.2.1 Engine versus Gameplay

From these realizations, we can specify two golden rules that apply to an architecture that mixes C++ code with script. These rules force our design to play to the strengths of both languages while minimizing their weaknesses:

- **Golden Rule 1:** C++ code belongs in the core engine of the game. Anything and everything that is CPU intensive should be implemented in C++.
- **Golden Rule 2:** Scripting code is best suited to gameplay. All high-level logic and program flow mechanisms should be implemented in scripting.

Of course there are always exceptions, but in general these rules mandate a dichotomy that provides a clean separation between the code in the game that is performance critical and functionally generalized, and code that is specific to the needs of the game design. Figure 14.1 illustrates this separation. On the left are some of the components of the engine that should be implemented in C++. On the right are the aspects of gameplay that should be implemented in script. Between them is the *engine/script interface*, which abstractly divides the two sides while also suggesting the presence of a mediating entity between the two worlds.

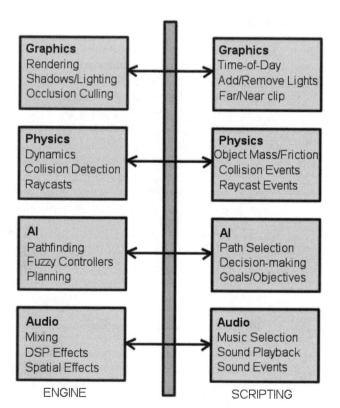

FIGURE 14.1 The basic architecture of a game that incorporates scripting contains an explicit interface between the core engine components (left), and the higher-level gameplay components (right).

To further illustrate the architecture, let's look at several of the components on each side of the interface and discuss the roles they play. The discussion in the following sections is not exhaustive, but it does cover enough of the elements in a game to sufficiently make the point about separation.

14.2.1.1 Graphics: Engine Side

The graphics system is an obvious choice for implementation in C++ (or assembly, of course). No other system screams out the need for performance like the graphics engine does. Some of the capabilities the engine-side graphics system provides are listed here:

- Low-level interface with the graphics hardware
- Scene management, frustum culling, and occlusion
- Shadows and lighting
- Shaders of all kinds

14.2.1.2 Graphics: Script Side

Just because graphics eats up a lot of CPU juice doesn't mean there isn't room for a counterpart on the scripting side of things. You would never try to implement the core functionality in script, but you certainly would (and probably should) expose as much of the graphics system as you can, according to the design needs of the project. Some of the features that can be manipulated in script include:

- Modification of the far and near clipping planes and the FOV
- Adjustment of ambient lighting and fog
- Addition, removal, and modification of dynamic lights
- Ability to add 2D graphics, such as overlays and HUD elements

These are but a few of the things you can expose for gameplay reasons. But there are also things you can expose for interactive debugging purposes, including scene-management settings, the selection of different renderers, and even shader parameters.

14.2.1.3 Physics: Engine Side

Physics is another CPU hog in a game, and the systems that drive it should definitely be as fast as possible. Anything dealing with collision detection, raycasts, or complex object dynamics involves a lot of math, which means it should be on the C++ side of the line. Of course, numerous aspects of each of these do not require tremendous CPU resources. For example, although the calculation of a collision between two objects is math intensive, the *result* of that collision might simply be the initiation of some high-level gameplay element, discussed next.

14.2.1.4 Physics: Script Side

Most of the time, the physics system in our game is busy calculating the outcomes of various object interactions. Or it's churning away on raycasts or similar calls. Although it's certainly appropriate that the core engine handle these operations, it is also reasonable that the characteristics of these interactions be described in data. The following is a brief list of the types of information that can exist on the scripting side of the physics system:

- Manipulation of object physics parameters, such as mass and friction
- Queries about object location, orientation, velocity, and other physical state properties
- Response to and handling of collision events for the purpose of generating sounds, particles, and other visual effects or events
- Initiation of raycasts used for AI, weapons, and other purposes

In short, everything that has to do with setting up physical interactions (or responding to them) are candidates for implementation in script.

14.2.1.5 AI: Engine Side

Yes, there is such a thing as an "AI engine." Generally, this term refers to the system that manages pathfinding, but in more sophisticated systems, the AI engine can also be responsible for processing fuzzy logic rules, managing the batching of raycasts and other sensors, formal planning, and numerous other features that are slowly making their way from the academic world into game development.

In the case of pathfinding, it is certainly desirable that the code driving it be as fast possible, not to mention cache friendly. At the same time, however, pathfinding and other core AI features are rife with opportunities for customization and modification at runtime (see Chapter 11, "Beyond STL: Custom Structures and Algorithms") to create a multitude of gameplay scenarios. Learning how to separate the core elements from the gameplay elements is not difficult, and a few ideas are listed next.

14.2.1.6 AI: Script Side

The scripting side of the AI system is rich with opportunity. AI usually manifests almost entirely as gameplay, and as such there are countless things you can do in script that don't require CPU-intensive operations. These include:

- The definition and execution of complex behaviors
- The specification of objectives and long-term goals
- Descriptions of personalities and emotion parameters
- Setting of pathfinding criteria, such as accessibility requirements, path usage, movement priorities, travel speeds, waypoint reservations, and so on
- Responses to sensory stimuli
- Inter-agent communication

14.2.1.7 Audio: Engine Side

The audio system is often associated with hardware management, although modern game audio increasingly includes sophisticated software algorithms for computing various effects, not to mention dynamic music and real-time synthesis. All of this is very CPU intensive, and therefore remains in the core engine. However, as with the other components we've seen, there is plenty of work to be done on the scripting side.

14.2.1.8 Audio: Script Side

The most obvious choice of tasks for the scripting side of the audio system is the triggering of sound playback. For example, when opening a door, the player might hear a creaking sound. But there are numerous other uses of scripting with respect to the sound engine:

- Setting of global sound parameters, such as volume, fade, or choice of supported effects.
- Dynamic triggering of music playback according to events in the game.
- Modulation of player-centric sounds. For example, in a racing game, the sound engine is probably responsible for generating the player's car engine sound, but the scripting system can respond to user input (such as gear shifting) to initiate a modification of that sound.
- Scene management in which the scripting side determines which sounds to activate according to the player's location.
- Soundbank I/O. The scripting side of the sound system can be responsible for loading sounds that are about to be used in the next section of a map, for example.

In the preceding discussion, you might have noticed a pattern in the types of things that appear on the scripting side. Although it was explicitly stated in the architecture golden rules, anything CPU intensive goes into the core engine. However, sometimes things that appear to be resource hogs actually contain elements that can be separated out and exposed in scripting. As a rule, you should examine every aspect of the engine component you are working on to see whether any part of it can be broken out without compromising performance. The more you can legitimately expose, the less you needlessly tie your engine down to a specific design, and the more you empower content creators to generate compelling gameplay you might not have even considered.

14.3 BEYOND GAMEPLAY: OTHER BENEFITS OF INTEGRATED SCRIPTING

We've taken a look at the many advantages scripting brings to gameplay in the preceding discussion. But the benefits hardly stop there. One of the best things about having a scripting language in your game is the way it significantly improves the development process itself. In this section, we examine how you can use scripting to increase productivity. We also see how to troubleshoot problems that are difficult or impossible to investigate by other means.

14.3.1 Working with a Scripting Console

If you are writing a game engine from scratch, there are two things you should do as close to the start of development as you possibly can. The first is to integrate scripting *immediately* so that you can achieve the ideal architecture right from the beginning and begin enjoying all the benefits it brings. The second thing you should do is implement an interactive *console* that provides runtime access to the scripting system. Even if you are working on a well-established engine, if you are going to add scripting, add a console.

Without a console, you still have a lot of power in that you can make changes to the script files and then immediately restart the game without having to recompile. But with a console, you can take things to an entirely new level. With a little effort, you can use your console as a shell for the scripting language, which means you can write *and execute* script directly in the console while the game is running. It simply isn't possible to exaggerate the utility of this facility—the benefits it brings are absolutely enormous. If you aren't convinced of this, read on.

14.3.2 Interactive Debugging

The single best advantage of having an embedded scripting language—gameplay reasons aside—is that it allows you to debug your application interactively. In this case, *interactive* doesn't mean just examining variables and checking function calls. It means actually changing the executable code at runtime to suit whatever debugging needs you might have.

Imagine a situation in which an AI character is exhibiting an inability to navigate an obstacle. You see the all-too-familiar "twitching" as the character oscillates between turning right and turning left, ad infinitum. You can, of course, break into the code and step through line after line, trying to figure out the problem. However, most likely this problem has to do with the data on which the AI pathfinding operates. Such data is spatial by nature, and trying to examine spatial data in the debugger is like looking at a Monet paint-by-numbers that hasn't been started; it just doesn't make sense.

No matter how powerful your debugging IDE is, you just can't compete with visual debugging. In this case, a picture is worth a thousand lines of code. But how do you visualize the underlying problem when the game renders only what the design calls for? The answer is to write a script that uses *debug-drawing* functionality that you can use to display the relevant information in the scene. If you haven't exposed a debug-drawing interface to the scripting system, then bite the bullet and expose it—it will pay for itself a hundred-fold in about a week, and it doesn't take much effort at all. Simply add some calls to the graphics system that allow you to draw lines, spheres, boxes, or other basic primitives in the scene, expose these calls to the scripting system, and you have everything you need to produce invaluable visual feedback that will help you debug many kinds of problems in the game.

Assuming that you have added some debug-drawing capability to the scripting system, you can visualize every aspect of the problem by writing a script to do just that. And if you've implemented a console, you can do so while the game is running, at the moment the problem occurs. In the case of the AI obstacle-avoidance problem, you can write a script that does all of the following:

- Draw a wire-frame box around the obstacle to represent its oriented bounding volume, which often serves as the footprint around which the AI will navigate.
- Display the AI's location, its destination, and any intervening waypoints that make up its current path, allowing you to see what its plan is versus its actual course of action.
- Display indicators on every object the AI is able to perceive, to determine whether the AI is, in fact, aware of the obstacle it is to circumnavigate.
- Draw triangles for every collision face in the vicinity so that you can verify the problem isn't caused by an unrelated environmental-collision glitch.

- Display formatted text on the screen that reveals numerous useful bits of data about the AI's current goals, behaviors, and other state information.

After you have written the script and executed it (specifying the problematic AI as the entity on which it operates), you will suddenly see in the game all this useful information. Most of the time you'll be able to spot the problem immediately, saving you countless hours of staring at the debugger trying to figure things out. As your collection of debugging scripts grows, you'll find yourself fixing bugs—and improving the script and C++ code that engendered them—at an ever-increasing rate.

The advantages of scripting as it relates to debugging do not stop with you, the programmer, and your daily dose of private bug hunting. Maintaining a growing library of debugging scripts allows you to easily make house calls to anyone on the team who might be having a problem you can address. If, for example, a tester comes across the AI navigation problem we just examined during beta testing on a release build, you can simply bring the appropriate test script to that tester's machine, run the script, and troubleshoot the problem on the spot.

Hopefully, you noticed mention of a *release* build in the preceding paragraph. If so, you read correctly. An integrated scripting system allows you to run debug code, in the form of a script, on a release machine because, although the underlying C++ code is compiled in release mode, the scripts are configuration agnostic. As long as you have exposed the necessary aspects of the engine to the scripting system, there is no reason you can't write scripts for debugging purposes and apply them to release builds. In fact, when you are done troubleshooting the problem with your handy debugging script, you can dynamically erase that particular script from memory, leaving the machine in a clean state and allowing the game to proceed as if nothing had been changed.

Incidentally, it really isn't even necessary for you to personally oversee the debugging process. The test scripts generated by the programming team could (and should) be added to source control, from which testers with read-only access can download scripts as necessary to their machines and run the test scripts themselves. The testers will initially still want to interact with you if they have questions, but in the case of common and recurring problems, they might eventually become experts in using your scripts to debug the problems they encounter.

One final point: it may have occurred to you that this "debugging portability" can be applied to end users outside the building as well. Gamers who have bought your game can make use of such scripts during communications with the tech support staff. Also, if you are in the serious-games arena, you might find these debug scripts especially useful when dealing with customers who have come across problems after they have left your site. Being able to email the customer a custom script that you wrote while on the phone with them is an impressive way to gain their trust and appreciation of your company's commitment to their needs.

14.3.3 Rapid Prototyping

Another fantastic benefit of having a scripting language is the ability it gives you to do *very* rapid prototyping of new algorithms or gameplay logic. Scripting gives a whole new meaning to the word *rapid* because nothing is faster than being able to test your code the moment you write it without waiting for a recompile.

Prototyping in script is also faster because scripting languages allow you to focus on the meat of the problem and not worry about details such as const correctness, template syntax, or correctly exposed library methods. Make no mistake—the concept of const in C++ is an elegant and very useful one that should be used as much as possible in production code. But it has no place in prototype code. When prototyping an idea—especially in the early phases of technical design—all you care about is getting results as quickly as possible. You need to validate your assertion that you have the correct solution to a given problem. Or you need to find out now that your proposed algorithm isn't going to work and will require a new design for the system that contains it.

As mentioned previously, scripting languages are complete languages, which means you can implement just about anything you can imagine in script—even things that normally would go into the core engine. When prototyping, you are free to ignore the golden rules of scripting because they generally don't apply. Your main goal is to get something working the way you designed it, so in many cases performance isn't an issue. Go ahead and implement a fancy new raycast function, or an improved collision routine. After you get it working, you can re-implement the logic in C++ and get all that performance back.

You might be wondering why you would "waste time" implementing something in script if you know you are going to move it into C++. Hopefully the answer is clear by now. When dealing with new algorithms or code in unfamiliar domains, it's very common to revisit the code numerous times after the initial implementation. Each time you do, you suffer a potentially long compile and link cycle. This is needless suffering: the bulk of game programming is not the typing you do, it's the problem solving. If you implement your new algorithm in script, you allow yourself to focus on just the problem, and you can get through numerous iterations of your solution very quickly. After the problem is solved, you'll find that a final "re-type" into C++ is a small price to pay.

14.3.4 Automated Testing

If you've ever spent time play testing a game, you know what an exhausting and arduous task it can be, especially when you are trying to recreate a problem that hasn't been seen for several days. Sometimes the solution is to simply give up and mark the bug as "cannot reproduce." You might never see the problem again, but it's equally likely that it will crop up after the game has shipped. You cannot continue to spend testing resources on this one bug with so many others in the queue, so what are you to do?

If the game engine has been generously exposed to scripting (as it should be), then writing scripts to do automated testing is the answer. Manual play testing is extremely important and will never go away. However, many studios have hundreds of computers running all night doing nothing but searching for aliens or folding proteins when instead they could be helping the testing process.

For some issues, you do indeed need human eyes to track down and report problems. However, numerous problems can be usefully addressed through automated scripts. Taking the time to implement these scripts pays off big in the long run because doing so establishes a formal and quantifiable procedure of testing that scales up with increased resource allocation. In other words, after the scripts are written, you can replicate them on numerous machines and really crank up the bug finding. The following subsections illustrate just a few ways you can use automated testing.

14.3.4.1 Automated Level Crawls

Many game levels (particularly in 3D) have places that break pathfinding for AI agents. Even worse, they can sometimes even break the player's movement because of cracks in the navigation mesh, for example. Manual level crawls are excruciatingly mind numbing, which makes them ripe for scripted automation.

Writing a script to direct one or more AIs to exhaustively navigate the level is easy, but the important thing is detecting error conditions in the level. These can take the form of any of the following:

- **Broken navigation data.** In this case, the underlying pathfinding information has been broken either by level-designer oversight or just plain buggy code. One very common cause of this problem is the addition, removal, or moving of objects in the level without rebuilding or adjusting the pathfinding information. The result is typically an object sitting on a path that an AI expects to be clear of obstacles.

- **Positive-collision bugs.** Sometimes there are places in the level where the player or AIs seem to be stuck against an invisible object. It's not uncommon for an object to be placed that has a collision component but doesn't have a visualization component. Or it could be that the collision model of a particular object is simply larger or shaped differently than the corresponding visual model. Either way, unfortunate placement of such objects can be the cause of extraneous collisions in places where you don't want them.

- **Negative-collision bugs.** In this case, there is no collision where it is expected to exist. This can be caused by the placement of objects that don't have a corresponding collision representation or, perhaps more commonly, by the placement of an object that has had its collision parameters (flags) mistakenly set to incorrect values. This problem can also occur because of negative-space issues in which the level itself doesn't properly bound the objects it contains, allowing them to fall to infinity or pass outside the world boundary.

All the errors just listed can be detected with robust collision callbacks or raycast results. In writing a script to automatically (and exhaustively) detect these problems, it's important that you very precisely define the error conditions so that the script can quantitatively evaluate situations and report problems in a meaningful way.

14.3.4.2 UI Stress-Testing

If you've ever been stuck with the task of "just going through all the menus and pressing all the buttons," you probably wanted to shoot someone after about 13 minutes. This kind of testing is particularly absurd because it's so easy to automate. If the input system is exposed to the scripting interface, you can simulate user-input commands without hacking the system. Doing so allows you to design exhaustive testing procedures that can do all that dirty work for you and report any problems to a log file that can be read the next day.

If you've implemented the UI in a graph structure as recommended in Chapter 11, automatically testing the user interface becomes a fairly simple exercise in applying a searching algorithm to every screen in the UI. With this technique, you can:

- Detect broken return links—as when the user isn't able to back up to the previous menu
- Find "lost" menus—as when there is no way to get to a certain screen from some other screen, even by way of the Main Menu

• Check for unnecessarily long input chains—as when it takes the user forever to get to a particular screen when there are shorter, more efficient (and less frustrating) paths to the same screen

14.3.4.3 Other Test Cases

There are countless other uses for automated testing, both for formal testing purposes used by the Q/A staff as well as for your own private testing. In general, with a little effort, you can write test scripts that do the following for every system in the game:

• Simulate user-input
• Test boundary conditions for all inputs to the system
• Test system outputs for valid ranges and expected values
• Procedurally generate test data
• Perform relevant hardware tests and evaluations
• Track and evaluate performance and resource use
• Generate save games that illustrate problems encountered during testing

This last point suggests a particularly powerful use of scripting that is available to you if your game has a solid event system with a playback mechanism. If you have such a system, you can have your automated test scripts generate *event bookmarks* that allow you to replay a save game that was created during testing and skip directly to the locations where the script detected the problems. In many cases, a simple report in a log file is sufficient feedback from a testing session, but there are times when you really need to see the problem yourself, and this method can really help.

14.4 Conclusion

This chapter was about theory rather than implementation, and deliberately so. Countless resources can explain the mechanics of hooking a scripting system up to your C++ code and can cover the basic syntax and features of a particular language (see the "Suggested Reading" section that follows). Instead of rehashing this information, we've chosen to focus instead on the larger issues that can make or break your architecture and to provide compelling reasons to add a scripting system to your next project.

The golden rules are the key to successful scripting integration. But they serve an even greater purpose in that they encourage highly modular and data-driven design, which is always a win in game programming. Scripting takes that purpose to the next level, so take the advice of this chapter: add a scripting system, add a console to interact with it, and watch the productivity of your entire team—not just the programmers—increase dramatically. Best of all, you might just find yourself enjoying writing code more than ever.

SUGGESTED READING

There is quite a bit of literature available for using scripting languages in games. The following resources are listed by language. Although the collection of represented languages is by no means exhaustive, it does cover the most popular scripting languages often found in commercial games.

Lua

Lua is the language of choice for a number of major commercial titles, thanks primarily to its simplicity, elegance, and tiny footprint. The main resource for the Lua language is the Web site of its creators, located online at *http://www.lua.org/*. Beyond that, there are numerous books and Web sites you can visit that will teach you the language and instruct you on the (simple) process of embedding Lua in your C++ project.

Some recommended books and articles include:

Celes, Waldemar, "Binding C/C++ Object to Lua." *Game Programming Gems 6*. Charles River Media, 2006.
Figueiredo, Luiz, "Programming Advanced Control Mechanisms with Lua Coroutines." *Game Programming Gems 6*. Charles River Media, 2006.
Ierusalimschy, Roberto, *Programming in Lua*, 2nd ed. Lua.org (publisher), 2006.
Schuytema, Paul, et. al., *Game Development with Lua*. Delmar Thomson Learning, 2005.

You might also find the following Web sites useful:

http://www.lua.org/pil/
http://lua-users.org/
http://www.tecgraf.puc-rio.br/~celes/tolua/tolua-3.2.html
http://luaplus.org/tiki-index.php

Python

Python is one of the most widely used scripting languages inside and outside of game development, in large part because of the large number of third-party tools and resources available for public use.

Here are some excellent books on the subject:

Lutz, Mark, et. al., *Learn Python*, 2nd ed. O'Reilly Media, 2003.
Norton, Peter, et. al., *Beginning Python (Programmer to Programmer)*. Wrox, 2005.

And here are some recommended Web sites:

http://www.python.org/
http://www.boost.org/libs/python/doc/
http://www.pygame.org/news.html

GameMonkey

GameMonkey is a scripting language inspired by Lua but cast more in a C++-like object-oriented light. It might be the language of choice for you if you prefer to stay closer to the C++ way of doing things. The following Web sites can tell you just about everything you need to know about GameMonkey:

http://www.somedude.net/gamemonkey/
http://www.evolutional.co.uk/gamemonkey/
http://gmcommunity.sourceforge.net/w/index.php/Main_Page
http://www.gamedev.net/reference/programming/features/gmscript1/

AngelScript

Another scripting language modeled very closely after C++, AngelScript is up and coming and appearing more frequently in discussions on game development. The following Web sites are good starting points for those interested in this option:

http://www.angelcode.com/angelscript/
http://sourceforge.net/projects/angelscript

RUNTIME TYPE INFORMATION

In This Chapter

- Working Without RTTI
- Uses and Abuses of RTTI
- Standard C++ RTTI
- Custom RTTI System

As games grow larger and more complex, the number of different classes involved during gameplay significantly increases. We might have thousands of objects of hundreds of different classes interacting with each other. In the middle of this chaos, sometimes we need to find out more information about the identity of the objects we are dealing with, such as the name of their class, or whether or not they inherit from a certain class. To achieve that goal, we need some sort of *runtime type information* (RTTI).

In this chapter, we learn about the RTTI system that C++ provides, its uses, and its cost. We can then see why sometimes it makes sense to roll our own RTTI system, and we then present a very simple, yet powerful custom RTTI system that can be used directly in your code.

15.1 WORKING WITHOUT RTTI

In a game that was designed in an object-oriented way, all our game objects should be interacting with each other and with the player, using encapsulation and polymorphism. Everything happens at a fairly abstract level, and we never have to worry about what type of object, exactly, we are dealing with.

That is an ideal situation. The higher the level at which we can interact with objects, and the higher the level at which they can interact with each other, the fewer dependencies we introduce in the code. Consider the simplified hierarchy structure for a real-time strategy game as shown in Figure 15.1.

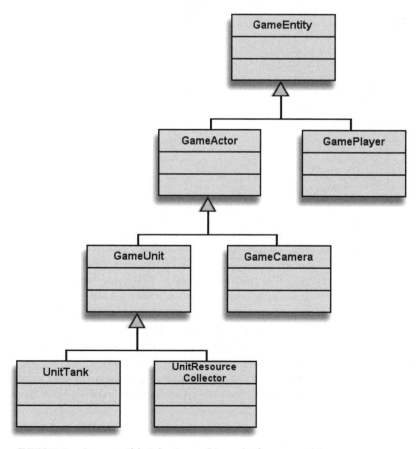

FIGURE 15.1   One possible inheritance hierarchy for game objects.

Most of the interactions between objects should happen through the GameEntity class. That is, a UnitTank should not know anything directly about a UnitResourceCollector. But we know what happens when a tank runs over one of our little resource-collector robots. So how can we implement that without having the tank check whether it is about to run over a UnitResourceCollector? Both the tank and the resource collector get a message saying they are colliding against another GameEntity object, without knowing the specific type. Then each can see the velocity and mass of the other GameEntity object it is colliding against and decide whether it takes any damage or not. In the case of our little resource-collector robot, this should be enough damage to squash it flat.

The same technique can be applied for other types of interaction. For example, suppose our game has barrels full of highly flammable fluid. When a tank runs into one of them, the barrel detects the collision and causes an explosion that will damage all entities within a certain radius. If the damage caused by the explosion is enough to destroy the tank, it will blow up in turn—all that without the tank ever knowing that what it collided against was an explosive barrel. The barrel also has no idea of what hit it; it just knows that the colliding object was able to make it blow up.

The main benefit of modeling object interactions in this way is that we do not introduce many dependencies in the code between all types of objects. Also, their interactions are generic enough that new interactions are bound to occur automatically as a result of how they were modeled. For example, now we do not need to do anything special about modeling a tank colliding with a car. Our generic way of handling collisions and damage can take care of that new kind of collision. If we need a land mine, it is very easy; a land mine is very similar to the explosive barrel. Whenever we add a new unit type, we can implement some generic ways of interacting with the rest of the world, and it should work just fine with all the other units.

15.2 Uses and Abuses of RTTI

Consider the alternative: the tank class specifically checks to see whether it is interacting with some of the other object types in the game. It needs to know about barrels, about resource-gathering robots, and about every other unit in the game. Whenever it collides against anything, it needs to find out what type of object it is and then react according to that type of object. Any time we add a new type of object, we would have to make all existing types aware of the new one, and we would have to hand-code how each would react to the new object. This sounds like a lot of unnecessary work. Sometimes it is more convenient, or even necessary, to find out exactly what type of object we are dealing with, perform a downward cast in the inheritance hierarchy, and continue using that object directly.

In our previous real-time strategy game example, imagine that the tank unit has the ability to combine itself with the aircraft unit to make a more powerful unit. To combine them, we need to land the aircraft and bring the two units together. If we just let the generic code handle it, they will probably blow each other up when they detect a collision. Instead, either the tank or the aircraft should have some special code in its collision-handler function that looks to see whether it is colliding against another special unit. If it is, it then triggers the metamorphosis into the new unit. In a case like this, finding out exactly what type of object we are colliding against is very useful, but it is nothing more than a shortcut.

In a more real situation, we probably would like several units in addition to the tank to be able to combine themselves with other units to create new unit types. In that case, a better design is to abstract that interaction through the GameEntity class. Maybe whenever any two units are brought together, they can send a message to each other, asking whether or not they can combine. If they can, the combination is triggered; otherwise, it is ignored and everything continues as normal. Maybe such functionality could be better exposed through an abstract interface, as we saw in Chapter 12, "Abstract Interfaces."

The moral to take from this example is that RTTI should be used carefully and sparingly. If you find yourself wanting to know the type of almost every object with which you interact, that is usually the sign of a poor object-oriented design. You should consider this technique as a quick shortcut to be used sparingly, not as a major design technique. Over-reliance on runtime type identification can lead to entangled class dependencies and programs that are hard to maintain, add new features to, and debug.

What are some situations where using RTTI is a good idea? Object and player interaction could benefit from RTTI, sparingly. Maybe RTTI could be used in the rare case in which we want to save the trouble of creating new abstract interfaces or adding some functionality to the base class when it should not really be there. The combination of two units is a good example—as long as it is just those two units that have the added functionality. Checking whether or not a node is a light when we are about to render a scene is also an acceptable usage. As soon as the interaction between those objects becomes a common situation, the solution is better handled by moving that functionality to a higher level in the hierarchy and avoiding RTTI altogether.

There is also the possibility that we cannot modify the parent classes of the objects in which we are interested. This could be because the specific class is in a library for which we have no source code, or even that it is in our own code base, but we cannot change it because of compatibility issues with other projects. Inheriting from that class to add our functionality might also be out of the question because objects of that type might be created directly inside the library, and we have no way to force it to use our new class instead. In a situation like this, using RTTI to detect specific classes and add some functionality or interaction with other objects based on their type might be the only possible solution.

Serialization is another situation where RTTI is essential (see Chapter 17, "Object Serialization"). Serialization is the process of saving and restoring an object. It can be done on disk, in memory, or even over the network. During the serialization process, an object is asked to write itself to a stream. One of the first pieces of data written to the stream is the type of the object that is about to be saved. This can be the class name of the object or some unique ID that identifies it. This is exactly the type of information we will get from an RTTI system. To restore the object at a later time, or from the other end of the network, we first look at the object type stored in the stream, create one object of that type, and then read all the appropriate information.

15.3 STANDARD C++ RTTI

How exactly do we find out what class an object belongs to? Or, in a more general sense, how do we find out whether an object derives from a particular class? The first solution we will cover is the standard C++ RTTI system. Then we will present a custom runtime type information system.

15.3.1 The `dynamic_cast` Operator

The first and most important part of the standard C++ RTTI system is the `dynamic_cast` operator. Its syntax is like any of the other C++ casting operators (see Chapter 3, "Constness, References, and a Few Loose Ends"):

```
newtype * newvar = dynamic_cast<newtype *>(oldvar);
```

The concept behind `dynamic_cast` is very simple: it casts the pointer or reference to the new type, but only if it is legal to cast the real type of the object to the type to which we want to cast it. If `dynamic_cast` succeeds, it returns a valid pointer of the new type. If it fails because the attempted casting was illegal, it returns a NULL pointer.

What does it mean for casting to be "legal"? A dynamic casting is legal if the pointer type we are converting to is the type of the object itself or one of its parent classes. It does not have to be its direct parent class; any ancestor class is considered a correct casting.

So `dynamic_cast` really does two things at once for us. It first checks whether the casting we are attempting is legal, which is the primary question. Then it actually converts the pointer to its new type. Most of the time, if we want to know whether a particular object derives from a certain class, we then want to manipulate that object through a pointer to the class we just checked against, so `dynamic_cast` does all this in one step and saves us some typing. Here are some examples of how `dynamic_cast` can be used with the inheritance hierarchy shown in Figure 15.1:

```
GameCamera * pCamera = new GameCamera;
// This works fine
GameActor * pActor = dynamic_cast<GameActor *>(pCamera);
// This is also fine
GameEntity * pEntity = dynamic_cast<GameEntity *>(pCamera);

// The next cast will fail because the object is of type
// GameCamera, which does not inherit from GamePlayer.
// The variable pPlayer will be NULL after the cast.
GamePlayer * pPlayer = dynamic_cast<GamePlayer *>(pCamera);
```

In the previous code snippet, all the conversions were done from a lower class type to a higher one. That type of conversion is called an *upcast* because it moves the pointer up the class hierarchy.

A more common type of casting in most applications is a *downcast*, which moves the pointer down the class hierarchy. This is particularly common when using polymorphism and when trying to get more specific information about a particular object.

```
// pEnt is of type GameEntity, but points to a
// GameActor object
GameEntity * pEnt = new GameActor;

// This is fine
GameActor * pActor = dynamic_cast<GameActor *>(pEnt);

// Not OK. This is a downcast, but the cast is not
// legal because GameUnit is now an ancestor of
// GameActor, which is the type of the object we
// are manipulating.
GameUnit * pUnit = dynamic_cast<GameUnit *>(pEnt);
```

You might have noticed that, so far, dynamic_cast looks remarkably similar to static_cast (see Chapter 3). It seems they both catch whether the upcast or downcast is legal, except that static_cast reports the problem at compile time instead of returning a NULL pointer at runtime.

The main difference is that static_cast has no idea about the actual type of the object pointed to by the pointer we are trying to cast, while dynamic_cast does. The static_cast lets any conversion go, as long as it is within the same inheritance hierarchy: up or down, it does not care; the cast is accepted. The dynamic_cast checks the type of the object and allows only valid casts to happen.

In addition to upcasts and downcasts on a single-inheritance hierarchy, dynamic_cast also performs casting on a multiple-inheritance hierarchy, including *crosscasts*. Consider the class inheritance hierarchy shown in Figure 15.2.

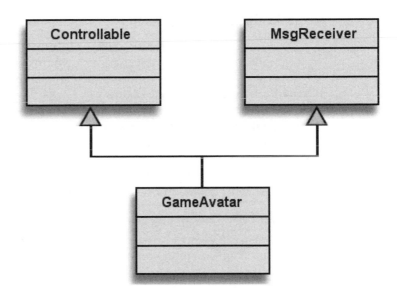

FIGURE 15.2   A class hierarchy using multiple inheritance.

Given a pointer to a GameAvatar object, we can correctly cast it up and down any of the branches of the hierarchy:

```
// Going up
GameAvatar * pAvatar = new GameAvatar;
Controllable * pCont = dynamic_cast<Controllable *>(pAvatar);
MsgReceiver * pRec = dynamic_cast<MsgReceiver *>(pAvatar);
```

```
// Going down
Controllable * pCont = new GameAvatar;
GameAvatar * pAvatar = dynamic_cast<GameAvatar *>(pCont);
```

You might remember from Chapter 2, "Multiple Inheritance," that casting up and down the hierarchy with multiple inheritance requires some runtime fix-ups. To make sure we are always accessing the correct class type, dynamic_cast takes care of adding or subtracting the correct offset from our pointer. We can also do crosscasts, going horizontally on the inheritance hierarchy:

```
// Crosscast
Controllable * pCont = new GameAvatar;
MsgReceiver * pRec = dynamic_cast<MsgReceiver *>(pCont);
```

15.3.2 The typeid Operator

The dynamic_cast mechanism gave us information about the inheritance relations of a particular object and allowed us to cast between the different types. C++ also offers another mechanism for finding out more information directly about one object.

The typeid operator returns information about the type of the object it is applied to. Going back to the class hierarchy of our previous example, we can use typeid in the following way:

```
Controllable * pCont = new GameAvatar;
const type_info & info = typeid(*pCont);
```

All the information about the object we asked about is contained in the type_info object returned by typeid. It turns out there is not a huge amount of information contained in type_info, and by far the most important piece of information is the class name (in its user-readable format as well as its C++-mangled version).

```
std::cout << "Class name: " << info.name();

// The output of running the above statement is
Class name: GameAvatar
```

One of the other uses of type_info is for comparing class types. If we wanted to make sure that two objects were of the exact same class, we could write code like this:

```
const type_info & info1 = typeid(*pObj1);
const type_info & info2 = typeid(*pObj2);
if (info1 == info2)
    // They are the same type. Do something...
```

Notice that we are comparing the type_info structures themselves, not just their pointers. It turns out that it is possible for objects of the same class to return identical type_info structures in different memory locations, so we must compare their *contents*, not their addresses.

The typeid operator also works with type names, not just with objects. This fact allows us to check whether an object is of a particular class by comparing the type_info structure returned from the object and the type_info from the class we want to check against.

```
if (typeid(*pEntity) == typeid(GameAvatar))
    // The object *pEntity is of the class GameAvatar
```

Something to keep in mind when using typeid is that it can be meaningfully applied only to polymorphic types—that is, to classes with at least one virtual function. If we use it on a nonpolymorphic class type, typeid returns information for the type of the reference, not the type of the object. This should never be a problem, though, because we should never have nonpolymorphic objects for which we do not know their real type.

15.3.3 C++ RTTI Analysis

The standard C++ RTTI system is certainly adequate for most tasks. It answers the question of whether an object inherits from a particular class, it supports casting between different parents in a multiple-inheritance hierarchy, and it even returns the name of a class. We get all that automatically, without any extra work on our part. So why would we ever need anything else?

One of the main drawbacks of the standard RTTI system is that it is either always on or always off if your compiler has a switch to turn it off completely (most compilers do). This means that every class with a virtual function (that is, polymorphic classes) has runtime type information associated with it, whether we want it or not. On the positive side, notice that only classes that already have a virtual function (and therefore a vtable) become part of this system. So all our simple, lightweight classes—such as points, vectors, and colors—remain unchanged.

What are the costs of all the polymorphic classes having runtime type information associated with them? It is not that bad. Remember, the information is per class, not per object, so RTTI does not increase the object size any. As usual, the specific details are up to the implementation of each compiler, but usually a pointer to class information is stored in the vtable, and the class information itself should be big enough to contain the class name and a few pointers and counters. So the cost is usually on the order of 30–50 bytes. Even if you have 1,000 classes (again, we're talking *classes*, not objects), which is on the high end, that only amounts to about 50 KB. This is a cheap price to pay for what we get in return with typical computers and game consoles, but it might be significant in the case of handheld devices with extremely limited memories.

What about the restriction of being able to do `dynamic_cast` and `typeid` on only polymorphic types? Even though it might appear restrictive at first glance, it really is not an issue. The only objects we need to get information from at runtime are ones of a polymorphic type; otherwise the type would be known at compile time, so there is no need for runtime type information for them.

The biggest drawback of the default C++ RTTI system is its performance, particularly its lack of consistency across platforms and compilers. On some implementations, `dynamic_cast` can do all sorts of checks to verify that the cast is valid, but under other implementations, it is reasonably fast. Performance also depends on whether the object in question is using multiple inheritance or not.

For a well-designed program that has minimal reliance on RTTI, the potential performance hit is probably not an issue. If it is used very sparingly during the game execution, or its use is restricted to serialization operations, then the C++ RTTI system is perfectly appropriate.

Unfortunately, we are not in an ideal world. There are games out there that, either for legacy reasons or simply because they were designed that way against common wisdom, make extensive use of RTTI operations during runtime. If every game entity performs several RTTI operations per frame, and we have on the order of 1,000 game entities, this would result in tens of thousands of RTTI operations per frame. Efficiency is now critical, and using a custom RTTI system is a necessity.

Finally, another reason to use a custom RTTI system is simply to have more control over it. As it turns out, a custom RTTI system is not particularly complicated. It is rather easy to write, actually, and it involves very little code. So for very little effort, we can have a guaranteed operation across platforms and compilers (and compiler versions; do not underestimate the changes in implementation from version to version of the same compiler), and we know what to expect from it in terms of performance.

15.4 CUSTOM RTTI SYSTEM

By this point, we have decided we want to have a custom runtime information system. We really must ask ourselves: what, exactly, do we need from it? There is very little point in writing our own RTTI system if we are just going to duplicate the standard C++ one. Let's start with a very simple approach and build our way up from there as our needs increase.

15.4.1 The Simplest Solution

The simplest possible RTTI query is to find out the exact type of a class. If that is all we need, it is really easy to do. If you are expecting some high-tech approach that uses all the latest C++ language features to discover the object type, you are going to be disappointed.

15.4.1.1 Using Strings

The simplest approach is to write a function by hand that returns the name of the class:

```
class GameEntity
{
public:
    virtual const char * GetClassName() const
                            { return "GameEntity"; }
    // ... Rest of the class goes here
};
```

This approach is very simple. We just wrote a function in a class that we are interested in that returns the class name. That is it. Actually, there is a little trick and an unspoken assumption in the preceding code. The trick is that the function is virtual. The function must be virtual because we asking what is the name of the class of the *object*, not what is the name of the class of the pointer. And that is exactly what virtual functions allow us to do— call the functions of the class of the object, not the class of the pointer.

```
GameEntity * pEntity = new GameEntity;
pEntity->GetClassName(); // OK, returns "GameEntity"

GameActor * pActor = new GameActor;
pActor->GetClassName();  // OK, returns "GameActor"
```

```
GameEntity * pObj = new GameActor;
pObj->GetClassName();    // Will only return "GameActor" if
                         // GetClassName is virtual!
```

The unspoken assumption is that the function that returns the class name has to be named the same for all classes. If it were not, then we would not know what function to call because we do not know the type of the object, which is what we were trying to find out in the first place.

To make sure the function name is the same everywhere, and to save a bit of typing, we can create a macro to add that function automatically to any class:

```
#define RTTI(name) \
    public: \
        virtual const char * GetClassName() const\
            { return #name; }
```

Using the macro is extremely simple:

```
class GameEntity
{
public:
    RTTI(GameEntity);
    // ... Rest of the class
};
```

This approach is extremely simple and flexible. It works with any class, whether the class is using single or multiple inheritance. Of course, it still does not answer the question of whether an object inherits from a certain class, but we will come back to that later.

The main drawback of this approach is its use of character strings. To do anything useful with the results we get from the function GetClassName(), we are forced to use strings. Strings are great for printing and reading in the debugger, but they are not particularly fast to compare, which is what we are likely to do in this situation. If on top of that we throw in a case-insensitive comparison, then things are even slower. A program that relies heavily on finding the class type of objects will quickly notice the hit of all the string operations.

15.4.1.2 Using Constants

One alternative that trades flexibility for performance is to return a constant or an enum instead of a string for identification. This is particularly handy when we have a small number of subclasses and are not planning to let other parts of the program extend it. We do not have to worry about creating new constants in the future or letting the users create new types, so there is no problem with the clashing of constants.

```cpp
class GameUnit
{
public:
    enum UnitType
    {
        UNIT_PAWN,
        UNIT_RESOURCEGATHERER,
        UNIT_TANK,
        UNIT_PLANE
    };

    virtual UnitType GetUnitType() const = 0;
};

class GameUnitPawn : public GameUnit
{
public:
    virtual UnitType GetUnitType() const
                        {return GameUnit::UNIT_PAWN;}
};

class GameUnitTank : public GameUnit
{
public:
    virtual UnitType GetUnitType() const
                        {return GameUnit::UNIT_TANK;}
};
```

We have replaced returning the class name as a string with a much more specific constant that applies only to the game unit types. The advantage of this approach is that checking whether a unit is a tank is a very fast computation, requiring the comparison of two integers.

One major draw of this approach is in how clear the code is. We are not doing dynamic_cast, typeid, or even inquiring about the class name. We are merely checking what type of game unit this object is, which is exactly what we need to know in our code. Do not underestimate the power of a simple solution with extremely obvious code.

15.4.1.3 Using Memory Addresses

We can combine the best benefits of the first two approaches and come up with a new implementation that is both completely general and very fast at checking the type of an object. To achieve this, we can use the memory address of a static class variable to uniquely identify a class. The variable itself contains the name of the class. This allows us to have some of the best characteristics of the previous two implementations (although the second approach still wins in the category for self-explanatory source code).

```
class RTTI
{
public:
    RTTI(const string & name) : m_className(name) {};
    const string & GetClassName() const { return
    m_className; }
private:
    string m_className;
};

class GameEntity
{
public:
    static const RTTI s_rtti;
    virtual const RTTI & RTTI() const { return s_rtti; }
    // ... Rest of the class goes here
};
```

We can use this approach in a very similar way to how we did it before, but now going through the RTTI object. If it looks like too much trouble just to keep a string, wait a bit because the next section expands on this example and makes the RTTI class a bit more useful.

```
GameEntity * pObj = new GameActor;
pObj->RTTI.GetClassName(); // Will return "GameActor"
```

We can check whether two RTTI objects are the same by comparing their addresses; we are guaranteed to have only one per class because it is a class-static variable.

```
// Comparing pointers directly

if (&pObj1->GetRTTI() == &pObj2->GetRTTI())
    // They are of the same class...

if (&pObj1->GetRTTI() == &GameActor::s_RTTI)
    // pObj1 is of type GameActor
```

This works. It is very fast because it is just a pointer comparison. But having to take the address of the RTTI object and compare it directly is quite awkward. Wouldn't it be better if it could all be encapsulated and we could just ask whether two RTTI objects are the same?

```
class RTTI
{
public:
    RTTI(const string & name) : s_ClassName(name) {};
    const string & GetClassName() const;
    bool IsExactly (const RTTI & rtti) const
                            { return (this==&rtti); }
private:
    string s_ClassName;
};
```

Now that we have hidden the pointer comparison under wraps, we can rewrite the previous code in a much simpler way:

```
// Comparing RTTI objects

if (pObj1->GetRTTI().IsExactly(pObj2->GetRTTI()))
    // They are of the same class...

if (pObj1->GetRTTI().IsExactly(GameActor::rtti))
    // pObj1 is of type GameActor
```

If you are really enamored with the idea, you could even provide an operator== for the RTTI class and use that instead of the IsExactly() function. It is just a matter of personal preference. The one good thing about using operator== is that it makes the code look more like the C++ RTTI system, so it might be a more familiar approach for programmers already experienced with RTTI.

We can update our macro to make adding runtime type information to our classes a snap. Unfortunately, we run into a minor snag with this new RTTI class: we need to provide both a declaration of the class static and a definition in the .cpp file. This means that if we want to use the convenience of macros, we have to create two macros: one for the header file and one for the .cpp file:

```
#define RTTI_DECL \
    public: \
        static const RTTI s_rtti; \
        virtual const RTTI & RTTI() const { return s_rtti; }
```

```
#define RTTI_IMPL(name) \
    const RTTI name::s_rtti(#name);
```

15.4.2 Adding Single Inheritance

So far our simple RTTI system has no concept of inheritance. We can ask whether an object is of a particular class, but we do not know anything about its parents.

If we are going to use RTTI as a part of our code, it will be much more robust if it thinks in terms of inheritance rather than in terms of specific classes. For example, imagine we write a function that, in every frame, goes through all the game entities in the world and puts aside those that are cameras, so we can use them for rendering later on.

```
// Shaky code checking for exact class
GameEntityList::iterator it = entities.begin();
while (it != entities.end())
{
    GameEntity * pEnt = *it;
    if (pEnt->GetRTTI().IsExactly(GameCamera::rtti))
        cameras.push_back(pEnt);
}
```

What happens if, at a later time, we introduce several types of cameras that inherit from GameCamera? Our code would ignore them. What we are really after are all the objects that are, or inherit from, GameCamera because anything that inherits from GameCamera "is a" GameCamera (see Chapter 1, "Inheritance"). So we really want to write something like this instead:

```
// More robust approach using derivation
GameEntityList::iterator it = entities.begin();
while (it != entities.end())
{
    GameEntity * pEnt = *it;
    if (pEnt->GetRTTI().DerivesFrom(GameCamera::rtti))
        cameras.push_back(pEnt);
}
```

We can extend our RTTI class to give it some knowledge of its parent. We can accomplish this by adding a pointer to the parent's RTTI static object, which gets initialized in the constructor—at the same time we pass in the class name. Our improved RTTI class looks like this:

```
class RTTI
{
public:
    RTTI(const string & className) :
        m_className(className), m_pBaseRTTI(NULL) {}
    RTTI(const string & className, const RTTI & baseRTTI) :
        m_className(className), m_pBaseRTTI(&baseRTTI) {}

    const string & GetClassName() const
                                { return m_className; }
    bool IsExactly(const RTTI & rtti) const
                                { return (this == &rtti); }
    bool DerivesFrom (const RTTI & rtti) const;

private:
    const string m_className;
    const RTTI * m_pBaseRTTI;
};
```

With the new changes, we can easily answer the question of who its parent is. But what about previous ancestors? We can find that from the parent's parent, and from its parent, and so on until we reach a class that does not have a parent. If we have not found the class we were checking along the way, then we know that the object does not derive from that class. This is how the implementation of DerivesFrom() looks:

```
bool RTTI::DerivesFrom (const RTTI & rtti) const
{
    const RTTI * pCompare = this;
    while (pCompare != NULL)
    {
        if (pCompare == &rtti)
            return true;
        pCompare = pCompare->m_pBaseRTTI;
    }
    return false;
}
```

We can wrap the latest changes in a macro again to make things simple. The only difference is that now we need two different macros: one for classes with no parent and one for classes with a parent. Actually, we could have made it with just one macro and passed NULL if there is no parent, but what follows is a bit cleaner:

```
#define RTTI_DECL \
    public: \
        virtual const RTTI & GetRTTI() { return rtti; } \
        static const RTTI rtti;

#define RTTI_IMPL_NOPARENT(name) \
    const RTTI name::rtti(#name);

#define RTTI_IMPL(name,parent) \
    const RTTI name::rtti(#name, parent::rtti);
```

The most interesting part is the `RTTI_IMPL` macro. At first glance, it looks a bit odd. We are passing the parent's RTTI static object as a parameter. But all this is happening at static-initialization time, before the game's main function has been called, so how do we know that the parent's RTTI object has been initialized? After all, there are no guarantees about the relative order of static initialization across different files. The answer is that we just do not know; but we do not care, either. All we are doing is storing that memory address for later; we are not trying to read any data from the parent's RTTI object or trying to call any of its functions. The memory address has been fixed since we compiled the program, so this turns out to be totally safe, even if a bit unorthodox.

At this point, every class that has RTTI information also knows about its parent and (potentially) all its previous ancestors. Even though our RTTI system is still very simple and small, it has become full featured. The only thing missing from the picture is multiple inheritance, and sometimes that is simply not necessary if we are either sticking with single inheritance or just using abstract interfaces, which have their own `QueryInterface()` functions. If that is the case, then our existing custom RTTI system is good enough to put straight into your game.

If you need multiple-inheritance support and are willing to pay for a bit of extra memory and performance cost, you should read the next section of this chapter. The source code for the RTTI system supporting single inheritance is included on the CD-ROM in the folder \Chapter 15. RTTI\, (the Visual Studio workspace is rtti.dsw).

ON THE CD

One thing you should be aware of is the performance of the `Derives-From()` function. All the other RTTI queries were extremely fast, usually involving returning a single pointer or doing a simple comparison. The `DerivesFrom()` function is different because it needs to loop until it either finds the class we are looking for or until it reaches the root of that particular inheritance tree. Granted, it should be pretty fast: it is not calling any other functions, and it is just comparing pointers along the way. But it is looping, nevertheless.

The worst case occurs when checking an object against a class that is not one of its ancestors. In that case, the RTTI query loops through as many levels as there are in that section of the hierarchy. If somebody were to design a class hierarchy tens or hundreds of levels deep, then the hit would be significant. Of course, at that point they would have much bigger problems to worry about than the performance of this simple loop. Still, it is worth keeping in mind; this function should not be overused.

15.4.3 Adding Multiple Inheritance

To add multiple inheritance support to our RTTI system, we just extend the single-inheritance implementation to allow for multiple parent classes. Then, the only change we need to make is to change the `DerivesFrom()` class to iterate through all the parent classes, not just the first one, as in the case of single inheritance.

Let's take things one step at a time. We will revisit the AI multiple-inheritance class hierarchy from Chapter 2. This particular hierarchy lends itself well to this RTTI approach, as opposed to the hierarchy from Figure 15.2, which is best implemented using abstract interfaces and a `QueryInterface()` method. The AI hierarchy is shown in Figure 15.3.

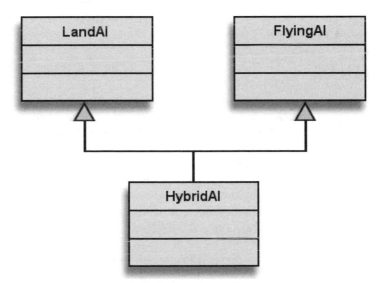

FIGURE 15.3   The AI class hierarchy using multiple inheritance.

Adding support for multiple parent classes requires several changes. In the single inheritance version, we kept one pointer to the parent's class RTTI object. Now we need to keep one pointer per parent. Using an STL vector of points sounds like a good idea, but this is such a low-level construct that we want to avoid using any more memory than we absolutely have to. We also want to keep tabs on all the memory we are allocating. In addition, the number of parent classes is not going to change at runtime, so a vector is definitely overkill here.

Instead, we can keep a dynamically allocated array of pointers. We can allocate the array in the constructor, which is when we know how many parent classes there are. In the case of no parent classes or just one parent class, this is how the constructors look:

```
RTTI::RTTI(const string & className) :
    m_className(className),
    m_numParents(0),
    m_pBaseRTTI(NULL)
{}

RTTI::RTTI(const string & className, const RTTI & baseRTTI) :
    m_className(className),
    m_numParents(1)
{
    m_pBaseRTTI = new const RTTI*[1];
    m_pBaseRTTI[0] = &baseRTTI;
}
```

There is nothing special here; it is just a bit more bookkeeping than we had before.

We also need another constructor that lets us specify as many parent classes as we want. We could create a constructor that takes two parent classes and another one that takes three. Chances are this will cover most cases with multiple inheritance, but it might not be sufficient if someone takes multiple inheritance to an extreme. Instead, we can use a constructor with a variable number of arguments and avoid imposing any limits on how our class is used.

This constructor needs to allocate enough memory, parse the variable list of arguments, and copy the right pointers to the array.

```
RTTI::RTTI(const string & className, int numParents, ...) :
    m_className(className)
{
    if (numParents < 1)
    {
        m_numParents = 0;
        m_pBaseRTTI = NULL;
    }
```

```
      else
      {
          m_numParents = numParents;
          m_pBaseRTTI = new const RTTI*[m_numParents];

          va_list v;
          va_start(v,numParents);
          for (int i=0; i < m_numParents; ++i)
          {
              m_pBaseRTTI[i] = va_arg(v, const RTTI*);
          }
          va_end(v);
      }
  }
```

One unfortunate consequence of having a variable number of parameters in the new constructor is that we cannot wrap it neatly in a macro as we did with the other two constructors. C (and C++ for that matter) does not have widespread support for macros with a variable number of parameters, and the little support there is does not allow the parsing of each individual parameter. We could provide a few macros for the cases of two and three parent classes if we really wanted to. For now, you would have to set it up explicitly. It is not that much more typing, but the code is not as clear as the macros at first glance.

Also notice that, in this case, we need to pass pointers to the RTTI objects of the parent classes, not references as we did before. That requirement is necessary because of the way functions with variable numbers of parameters are handled in C, which does not allow those parameters to be references.

```
// In the HybridAI.cpp file
const RTTI HybridAI::rtti("HybridAI", 2, &LandAI::rtti,
                                         &FlyingAI::rtti);
```

Classes with a single parent or with no parent at all can use the same macros as before. In this case, both of our AI classes have no parent, so they can use the RTTI_ROOT_IMPL macro:

```
RTTI_ROOT_IMPL(LandAI);
RTTI_ROOT_IMPL(FlyingAI);
```

The only thing left is to implement the new version of the function DerivesFrom(), which checks through all its parents:

```
bool RTTI::DerivesFrom (const RTTI & rtti) const
{
    const RTTI * pCompare = this;
    if (pCompare == &rtti)
        return true;

    for (int i=0; i < m_numParents; ++i)
        if (m_pBaseRTTI[i]->DerivesFrom(rtti))
            return true;

    return false;
}
```

The version presented here uses recursion to iterate through all the parent classes, which has the disadvantage of multiple function calls and the need to unwind the stack whenever we finally find a match. It is possible to write a more efficient version that replaces recursion with a stack and avoids doing any extra function calls.

Even the improved version using a stack is slower than the equivalent function in the single-inheritance case. This is because of the extra checking and indirections that must be done to traverse through the parent classes. It is for this reason that this version of the RTTI system is included separately on the CD-ROM in addition to the single-inheritance version (it is available in \Chapter 15. RTTIMulti\rtti.dsw).

ON THE CD

If we know we are going to be limiting our design to single inheritance, we should choose the single-inheritance version. We can always switch to the custom version if we decide to use some multiple inheritance. The change is totally transparent, and there is no need to modify any existing code.

15.5 CONCLUSION

In this chapter, we saw that when we are manipulating objects polymorphically, sometimes it is necessary to find more information about them. That information is called runtime type information because it is gathered while the program is running, not at compile time. More importantly, we also saw how there are often better design alternatives that do not require any specific information about objects, and we can continue treating them polymorphically. We then saw what provisions the C++ language has for runtime type information, and we learned their uses and limitations.

Finally, we developed a custom RTTI system from scratch that can be dropped into any existing game with minimal effort. We saw several versions of this system, in increasing order of complexity, including one that supports multiple inheritance at the cost of a bit more memory and performance.

SUGGESTED READING

This is a good reference for the standard C++ RTTI system. It covers all the details and even some advanced uses.

Stroustrup, Bjarne, *The C++ Programming Language*, 3rd ed. Addison-Wesley, 1997.

There is not much information on custom RTTI systems. These are some of the few references that cover it in any detail:

Eberly, David H., *3D Game Engine Design*. Morgan Kaufmann, 2001.
Wakeling, Scott, "Dynamic Type Information." *Game Programming Gems 2*. Charles River Media, 2001.

16

OBJECT CREATION AND MANAGEMENT

In This Chapter

- Object Creation
- Object Factories
- Shared Objects

M ost of the time when we envision a program running, we visualize the function calls between objects, the transfer of data, and the modification of memory. That aspect is called the *steady state* of the program. However, that is only part of it. Another, equally important part of program execution deals with the creation of objects, and this is called the *dynamic state* of the program. After all, a C++ program starts out with only the statically declared objects, and everything else has to be constructed from scratch.

This chapter examines effective ways of creating different types of objects through the use of *factories*. These factories allow us to be much more flexible with how we create objects than a plain new call would be. They also offer us the opportunity to extend our program more easily in the future.

Then we examine the thorny problem of what to do once we have created the objects. Typically, more than one part of the code has a pointer or a reference to an object. How do we go about deleting those objects without breaking the program? The last part of the chapter offers different methods for doing this, including handles, reference counting, and smart pointers.

16.1 OBJECT CREATION

Every game has to create objects at one point or another. Whenever we load a new level, we have to create all the objects in that level. If we exit back to the main menu, we destroy those objects and create the objects that represent the user interface.

Object creation is not limited to loading new levels, though. It can also occur during gameplay: a shot is fired and a projectile object is created; the projectile hits the wall and an effect is created that displays some sparks and creates a sound effect; a person walks through a pool of water and splash effects are created; your units finish creating a new type of building, so that object has to be created.

There are also more subtle forms of object creation: you push the gamepad button, and a message is created that gets passed to the input-processing system; another player takes control of the ball, and a network packet is created and sent to you through the network. In other words, object creation is everywhere.

16.1.1 When new Is Not Enough

What is wrong with using new whenever we want to create an object? This is how we have most often done it. Usually there is nothing wrong with this method, but the type of object we create with it is determined at compile time. If we write the code as follows, the program always creates an object of type GameCamera. There is no way around it.

```
// This will always be a game camera
GameEntity * pEntity = new GameCamera;
```

In C++, we can manipulate objects in a polymorphic way, which (as you should remember from Chapter 1, "Inheritance") means we can work on an object without knowing its specific type and refer to it through a pointer or a reference of the type of one of its parent classes. The key to polymorphism is virtual functions.

Unfortunately, C++ does not allow a similar type of polymorphic access for the creation of objects. On the other hand, because C++ is so flexible, we can come up with acceptable solutions, but we have to write them ourselves.

What are some circumstances where using new is not good enough? The best example is during the loading of a level. We have a file that contains all the information we need to restore the state of a game that was previously saved. That file contains information about what types of objects there are in the game as well as all the data each object needs. (We see this in much more detail in Chapter 17, "Object Serialization.") Consider the following pseudocode to see the need for dynamic creation of objects:

```
// Pseudocode for object loading
for (each object in the file)
{
    ObjectType type = LoadObjectType();
    GameEntity * pEntity = CreateEntity(type);
    pEntity->Load();
}
```

The LoadObjectType() function returns what type of object we have to create, and the next function creates the correct type of object. That is exactly what we are after.

16.1.2 Big Switch

How can we vary the behavior of the code at runtime without using virtual functions? This is achieved in the ways we are used to: if statements, switch statements, or even function pointers. Here is how the loading code looks with a switch statement:

```
// Pseudocode for object loading
for (each object in the file)
{
    ObjectType type = LoadObjectType();
    GameEntity * pEntity;
    switch (type)
    {
        case GAMEENTITY: pEntity = new GameEntity; break;
        case GAMECAMERA: pEntity = new GameCamera; break;
        case GAMEPLAYER: pEntity = new GamePlayer; break;
        case GAMEACTOR: pEntity = new GameActor; break;
        case GAMEENEMY: pEntity = new GameEnemy; break;
```

```
                // Add *all* the other possible types of game
                // entities here
                default: // Error entity type unknown
        }
        pEntity->Load();
    }
```

If you feel a bit uncomfortable writing code like this, then you have the instincts of a good object-oriented programmer. This example has all the usual problems of code that explicitly depends on object types. The more immediate problem is that it has to be updated every time a new object type is introduced, or an existing object type is removed or changed.

Another problem is that this example requires the program to know about all the specific types of objects. This is a theme that keeps coming up repeatedly in this book: the least amount of information about the rest of the program a particular section has, the better. The program will be easier to test, maintain, and improve in the future. (We see this in more detail in Chapter 18, "Dealing with Large Projects," when we cover the physical structure of a program.)

A consequence of having all the information about object creation concentrated in this one function is that it will be very difficult to extend in the future. As we saw in Chapter 12, "Abstract Interfaces," and Chapter 13, "Plug-Ins," it is often desirable to be able to create new object types after the game ships, or at least without having to recompile and redistribute the original program.

For example, imagine we add a new level to our game that uses a new type of object: a dynamic weather entity that adds an extra level of realism to our game. With our current approach, the only way we can create a new type of entity is by modifying the big `switch` statement and checking for the new type. If we cannot update the executable, we are out of luck. If we decentralize the responsibility of object creation, we have a much easier time extending our program, and we can fix the other drawbacks of this approach at the same time.

16.2 Object Factories

An *object factory* is simply code that creates objects based on a parameter that indicates their type. That code can be something as simple as a function that takes an `enum`, or it can be a full-blown class that takes multiple parameters to describe exactly what type of object is created. Encapsulating all the object creation into a factory has several benefits:

- If any other parts of the code need to create the same type of objects, they can all use the same object factory.
- Only the factory has to know about all the object types and include all the necessary headers. The rest of the program does not have to know anything else about them.
- Usually, we want to do more than just create objects. We often want to keep track of all objects of a particular type, or at least the number of them that are currently allocated. By having a single point of creation, we can keep track of these things more easily.

Object factories often end up being used at many different places in the code. They also usually keep some bookkeeping data around, so they are a perfect match for the Singleton pattern: there is only one object factory for each major object type, it keeps all its associated data with it, and it is easily accessible anywhere in the code.

16.2.1 A Simple Factory

In a way, the function with the big `switch` statement we saw in the last section was almost a very rudimentary type of object factory. We need to refactor it so the creation happens in a separate function from the loading, and then it really becomes an object-factory function:

```
GameEntity * CreateEntity(ObjectType type)
{
    GameEntity * pEntity;
    switch (type)
    {
        case GAMEENTITY: pEntity = new GameEntity; break;
        case GAMECAMERA: pEntity = new GameCamera; break;
        case GAMEPLAYER: pEntity = new GamePlayer; break;
        case GAMEACTOR: pEntity = new GameActor; break;
        case GAMEENEMY: pEntity = new GameEnemy; break;
        // Add *all* the other possible types of game
        // entities here
        default: pEntity = NULL;
    }

    return pEntity;
}
```

This is very similar to the object factory we saw in Chapter 12 that allowed us to create different implementations of an abstract interface.

16.2.2 A Distributed Factory

Other than creating a more focused function, splitting that code into a function by itself and calling it a factory has not helped our situation any. We still have the same ugly code to maintain and too much centralized knowledge about all the objects types we can create. To really improve things, we need to create a *distributed factory*.

The idea behind a distributed factory is to avoid hardwiring the possible types of objects in the source code. By dynamically maintaining a list of possible object types, we can easily add more object types later on or change existing ones without any difficulty.

Up until now, we have been associating some sort of type ID with each class type. Whenever we passed that ID to the factory function, a new object of the correct type was created. That association was explicit in the code by using the `switch` statement.

Now we are going make that association dynamic. We would like to create a map, or some other type of data structure, that associates type IDs with the actual classes to be instantiated. To accomplish this, we will create a set of very small creator objects whose only purpose is to create objects of a particular type. We need one of those objects per class type that we want to create. This is what a typical creator object looks like:

```
class CreatorCamera : public Creator
{
public:
    virtual ~CreatorCamera() {}
    virtual GameEntity * Create() const
            { return new GameCamera; }
};
```

Why go through this extra indirection? Because now we are dealing with terms we can work with more easily in C++. We are not associating type IDs with class types, which there is no way to do. Instead, we are associating type IDs with specific creator objects. Then, whenever we need to make a new object, we call the `Create()` function on the creator object. Our factory class can implement the map and the object creation like this:

```
class EntityFactory
{
public:
    GameEntity * CreateEntity(ObjectType type);
private:
    typedef map<ObjectType, Creator*> CreatorMap;
    CreatorMap m_creatorMap;
};
```

```
GameEntity * EntityFactory::CreateEntity(ObjectType type)
{
    CreatorMap::iterator it = m_creatorMap.find(type);
    if (it == m_creatorMap.end())
        return NULL;

    Creator * pCreator = (*it).second;
    return pCreator->Create();
}
```

Notice that we are taking advantage of the STL map class. In just a few lines, we can create and use a complicated and well-optimized data structure. Refer to Chapter 9, "Standard Template Library: Containers," if you want to refresh your memory on STL containers.

The entity factory class is in place. Now we can create objects dynamically without knowing anything about their specific class type.

```
ObjectType type = LoadTypeFromDisk();
GameEntity * pEntity = factory.CreateEntity(type);
```

16.2.3 Explicit Creator Registration

Of course, for everything to work, we need to tell the factory about what types of objects we support and pass one creator object for each of those types. That is exactly what the Register() function in the factory does. It lets us pass one object ID and one creator object, and the factory keeps track of this association and uses it whenever an object of that type is to be created.

```
bool EntityFactory::Register(ObjectType type,
                             Creator * pCreator)
{
    CreatorMap::iterator it = m_creatorMap.find(type);
    if (it != m_creatorMap.end())
    {
        delete pCreator;
        return false;
    }
    m_creatorMap[type] = pCreator;
    return true;
}
```

Registering a new type of object is now simple. It just requires creating a new Creator class and calling the Register() function.

When should we call the `Register()` function? It depends on each project, but usually on initialization of the system that has to create those objects. In the case of game entities, a good moment is as soon as the game is initialized, before we try to create or load any entities. The initialization function of the game could look something like this:

```
factory.Register(GAMEENTITY, new CreatorEntity);
factory.Register(GAMECAMERA, new CreatorCamera);
factory.Register(GAMEPLAYER, new CreatorPlayer);
factory.Register(GAMEACTOR, new CreatorActor);
// ... Register the rest of the entity classes
```

We have decentralized the information of the object types that can be created. A plug-in could add new object types just by calling the `Register()` function whenever it is initialized. Whenever an object of that new type is loaded or created by any other part of the code, the correct factory function is called.

16.2.4 Implicit Creator Registration

We can take this system a step further and make it even easier to use. And, if we do things just right, we can avoid even having to call the `Register()` function explicitly. That would make the whole system even more transparent, and adding new types would just be a matter of creating new `Maker` objects.

We could write it so the constructor in the `Maker` object registers itself with the factory. Then all we have to worry about is making sure that at least one creator object is instantiated so its constructor gets called. We can do that easily by declaring an object statically and letting the C++ initialization code deal with calling its constructor for us. The creator object would look like this now:

```
class CreatorCamera : public Creator
{
public:
    CreatorCamera() { GameFactory::Register(
                        GAMECAMERA, this); }
    virtual ~CreatorCamera() {}
    virtual GameEntity * Create() const
                {return new GameCamera;}
} instance;
```

Notice the new constructor that registers itself and, in particular, the variable `instance` created right after the class declaration. With this in place, we do not even need to call `Register()` anymore. As it turns out, the extra convenience gained by not having to call `Register()` might cause more problems than it is worth.

The first thing to keep in mind is that the creator class will be created at static initialization time. Unfortunately, C++ makes no guarantees about the order in which static variables are initialized if they reside in different files, so we have to make sure that all the initialization code does not depend on other objects being already initialized. If we need other objects, then we should probably use explicit initialization instead, which happens whenever we want.

The second problem is that we do not have very much control over what creators get registered. As long as they are processed by the compiler, they are registered, whether we want them or not. This might be fine for game entities, but it might not be acceptable if we are registering creators for graphics resources. We probably want different creator types for different platforms, or even for different graphics APIs in the same platform. If so, we want to be able to choose whether we are registering the OpenGL creators or the Direct3D ones at runtime, based on the user's hardware or some configuration file.

Even if none of the previous drawbacks are a problem for you, there is one more annoyance about implicit registration of creator objects. Some compilers perform some very aggressive dead-code elimination steps at link time. They consider dead any code that is not actively called from anywhere else, with the goal of keeping the executable as small as possible. As commendable as this is, it has some unfortunate consequences when the compilers are overzealous about dead-code elimination. For instance, look at the `CreatorCamera` class. Nowhere in the rest of the program is that class used directly, and neither is the static variable instance we created. So, much to our annoyance, some compilers eliminate the instance variable altogether, which prevents the creator class from being registered at all.

You will quickly find out whether your compiler falls in this category. Sometimes this problem appears only if the creator class is in a static library, which is often the case in large projects. You might be able to find ways around it and force your compiler to include the code, but this process is generally unpleasant and changes from platform to platform. It might be enough to force the compiler to use some other variable in the same file, and some compilers provide a compiler-specific `#pragma` directive to force all the symbols in the file to be linked. Or we might be able to turn off the dead-code removal optimization, but that might cause the executable size to grow too large in size. So in the end, unless you are sure that none of these drawbacks are going to affect you, it might be best to simply be explicit and call `Register()` by hand.

16.2.5 Object Type Identifiers

Thus far we have totally glossed over the specifics of how we specify the object type. We have been using variables of the type `ObjectType`, but what are they exactly? As usual, it depends on your specific needs.

The easiest way to specify object types is to use a string that contains the class name. Strings are very easy to debug because it is possible to read their contents from the debugger. Also, it is easy to come up with unique strings for each class. You could even use the string for the class name returned by the RTTI system (either the standard C++ one or your own custom one). On the other hand, strings take more memory to store (although you need only one per class type in the factory, so the cost is not exorbitant), but more important, their comparison operation is slower than that of an integer or an `enum`.

If objects are mostly going to be created at level-load time, then these string issues should not be a problem. Any performance losses are going to be totally overshadowed by IO access to the hard drive or the CD-ROM. On the other hand, if we intend to use the factory to create many objects at runtime, that extra performance loss might start to add up and become noticeable.

The alternative is to use some sort of integer or `enum`. Using an `enum` seems like an attractive idea: it is small, fast to compare, yet it is just as easy to read from the debugger as a string. This is true, but it is not possible to extend `enum`s once they have been defined. Remember, we want to add new object types through plug-ins, so using an `enum` to describe all the object types returns us to the original problem of hardwiring all the possible types in one place.

So we are left with the option of using integers or some other light-weight object to uniquely describe object types. To make them unique, we cannot just increment the identifier for every object type, because we do not know how many other object types are out there, especially not from the perspective of a plug-in. The best solution is to attempt to generate a pseudo-unique ID based on the class, such as using the CRC of the class name or the memory address of a class static variable. If we need a bombproof solution, we can generate full UIDs, which are numbers guaranteed to be unique.

16.2.6 Using Templates

What if we have several totally different types of objects that we want to create through a factory—for example, game entities like we have seen so far, but also resources, or animations, or anything else that does not share a base common class with the game entities? We just create one factory for every one of those groups. Game entities can have their own factory and so can resources. We need to register the creator objects with the correct factory and call `Create()` on the correct factory.

Suppose that after we write one factory, we realize that the code for the second one is not all that different. As a matter of fact, it is probably exactly the same, but it uses a different base class. The same holds true for all the `Maker` objects. Does this sound like a familiar situation? This is a good time to use *templates*. We need the same code, but we want to vary the class on which the code works. This is how the declaration of a templated factory would look:

```
template<class Base>
class Factory
{
public:
    Base * Create(ObjectType type);
    bool Register(ObjectType type,
                    CreatorBase<Base> * pCreator);
private:
    typedef std::map<ObjectType, CreatorBase<Base> *>
                                        CreatorMap;
    CreatorMap m_creatorMap;
};
```

The creator classes must also be templated. Previously, all creators inherited from a common `Creator` class, which is the type of the pointers that was stored in the factory. Because the `Create()` function of the creator base class returns a pointer to the base class of the objects we are creating, we must also template the creator base class itself so that the type of the pointers returned match up in the proper way.

```
template<class Base>
class CreatorBase
{
public:
    virtual ~CreatorBase() {}
    virtual Base * Create() const = 0;
};


template<class Product, class Base>
class Creator : public CreatorBase<Base>
{
public:
    virtual Base * Create() const {return new Product;}
};
```

ON THE CD

The implementation of the factory functions is similar to the non-templated version presented earlier, but with the generic type parameters instead. Refer to the source code on the CD-ROM for the details on the templated implementation. The Visual Studio workspace is located in \Chapter 16. ObjectFactory\ObjectFactory.dsw.

With these templates, making new factories and creators is easy:

```
Factory<GameEntity> factory;
factory.Register(GAMECAMERA,new Creator<GameCamera,
                 GameEntity>);
factory.Register(GAMEENTITY,new Creator<GameEntity,
                 GameEntity>);
```

And using them is just as easy as it was before:

```
GameEntity * pEntity = factory.Create(GAMECAMERA);
```

As long as all your object types are created with a default constructor, and you do not have to do any extra processing or bookkeeping in the factory, then using templated factories and creators is probably a great way to go. However, it falls short if your objects have special creation needs. Maybe they need a parameter passed on to their constructor, or maybe a function has to be called right after they are created. These are things a templated solution cannot do for you. Similarly, the templated solution does not allow you to keep a list of objects in your factory or some statistics about them. In these situations, the non-templated solution gives us the flexibility we need at the cost of some extra typing.

16.3 SHARED OBJECTS

Creating objects is only half the fun. After they are created, we have to keep track of them, manage their life spans, and delete them correctly. This is more difficult that it looks when more than one part of the code refers to the same object.

C++ does not have any sort of native automatic *garbage collection*, and instead, programmers must manage the memory by hand. With automatic garbage collection, programmers are free from worrying about what memory is allocated and what memory is freed. Instead, the run-time code takes care of releasing all the memory that the program is no longer using. Of course, garbage collection has its own share of problems, such as taking time away from the processing of the program at an inopportune moment and making us miss the next vertical synch for a frame.

What the lack of garbage collection means is that we have to be very meticulous about the memory we allocate and the objects we create. We have to keep track of the objects, and when we no longer need them, we need to delete them. Unfortunately, things are a bit more complicated than that. Consider the following code:

```
// Create a new explosion and point the camera to it
GameEntity * pExplosion= new GameExplosion;
camera.SetTarget(pExplosion);

//...
// Some time later, the explosion dies
delete pExplosion;
```

The camera class is keeping a pointer to the entity it is focused on. What happens if that entity is deleted? How is the camera going to know? The pointer still looks the same: it is just a memory address, and that has not changed. But now that memory address either does not belong to the process or is taken up by something totally different from the original entity it was pointing to. This condition is called a *dangling pointer* because the memory location the pointer was referring to is gone or has totally changed.

This is the fundamental problem of shared objects. The rest of the chapter presents several approaches to dealing with shared objects in our programs.

16.3.1 No Object Sharing

As usual, one of the possible solutions to a problem is to not get in the situation in the first place. If we totally avoid shared objects, our problem is nonexistent. Unfortunately, it is not always possible or desirable to do without object sharing completely, but sometimes it might make sense.

In most games, if two game objects use the same expensive resource, it makes sense for them to share it instead of keeping two duplicate copies in memory. For example, all buildings of a certain type can share textures, and all tanks can share the same engine sound. It would be wasteful to create new copies of the same resource for each entity in the world.

In our previous example, the camera has to point to an existing object in the world. It does not make any sense for the camera to have its own copy of the object, because the other object would move away, and the camera would stay pointed to its stationary copy. That is another case where some type of object sharing is necessary.

However, if object sharing is not necessary, then avoid it. Doing so keeps the code a lot simpler, more efficient, and easier to maintain. There is no need to introduce complexity when a plain pointer can do just fine.

For example, a camera entity can keep a pointer to a rotation matrix as a private member variable. That pointer does not have to be exposed to the rest of the world. Only the camera knows about it, and it has full responsibility over it. Whenever it decides to delete the matrix, there are no other pointers to it, so we do not run into any problems. The camera itself might set the pointer to NULL after the camera has been deleted, so it knows not to access that pointer anymore.

16.3.2 Ignore the Problem

Sometimes, for very simple problems and small projects, the ostrich approach works just fine: bury your head in the sand and ignore the problem. Granted, this approach could potentially lead to trouble, but if the project is small, we can probably foresee that nobody is going to access the shared pointer after it has been deleted. It is a bit like playing with fire, but if we do not get burned, then no harm is done.

This is definitely not an approach recommended for a project of any reasonable size—maybe a technology demo or a quickly produced, throwaway prototype—but that is about it. Also, if the team involves more than one programmer, this approach is bound to fail because the other programmers will most likely forget the implicit rules governing deleted objects and accidentally introduce some bugs.

A game that has virtually no dynamic allocations at runtime might also be able to get away with the ostrich approach. If everything is allocated statically, then objects are never deleted and pointers remain valid. We must always check that the object we are accessing through a pointer is active or valid before using it, though. If your game is architected that way, then this approach might be fine. (Refer to Chapter 7, "Memory Allocation," for a comparison of static and dynamic memory allocation strategies.)

When problems arise with the ostrich approach, there are no easy fixes, either. The bugs are not simple to track down. Trying to find out who deleted some memory at some point in the past is not a pleasant task to do in the debugger, and even determining that the crashes are caused by a shared pointer deletion is not simple.

When a project grows larger than expected, trying to change from ignoring the shared-object problem to implementing one of the other methods described in this chapter becomes quite involved; it is possible, but time consuming. Forethought and planning can save us a lot of time down the line, especially as milestones approach and time becomes more precious.

16.3.3 Leave It Up to the Owner

A possible way to deal with the shared-object problem is to designate a section of code, or in our case a particular object, as the *owner* of a shared object. A shared object can have many pointers and references to it from different objects, but only one of those objects is its owner.

The owner is solely responsible for creating, managing, and eventually destroying the shared object. Like the previous approach, there really is nothing preventing a non-owner object from deleting the shared object; it is more of a rule that the code has to follow for everything to work correctly. Because it is more concrete than the previous approach, this method is something that could be used in a larger team project without too much difficulty, as long as everybody is careful.

So the owner can now freely delete the object, but what happens to the pointers held by the non-owner objects? They have to know whenever the object is deleted so they can update their pointers to NULL or just change their state, so they do not attempt to use that pointer anymore.

This notification can be done by using an arrangement similar to the Observer pattern, where the non-owner objects are *observers* that subscribe themselves to notifications from the subject, which can be the owner or even the shared object itself. Whenever the shared object is deleted, all the observers receive a message with the news.

Just because something is the owner of a shared object, it does not have to remain this way forever. As long as all the objects involved agree, we can transfer ownership of an object as needed. For example, in a multiplayer strategy game, all the units a player controls can be owned by that player. If a player happens to get disconnected, we could create an AI player and transfer the ownership of all that player's units to it, so that everybody can continue playing.

This method requires that we decide who the owner is, and how it is going to manage the lifetime of the shared object. It also requires that we write the non-owner objects in such a way that they can deal with the shared object being destroyed at any time.

Finally, if there are a lot of observers and objects are created and destroyed very often, the performance costs of notifying every observer and the memory necessary to store all the observers in the list could be significant. This approach works best for relatively large objects that are not destroyed many times per frame.

16.3.4 Reference Counting

Another more egalitarian approach is to use *reference counting*. In this method, there is no need for an owner of a shared object. Instead, that object is kept around for as long as someone needs it. As soon as the last reference to that shared object goes away, we detect that nobody needs it anymore, and it is deleted. Reference counting is like a rudimentary garbage collection system.

16.3.4.1 Implementation

To be able to use reference counting, our shared objects have to implement two functions: `AddRef()` and `Release()`. Whenever any part of the code acquires a pointer to the object, `AddRef()` is called. Whenever any part of the code is done with an object, instead of deleting it, it calls `Release()`.

The reference-counted object keeps track of how many references it has. Every time `AddRef()` is called, it increases that reference count. Every time `Release()` is called, the reference count goes down by one. If the reference count ever reaches zero, the object is deleted.

This is exactly how COM manages its shared objects. You will also use these calls often if you use the DirectX API because it is based on a COM system.

To make things easy to use, we can place all the reference-counting functionality in a class and allow any class that inherits from it to automatically become reference-counted.

```
class RefCounted
{
public:
    RefCounted();
    virtual ~RefCounted() {};

    int AddRef() { return ++m_refCount; }
    int Release();
    int GetRefCount() const {return m_refCount;}

protected:
    int m_refCount;
};

int RefCounted::Release()
{
    m_refCount-;
    int tmpRefCount = m_refCount;
    if ( m_refCount <= 0 )
        delete this;
    return tmpRefCount;
}
```

To use it, a class just inherits from the RefCounted class. If we want to make the class more foolproof, we could declare its destructor as protected; that way the only way the object is going to be destroyed is through its Release() call. Any attempts by external code to destroy the object directly result in compiler errors.

```
class GameEntity : public RefCounted
{
public:
    // ...
protected:
    virtual ~GameEntity();
};
```

There are a couple of interesting aspects of the RefCounted implementation that are worth paying attention to. First of all, notice that the AddRef() and Release() functions return an integer. The returned value is the current reference count after the call takes place. This value is sometimes required by code that deals with reference-counted objects in order to be aware of whether or not an object is being destroyed.

The second interesting item is the Release() call. You might not be used to seeing code that says delete this. It looks a bit dangerous to call it from within a member function, but it is quite safe. The object is deleting itself; it is no different than if somebody else had deleted it. What we have to be careful about is not to make any other function calls or touch any member variables after the delete call, which is why we have to go through some contortions to keep a temporary variable with the value of the reference count on the stack. If we attempt to return the value of m_refCount directly, everything would work fine until the reference count reaches zero, at which point the object would be deleted and we would be trying to read one of its member variables. As you can imagine, the program would then most likely crash. But if both that value and the return address are stored on the stack, we can safely return from the function without incident.

16.3.4.2 Recommendation

Are there any drawbacks to reference counting? Unfortunately, there are a few. It might appear that this method is totally foolproof. As soon as the reference count reaches zero, the object is deleted. Nobody has to remember to delete it in one place and notify other objects. Unfortunately, they have to remember to call AddRef() and Release() correctly. As soon as there is an unbalanced number of AddRef() and Release() calls, objects either never go away because their reference count keeps going up, or they are destroyed prematurely because their reference count accidentally reached zero. Tracking down unmatched `AddRef()` and `Release()` calls is not easy, and usually it only takes one unmatched call to break the system down.

Still, reference counting is a much more robust system than trying to ignore the problem, and it has the advantage that there is no need to designate an owner to keep track of the object. This method is best suited for situations where there is no strict ownership of the shared object. A perfect example is the graphic resources used by the game. Textures, geometry, and animations can keep a reference count of how many game objects use them. As soon as all game objects that use a particular texture are removed, the texture is also destroyed.

This brings us to the second drawback of the reference-count approach: objects might get destroyed a bit too easily. Maybe we just released a texture, but we are about to create a new entity that needs that texture. Now we are forced to load the texture from the disk again, when we would have preferred that it had stayed in memory. You can work around that problem by having a resource manager that keeps one extra reference to all the textures. That way, even if there are no entities in the game that use a particular texture, it will stay around as long as the resource manager wants it to.

Finally, the last drawback of this approach is that it causes verbose, awkward code. Do not discount this problem as a capricious remark. It is similar to doing error handling by returning and checking error codes from functions. Your code might have more lines for checking error codes than for doing the actual work. The same thing can happen to reference counting. The code can soon be filled with `AddRef()` and `Release()` calls everywhere.

To make things worse, functions that fetch pointers to reference-counted objects often take those pointers as parameters instead of returning them directly, which makes the code even more convoluted and verbose.

Consider the following code:

```
GameEntity * GameCamera::GetTarget()
{
    // We assume that the target always exists
    m_pTarget->AddRef();
    return m_pTarget;
}
```

Now, it would be too tempting for someone to write a line of code like this:

```
cout << pCamera->GetTarget()->GetName();
```

The `return` value of the `GetTarget()` function was used directly from a temporary variable; after that statement, we no longer have access to it. This means that the reference count to the target object was increased, but `Release()` was never called. To avoid this problem, a function is typically written this way:

```
void GameCamera::GetTarget(GameEntity *& pEntity)
{
    // We assume that the target always exists
    m_pTarget->AddRef();
    pEntity = m_pTarget;
}
```

The function is used this way:

```
GameEntity * pEntity;
pCamera->GetTarget(pEntity);
cout << pEntity->GetName();
pEntity->Release();
```

What should have been a single line is now four different lines. Still, sometimes it is worth paying that price to get a more robust way of managing shared objects.

16.3.5 Handles

The root of the problem of having shared objects is that there are multiple pointers to the same object. *Handles* prevent that situation from happening, so there are no longer any problems with objects being deleted and dangling pointers being left around.

The principle behind handles is to use some sort of identifier (a handle) instead of a pointer to a shared object. Then, anytime we want to work on a shared object directly, we ask the owner of the shared object to give us the pointer to the object that corresponds to a certain handle. We perform any operations on that object through the pointer; when we are done, we throw the pointer away. We do not keep that pointer around.

This way there really is only one pointer to each shared object: the pointer of the owner of the object. Any time someone else wants to use the object, they must pass in the handle first. If the object has been deleted, we can return a NULL pointer. At that point they know the object does not exist and can deal with it appropriately.

Handles can be just a plain integer. This is convenient because integers are small enough to be copied and passed around very effectively, but they also have a larger range of unique values they can cover. For this method to work, it is essential that we map every handle uniquely to each object.

How do we guarantee that we can give entities unique handles? Just using a 32-bit number and incrementing it every time we need a new entity gives us about 430 million different numbers. These should be more than enough for any game. Here is how we would use handles in a real situation when dealing with textures:

```cpp
typedef unsigned int Handle;

Handle hTexture = CreateTexture("myTexture.tif");
// ...
Texture * pTexture = GetTexture(hTexture);
if (pTexture != NULL)
{
    // The texture was still around, do something with it
    // ...
}
```

One side effect of dealing with 32-bit number handles is that it is impossible to tell a valid handle from any random number. This can be a problem if memory is being accidentally corrupted, if there was a problem copying a handle correctly, or (a much more likely situation) if a handle variable was never initialized and it contains random data in it. Wouldn't it be nice if there were a way to tell valid handles from invalid ones?

We can sacrifice a few bits off the top and use them to store a unique bit pattern. We could use the top eight bits, which still leaves us with 2^{24} different handles. We could even go with as many as 16 bits for the unique identifier, and we would still have over 60,000 handles for our entities. That should still be more than enough for most games, especially if you consider that we need unique handles for only each major type of shared object. For example, all resources could use one handle system, but all game entities could use a different one. There really is no truly unique bit pattern, but the chance that a random number will match our bit pattern is pretty slim, and it gets slimmer the more bits we use.

Whenever we attempt to translate between a handle and a pointer, the program can first verify that the handle has the proper bit pattern and assert right away if it is invalid (see Chapter 19, "Crash-Proofing Your Game," for the proper use of asserts). This verification is something we might want to do only in debug mode if performance is a problem, and bypass it completely in release mode.

Handles can be somewhat cumbersome because they require the translation step to get a pointer to the shared object. However, handles can be quite effective for tasks for which we do not have to get to the underlying pointer very often. For example, there are not going to be many places in the code where we try to get a pointer to the texture of a mesh. That is probably going to happen only when we load the mesh and when we render it, so using handles in that situation is not going to be very painful.

Handles are also quite effective when the shared objects are deleted but have to be re-created at a later time. If we make sure that the newly created object maps to the same handle it used to have, then all previous handles become valid once again. This is perfect for situations where we are caching resources in and out during the game as the player moves to different locations.

The translation from handle to pointer should be implemented in a way that is very fast. Usually, a hash table or a map is a good implementation, but we could even consider using an array (or a vector) of pointers so that each handle is just the index into the array. The main performance hit is going to be caused by the extra indirection level added by the translation table and its effect on the data cache.

16.3.6 Smart Pointers

Handles, reference counting, and all the different approaches we have discussed for dealing with shared objects are trying to solve one problem: having dangling pointers if the shared object is deleted. Wouldn't it be great if either the pointer knew it was pointing to a deleted object or that the shared object would not be deleted as long as there were any pointers referring to it? This is what *smart pointers* can offer us.

C++ pointers are best described as dumb pointers. They really do not do much: they point to a memory location, and they know what type of data we expect to find there. They are not aware of what is really going on at that location, and they do not seem to be aware of people using them or making copies of them.

It turns out we can tap into the flexibility and power of C++ to create objects that look and feel like pointers, but that can do some extra work for us along the way.

There is really no single definition of what a smart pointer does. Different smart pointers can do different things: check that the memory is valid, keep reference counts, apply different types of copying policies when the pointer is copied, keep statistics, or even delete what they are pointing to when the pointer itself is destroyed.

We actually already saw some smart pointers in Chapter 5, "Exception Handling," when we dealt with exceptions. There is one type of smart pointer, auto_ptr, that, when destroyed, deletes the object to which it is pointing. This ability is extremely useful for correctly freeing all resources, even in the face of exceptions and the unwinding of the stack.

For smart pointers to be effective, they must behave like real pointers. That is, we should be able to use them in the way we have come to expect pointers to work in C++: we should be able to dereference them using -> and *, we should be able to copy them very efficiently, they should be type-safe, and they should be small and not take much memory. We can accomplish all those goals.

There are two main types of smart pointers that can help us with shared objects. They both implement two of the previous solutions we have discussed, but they wrap them in the convenience of a pointer-like object, which makes them more foolproof and actually helps to remove a lot of extraneous code when dealing with handles and reference counting directly.

16.3.6.1 Handle-Based Smart Pointers

A handle-based smart pointer is simply a wrapper around a handle. It does not need to have any other data. That is handy because it means that, on most platforms, we can make a handle-based smart pointer be just as small as a regular pointer.

The pointer takes care of doing all the legwork for us. Remember that to use a handle, we had to first translate from the handle to the actual pointer? The smart pointer takes care of doing this under the hood. We just go ahead and use it as a regular pointer. To do so, we must override some of the more esoteric operators defined in C++, such as operator -> and operator *. This is the skeleton for a handle-based smart pointer:

```
class EntityPtr
{
public:
    EntityPtr(Handle h) : m_hEntity(h) {}
    bool operator == (int n)
                     { return (n == (int) GetPtr(m_hEntity); }
    bool operator != (int n) { !operator==(n); }
    GameEntity * operator->() { return GetPtr(m_hEntity); }
    GameEntity & operator *() { *return GetPtr(m_hEntity); };

private:
    Handle m_hEntity;
};
```

Notice how, thanks to the overridden operators, we can treat it as a real pointer:

```
EntityPtr ptr(GetEntity());
if (ptr != NULL)
{
    cout << ptr->GetName();
    const Point3d & pos = ptr->GetPosition();
}
```

We can even check against NULL like we normally do with any pointer because we have overridden the operator== function, which checks whether a corresponding pointer exists and that it is not NULL.

The preceding smart pointer works only for pointers of GameEntity types, but we really want to use it with any other pointer, including resource pointers or anything that uses handles. Because the only thing that changes is the type of the pointer, we use a template to create the type of pointer we want:

```
template <class DataType >
class HandlePtr
{
public:
    HandlePtr(Handle h) : m_hEntity(h) {}
    bool operator == (int n)
                    { return (n == (int)GetPtr(m_hEntity); }
    bool operator != (int n) { !operator==(n); }
    DataType * operator->() { return GetPtr(m_hEntity); }
    DataType & operator *() { *return GetPtr(m_hEntity); };

private:
    Handle m_hEntity;
};
```

To use it, we just instantiate the template with the type to which we want to point:

```
typedef HandlePtr<Texture *> TexturePtr;
TexturePtr pTexture = CreateTexture("smiley.tif");
```

Suddenly, we have all the safety of handles with the convenience of pointers. That is all that smart pointers are about.

16.3.6.2 Reference-Counting Smart Pointers

Reference-counting smart pointers wrap the reference-counting approach into a smart pointer. Conceptually, every time a smart pointer is created to an object, the reference count is increased. Whenever that object is destroyed, the reference count is decreased. In a way, they are doing the calls to `AddRef()` and `Release()` automatically, based on the life of the smart pointer itself. As usual, if the reference count of the shared object reaches zero, it gets deleted.

In practice, things are a bit more complicated. We have to deal with the mechanics of copying smart pointers, as well as loops in reference-counting graphics, and we might even want to move the reference counting outside of the shared object and into the smart pointer itself. (See "Suggested Reading" at the end of this chapter for many more details on different effective implementations.)

The Boost Smart Pointer Library provides different types of smart pointers for different purposes. One of them, the `shared_ptr`, implements exactly this reference-counting approach. Just as are the handle-based smart pointers, the reference-counting pointers are also templated for type-safe use with any pointer type.

16.3.6.3 Recommendation

Smart pointers can be the best of both worlds. If you are prepared to invest a bit of time and plan from the beginning how they can be integrated with the rest of the engine, they can be an ideal solution.

Implementing a smart pointer from scratch can be fairly simple and very enlightening. But if the mechanics it implements are complex, it can be difficult to make it work correctly under all circumstances (for example, temporaries generated, copies in the stack versus the heap, and so on).

If what you need is already provided in one of the smart pointer types in the Boost library, then go ahead and use it. Just make sure you read carefully through the documentation to find out what its exact memory and performance cost is, and what its behavior is when copied, deleted, or passed around.

One of the situations in which smart pointers do not always behave exactly like a normal, dumb pointer is when casting to different types. The conversion from a pointer to a child class to a pointer to its parent class happens automatically in C++. Unless you provide some special constructors, that same conversion does not happen with smart pointers. The most common way of dealing with conversions is to provide special templated functions just to perform the casting.

16.4 Conclusion

In this chapter, we have seen how we can use object factories to create any object type in a very flexible way. Object factories allow us to create objects of a type that is determined at runtime instead of at compile time. This allows us to create and load objects very easily, as well as to dynamically extend the types of objects in our game.

We then saw how having shared objects can be problematic in C++. If multiple objects are keeping pointers to a shared object, who is responsible for deleting that object? And most important, what happens when that object is deleted? We covered several different techniques for dealing with shared objects, including these:

- Not sharing any objects
- Not worrying about object sharing and destruction
- Letting the owner deal with the destruction of the object and the responsibility to notify all the objects that kept pointers to the shared object
- Applying reference counting through the use of the `AddRef()` and `Release()` functions
- Using handles to avoid keeping any extra pointers around
- Using smart pointers to implement reference counting or handle usage, but in a pointer syntax

Suggested Reading

These are some good references that deal with object factories. In particular, Alexandrescu's book goes into a lot of depth on the implementation details of a templated factory. The *Design Patterns* book also contains a good general description of the Observer pattern.

Alexandrescu, Andrei, *Modern C++ Design*. Addison-Wesley, 2001.
Gamma, Erich, et al., *Design Patterns*. Addison-Wesley, 1995.
Larameé, François Dominic, "A Game Entity Factory." *Game Programming Gems 2*. Charles River Media, 2001.

Here is a good article on how to use handles for resource management:

Bilas, Scott, "A Generic Handle-Based Resource Manager." *Game Programming Gems*. Charles River Media, 2000.

The following books explain reference counting in more detail and delve into the intricacies of implementing robust smart pointers:

Alexandrescu, Andrei, *Modern C++ Design*. Addison-Wesley, 2001.
Eberly, David H., *3D Game Engine Design*. Morgan Kaufmann, 2001.

Hawkins, Brian, "Handle-Based Smart Pointers." *Game Programming Gems 3.* Charles River Media, 2002.

Meyers, Scott, *More Effective C++.* Addison-Wesley, 1996.

Rogerson, Dale, *Inside COM.* Microsoft Press, 1997.

Finally, the Boost library provides several smart pointer classes, along with extensive documentation for each of them:

C++ Boost Smart Pointer Library. Available online at *http://www.boost. org/libs/smart_ptr/index.htm.*

17

OBJECT SERIALIZATION

In This Chapter

- Game Entity Serialization Overview
- Game Entity Serialization Implementation
- Putting It All Together

*S*erialization is the ability to store an object into some medium and then restore at a later time. The medium can be any type of data storage: memory, disk, or even a network pipe.

Serialization is an essential component of games. At the very least, a game has to load its levels, assets, and game state for the game to start. Most games also allow some form of in-game save, which can be later restored so the user can continue playing from that point.

Unlike other languages, C++ does not offer built-in serialization facilities, so we must manually implement what we need. This chapter looks at how to effectively apply serialization to games, examines the challenges presented by serialization, and proposes solutions for dealing with both game entities and game resources.

17.1 GAME ENTITY SERIALIZATION OVERVIEW

Just about every game has to save the state of its game entities. Sometimes this is in the form of a mid-game save or a checkpoint to allow the user to come back later and continue from that point. Even if a game does not offer a mid-game save feature, it still has to create an initial state for all the game entities at the beginning of each level. Most of the time, that initial state is generated by a level-editing tool the designers can use to place game entities in the world, set their parameters and the relationships between them, and save them to create a new game level.

17.1.1 Entities versus Resources

Game entities are objects that represent the information about specific things in the game. They are the objects we interact with: the enemies that shoot at us, the objectives we are trying to accomplish, and even the camera through which we are looking at the world. All these things can, and probably will, change during gameplay. We care about saving them in order to preserve the state of the game world.

It is important to distinguish between game entities and game resources. *Resources* are some of the parts that make up game entities. Resources typically do not change during gameplay, and they do not have any information specific to a game entity. They just exist so that entities can use them. Some examples of resources are textures, geometry data, sounds, and script files.

The key difference between entities and resources is that resources do not change after they are loaded (they might change under some rare circumstances, but we explore that possibility later). We do not have to save the resources to capture the state of the game. They have not changed from the time they were loaded from the DVD when the level started. It is possible to load a previous state just by restoring all the game entities because the correct resources are already loaded in memory.

Entities and resources present totally different challenges. Entities must be both saved and loaded, while resources just have to be loaded. Entities tend to be relatively small objects, but they are made out of very heterogeneous data and are highly interconnected among themselves. Resources, on the other hand, are large, fairly homogeneous, and without many interconnections to other resources. This chapter deals only with the serialization of game entities because they present very different challenges from resources.

17.1.2 The Simplest Solution That Does Not Work

Game entity serialization is one of those problems that seems very simple and straightforward at first, but becomes complicated and hard to get to work correctly when you start implementing it. At first the problem seems trivial: go through every entity in the world and save the object to disk. Then, to restore the game state, we just load that data back into memory. What is wrong with this approach?

There are many things wrong with it. The most significant problem is caused by pointers. The value of a pointer is just a memory address, but memory addresses change from one run of the game to the next. If we were to save the value of a pointer and later restore it and try to use it, it would most likely cause the program to crash because it would probably be pointing to some random memory location that the program is not using. It certainly will not be pointing where it was when we saved it.

The second problem is how to restore the objects. Just saving the data from each entity is not enough. Later on, when we are loading that data to restore the game, how do we know what to do with the data? How do we know whether we are reading data for a projectile entity or for a camera entity? We do not. We need some additional information to restore things correctly.

The third problem is that we probably cannot treat our game entities like plain C structures. It is not enough to create them and fill them with the correct data. We need to ensure that the initialization for each entity happens as it would normally happen. That means that its constructor gets called, and that it receives any other initialization calls. That gives the entity the chance to register itself with some other manager class, or to acquire resources or anything else it might normally do.

17.1.3 What We Need

Given than we cannot just dump the bits on the hard drive and load them again, what is the ideal solution? Let's first examine what we want in high-level terms, and we will worry about the specific implementations of it in the next section.

We want to be able to save the state of any game entity at any time. We clearly want this system to deal correctly with pointers and relationships in general. If an end-of-mission trigger entity was supposed to go off when a certain entity was destroyed, we still want that trigger to be associated with the same entity when we load the game, even if each resides in totally different memory locations.

When we consider what to save, we have to make a distinction between instance data and type data. *Type data* is usually created by the designers, and it includes the general characteristics of all the objects of that type. For example, a particular enemy unit type can have maximum hit points, certain types of weapons, a maximum speed, and a flag indicating whether or not it has flying capabilities as part of its type data. If the type data never changes, there is no need to save it. If it does change, we have to save it, but only once and not for every entity of that type. The *instance data* of our enemy unit, on the other hand, includes its current position and velocity, its current hit points, and how many rounds it has left in its weapons. It's the instance data we care about saving.

When thinking about the data we want to save, we must also consider how important it is to save all the little details. Does our game require that every single detail be saved exactly right, or can we approximate things? For example, if a fire is burning in the fireplace when we save the game, it is important that the logs be still burning when we load the game. But does it matter whether the flames have the exact same number of particles as they did before? Do they have to be in the exact same position? Probably not. In this case, it is enough to note that there is a fire effect and that it has been burning for a while. On the other hand, it is important that we store the exact location, velocity, and maybe even acceleration of some other objects. If an arrow was in the air when we saved the game, we definitely want it to be there and to continue its trajectory as expected when we load it back up.

One aspect that is not particularly difficult, but would be great if our solution could support it, is to be able to use different formats for saving and restoring the entity data. Doing so would allow us to have a very fast binary format that we can use when the game ships, but also have a slower, but much easier-to-debug-and-read, text-based version. In general, this is a good approach to take with almost any type of serialization, especially if loading efficiency is important.

We also want to be able to serialize the entities to and from any type of storage media. At the very least, we want to be able to save them to and load them from disk and memory, while also having the flexibility to use other types of media, such as memory cards or even a network pipe. Being able to use different types of media, such as memory, can come in very handy when we have already loaded a file in memory and we want to create the appropriate entities from its contents.

Serialization can also be used to transfer entities across a network. However, even though it might seem tempting to reuse this technology, do not expect to be able to create a fully network-enabled game just by supporting a network pipe as one of your media targets. This feature can be used to create new entities on other machines or to pass the data for a new type of entity that only the local machine knows about. It is definitely not enough to support all the real-time updates necessary for a full multiplayer game. Updating of game entities is a difficult topic that requires a book all by itself.

We have not discussed the difference between a full game save and a checkpoint. *Checkpoints* are more often employed in console games; they store the state of the game world at a particular place in the level, but usually with most entities reset to their original states. Only a handful of states are preserved, such as the player's position and what objectives have been accomplished so far. Everything else—such as doors, secret passages, enemies, and power-ups—are usually back at their initial states.

Checkpoints can be implemented using the same technique as game entity serialization, but saving the state of only a few selected entities. Whenever we need to revert the state of the game to one of the checkpoints, we can reset the level to its initial state and then serialize the few selected entities.

Size can be an important aspect of saved games. On PCs, or even on consoles with large amounts of permanent storage, the size of a saved game file does not matter very much. Hard-drive space is cheap and fast, so taking 5–10 MB per file is not unheard of. However, sometimes we have to save our games to small devices, like memory cards, so saved games must be kept as small as possible. Keeping the saved game file size under control can make the difference between fitting dozens of saved games or taking up the whole card with just a couple of saves. Sometimes this is enough of an incentive for games to implement the checkpoint save system because saving a checkpoint requires much less data.

17.2 GAME ENTITY SERIALIZATION IMPLEMENTATION

So far, we have put together a sort of wish list of what we want as far as serialization goes for our games. This section turns those wishes into reality.

17.2.1 Streams

Streams allow us to abstract out the media we use for serialization. A stream is just a sequence of bytes in a particular order that can be read and written to. Additionally, we might want to provide other useful operations, such as rewinding or moving to a particular location.

The standard C++ library provides us with streams for general input and output with the `iostream` classes. It also provides a set of templated classes for input, some for output, and some that do both. Should we take advantage of these pre-built classes for our serialization needs? It depends on our specific situation. Most of the time, these classes are too heavyweight for what we really want. We want something small and easily customizable to deal with unusual requirements and strange media types. Most of the time, we have no need for the flexibility these templated classes provide with locales and character traits. Therefore, we will go ahead and create our own versions; but if it makes more sense to reuse the standard C++ ones in your project, go ahead and use their interfaces instead.

The `IStream` interface describes all the operations that we want to make available to streams. As we saw in Chapter 12, "Abstract Interfaces," having an abstract interface allows us to easily switch specific implementations of the streams at runtime without the rest of the code noticing the switch. This fulfills one of our wish-list items: being able to serialize entities to any media type. As long as we have a stream for that type of media, everything should work correctly.

```
class IStream
{
public:
    virtual ~IStream() {};
    virtual void Reset() = 0;

    virtual int Read (int bytes, void * pBuffer) = 0;
    virtual int Write (int bytes, void * pBuffer) = 0;

    virtual bool SetCurPos (int pos) = 0;
    virtual int GetCurPos () = 0;
};
```

Then we can inherit from this class and provide specific implementations for memory streams, file streams, or any other type of media we need. We might also want to provide very platform-specific stream types that take advantage of all the functions available to that particular platform so that we have the most efficient implementation possible. For example, a default file stream could be implemented with just `fopen` and `fread` operations, but we could write a special stream that is optimized to read from a DVD, taking into account goals such as reducing the number of seeks, or that is optimized to read from a hard drive in a specific console, using console API calls for low-level hard-drive access.

The specific stream implementations each has constructors or initialization functions that create the specific constructor with the correct parameters we want. For example, the file stream could take a filename and maybe another parameter indicating whether to open it in read or write mode. The memory stream could take a specific memory location and a size to use as its source, and a default constructor with no parameters that just creates the stream contents anywhere in memory. Alternatively, we can provide that functionality with the regular member functions of the stream classes instead of using constructors.

```
class StreamFile : public IStream
{
public:
```

```
        StreamFile(const string & filename);
        virtual ~StreamFile();
        // ...
};


class StreamMemory : public IStream
{
public:
        StreamMemory();
        StreamMemory(void * pBuffer, int size);
        virtual ~StreamMemory();
        // ...
};
```

In addition to this minimal interface, we might also want to provide some helper functions so that common data types can be read more easily. Keeping with the spirit of trying to have the simplest possible interface, those kinds of functions make more sense as nonmember functions. If you really like the C++ stream syntax, you can use operator << and operator >> to manipulate the streams. Otherwise, you can just use more straightforward functions, such as read and write.

```
int     ReadInt     (IStream & stream);
float   ReadFloat   (IStream & stream);
string  ReadString  (IStream & stream);

bool WriteInt      (IStream & stream, int n);
bool WriteFloat    (IStream & stream, float f);
bool WriteString   (IStream & stream, const string & s);
```

We can also implement special types of streams that read and write compressed data, for example. That way, we can move the complexity of compressing and uncompressing the data out onto the specific implementation of the stream class, and any type of object can then take advantage of it.

It is also possible to create more complex file types on top of a stream. For example, we can implement a binary chunk-based file format, an .ini file format, or even an XML file format on top of a stream.

As an example, here is how the integer read and write functions are implemented:

```
int ReadInt (IStream & stream)
{
        int n = 0;
```

```
        stream.Read(sizeof(int), (void *)&n);
        return n;
}

bool WriteInt (IStream & stream, int n)
{
        int iNumWritten = stream.Write(sizeof(int), &n);
        return (iNumWritten == sizeof(int));
}
```

If you find yourself writing certain types of objects to a stream very frequently—such as points, vectors, or matrices—you can write helper functions for each of those types. Doing so makes it easier for the rest of the code to serialize them.

17.2.2 Saving

When it comes time to save game entities, it is best if each entity decides for itself how to save itself to the stream. To this end, we can make a pass through all the entities we are interested in saving and give them the chance to serialize themselves.

17.2.2.1 ISerializable Interface

We can call the write function for each entity we want to serialize. We could just make that function part of the base GameEntity class, and everything would work fine. Entities that did not want to be serialized could just leave it blank, and all the others would implement the function, depending on their contents.

A better approach is to make the serialization-related functions part of an abstract interface, ISerializable. Then the GameEntity base class can inherit from it and everything would work the same way. However, splitting those functions into a separate interface allows us to easily serialize other types of objects that are not necessarily game entities. If we really have to discover whether or not an object implements the ISerializable interface, we can use the QueryInterface approach described in Chapter 12. For now, we just assume that all game entities implement the ISerializable interface.

What does the ISerializable interface look like? The interface is very simply along these lines:

```
class ISerializable
{
public:
```

```
        virtual ~ISerializable() {};
        virtual bool Write(IStream & stream) const = 0;
        virtual bool Read(IStream & stream) = 0;
    };
```

Clearly, we also use the ISerializable interface during the load process. This is why it has a Read() function as well.

Again, if we really prefer the C++ stream syntax, we could have used the operator >> and operator << method. Or if we want to be really fancy, we could have written two functions called Serialize, but with one of them being constant and the other non-constant. The constant one can do only the writing, and the non-constant one does the reading. However, this is more trouble than it is worth, and it makes it unclear which function is being called when. A terser interface cannot beat being explicit and clear about our intentions.

17.2.2.2 Implementing **Write()**

Implementing the Write() function for each entity is a very straightforward task. We have to decide what data we want to save. Then, for each member variable we want to save, we serialize it to the stream.

For integers, floats, and other standard data types, we just stream them directly. But what if our entity contains a member variable of its own that we have to serialize? We simply have to ensure that the variable also implements the ISerializable interface, and we just call its Write() function, which in turn is implemented in the same way. This way, we can save any number of nested objects without any difficulty. If the entity contains pointers or references to other objects instead of the object itself, we have to deal with them in a different way (as described in the next section).

If our entity classes use inheritance, we might want to let the parent classes deal with the serialization for their own data. Derived classes have to worry about only the new variables they add.

Here is some potential code for the Write() function of a camera class:

```
    bool GameCamera::Write(IStream & stream) const
    {
        // Let the parent class write common things like
        // position, rotation, etc.
        bool bSuccess = GameEntity::Write(stream);
```

```
// These are basic data types, serialize them directly
bSuccess &= WriteFloat(stream, m_FOV);
bSuccess &= WriteFloat(stream, m_NearPlane);
bSuccess &= WriteFloat(stream, m_FarPlane);

// This is an object that needs to be serialized in turn
bSuccess &= m_lens.Write(stream);

return bSuccess;
}
```

What we have implemented so far is a pure binary format—no headers, no extra information—just the raw data. It might be a fine format for whenever we need to load entities as fast as possible, such as in the released game, but it is not a very friendly format for game development. As soon as a minor change is made to an entity class, all the previously saved games become unusable. Worse, there is no way to detect that something is wrong, and we will most likely read garbage data.

For this reason, it is a good idea to implement at least two types of formats: a fast one like the one we just saw, and a slower one that is easier to debug, and that still works when the format changes. We might even want to make that slower format text based, so it is easier to debug and examine during development.

17.2.2.3 Unique Identifiers

We still have not solved one of the major problems: what to do about saving pointers. It turns out we have several choices.

The first possibility is to completely avoid pointers, or at least pointers to other game entities. Instead of a pointer, we could refer to any other game entities through unique IDs (or UIDs). If every game entity has a UID that is guaranteed to never be repeated, then we can just keep that number. Anytime we have to work directly with the entity, we ask the game entity system to give us a pointer to the entity corresponding to that number.

In addition to solving the problem of not having to save pointers, this approach also simplifies the bookkeeping necessary between game entities. If we keep direct pointers to entities, but one entity is removed from the world, what happens when another entity tries to access it? In theory, we could never delete any entities; we'd have to keep them around, just making sure they never get updated or rendered. If we use the UID method, and an entity does not exist anymore, we just get a NULL pointer back and we know not to use it.

For example, the following code updates the position of a homing projectile that has locked on to some target, all using the UID method:

```
void HomingProjectile::Update()
{
    if (!m_bLocked)
        return;

    GameEntity * pTarget = GetEntityFromUID(m_targetUID);
    if (pTarget == NULL)
    {
        m_bLocked = false;
        return;
    }

    // Do whatever course correction is necessary here...
    // ...
}
```

This is exactly like the solution to the shared-object problem using handles that we saw in Chapter 16, "Object Creation and Management." The same comments about the construction of handles and how the translation is implemented also apply here.

17.2.2.4 Resources

What about pointers to resources instead of entities? Usually, this is less problematic. Entities point to resources because they were created that way, and their data was set up that way from the beginning. For example, one of the properties of a certain player-avatar entity is the mesh it uses to be rendered, along with all its animations and textures. Usually, entities refer to resources by filename or by some resource ID, and that is all that we need. If the resource it points to is going to change during the program, the entity should save that filename or ID to be restored later on. Otherwise, it always remains the same, so there is no need to save it.

17.2.2.5 Saving Pointers

There is an argument in favor of using pointers between game entities, which makes life simpler and code easier to write. We still have to deal with the problem of entities disappearing in the middle of the game, but if that is not an issue, changing everything to use UIDs can be more trouble than it is worth.

It is also possible that our game entity system has been developed without plans for serialization, and saving the game was a feature that was left for the very end of the development cycle. Or maybe it was purposefully left out of the first release of the game, but we want to add it for the sequel while we reuse the source code.

In that case, changing an existing code base from using pointers to using UIDs can be quite a task. Imagine wading through hundreds or thousands of classes, changing all the pointers and the code that uses them to UIDs. If all we want is a quick way of serializing entities, there is a better alternative: we can save the pointers straight to disk.

We know that the memory address contained in the pointer will not point to the correct memory location when we load the game again. Clearly, something has to be done to solve that problem when we load the game entities. For now, we will save the raw pointers and leave it at that. The next section covers what has to be done at load time to get everything to work.

17.2.3 Loading

All we have done so far are preparations for being able to load the game entities and restore the game state. Now comes the actual game load itself.

17.2.3.1 Creating Objects

A requirement when restoring different types of objects is to be able to create any object type based on the data we read from the stream. It is not enough to be able to read the data that should go in a GameCamera class; we have to know that it belongs to a GameCamera class, and we have to actually create an object of that type.

If the problem sounds familiar, it should, because we covered it in detail in Chapter 16. A good game entity factory should be able to create any entity type we want just by passing the class name or a type identifier. Then we can call Read() on the newly created object to load all its data from the stream.

```
string strClassName = ReadString(stream);
GameEntity * pEntity = EntityFactory::Create(strClassName);
// ... Some bookkeeping here ...
pEntity->Read(stream);
```

Depending on what type of factory system we have, we can save full strings for the class name of our entities and create them again by passing the strings to the factory system. Using strings has the usual tradeoffs:

they are easy to debug and very readable, but they are slower and take more memory than using simple identifiers. Although they are more efficient, 32-bit identifiers do not immediately tell us what type of object we are trying to create when we look at the identifier in the debugger.

17.2.3.2 Loading Pointers

How do we deal with the thorny issue of pointers? As previously mentioned, we could just save them straight in the code, and they would restore correctly. Here is how to do it.

We know that every memory address is unique. By storing the memory address of an entity, we are uniquely identifying it. If along with every entity we also store its memory location when it is saved, we can construct a translation table at load time that can allow us to go from the old memory address to the new memory address.

For the translation to work correctly, it must be done after all the entities are loaded, otherwise we might try to look up a memory address that we have not loaded yet. The load process is as follows: first we load all the entities and construct a table mapping old addresses to new ones; then we make a "fix-up" pass through all the entities and give them a chance to fix any pointers they have to point to the new, correct memory locations.

To accomplish this fix-up of addresses, we need a bit more support from the loading system and the ISerializable interface. After we are done loading all the entities, we give all the entities a chance to fix up their addresses in their pointers. To accomplish this, we extend the ISerializable interface to include a Fixup() function.

```
class ISerializable
{
public:
    virtual ~ISerializable() {};
    virtual bool Write(IStream & stream) const = 0;
    virtual bool Read(IStream & stream) = 0;
    virtual void Fixup() = 0;
};
```

The same way that entities implemented their own Write() and Read() functions, they can now implement a Fixup() function that takes care of translating old pointer addresses to correct addresses for each saved pointer. If an entity saved no pointers, it does not have to implement the Fixup() function because the base GameEntity class implemented an empty one. As with the other serialization functions, an entity must call its parent's version of Fixup() in addition to doing its own pointer translations.

To make this fix-up step possible, each entity must be associated with its old address when it is loaded back in memory. This is done by simply saving the address of each entity when it is written out to the stream.

With all this information in hand, we are ready to deal with pointers correctly. Whenever an object is created from the stream, we also read what its old address was and enter it in the translation table along with the new address. The class `AddressTranslator` is in charge of keeping track of all the addresses and providing us with a translation during the fix-up pass.

```
GameEntity * LoadEntity(IStream & stream)
{
    string strClassName = ReadString(stream);
    GameEntity * pEntity = EntityFactory::Create(
                                    strClassName);

    void * pOldAddress = (void *)ReadInt(stream);
    AddressTranslator::AddAddress(pOldAddress, pEntity);

    pEntity->Read(stream);
    return pEntity;
}
```

The `AddAddress()` function puts the new address in a hash table, indexed by the old address, so it is very efficient to translate from old address to new address.

To implement the `Fixup()` function, we can use the other function provided in the `AddressTranslator`, `TranslateAddress()`. This function looks through the hash table for an old pointer value and fetches the new value. This is how the `Fixup()` function for our `HomingProjectile` class might look:

```
void HomingProjectile::Fixup()
{
    m_pTarget=(GameEntity *)AddressTranslator::
                      TranslateAddress(m_pTarget);
}
```

After the load is complete and all the pointer fix-ups are done, we should reset the translation table to save memory because it is not needed any longer.

One important thing to notice is that this method works only for pointers that we explicitly saved and then added to the table. In this case, it happens automatically for all game entities. If we were to attempt to do this with a pointer that had not been added to the translation table, it should assert or print a big warning to let us know something went wrong in the translation process. Otherwise, the problem might go unnoticed, and the bug might not be found until after exhaustive testing.

The problem is a little bit more subtle, though. We have to be very careful about saving the correct memory address of an object. That address must be the exact address pointed to by other game entities. If it is the slightest bit different, the translation step will fail. How could the address be "slightly" different? Multiple inheritance could make it so. When multiple inheritance is involved (see Chapter 2, "Multiple Inheritance"), casting to the different parent classes could result in an offset to the value of the pointer itself. Fortunately in this case, GameEntity inherits only from IRenderable, so we have nothing to worry about. If it inherited from another abstract interface or from a separate base class, then we would have to be extremely careful to always save the pointer of type GameEntity.

17.3 PUTTING IT ALL TOGETHER

ON THE CD

The serialization example on the CD-ROM has source code for a fully functional program that saves and restores the state of a game. It creates a simple tree of GameEntity objects, saves it to disk, deletes it, and loads it again. To verify that it indeed works as expected, it prints the contents of the tree before it is saved and after it is restored from disk.

The program is intended only as a working example of how to apply the concepts in this chapter. It is not robust code that can be thrown into any development environment. It does not handle errors well, if at all, and the file format is too raw and basic. By keeping the code small and simple, it is easier to understand the concepts behind it instead of getting lost in layers of complexity and error checking. For example, the game entity factory is just one function with hardcoded entity types. It is the simplest solution that works, but we saw much better ways of implementing it in Chapter 16.

Of particular interest is how all the pointers of all the entities are saved and restored correctly. All game entities have a vector of pointers to child entities. Those pointers are simply stored and then translated in the fix-up pass. Additionally, the camera has a pointer to another game entity that it uses to focus on. That pointer is treated the same way, and it is restored correctly. Figure 17.1 shows the structure of the game entity tree that is serialized in the sample code on the CD-ROM.

ON THE CD

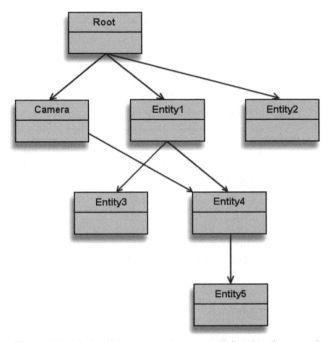

Figure 17.1 A simple game entity tree serialized in the sample code.

17.4 CONCLUSION

In this chapter, we have seen how something that sounds as simple as implementing in-game saves can be quite difficult to implement correctly. In-game saves are just one example of the problem of serialization: storing the state of an object in some data medium and being able to completely restore it at a later time.

Other languages offer better built-in facilities for serialization; but in C++, we have to take the hard road and implement them ourselves. In particular, when dealing with any complex object structure, we have to deal with the issue of saving and restoring pointers to memory locations.

This chapter presented several different variations on serialization. All of them rely on the use of streams, which allow us to abstract out the actual media to which we are serializing our entities. We can provide streams that work on disk files, memory, or even over a network.

We then saw how we could save the state of game entities by using the `ISerializable` interface, making each entity responsible for determining what to save. We also discussed the possibility of using UIDs instead of pointers to model relationships between entities. However, if the program has not been implemented to use UIDs from the beginning, changing it is a time-consuming task.

Finally, we saw how to restore the objects from a stream. We also learned how to translate raw memory pointers so they work correctly, even after the game entities have been loaded in different memory locations.

SUGGESTED READING

In-game saves is not as glamorous a subject as using the latest pixel shaders for photorealistic effects, so we are left without much literature on the subject. The following books have some short but interesting sections on object serialization in games:

Brownlow, Marin, "Save Me Now!," *Game Programming Gems 3.* Charles River Media, 2002.
Eberly, David H., *3D Game Engine Design.* Morgan Kaufmann, 2000.

The original factory pattern is described in the Gang of Four book:

Gamma, Erich, et al., *Design Patterns.* Addison-Wesley, 1995.

18

DEALING WITH LARGE PROJECTS

In This Chapter

- Logical versus Physical Structure
- Classes and Files
- Header Files
- Libraries
- Configurations

S o far in this book, we have covered logical concepts of game programming: memory allocation, plug-ins, and runtime type information. That knowledge is adequate for a small project or a quick demo,
but it falls short when dealing with a full-size game project. Even the best
data structures or slickest algorithms in the world cannot help when a full
compilation of the game takes over an hour, or when the process of releasing a gold candidate becomes cumbersome and error prone.

This chapter deals with the realities of working with a large code base
for a game project. We see why excessive dependencies between files
should be avoided as much as possible and present some rules to improve
that situation as well as speed up compile times. We also deal with how
projects should be structured so that we can easily create different versions of the game or deal with targets in different platforms.

By the end of this chapter, you should have enough tricks in your
portfolio to feel confident enough to tackle a large game project.

18.1 LOGICAL VERSUS PHYSICAL STRUCTURE

The *logical structure* of a program, which is the only subject covered in most C++ books, deals with classes, algorithms, data, and their relationships. Clearly, the logical structure is crucial for the success of a program; the choice of data structures determines how efficient the program is, and the relationship between classes make the program easier or harder to maintain and debug.

The *physical structure* of a program, on the other hand, deals with more concrete items such as files, directories, and even project or make files. It is a much less glamorous topic, and one that does not get the attention it deserves, but it becomes almost as important as the logical structure as the project size grows. The exact same program can be implemented with many different physical structures, but some of them allow for fast compile times, easy expansion, and the building of different targets, while others cause extremely long and painful build times and difficulty in creating different versions of the program.

Just to put things in perspective, let's look at some real numbers. A normal PC or console game project can easily have a code base on the order of 4,000–5,000 different files, all of which must be compiled to create the game. That number does not even come close when we consider behemoths such as massively multiplayer online games, which can have a code base many times that of a regular game, plus all the code for their servers, billing, backup, and so forth. With a project of that size, the physical structure of the program becomes crucial. A well-structured project has compile times of perhaps 5–10 minutes, and small changes require almost no recompilations. On the other hand, a badly structured project can easily run into compile times of over an hour, and even a minor change can trigger a compilation that lasts for 10 to 20 minutes. Which project would you rather work on?

Physical structure is determined by which files need other files in order to compile. In C++, "needing" another file means including that file through the #include preprocessor directive. In an ideal world, every file would compile by itself. But this is clearly not possible because a program is made up of interacting objects; they have to know about each other to a certain extent. Minimizing the number of connections between files is a goal toward achieving an acceptable physical structure. The level of connections between a file and the rest of the source code is called *insulation*, and the fewer connections, the more insulated the file will be.

Fortunately, a good physical structure goes hand in hand with a good logical structure. A class that hides its implementation from the outside world is said to be well encapsulated. The better encapsulated a class is, and the less other classes depend on it, the cleaner the logical structure is, with all the usual consequences: ease of maintenance, clear debugging, and simpler testing.

As a general rule, whenever a file is modified, all the files that included it are considered modified and must be compiled. Ideally, a change to a single file should result in the recompilation of only one or two files. A really tangled physical structure causes most of the files in the project to be recompiled as a result of an innocent-looking change to one file. The turnaround time in these situations, from making a code change to being able to run the game and test the results, quickly becomes unbearable, and it can result in lower quality work, untested features, and hacked shortcuts in the code to avoid major recompilations.

The rest of this chapter looks at different aspects of physical structure. We explain some possible organizations and solutions for achieving a good physical structure and maximizing programmer efficiency in a large-project environment.

18.2 CLASSES AND FILES

At the core of the physical structure of a program, we have files. Organizing them correctly is the first step toward an effective physical organization. A lot of this information is available just by browsing through existing C++ code; some of it is not as common, though, so it might come as a surprise. This section should give you a solid understanding of how and why classes are split into different files.

In general, a good rule to follow is to have two files for every C++ class: one header file (usually with the extension .h or .hpp) and one implementation file (with the extension .cpp). This organization has several advantages. First, it is convenient to browse through the files and locate a particular class just by looking at the filenames. Even with fancy IDEs and other source-browsing tools, such a simple system is still very useful.

Second, this rule strikes a good balance for minimizing compile times, especially incremental compile times, which are the ones we are most concerned about because we do them many times a day while we are developing new code or fixing bugs. If we had packed several classes per file, compile times would be faster; but we would have to compile more code, even for a simple change to one class. Splitting a class into more files does not give us any extra advantages because most likely the whole class has to be compiled when a change is made.

Finally (and this is very subjective), having the full class implementation in one file seems like a perfect unit to work with. A file should hopefully never be so long as to become unmanageable and cause us to get lost, but it should also not be so small that it becomes meaningless. If your class ever starts to get so large that you feel the urge to split it into more files, chances are it should really be split into multiple classes.

18.3 HEADER FILES

A *header file* is the window through which the outside world looks into a class. The information there lets other code know about our class and how to use it, nothing else. A header file is used by other parts of the code, by using the #include directive in their own files.

18.3.1 What Goes into a Header File?

So what should go in the header file? The quick answer is that the header file should have the minimum amount of code that still allows everything to compile and run correctly. That is easier said than done, especially if you are coming from a C background where header files were used to dump everything that was not implementation code.

Preprocessor #include statements are extremely important to the structure of the program and deserve a whole section devoted to them, so they are the subject of the next subsection. For now, we will carefully ignore them in our discussion of header files.

As a first step, move any nonessential information out of the header file and into the implementation file. Constants that are used only in the class implementation, or small private structures or classes are good candidates to move out of a header file. Always ask yourself, is this something other classes need to interact with this class?

Unfortunately, C++ muddies the water a bit by forcing us to put some things in the header file that would be best placed in the implementation file. The whole private section of a class is only of interest to the class itself, yet we are forced to declare all private member functions and variables in the header file. This has the unfortunate consequence of leaking out some extra information through the header file. We see some possible solutions to this problem in the next section.

Something else to keep in mind when creating header files is how they are used in the rest of the program. Class header files are reasonably straightforward: they get included everywhere the class is used. This is usually not a problem, and only a small number of files include a particular header file. However, sometimes there are special classes that we seem to need everywhere: an error class with all the error codes for the whole program, a resource file, or a header file with a lot of the text IDs for the translation table.

Header files that become that ubiquitous are dangerous, but they can be tolerated if they hardly ever change. However, if they are likely to change during the program development, they should be avoided as much as possible. A file containing all the global error codes is likely to be included everywhere and updated frequently as we add more error codes. For example, we decide we want to add a new error code to indicate that one of the network clients has dropped out. We add it to the header file, do a quick recompile to test our changes and find out to our dismay that it has triggered a full project rebuild. Every library, every DLL, and every single source code file in the game has to be rebuilt. This could take up to several hours on really large projects.

Instead, a file like that is best split into several unrelated files, each containing error codes for different subsystems. The graphics renderer could have one, the network code another, the file IO another. Adding a new network error code would simply cause a recompile of the network subsystem and a full link, drastically decreasing our time for the change to about five minutes.

18.3.2 Include Guards

An `#include` is a *preprocessor directive*—a statement that allows the preprocessor to modify the source code before the compiler ever sees it. In this case of including files, the preprocessor scans every single file for the `#include "filename"` directive, opens up the specified filename, reads all its contents, and inserts them where the `include` statement is.

There really are no rules about using the `#include` directive for only header files. We can use it for just about anything: header files, implementation files, parts of a file, or any random text file. However, traditionally, `#include` is used to include header files only, with either class declarations, function declarations, or global constants and defines, although you see some other different uses from time to time.

Consider the following code:

```
// Game.h
#define MAX_PLAYERS    16

// Game.cpp
#include "Game.h"
Players players[MAX_PLAYERS];
```

This code is transformed by the preprocessor into something like this:

```
// Game.cpp
#define MAX_PLAYERS    16
Players players[MAX_PLAYERS];
```

This translated version is what the compiler sees and proceeds to compile.

There are some potential problems that can be caused by `#include` directives, which are not all that obvious at first. Consider the following extra header file and modification to the previous example:

```
// FrontEnd.h
#include "Game.h"
// Rest of the front end declarations...

// Game.cpp
#include "Game.h"
#include "FrontEnd.h"
Players players[MAX_PLAYERS];
```

Just by looking at `Game.h`, nobody would think that there is a problem; yet, trying to compile that code results in a compiler error. In this case, the compiler complains about attempting to `#define` the same constant twice.

The problem is that the contents of the file `Game.h` were included twice in the same file. This is how it looks after the preprocessor is done with it:

```
// Game.cpp
#define MAX_PLAYERS    16
// Rest of the front-end declarations...
#define MAX_PLAYERS    16
Players players[MAX_PLAYERS];
```

Now it becomes very obvious that we are trying to define the constant `MAX_PLAYERS` twice. Without us realizing it, the preprocessor included the same file twice. Not only was it a waste of compilation time, it also led to compiler errors.

To solve that problem we use *include guards*. Include guards are preprocessor directives that prevent the same file from being included more than once in the same compilation unit. Include guards are used extensively in most C and C++ programs, and are usually implemented in this form:

```
// Game.h
#ifndef GAME_H_
#define GAME_H_

#define MAX_PLAYERS    16

#endif // #ifndef GAME_H_
```

If every header file has guards around it, we can guarantee that it is never included twice. The first time the preprocessor includes it, the guard symbol (`GAME_H_` in this case, but it should be different with each header file) is not defined, so it immediately defines it and proceeds to include the rest of the file. The next time we try to include the same file, the guard symbol is already defined, and the preprocessor skips that file completely.

The choice of the actual guard symbol is not that important, unless you have such a large code base that you can get duplicate guard symbols in the same compilation unit. Usually, just making a variation on the header file name itself is the simplest solution and works perfectly well for most projects.

One related technique you might come across when looking through source code is the use of the preprocessor directive `#pragma once`. That directive prevents the preprocessor from ever including (or even opening again) the file that contained `#pragma once` in the same compilation unit. So it seems to do the same job as our more cumbersome include guards by preventing a file from being included multiple times, but also prevents it from even being opened a second time, which should speed up compilation times somewhat.

As it turns out, `#pragma once` is not a particularly good substitute for include guards. Its main advantage is that it is clearer and easier to type, but that is about all. The major blow against it is that it is not part of the C++ standard. There are a fair number of C++ compilers that understand it and apply it correctly, but not all of them do. If you are doing multi-platform development, you should take this into consideration.

What you often see is both of these directives used in the same file at once—the include guards to prevent double inclusion in compilers that do not support `#pragma once`, and `#pragma once` to avoid opening the file multiple times in compilers that do support it. Because not all compilers understand the `#pragma once` directive, it is usually surrounded by conditional statements that allow its processing only in compilers that support it. The typical header file is written this way:

```
#ifndef MYHEADERFILE_H_
#define MYHEADERFILE_H_

#if _MSC_VER > 1000
#pragma once
#endif // _MSC_VER > 1000

// Contents of the header file here
// ...

#endif // MYHEADERFILE_H_
```

In this case, the `_MSC_VER > 1000` means we want to use `#pragma once` only on Microsoft compilers after a certain version. This certainly did not save us any typing or make things cleaner and clearer; but if it at least helped with compilation times, it would be bearable, even at the cost of having to modify all the header files every time we add a new compiler that supports `#pragma once`.

As it turns out, most of the time `#pragma once` is not even necessary. Most preprocessors that understand the `#pragma once` directive are smart enough to detect the pattern of include guards and automatically avoid opening the same file multiple times. So in the end, just adding include guards to our header files is the best solution.

If you ever find yourself trying to debug a problem that you think might be caused by the preprocessor, you might want to turn to your compiler's documentation. Most compilers have a handy feature for saving out the source code the way it is after the preprocessor is done with, so that you get to see exactly what the compiler is processing and compiling. This feature allows you to debug macro expansions more easily and to detect any strange or out-of-order inclusions.

Another handy utility provided by some compilers is a switch that forces the compiler to print out every included file in the order in which it is included. Not only is this handy for tracking down include problems, but you might discover that your innocent-looking class is pulling in hundreds of other header files all by itself.

18.3.3 Include Directives in .cpp Files

The `#include` directives totally determine the shape of a program. If your code is lean, efficient, and streamlined, or if it is an ugly beast of a program with long tentacles reaching to every single source file, it is all caused by the `#include` directives.

We want to minimize the number of header files included in each implementation file, not only the actual `#include` statements in the .cpp file, but also any `#includes` in each of the header files pulled in. In some extreme cases, compiling a .cpp file could cause the inclusion of hundreds of header files. Just the time to access and open all those files is probably quite significant (a second or two per .cpp file). Multiply that times the number of .cpp files in the project, and all of a sudden we are talking about compile times of half an hour or more.

The first step toward minimizing how many files are included—and consequently compilation times—is to untangle the `#include` web and organize it in such a way that we can make sense out of it.

Usually, .cpp files include several header files at the very top of the file. The number of files included can range from just a couple to many dozens. Each `#include` directive literally brings in all the contents of the file it refers to and adds those contents to the file that used the directive. Then the file, with all the #include statements expanded out to their file contents, is compiled as normal.

A key observation is that the #include statements are expanded in place in the same order they appear in the code. Compilation also proceeds from top to bottom, so by the time the code contained in the second header file is compiled, it has the knowledge of the contents of the first header file, but not of what is coming up in subsequent header files. This means that if we are not careful about how we organized our includes, the same header file could compile perfectly fine in one .cpp file, but fail to compile in another, just because of the #include statements that were preceding it.

We can untangle this seemingly complicated situation by following a very simple rule: in a .cpp file that contains the implementation for a class, the first included file must be the header file corresponding to that class. We will make an exception for this when dealing with precompiled headers later on, but otherwise you should consider it a universal rule.

Following this rule, our source code should look like this:

```
// MyClassA.h
class A
{
    // ...
};

// MyClassA.cpp
#include "MyClassA.h" // <- First include is the
                      //    header file for the class
#include "MyClassC.h"
#include "SomethingElse.h"

// The rest of MyClassA implementation
// ...
```

What exactly have we accomplished? We avoid ever having the problem of header files depending on other header files that came earlier. We guarantee that our header file compiles correctly, even if it is the first one in the inclusion list. By following this rule for all the classes, the order of the rest of the header files should not matter.

One of the consequences of this rule is that some header files must include other header files to compile properly. That is fine. If they needed those files, we might as well put the #include in the header file and not have to remember to include them in every .cpp file that uses them.

18.3.4 Include Directives in Header Files

First in the list of things to remove are any unnecessary #include statements from the header files themselves. It sounds strange, but unfortunately it is far too common to have unnecessary #include statements cluttering up your headers. For example, some header files might have been included at some point, but then things changed, and they were not needed any more, but nobody remembered to remove the #include statements. It does not matter whether they were needed or not, you pay the price every time you compile the program—so out with them. In general, include in the header file only those files whose omission would cause the compilation to fail.

After we have removed all the useless includes, we can turn our attention to the ones that are necessary but can be replaced by other means. The only reason we include a file in a header file is because the header file uses something that was declared in the included file. For example, when one class derives from another, we must include the header file for the parent class.

```
// B.h

#include "A.h"

// B inherits from A, so we must include A here.
// There is no way around it
class B : public A
{
  // ...
};
```

Inheritance is one of those cases where we have to include the header file for only the parent class. There is simply no way around it because the compiler must have seen the full parent class to know how to build the derived class correctly.

However, there are times when the compiler does not have to see the full declaration of a class; all it needs to know is that there is a class with that name. This situation happens whenever we are using only pointers or references to a class. As long as we assure the compiler that there is a class of that name, we do not have to include that class declaration. Instead, we use a *forward declaration* with the class name. Consider the following two files describing the class GameCamera:

```
// GameCamera.h
#include "GameEntity.h"
#include "GamePlayer.h"
```

```
class GameCamera : public GameEntity
{
    GamePlayer * GetPlayer();
private:
    GamePlayer * m_pPlayer;
};

// GameCamera.cpp
#include "GameCamera.h"

// Rest of GameCamera implementation...
```

At first glance, it might appear that the two #include statements in the GameCamera.h file are necessary. Clearly, the first one is necessary because GameEntity is the parent class. On the other hand, the only reason we had to include GamePlayer.h is because we use a few pointers to objects of that class in the functions and as a member variable. Because they are only pointers, we can instead use a forward declaration and avoid including the file altogether:

```
// GameCamera.h
#include "GameEntity.h"
class GamePlayer;    // Forward declaration is enough

class GameCamera : public GameEntity
{
    GamePlayer * GetPlayer();
private:
    GamePlayer * m_pPlayer;
};

// GameCamera.cpp
#include "GameCamera.h"
#include "GamePlayer.h"

// Rest of GameCamera implementation...
```

Notice that when we removed the #include statement from the header file, we had to add it to the implementation file. That is because GameCamera uses the GamePlayer somewhere in its implementation, and that requires that the compiler sees the GamePlayer class declaration.

Notice that we could have saved an #include statement in the header file, but we moved it to the implementation file instead. What kind of gain is that? It is a tremendous gain, actually. Imagine that 100 other classes need to include `GameCamera.h`. By removing the `#include` of `GamePlayer.h` from `GameCamera.h` into `GameCamera.cpp`, we prevented the `GamePlayer.h` file from being opened and included 100 times during the compilation of the program. If `GamePlayer.h` in turn included 10 other files, then we prevented the opening and reading of 1,000 files! Instead, now `GamePlayer.h` is included only in the `GameCapera.cpp` file, which is compiled only once. Imagine applying that simple example across the thousands of files that make up a project, and you can start seeing the huge difference that proper use of forward declaration can make in the physical structure and compilation times of a large project.

18.3.5 Precompiled Headers

Even after all our code follows the inclusion rules presented in this chapter, we might still notice how many of our files include the same headers over and over because a large section of our code depends on the C standard library header files, STL, Windows, OpenGL, or any other common API. So every file ends up including some of the same headers:

```
// MyClass.cpp
#include "MyClass.h"
#include <vector.h>
#include <list.h>
#include <algorithm.h>
#include <stdio>
#include <windows.h>

// Now we can start including the other files from our code
#include "MyClass2.h"
#include "MyClass3.h"
```

This is even worse than it seems, because those large APIs typically have really large and complex header files, which can in turn include many other files. The most frustrating part is that we know those header files are not going to change during development. Yet we keep including and processing them every time we compile any file. Compile times could slow to a crawl in a situation like this.

Fortunately, several compilers provide a solution: *precompiled headers*. Granted, using precompiled headers is an option that is available only in specific compilers, so you cannot rely on it across multiple platforms. Still, it is such an incredibly useful feature that it is well worth taking advantage of it whenever possible. If you are not sure about your specific compiler, check the documentation and find out how to turn it on.

What exactly are precompiled headers? It is more or less what it sounds like. With this option turned on, some files are compiled only once, and the results are saved to disk for later use during the compilation of the rest of the program and subsequent compilations. This means that all the headers included by the files used to create the precompiled headers are loaded and processed only once.

Additionally, every time the program is compiled, as long as none of the files used to generate the precompiled headers have changed, the same generated precompiled header file can be used without the need to compile it again. This is an ideal situation for those large, external API header files that just about every file in our program depends on. They get compiled once, and from there on, they are almost free as far as compilation time goes.

Different compilers have different rules on how a file can take advantage of the precompiled headers. In the case of Microsoft's compilers, you have to make sure you include a specific header file as the first inclusion in your .cpp file. Check your compiler documentation for all the details. This is the only allowable exception to the inclusion rule that the first include statement in the .cpp file for a class must be the header file for that class. Using precompiled headers, a normal .cpp file would look like this:

```
// MyClassA.cpp
#include "precomp.h"  // Precompiled header files
#include "MyClassA.h" // First real include is the
                      // header file for the class
#include "MyClassC.h"
#include "SomethingElse.h"

// The rest of MyClassA implementation
// ...
```

The effects of precompiled headers can be dramatic, so it is well worth investigating their use for your project if you are not doing so already. It is possible for a project to compile 10 times faster with precompiled headers than without it, depending on how the project was structured to start with and how much it uses other large header files. In a less extreme case, you might still expect compile times to be two to three times faster when using precompiled headers.

The major drawback of precompiled headers is that because including headers is pretty much free, the number of headers included that way grows over the course of the project. This means that every file that uses precompiled headers (which ends up being most of them) automatically knows about all the files that are part of the precompiled headers. This is not a bad thing in itself because it does not increase compilation times, but it makes header files available to source files that were never intended to know anything about them.

For example, adding `windows.h` to the precompiled header section causes every file that uses precompiled headers to know about all the Windows structures, constants, and functions. It will only be a matter of time before you start seeing functions and data types popping up all over the program. If you are doing multi-platform development, this is a good way to break the build on other platforms. Even worse, if you are not currently working on multiple platforms but later decide to port your code, you might be in for a bit of a shock.

In addition to bringing in more information than is necessary, the other drawback of relying on precompiled headers in is switching between platforms or compilers. The code still compiles fine without precompiled header support because each file includes the precompiled header file `precomp.h`, which in turn includes all the needed header files. The problem is that `precomp.h` includes all the big header files that the entire program needs, not just the ones that each individual .cpp file requires. This means that if a project was laid out with the use of precompiled headers in mind, compiling it without precompiled headers will probably result in significantly slower compilation times than if it had been laid out without precompiled headers from the start.

To alleviate this problem, we can substitute the inclusion of the precompiled header file with the minimum number of inclusions necessary to compile that file in the case of platforms that do not support precompiled headers—something along these lines:

```
// Precomp.h
#include "LargeAPI1.h"
#include "LargeAPI2.h"
#include "LargeAPI3.h"
#include "LargeAPI4.h"
#include "LargeAPI5.h"

// MyClassA.cpp
#ifdef PRECOMP_SUPPORT
#include "precomp.h"
#else
// This file only needs LargeAPI3.h
#include "LargeAPI3.h"
#endif

#include "MyClassA.h"
#include "MyClassC.h"
#include "SomethingElse.h"
```

```
// The rest of MyClassA implementation
// ...
```

18.3.6 The Pimpl Pattern

If you have followed all the advice up to now, your header files should be self-sufficient (they do not rely on another header file being included for them), should be included only once, and should have the minimum number of includes that still allows them to be compiled correctly. In addition to all that, you should be using precompiled headers effectively if your compiler supports them.

It is possible that, even given all that restructuring of header files, a large project still compiles very slowly, or that small changes often trigger long compilations. We really need to do something about these issues. Nobody likes working with projects that take several minutes to compile a minor change, or that require you to go out to lunch every time you do a full compile.

The problem is probably still caused by there being too many tangled headers. This might be a good moment to see whether your compiler has a switch to display all included files in the order the preprocessor opens them. If every .cpp file ends up including dozens or hundreds of header files, we can probably improve on our design. If, on the other hand, only a handful of files are included per .cpp file, then the problem lies elsewhere. Maybe you just have a lot of code, and it simply takes a long time to compile it. In that case, upgrading your hardware to a faster CPU and faster hard drives might be more beneficial than any another solution.

Before attempting to improve the physical organization of your project, have a good look to see whether the project would benefit from a better logical organization. If the whole game is just one huge project with several thousand files, it will probably benefit from some subdivision into smaller, more self-contained systems. Some of the systems that should be able to be isolated are rendering, input, sound, AI, collision, and physics.

A project that is divided into several fairly independent subsystems has many advantages (which we will see in more detail later in this chapter). One of the major benefits is the reduced physical dependencies between files on different subsystems. In particular, if the subsystems use abstract interfaces or a façade pattern to hide their contents from the rest of the world, then the only physical dependencies we need to worry about are the ones between files within the same subsystem, which becomes much more manageable.

Assuming that the problem is still caused by too many include files, the Pimpl pattern might help. Pimpl, which stands for Private IMPLementation, is also known as the Cheshire Cat pattern. Let's first look at an example of a situation that might be helped with a Pimpl. Consider a minor variation on our previous `GameCamera.h` header file:

```
// GameCamera.h
#include "GameEntity.h"
#include "CameraLens.h"
class GamePlayer;

class GameCamera : public GameEntity
{
    GamePlayer * GetPlayer();
private:
    GamePlayer * m_pPlayer;
    CameraLens m_lens;
};
```

The only difference from the previous `GameCamera` header file is that now we show an extra member variable, `m_lens`, which represents the camera lens that the camera is using. By default, it can just be a totally transparent lens, but we could use colored lenses to give the whole scene a specific tint, a black-and-white lens to filter out all the color, or even some sort of dynamic lens that we can use to flash the screen with red patterns whenever the player gets hit. Even better is the ability to have multiple lenses at once, but we are restricting ourselves to one to keep the example as simple as possible.

A consequence of adding the `m_lens` variable to the header file is that now we are forced to include the header file that contains the declaration of the `CameraLens` class. We cannot just do a forward declaration, because we are dealing with a full variable, not just a pointer or a reference. The same thing will happen for every variable we add to the class.

This is particularly frustrating because `m_lens` is a private variable. That means that only the `GameCamera` class will have access to it, so it is frustrating to have to include the header file for `CameraLens` in the `GameCamera.h` file and force everybody that uses the camera to include it as well. We saw how the inclusion of files can proliferate if `GameCamera` is a popular class used in many places in the code.

The Pimpl pattern allows us to avoid including in our header file files that are required only by private variables. We accomplish this by putting all the private implementation inside a simple structure and taking care of creating it and destroying it along with the object. This is how a Pimpl that contains the camera lens would look for the `GameEntity` class:

```
// GameCamera.h
#include "GameEntity.h"
class GamePlayer;

class GameCamera : public GameEntity
{
    GamePlayer * GetPlayer();
private:
    GamePlayer * m_pPlayer;

    class PIMPL;
    PIMPL * pimpl;
};

// GameCamera.cpp
#include "GameCamera.h"
#include "GamePlayer.h"
#include "CameraLens.h"

struct GameCamera::PIMPL
{
    CameraLens m_lens;
};

GameCamera::GameCamera()
{
    pimpl = new PIMPL;
}

GameCamera::~GameCamera()
{
    delete pimpl;
}

// Rest of GameCamera implementation...
```

Notice that we were able to remove the inclusion of CameraLens.h from the header file, which was our goal. If we had any more private variables that would require including other files, we would add those to the Pimpl structure as well.

By using the Pimpl pattern, we have traded a reduction in the physical dependencies between classes for a bit of extra complexity and the dynamic allocation of the private implementation of the object. The extra complexity is not too bad. The Pimpl has to be created only once, regardless of how many variables it contains, and accessing one of those variables just requires prefixing it with the name of the Pimpl object.

The more worrisome drawback is the dynamic memory allocation caused by every object that uses the Pimpl pattern. This might be perfectly fine for large objects with relatively few instances, but it might cause problems for small objects with many hundreds or thousands of instances. If we still want to use the Pimpl pattern in these cases, we might want to use a memory-pooling system like the ones described in Chapter 7.

18.4 LIBRARIES

The techniques that work with a small code base often break down when dealing with a large project. Most of the source-code examples you find with APIs, or those available on the Internet, are very small and are simply thrown together to demonstrate some particular feature or to illustrate a point. Because of their size, these small projects are structured as a single system that compiles into an executable.

This approach works fine for a relatively small code base, but it quickly becomes inadequate for a larger project of the size of most games produced today. The dependencies between files quickly become unmanageable, compile times go up, things that should be simple become very complicated, and programmers suffer.

When dealing with large projects, it is usually a much better approach to break down the massive code base into relatively independent subsystems. Each subsystem is a set of related source code that has a logical, cohesive objective. It exposes the minimum amount of functionality to the outside world, but still allows everybody to use it to its full extent. Subsystems are compiled separately from the main executable and create a static or dynamic library. That library is then linked with the main executable to create the full program. Some of the perfect candidates that come up often during game development that can be split into separate libraries are memory management; graphics rendering; input handling; collision detection and physics response; animation, music and sound playback; user-interface widgets; and generic AI functions.

The first advantage of separating subsystems into libraries in this way is the reduced dependency between classes and between files, so we improve both the logical and the physical structure of the project. Figure 18.1 illustrates how dependencies are reduced by separating a project into libraries, thus presenting a simple interface to the rest of the code.

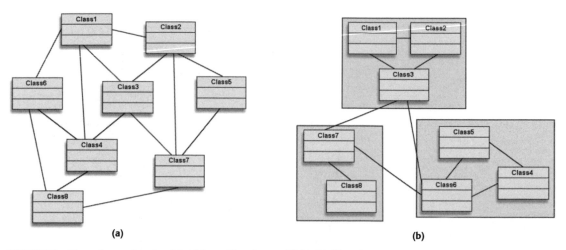

FIGURE 18.1   Class dependencies **(a)** without libraries and **(b)** with libraries.

The same effect can be achieved without a subdivision into libraries, but such a project is much more difficult to maintain. Programmers have to be constantly aware of the artificial divisions they are trying to enforce, because in any real project, things can degenerate very quickly into a mass of chaotic dependencies. By explicitly creating subsystems, we are enforcing that subdivision and making sure no extra dependencies are introduced.

Now that we have a higher-level view of the project by looking at the libraries, it should be possible to determine which libraries depend on other libraries. One very desirable (but not absolutely necessary) property is to make sure that there are no cyclical dependencies between libraries. That is, libraries can depend on other libraries "below" them, but no library should depend on a library "above" it. An example of correctly organized libraries is shown in Figure 18.2.

When libraries are organized this way, we keep the code base from being a confusing mass. We can treat any section of the code independently of the rest by taking one library and including all the libraries it depends on, all the way to the bottom. There are many beneficial consequences of such an organization:

- **We can test each library in isolation, working our way from the bottom up.** This is particularly useful when trying to isolate a bug, and we have no idea whether it is being caused by a low-level library or something much higher up. We can even create simple test applications that rely on a small subset of the libraries to test certain behaviors.

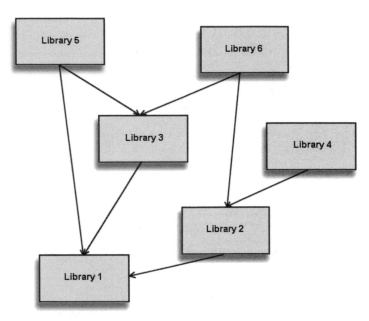

FIGURE 18.2   Library dependency without cycles.

- **In-house tools can pick and choose the libraries they need.**
  When dealing with a big mass of code, tools tend to either include all
  the game code (with the subsequent bloating, slowness, and restrictions) or not share any code at all with the game, which prevents us
  from seeing things exactly as they will behave in the game, and
  which requires us to write a lot of duplicate code. With a layered
  library approach, a tool that needs only the graphics renderer can
  include that library plus all the libraries all the way down, but no
  more. A more complex tool could include a few more libraries, and a
  tool that requires virtually all of the game functionality could include
  most libraries and the game code.
- **It becomes easier to share already-built code.** With a layered
  library system, it is possible to build some of the lower-level libraries
  and distribute them to the rest of the team. That way, programmers
  (as long as they are making localized changes) have to build only the
  libraries they are working with, not the libraries for the whole project. By itself, this can mean considerable timesavings. To take the
  idea even further, an automated build system could do a full build of
  all the libraries and game code every night, and make the compiled
  versions available to all the programmers every morning.

- **Separating engine and game-specific code becomes easier.** When code is structured in relatively independent libraries, the game-engine boundary becomes a natural separation point. As a consequence, with little effort, some libraries will be completely game independent, and some will be totally game specific. That allows much easier code reuse across different projects and even makes it easier to start a new project with an existing code base because it is very clear what code was game specific and has to be replaced.
- **We can take a modular approach to the code.** If the code is structured in separate libraries, it becomes relatively easy to replace a whole library with a new implementation. That allows us to customize many parts of the engine, as well as the game itself for the current project. For example, we could replace a portal visibility system with a quadtree-based one just by swapping libraries, and almost no other code changes would be necessary. It also makes multi-platform development a lot easier by allowing us to replace platform-specific libraries with new libraries for the new target platform.

18.5 Configurations

In a real project situation, it is not enough to be able to compile the game only one way. You will want to compile it with different settings for different uses. Each of these different settings is called a *configuration*. Each configuration uses different levels of error reporting, code optimizations, and debug facilities.

It is often a good idea to add a postfix to all the executables and libraries produced by each configuration, instead of all of them having the same name. That way, we can have several executables of the game in the same directory and run whichever one is appropriate.

It is fairly common to have at least two configurations per project: debug and release.

18.5.1 Debug Configuration

The debug configuration is usually used only by programmers when they are debugging the program or adding new features. Compiler optimizations are completely disabled, and all the debug information is included. That makes stepping into the program with a debugger very easy, and all variables are easily accessible from the debugger's watch windows.

This configuration can also have all sorts of guards and protections enabled, at the expense of performance, to help the programmer catch logic bugs in the code. For example, this version could automatically do bounds checking with every array access, or it could fill freed memory with a certain bit pattern to make it easier to find situations in which pointers lead to memory that has been released.

Performance in this configuration is going to be poor, easily two to four times slower than the final product. The debug configuration makes things slow enough that playing the game might not be particularly easy because of the low frame rate, but performance is not the focus of this configuration. Also, the debug configuration typically requires more memory to run because it has extra code as well as all the debugging symbols.

18.5.2 Release Configuration

The release configuration is the opposite of the debug configuration. All the optimizations are on, all the debugging aids are removed, and all the guards and safety tricks are gone. The executable that comes out of this configuration is what is usually sent to the manufacturer to create the CD-ROMs, DVDs, or cartridges of the final product. This is what the end user gets.

Performance is as good as it is going to get, but trying to debug this configuration is virtually impossible. Also, if all the debugging code has been removed and the game crashes, it might not report any useful information to help track down the bug.

18.5.3 Debug-Optimized Configuration

The debug and release configurations are opposite extremes. They are both useful, but we need some intermediate solution. This intermediate configuration strikes a balance between performance and debugging facilities, and chances are that most of the work with the game will be done using it.

This configuration often has code-debugging information, as well as all the debugging tools, such as in-game consoles or full error reporting, but it also has all the optimizations turned on, which allows it to run at close to full speed. This configuration uses more memory than the release version because it incorporates all the debugging symbols.

Some projects use another intermediate configuration, one without any debugging information but which can still produce meaningful error reports whenever the game crashes. This version can be used to iron out any problems that appear only in the release configuration. Depending on your game and platform, sometimes the shipped version of the game is intended to have some level of error reporting. In this case, error reporting is built into the release configuration, and there is no need for an intermediate version.

18.6 Conclusion

In this chapter, we saw the difference between the physical and logical structure of the source code and how it is possible to have a good logical structure yet still have a bad physical one. The physical structure refers to the relationship between files, not classes. A good physical structure results in fast compile times, short recompilations for small changes, and easier testing and maintainability of the code. Physical structure plays a much more important role in large projects than in small ones.

We then saw the proposed organization of classes into two files: one for the class declaration and one for the implementation. The management of header file inclusions is at the heart of a good physical structure, so we saw several suggested rules to tame the potential tangle of includes, how to minimize the number of header files included, and how to avoid having header files that depend on other header files. We also covered two techniques that help with compilation times: precompiled headers and the Pimpl pattern.

Having a good higher-level organization of the project, divided into relatively independent libraries and with a clear dependency chain, can have many benefits. These include code reuse, replacement of libraries, ease of testing, and the potential to use only part of the libraries when building tools or running tests.

Finally, any project of a reasonable size must have multiple configurations that produce different executables or libraries. The most common are debug, optimized debug, and release.

Suggested Reading

The great majority of the C++ literature seems to cover only the logical structure of the program. These are a few of the books that actually cover the physical structure in any depth. John Lakos' book is especially detailed.

Lakos, John, *Large Scale C++ Software Design*. Addison-Wesley, 1996.
Stroustrup, Bjarne, *The C++ Programming Language*, 3rd ed. Addison-Wesley, 1997.

The following book is a true classic and has many useful patterns. Of relevance to this chapter is its discussion of the Façade pattern, used to reduce the number of dependencies to files in one library or module.

Gamma, Erich, et al., *Design Patterns*. Addison-Wesley, 1995.

Many articles and books talk about Herb Sutter's Pimpl pattern. The following book offers several chapters on that topic:

Sutter, Herb, *Exceptional C++*. Addison-Wesley, 2000.

CRASH-PROOFING YOUR GAME

In This Chapter

- Using Asserts
- Keeping the Machine Fresh
- Dealing with "Bad" Data

As you have most likely realized by now, C++ is not forgiving. We have to be very explicit about what we want it to do. Sometimes, against all principles of good software engineering, we even have to be redundant, such as when writing both the function name and arguments in the declaration and definition of the function.

C++ is just as unforgiving at runtime. A minor miscalculation on our part, and the program will at best crash with some cryptic message; at worst it will lock up the user's computer, possibly inspiring them to uninstall our game and return it to the store right away.

Obviously, we would like to avoid the latter situation as much as possible. This chapter deals with several techniques we can apply to crash-proof our game. We will see the most effective use of asserts to catch bugs as soon as they happen, how to keep the machine fresh to avoid bugs that creep up after running for a while, and how to deal with bad data in our own functions without wasting performance or sacrificing safety.

19.1 USING ASSERTS

The assert() function is part of the standard C++ library and will soon become one of your favorite tools. Put simply, all it does is stop the program right away if a specific condition does not evaluate to true.

19.1.1 When to Use Asserts

If we are trying to crash-proof the game, why would we want to use asserts? In a way, we are "crashing" the program ourselves in order to avoid having it crash by itself. The main difference is that we are doing it in a much more controlled manner, collecting useful information for debugging, and doing it as close as possible to the source of the problem. There is nothing more frustrating that tracking down a crash produced by something that occurred several frames ago and that went by completely unnoticed. By asserting often, we will know as soon as something goes wrong, and it will make debugging much easier.

These are the most frequent scenarios for an effective use of assert():

- **Stop the program if the parameters passed to a function are something that we cannot (or do not want to) deal with.** Not every function has to deal with all possible combinations of parameters, especially private functions of a class or functions that are not exposed to the final user. Catching the misuse of a function right away is much better than letting it exhibit the old result of garbage in, garbage out.

  This scenario is often called *checking the preconditions of a function*. Each function has a set of preconditions, and if they are not met, the function does not execute.

  For example, consider a function that adds an object to the player's inventory. This function takes a pointer to a game object. To make things simple, we decided early on that it is illegal to pass a NULL pointer to that function because it makes no sense and we would never want to do that. Using assert() at the top of the function makes sure that the pointer is not NULL.

```
void Inventory::AddItem (Item * pItem)
{
    assert(pItem != NULL);
    // Add it to the inventory here, since now we
    // know for sure it's not NULL
    // ...
}
```

- **Check that the program is in a consistent state.** Sometimes before we do an operation, we want to make sure that it is safe to go ahead and perform that action. By using an assert in that situation, we catch a problem before it even surfaces. This is also useful as a future safeguard: we know what we are doing right now, so the checking might be unnecessary, but chances are the code will be updated in the future. At that point, having those extra asserts could make a huge difference in finding problems early on.

  Take as an example the function that handles a game entity's death. We know from past experience that sometimes several kill messages can sneak through, but it is not supposed to happen, so we guard against that eventuality. That way if it happens, instead of either ignoring it or having something unexpected happen, we can just deal with it right away and fix the bug.

```
void GameEntity::HandleKillMessage (const Msg & msg)
{
    assert (!IsDead());
    SetIsDead (true);
    // Do the rest of the killing process here...
}
```

- **Check that a complicated algorithm is working the way we expect.** Complex algorithms are also commonly referred as "sanity checks." We know that something should be in a certain state after we perform a set of operations, but because it is somewhat complicated, it is hard to say for certain that it will always be true. To make really sure, we can insert an assert() call, and we will know right away if it ever fails.

  These are postconditions, the counterparts of preconditions. Like preconditions, they check that certain conditions are true, but unlike preconditions, they happen at the end of a function or a code segment instead of the beginning. Checking them is not as crucial as checking the preconditions, but performing these checks can help catch bugs during development and make us feel more confident that the code is working as it should.

  The following function processes all the messages in the queue. However, as a message is processed, more messages might be sent. A postcondition for this function states that there should be no more messages in the queue when the function finishes. We can express that postcondition with an assert().

```
void MsgQueue::ProcessAll()
{
    // Do all the processing here. Maybe from different
    // queues, so it isn't a straightforward process
    // ...

    // Before we finish, double-check that there are no
    // messages left.
    assert (IsEmpty());
}
```

- **Stop the program if a function fails and we cannot recover.** Something bad has happened—really bad. We have tried to allocate a block of memory, and a NULL pointer was returned, or we tried to move an enemy entity only to realize that that entity does not exist anymore. Obviously, there is a major problem in the code. Now is the time for an assert so the problem can be fixed right away.

Sometimes we would like our programs to detect parts that fail and recover gracefully. That is a nice goal, but often unnecessary for games. It does not mean we never want to recover, though; see the next section for advice on when *not* to use asserts.

19.1.2 When Not to Use Asserts

So far, it seems that we should use asserts as soon as something unexpected happens. That is generally true, but there are some situations in which we want to handle errors gracefully.

A good rule of thumb is that a designer or an artist should never be able to trigger an assert (or even worse, crash the program outright) unless they come up against a code bug. In other words, someone using our game or tools should not be able to crash it. If we follow that rule, we make everybody happier and minimize the downtime caused by non-functional games and tools. What does this mean? It means we should not assert in the following situations:

- **Trying to open or load a file that does not exist.**
- **Trying to load a file of the wrong format or an older version.** This does not mean we have to support old versions forever, just that we should handle them without stopping the program.
- **Entering "bad" data.** Suppose that the user can specify a near and far plane for the camera settings, and he enters a smaller number for the far plane than for the near plane. The best method would be to prevent the user from doing that to begin with through the user interface, rather than using assert().

- **One of the objects in the game did not load correctly.** If it is not a required object to run the game, we should put in a warning message and then run the game as usual. If it is a required one (like a player camera), then we should print a message explaining the problem and stop. That solution is still be better than an `assert()` when the level designers see it come up.

On the other hand, if a tester manages to make his character walk into a room that doesn't exist, this is a perfect time to assert because it is something that should not be possible to do. What it all boils down to is that asserts are messages by programmers *for* programmers. If ever an assert is triggered, it should be up to a programmer to fix it, hopefully right away.

19.1.3 Custom Asserts

It is great that `assert()` is part of the standard C++ library. It is a very handy function that we can use right away. However, when we start using it extensively in a large project, it becomes clear that it is too simple, and we would like to get more functionality out of it. It is time to roll our own `assert()`.

What we want is more information and more flexibility. Remember that asserts are messages for programmers. If they happen while we are running the game from the debugger, we do not need much more than what the default assert function already gives us. However, if they happen while the testing department is hammering on the game, then we need all the information we can get to try to identify the problem. Even if the testers are running the game from the debugger, there might not be any programmers around who can look into the crash right away; so displaying all the relevant information becomes even more important.

Specifically, these are some of the options we might want to consider having in a custom `assert()`:

- **Gather and display more information on the screen.** The default `assert()` stops the program, shows the failed condition, and perhaps displays the file and the line number where the error occurred. This is not bad for a start, but we might want more, such as the ability to see the call stack, the register state, or the build version.
- **Save information to a file.** Not only do we want to display information, we probably also want to save all that information and more to a file so it can be easily emailed to the right person or added to the bug database to be fixed later. In the file, we want to have the same information as was displayed on the screen, and maybe a code and memory dump of some potentially interesting places (such as the stack, instruction pointer, and so on) to investigate.

This can be taken a step further: we can do a *core dump*, or the equivalent, in our working platform. A core dump is a binary snapshot of the state of the machine that allows a programmer to restore that state in a different machine later on for debugging purposes.

- **Email information directly.** A nice touch is to enable all the assert information to be emailed right from the assert display. This is usually feasible only from a PC and not a game console, but it is very handy and worth considering. Alternatively, if you have a bug database, you can provide the option to enter it directly in the bug database, along with the comments from the testers, describing the situation that led to the assert.

An option that often comes up when considering custom asserts is the ability to continue even after an assert goes off. The argument for adding that option is that sometimes it is possible to continue running the game, even though one assert was triggered, so why force people to stop? This is typically a bad idea for several reasons.

First of all, asserts are indicating absolute conditions that must be true for the program to continue. The code relies on that for its proper execution, so continuing if an assert condition is not met is an almost guaranteed failure. In the presence of nonstopping asserts, people stop relying on the conditions that have been asserted and are forced to check for them in the code. That makes the code messier, more bloated, slower, and much harder to maintain.

Another consequence of nonstopping asserts is that they are inevitably used to flag errors and warning messages. For example, if a file does not exist, or an object is not initialized correctly, instead of coming up with a correct error-reporting scheme, programmers under pressure might instead choose to put in a non-stopping assert and let people press the "continue" button to move on. This causes numerous problems: error messages are not batched, so there might be hundreds of assert boxes to wade through before we can play the level; the errors might not be reported and saved correctly, or real asserts might be lost in the shuffle among all the meaningless ones.

Finally, the worst problem of all: if the program crashes some time after a non-stopping assert was bypassed, it will be very hard to determine whether it was because of a bug in the code or whether it was because the testing continued after an assert was triggered.

19.1.4 What to Do in the Final Release

Typically, all the assert() calls are automatically removed in the final build. The reasoning is that all the bugs have been ironed out, and leaving the asserts in only slows down the game and makes its memory footprint larger (because of all the assert() statements and the messages associated with them). In other words, it would be best to have the game act weirdly or crash, rather than show an assert message to the player.

Unfortunately, the issue is not that straightforward. What we decide to do depends on our target platform and our development plans.

The big problem is that no matter how much testing we have done on the game, somebody is going to come across a situation that will trigger an assert. If you find that hard to believe, consider this possible scenario: imagine we have a large testing department, and we have 40 people hammering on the game for 20 weeks, 40 hours per week. (We will gloss over the fact that the game will be changing over those 20 weeks, and will consider this a best-case scenario.) That is a total of 32,000 man-hours of testing, which translates to about three and a half years.

After we are confident we have removed all the bugs, the game is released and becomes an instant hit: one million copies are sold in the first month. Now we have one million people playing the game on an average of one hour per day for two weeks. That works out to 14 million hours, or 1,639 years of testing—three orders of magnitude more time than was spent in our exhaustive testing. And that is only in the first month. These numbers are very conservative; they could in reality be much higher, depending on sales and how much people play. In addition, those assumptions do not take into account different user configurations, incompatible hardware, or defective media.

Things might be improved a bit by doing open beta tests, but that is not always feasible (especially with console games). Also, with beta tests, you will probably be testing only a small fraction of the game, so bugs are bound to show up in other parts that did not receive the same attention.

In other words, it is virtually impossible to ship a game without bugs. So let's accept it, get over it, and do our best to deal with it.

We need to think about how we are going to deal with the bugs once the game has been released. Just because we admit that we are going to ship a game with bugs does not mean we have an excuse for not fixing them or for shipping a game that we know has bugs. We still want to do everything in our power fix every single bug, but we have to accept the fact that we will not find them all.

As previously mentioned, an all-too-common way of dealing with bugs is simply to ignore them. All the assert() calls are removed and we hope for the best. However, if something goes wrong, it might simply cause some weird behavior, but it can also freeze the game, which is not a good experience for the player.

As an alternative, especially for the PC platform where patching games is very common, we could leave the asserts in—along with the ability to email all the crash information to us, including information about the user's system configuration and driver versions, with the click of a button. After the first few weeks of the game's release, we can process all these reports and iron out most of the problems. This is a particularly attractive option for PC games because there is so much variation in user configurations that it is completely impossible to test even a good sample of them before the game ships.

Console configurations are much more limited, so hardware testing can be much more thorough. Besides, in the console world, patching is not as accepted, even if it is possible, so patching is probably not a viable option.

If we do not want to report the assert to the player, but at the same time we do not want a crash, what can we do? There is no obvious answer. Here are some possibilities you can consider:

- **Recover from the error.** If we have an assert in the graphics subsystem, we can try shutting it down completely, restarting it, and continuing the game from there. This is a very difficult option to implement because by the time we get an assert, the state of the system could already be compromised.
- **Restart the console.** We could try saving the game (assuming that the assert does not affect the integrity of the save-game data), reboot the console, and reload it as quickly as possible. The player has an interruption of a few seconds, but this is clearly a much better option than crashing.
- **Finish the level.** If something bad happens, we could just finish the level and bring them back to the front end. We could even make up an in-game reason for ending the level early.

An intermediate solution is to remove the asserts completely in the final release but deal with all uncaught exceptions. By removing the asserts, we hope for the best. Maybe a situation will arise that would have triggered an assert, but it does not cause the game to crash. However, if something really bad happens, depending on your platform, there is a good chance that it might result in an exception (for example, accessing an incorrect section of memory, using the hardware incorrectly, and so on). We can then catch that exception and try to do the best we can with it.

19.1.5 Sample Custom Assert Implementation

Whichever method we end up choosing for dealing with errors after the game is released, it is clear that having a custom version of `assert()` is very useful. We also want to be able to change the actual implementation of `assert()` depending on the type of build, with the option to disable it completely and totally remove all performance costs.

This sample implementation is enabled only in debug builds, and it is totally turned off in release builds, but we have the flexibility to turn it on and off independently of the build type, through the preprocessor define DO_ASSERT.

```
#ifdef _DEBUG
#define DO_ASSERT
#endif

#ifdef DO_ASSERT
#define Assert(exp,text) \
    if (!(exp) && MyAssert(exp,text,__FILE__,__LINE__)) \
        _asm int 3;
#else
#define Assert(exp,text)
#endif
```

The way the macro works is that it always evaluates the expression, and if it is false, it calls our own function MyAssert() with the expression that failed, the explanatory text, and the file and line where the assertion occurred. If the function wants to stop the execution of the program and break into the debugger, it can return true, otherwise it can return false, and the program continues executing as normal. That is the purpose of the _asm int 3 line after the if statement. On a PC, this statement causes the program to break into the debugger. If there is no debugger hooked up, the call is ignored and the program resumes execution. Other platforms have similar functionality that allows you to break the debugger execution. By having the _asm int 3 line in the macro itself, the debugger breaks at the line with the assert() call itself, not in some internal implementation file like the standard assert() function does.

What the MyAssert() function does is totally up to us. It can simply print the explanatory text to the debug channel, along with the filename and line number, or it can bring up a fancy dialog box with that information, or it can simply save it to a file for future processing.

19.2 Keeping the Machine Fresh

The following situation is not uncommon: the game runs without any problems for quite a while, but then testing starts and we have reports of crashes after five, six, or even more hours of continuous playing. What is going on?

These can be some of the most frustrating and difficult bugs to fix because they are not easy to reproduce. They happen only after a lot of continuous play—maybe a few hours if we are lucky, maybe after a few days if we aren't. These errors can occur for several reasons.

19.2.1 Memory Leaks

Memory leaks are unfortunately all too common in C++. Some bytes are allocated dynamically and are never released. The big offenders are usually caught pretty quickly during development, but sometimes there are just a few bytes that sneak through. They might have no ill effect in the short term, but when they start accumulating, they can bring a system to its knees. The system eventually runs out of memory and crashes, or it starts swapping out virtual memory and suffers a major performance hit.

Imagine that we are leaking 200 bytes every second (maybe as the AI is refreshing its pathfinding information). That is a leak of 4.5 MB in five hours. This might not be much for a PC with a large amount of RAM, but it will certainly be a big problem in a console with much more limited resources. If the leak happens not once every second but once per frame, even a small number of bytes can become a huge problem for a PC in just a few hours.

19.2.2 Memory Fragmentation

Dynamic memory is allocated from a heap. At first, all memory in the heap is available for allocation in one large, contiguous block. As requests to allocate and free memory blocks are made, the heaps becomes *fragmented*, meaning that the free memory blocks are interleaved with many blocks of used memory. In the end, this can have an effect similar to a memory leak: we might request an allocation of a certain amount of memory, and because there is no single block that large, the memory allocation fails.

This problem is much more of an issue in consoles than in PCs because PCs typically have much larger memories. Sometimes developers completely give up on dynamic memory allocations to prevent this problem (and memory leaks along with it). However, that is a very drastic measure; it is inefficient with resources and is very limiting. Other solutions, such as memory pools, are usually preferred. (See Chapter 7, "Memory Allocation," for details on memory-allocation techniques.)

19.2.3 Clock Drift

Sometimes elapsed game time is implemented as a float in the game code. In principle, this sounds like a fine idea. However, unless we are careful, it can have some unfortunate side effects down the line. Because of the nature of a float number, the larger the number becomes, the less precision it has. Up to one second, it will have all 32 bits dedicated to subsecond precision; after two hours, the precision dedicated to subsecond time is reduced to 11 bits; and after 18 hours of running time, it is down to 8 bits, which means that the smallest time increment is roughly 8 ms. At this point, things start to become dangerous. Time steps are not reliable anymore, and strange effects can occur in the game, especially with some of the more time-sensitive systems such as physics or collision detection.

Another common representation for time is as a 32-bit integer containing the number of milliseconds since the start of the game. The integer does not have any loss of precision, but it eventually runs out of bits after 49 days. That is usually long enough for most games (other than game servers that must be on all the time).

19.2.4 Error Accumulation

Another type of error caused by running the game for a long time is the accumulation of mathematical imprecision. Sometimes we are not calculating a new value from scratch, but instead, we are always adding to it or concatenating it with a new value. This can happen with the camera position and orientation, the location of game objects, and many other things. Sometimes the mathematical error accumulates and shows up as strange effects after several hours of play.

19.2.5 What to Do?

We have seen that running the game for a long time has its own set of problems, aside from the fact that long play times are also more likely to uncover some normal bugs. Is there some way we can avoid these types of problems?

The answer is to keep the machine *fresh*, that is, to keep it in a state as close as possible to how it was when the game started. In a console game, the best way to do this is by doing a reboot of the machine between levels. Usually, consoles have a fast reboot mode, and the user cannot even tell that the machine was rebooted. Doing so is the perfect solution to all these problems because technically your game only runs for the duration of one level. Everything, including the memory systems and the clock count is completely reset.

Unfortunately, not everybody can reboot between levels. We cannot do it on a PC, and maybe we cannot do it on a console, either, given the particular circumstances of the game (for example, if we have to keep the network connection open). In that case, we have to do much more work by hand.

Between levels or at convenient moments (such as when the game is paused or the system is not loaded at 100%), we should take care of resetting as many systems as possible—at the very least, the memory and clock systems. The memory heaps should be compacted, and we might even want to run some form of garbage collection or do a pass through all the memory to identify memory leaks. The clock should also be reset at certain intervals. We might also want to completely reset the graphics system, sound system, physics, or AI to avoid any accumulated errors. This is not as ideal as rebooting the machine, but it can prevent, or at least delay most of the preceding problems.

If rebooting is not an option, we should also consider tearing down whole levels at once. At the end of the level, instead of freeing every single dynamically allocated object, we could instead just reset all the memory that was used by the level data itself. As long as we took precautions so there were no pointers or other code that depended on anything in that area, totally wiping that memory can prevent any fragmentation and be much more efficient. This is particularly easy to do if we are using memory pools (as explained in Chapter 7) to hold a lot of our level data.

19.3 Dealing with "Bad" Data

What is "bad" data, and why is it a problem? Let us consider the following simple function that normalizes a vector:

```
void Vector3d::Normalize()
{
    float fLength = sqrt(x*x+y*y+z*z);
    x /= fLength;
    y /= fLength;
    z /= fLength;
}
```

Your programmer alarm bells are probably going off—we might divide by zero! That is true; if someone calls `Normalize()` on a zero-length vector, our code will attempt to divide by zero. That is bad data because it makes no sense from the function point of view. To normalize a vector is to set its length to exactly one unit but leave its direction unchanged. What exactly does it mean to normalize a zero-length vector? It does not really have a direction to start with. It is pretty meaningless.

One of the aspects of bad data that makes it difficult to deal with is its tendency to propagate. If a function like the preceding one goes ahead and runs with bad data, either an exception is triggered (if the system is set up to trigger that particular type of exception) or the values computed will be NAN (Not A Number). NAN is a special float value that indicates an invalid result. The problem is that doing any operations on a NAN always results in a NAN, so those values propagate throughout all the calculations. Such propagation was originally designed in the IEEE 754 standard, but it had standardization of floating-point computations for scientific purposes in mind, not game programming. So, how do we deal with this problem? There are two main opposing views.

19.3.1 Assert on Bad Data

We apply what we learned in the first section of this chapter and we do not allow any bad data in any function by using asserts. This approach has the advantage of flagging bad data as soon as it happens so that it can be fixed right away. The drawback is the same as for the general use of asserts: if we leave them in the final build of the game, somebody will most likely come up with a situation when it will be triggered; if the asserts are removed, then the function returns NAN with unexpected results to the rest of the game. Specifically, this is how the `Normalize()` function would be implemented:

```
void Vector3d::Normalize()
{
    float fLength = sqrt(x*x+y*y+z*z);
    assert (fLength != 0);
    x /= fLength;
    y /= fLength;
    z /= fLength;
}
```

Something that makes math functions particularly susceptible to this problem is the nature of the problem itself. Unlike most other functions, there is not a range of good data and a range of bad data; things are a bit fuzzier. For example, the preceding normalize function can deal with any vector of any length, except for a vector that is all zeros. Similar situations happen with other math functions that cannot handle exactly parallel vectors or two points that are in the exact same place in space. For instance, a game might run without any problems until the player aligns the camera exactly with some other object, which causes both the camera vector and the alignment vector of that object to be exactly parallel, causing a function to fail. Reproducing that case might be very difficult, and it might be rare enough to go unnoticed even during internal testing.

19.3.2 Cope with Bad Data

The opposite view claims that we should make sure our function does not crash, does not trigger an assert, and returns the most meaningful values possible. What can we do in the case of normalizing a zero-length vector? We can detect that situation and leave the vector alone. Unfortunately, the resulting vector is not of unit length. An alternative approach is to return a unit vector along some arbitrary axis; that would satisfy the postcondition of the function, even if the direction of the vector is not meaningful. This is how the `Normalize()` function is implemented to cope with bad data:

```
void Vector3d::Normalize()
{
    float fLength = sqrt(x*x+y*y+z*z);
    if (fLength > 0)
    {
        x /= fLength;
        y /= fLength;
        z /= fLength;
    }
    // Return a unit vector along the x axis if
    // this is a zero-length vector
    else
    {
        x = 1.0f; y = 0.0f; z = 0.0f;
    }
}
```

The advantage of this approach is that the functions become much more robust. It should be impossible to pass any data that returns NAN (other than passing NAN in the first place as a parameter). There is no need for asserts, so even if something unexpected happens, the functions can handle it reasonably well without crashing the game.

This approach is not without drawbacks, however. These functions are all at a fairly low level, and they can get executed many times per frame (easily thousands of times). By adding the extra logic, we make them slightly slower—and even worse, slightly larger, which could prevent them from being inlined. The performance hit could be noticeable.

Another drawback is in the data returned. At least it is not NAN, but it might not be particularly meaningful and could cause strange behavior in the game. In this case, imagine we are normalizing the normal of a collision between the player and an object. For whatever reason, that normal was zero-length, but we went ahead and attempted to normalize it anyway. This function now returns a vector along the x-axis, which is clearly incorrect and could cause the player to get stuck in a wall.

Finally, and probably the greatest drawback of all, is the reliance on the fixed results. After all the math functions that fix bad data are in place, people will start using them without a second thought, relying on their implementation as part of the game. We will be normalizing zero-length vectors, doing square roots of negative numbers, dividing by zero, and so forth. If at some point that behavior changes (for example, when porting the game to another platform or when optimizing a function), it might be extremely difficult to fix all the code that relied on that behavior.

Interestingly, this is the approach that some of the standard math libraries included for some consoles' use. They realized that there was no point in doing exceptions or creating NAN because we are developing a game; instead, they expect us to try to deal with the data in the best way possible. For example, in those consoles, dividing a number by zero results in zero. The problems come when a program that was developed for that console needs to be ported to a different platform because it typically results in continuous crashes until all the logic has been straightened out.

19.3.3 A Compromise

Neither of the two options we have seen so far seems particularly promising for games. They both have some major drawbacks. Instead of offering a third solution, a good option is to compromise on the two approaches just described.

To get the best of both worlds, one possible approach is to alternate between the two techniques. By default, we take the second approach and deal with the bad data the best way we can. That guarantees that the game does not crash, but it makes the code rely on the meaningless returned values. The key is to occasionally switch to the first method and assert as soon as bad values are passed in. This approach can help you find as many bugs as possible and fix them. Doing this once every few weeks should help you catch most of the bad data being passed around. To switch back and forth easily, it is best to surround those specific asserts with an `#ifdef` statement and compile them in only when needed:

```
void Vector3d::Normalize()
{
    float fLength = sqrt(x*x+y*y+z*z);
    #ifdef ASSERTBADDATA
    assert (fLength > 0);
    #endif
    if (fLength > 0)
    {
        x /= fLength;
        y /= fLength;
        z /= fLength;
    }
    // Return a unit vector along the x-axis if
    // this is a zero-length vector
    else
    {
        x = 1.0f; y = 0.0f; z = 0.0f;
    }
}
```

The advantage of this approach is that it discourages passing bad data to math functions (and therefore relying on their meaningless results); at the same time, it ensures that the game works correctly if that situation every happens after the game has been shipped.

The main drawback remains the potential performance hit for all the extra conditionals and lack of inlining. It might therefore be worthwhile to provide two functions for the same operation: one that is safe and does all the checking, and another one that is very fast and does no checking at all. The difficult part is in deciding which one to use, and that might require some discipline. It is very important that the fast version be used only if it is called from a function that is already guaranteed not to contain any bad data. Otherwise, we are back to square one, with anybody potentially calling the unsafe versions with bad data. A potential solution might be to make the unsafe versions available only within the math library and not expose them to the rest of the game. This solution can help remedy the problem, but it prevents the use of the faster functions from a few places where their use was justified. Our normalize functions would look like this:

```cpp
void Vector3d::Normalize()
{
    float fLength = sqrt(x*x+y*y+z*z);
    #ifdef ASSERTBADDATA
    assert (fLength > 0);
    #endif
    if (fLength > 0)
    {
        x /= fLength;
        y /= fLength;
        z /= fLength;
    }
    // Return a unit vector along the x-axis if
    // this is a zero-length vector
    else
    {
        x = 1.0f; y = 0.0f; z = 0.0f;
    }
}

inline void Vector3d::NormalizeUnsafe()
{
    float fLength = sqrt(x*x+y*y+z*z);
    assert ( fLength != 0 );
```

```
    x /= fLength;
    y /= fLength;
    z /= fLength;
}
```

19.4 CONCLUSION

The focus of this chapter was on techniques that avoid having the game crash in the hands of the final user, thus ruining their experience (and our reputation). The first part dealt with how to use assert() effectively in our programs. We saw when it is appropriate to use assert(), and when it is better to handle the error in a different way. We debated the merits of the different possibilities of what to do with asserts after we release the game and presented a very basic custom assert we can use in our own programs.

The next section dealt with the problems that creep up when the program has been running for a while. Memory leaks, memory fragmentation, and clock drift are some of the problems that can occur in that situation.

Finally, we suggested some solutions to the problem of dealing with bad data. Bad data is when meaningless data is passed into a function. On the one hand, we do not want our program wasting time so that every low-level function can accept any parameter; on the other hand, we want to make sure that our game does not crash if this ever happens. A good compromise is to switch between reporting every instance of bad data with an assert for a few weeks, and then ignore it for a few more weeks. That way, hopefully, the code develops resilience to bad data, but we can still manage to catch most of the bugs that cause the bad data in the first place.

SUGGESTED READING

This is one of the few books that discusses how assert() calls should be used and why using them is a very good idea. It seems that most other books have decided to ignore assert() as a simple "implementation detail."

McConnell, Steve, *Code Complete*. Microsoft Press, 1993.

This article explains in great detail how to set up your own custom assert:

Rabin, Steve, "Squeezing More Out of Assert." *Game Programming Gems*. Charles River Media, 2000.

A

ABOUT THE CD-ROM

The CD-ROM included with this book contains the source code for several programs that demonstrate some of the more complex concepts in this book. All the programs have been kept to a minimum size to allow you to concentrate on the point they are trying to illustrate; at the same time, they are fully functional programs that show how all the different ideas interrelate and come together.

Instead of boring you with page after page of program listings in the book, only the most important sections are included in the chapter text; you can refer to the source code on the CD-ROM for the rest of the details. If you prefer to have a lot of source code, you can open the source code files and have them by your side while you are reading the chapter.

The best way to use the source code is to compile the program and verify that it works. Step into it with the debugger if you want to verify a particular sequence of operations, or make modifications to it to see how you can extend them or improve them. Each program is in a separate folder with all its source code and project files.

FOLDERS

The files on this disc are organized into folders as follows:

- **Chapter 07: MemoryMgr.** A fully implemented memory manager and a small test application.

- **Chapter 13: Plugins.** A simple Win32 application with plug-ins. The application displays the currently loaded plug-ins, and the plug-ins themselves add some menu entries to the main application. Plug-ins can be loaded and unloaded dynamically.
- **Chapter 15: RTTI.** A custom runtime type information system, this one is intended to work only with single inheritance.
- **Chapter 15: RTTIMulti.** This is a variation on the previous custom runtime type information system. It supports multiple inheritance at the cost of some extra performance.
- **Chapter 16: ObjectFactory.** This is a templatized object factory for game entities.
- **Chapter 17: Serialization.** A very simple implementation that serializes a full game-entity tree to disk and loads it back. It uses a custom stream class and the pointer fix-up method.

SYSTEM REQUIREMENTS

All the programs were compiled using Visual Studio C++ 6.0 and were tested under Windows 2000. However, except for the plug-ins example, they should all be platform and compiler independent, so they should be easy to compile and run in your favorite environment. The executable for the plug-ins example program is also provided. You can experiment with it without having to compile it first.

INDEX